SOCIAL ANTHROPOLOGY AND LANGUAGE

Edited by Edwin Ardener

TAVISTOCK PUBLICATIONS

First published in 1971
by Tavistock Publications Limited
11 New Fetter Lane, London EC4
SBN 422 73700 3
First published as a Social Science Paperback in 1973
SBN 422 75560 5
This book has been set in Modern Series 7
and was printed by Butler & Tanner Ltd,
Frome and London

This volume derives mainly from papers presented at a conference on linguistics and social anthropology sponsored by the Association of Social Anthropologists of the Commonwealth and held 9–12 April 1969 at the University of Sussex

Distributed in the USA by
Harper & Row Publishers, Inc.
Barnes & Noble Import Division

The husband and wife ongon
(Museum of Anthropology and Ethnography, Leningrad, collection no. 654-7)

Contents

Editor's Preface

The Conference on the topic to which this volume is devoted took place at the University of Sussex in April 1969. The papers included were all circulated and discussed on that occasion, except for those by Miss Henson and Professor Whiteley, which were specially written for publication here. I should like to thank Dr Edmund Leach, Dr Jean La Fontaine, and Dr Anthony Forge for leading the discussion on three of the papers. The ASA is particularly indebted to its guests Dr Crystal (Reading), Dr Denison (London School of Economics), Professor Hymes (Pennsylvania, and Clare Hall, Cambridge), Dr Milner (School of Oriental and African Studies), Dr (now Professor) Pride (Leeds, now Wellington), and Professor Robins (School of Oriental and African Studies). I would also like to thank especially the younger contributors Mrs C. Humphrey (Cambridge), Miss H. Henson (Oxford), and Miss (now Dr) E. Tonkin (Oxford, now Birmingham), for giving papers from their current researches.

Warm thanks are due to the University of Sussex, which accommodated the Conference, and to Dr Peter Lloyd, who was responsible for the local arrangements.

Finally, I am grateful to my wife Shirley Ardener, and to Rosamund Robson of Tavistock Publications, for invaluable assistance in putting this volume through the press. Mr Malcolm Crick kindly prepared the indexes.

Edwin Ardener

Introductory Essay: Social Anthropology and Language

The failure of the great middle generation of social anthropologists to respond to the challenge of language has long been one of the curiosities of the British school of the subject; and possibly nothing today so clearly exemplifies that sadly widening rift between the older and the newer social anthropology than the different attitudes to language to be found on either side. This is in great contrast to the 'cultural anthropology' of the United States, in which the study of language has never lost its place. There, indeed, even linguistic anthropology has developed far beyond the proportions of a mere sub-field of anthropology – its vast literature is beginning to exceed what anyone but a full-time specialist can assimilate. Of course, the autonomy as an academic discipline of linguistics without special labels has everywhere been long established, and it might therefore appear both economical and logical that its study should be left to specialists. This may once have seemed a reasonable view to take. During the forties and fifties, however, when British theoretical social anthropology often gave the impression of resting after the exertions of the Malinowskian period, scientific linguistics made one or two striking advances of sufficient importance to begin to bear upon thought in neighbouring disciplines. As far as British social anthropology as a whole was concerned, it became aware of these advances with the growing influence of Lévi-Strauss. It is something of an irony that this situation should exist: that the influence of thought purportedly derived in some part from linguistics should have come to be so important in British social anthropology, when the direct study of linguistics had for so long lapsed.

The importance of Malinowski for the London school of linguistics obscured this situation. As Miss Henson shows, British social anthropologists have been ill at ease with language ever since the nineteenth-century beginnings. The early developments in comparative philology were, it is true, in many ways a hindrance rather than a help to theoretical development, encouraging as they did some of the less fruitful speculations on race and primitive origins. At Oxford the German Max Müller tried to express before his time, although in a form subsequently much criticized (Evans-Pritchard, 1965: 20–23), some of the links between language and myth, which were not explored again in this country with official approval for another half-century. The philological movement of the 1870s under Brugmann and his colleagues seemed to make no impact. As far as British anthropology was concerned, the Neogrammarians lived and died unnoted. Ferdinand de Saussure lectured in the first decade of this century on topics such as synchrony and diachrony, and subsequently remained uncited by anthropologists whose treatment of these subjects was less skilful. Malinowski taught his pupils to 'learn the language', and it is a tribute that many so successfully made the attempt with what seems in retrospect so relatively little awareness of the main advances in descriptive linguistics in the twenties and thirties. In the United States anthropological linguistics flowed from decade to decade, from Boas to Sapir, up to the present day, almost unremarked. Glottochronology rose and fell. Information theory appeared in 1948, fructified linguistics and psychology, and slowly went out of fashion, while few British anthropologists noticed. Chomsky flourished for a decade before many could haltingly spell his name. Only in one or two academic centres that had preserved links with a wider intellectual world was it possible in the later fifties and the sixties for influences from the French and American schools to be gathered together and fed into the British tradition.

Had all this truly been the expression of supreme disciplinary self-confidence, it might have been wholly admirable. But in fact, after 1960, at the same time that the most lively issues were being raised as a result of the newer movements, the image-makers of the profession seemed to be sunk in a mood of breast-beating (below, p. lxviii) which ran the risk of being taken at its face value by the growing 'social science' establishment. The idea of the relevance of theoretical linguistics to social anthropological theory never made much practical headway in anthropological circles in London after Malinowski (despite pioneering efforts by Milner, 1954, and more recently by Whiteley, 1966), and in the social structure of British anthropology London has carried considerable weight, even in her more somnolent periods.

By 1969, when the ASA symposium on language was convened, the number of full members of the Association who yet felt qualified to offer formal papers was still very few. Even some of these were for one reason or another unable to present papers, and are therefore not represented here, except by citation of their writings. Others made valuable oral contributions. The linguists who came as our guests, and who are represented here, have been very generous in their support of our relatively untutored steps.

This volume, accordingly, has to try to achieve several aims (whatever may be the chances of success). Its first aim is to be read *primarily* by social anthropologists, and by them not as a merely specialist branch of their subject, but as an illustration of certain post-functionalist trends of general relevance. Second, to provide an introduction to the range of possible work that may be or has been done, and to put it in the perspective of earlier trends both in social anthropology and in linguistics. Third, to offer some collaborative insights to the growing body of linguists and other scholars with 'sociolinguistic' interests.

For the first aim, much of this introductory essay especially will restate a number of linguistically well-worn themes in what may at times be a rather elementary manner. It is, however, generally in an anthropological manner, if not in the only possible anthropological manner. I have drawn here on some of my lectures at Oxford between 1964 and 1969. It is possible that the discussion may at times be directed rather closely to illumination of the failings of the past, while leaving itself open to more serious criticisms from social anthropologists who take its purpose for granted, but may doubt the skill of its achievement. Even since the Conference was first planned in 1967 there have come to be a greater number of linguistically trained anthropologists in the ASA itself. The weaknesses will, I hope, be accepted in a tolerant manner as due to the particular period at which this volume was compiled. Possibly it will be received across the Atlantic as yet more evidence of past and present 'insularity' and 'parochialism', charges which are seemingly now inseparable from the American view of British social anthropology (Murdock, 1951; R. Firth, 1951; M. Harris, 1969). We may perhaps be shielded in part by the contribution of one of their most eminent linguistic anthropologists. It is no doubt true that 'ASA' social anthropologists should educate themselves about language by turning to the copious work in anthropology at large. There should be no need for an internal debate mediated by special interpreters. All of which having been said, any approach to language the British school may have, is, or is likely to be, distinctive and must grow from its own interests.

For the second aim, the whole volume is offered, with its contributors' cited bibliographies as partial evidence. Here we depend most heavily on our linguistic colleagues. Certain topics are not represented: in particular the contribution from philosophers which would illuminate many of the topics touched upon. The major deliberate omission from the social anthropological point of view is the direct consideration of kinship terminology, since the next volume in this series is devoted to the study of kinship, under the editorship of a foremost specialist (Needham, 1971). A later volume is to concern itself with other aspects of cognition. The approach here is, however, clearly in line with and owes very much to the main developments in these fields.

The third aim may at first sight seem unlikely to be implemented in the light of the long absence of British social anthropology from linguistics. This we did not believe was shown to be the case at the Conference. Absence from the direct study of language had had some advantages. Social anthropology had developed independently insights that had some relevance to linguistic movements, and as a professional subject in its own right it is perfectly well equipped to evaluate the 'social' component of any proposed sociolinguistics, if it is asked to do so. The subject has its *Junggrammatiker*, even though Leitner's view of the early Neogrammarians ('literary terrorism exercised by a set of Sanscritists' – below, p. 25 n. 2) serves as the prejudicial model for much anthropological comprehension of the 'neo-anthropological' movements! For linguists, it may be sufficient to offer as our justification, and aspiration, a text suitably amended from Hjelmslev (1963: 127):

'A temporary restriction of the field of vision was the price that had to be paid to elicit from [society] itself its secret. But precisely through that immanent point of view and by virtue of it, [social anthropology] itself returns the price that it demanded.'

SOCIAL ANTHROPOLOGISTS AND LINGUISTICS: LEVELS OF RELATIONSHIP

We may as well begin with Lévi-Strauss's three levels of contact between the subject-matters of the two disciplines: (1) the relationship between a [single] language and a [single] culture, (2) the relationship between language and culture, and (3) the relationship between linguistics as a scientific discipline and anthropology (Lévi-Strauss, 1963a: 67–68; J. R. Firth, 1957b: 116; Hymes, 1964: xxi; Whiteley, 1966: 139). These divisions are hardly exhaustive, however, and the first two are very closely linked. Hymes (1964) shows how difficult they are to use in practice, and suggests a score of distinctions that must be taken into account (pp. xxv–xxviii). Not least, of course, among the many long debates that are possible is whether 'language' is to be classed as part of 'culture', to be opposed to 'culture', to be a determinant of 'culture', or what – as if 'culture' (and 'language' too?) in this context was not itself a term of art obscuring any solution.

I prefer to introduce the matter here from a somewhat different point of view, by taking three levels on which social anthropologists in this country have viewed the relevance of linguistics to their subject over the last generation or two. The idea of levels here derives from the observed tendency of British social anthropologists to *isolate* pieces of the study of language for their own purposes. They may be labelled in this way:

1. A *technical level*: on which social anthropologists might seek and receive help in actually learning languages, especially those exotic and unwritten languages with which they characteristically have to work.

2. A *pragmatic level*: on which they might seek what help, if any, linguistic data can give in the interpretation of anthropological data in a given region or among a given people.

3. The *level of explanation*: on which they might seek the relevance, if any, of theories *about* language, even of theories about linguistics, to theories *about* society, or about culture, or about the place and aims of social anthropology.

In this country, as I have said, the three levels tend to have been treated separately. At all times there has been some interest at level (1). Sometimes there has been interest at level (2). Nowadays there has been considerable interest at level (3). These split relations with linguistics have correspondingly split the apprehension of language as a whole, especially among post-Malinowskians. These levels, then, form a useful starting-point for discussion on the way to disposing of them.

THE TECHNICAL LEVEL

Among the main body of social anthropologists since Malinowski a knowledge of the language is taken for granted as a *sine qua non* of good fieldwork. As it has been summarily put:

> 'Sociologists usually speak the same language (more or less) as the people they study, and they share with them at least some of their basic concepts and categories. But for the social anthropologist the most difficult task is usually to understand the language and ways of thought of the people he studies, which may be – and probably are – very different from his own. This is why in anthropological field-work a sound knowledge of the language of the community being studied is indispensable, for a people's categories of thought and the forms of their language are inextricably bound together' (Beattie, 1964a: 31).

This view, with its stress on categories of thought, was an important advance on the more mechanistic attitude of many writers, among whom there was often an unreflecting faith in the linguistic ability of the average social anthropologist. Interpreters seemed to be abhorred – even hated. Now, there are many very good reasons why interpreters should not be relied upon in social anthropology. No doubt most writers had in mind the khaki-uniformed figures (frequently corrupt) used by the colonial administrations. We must only comment on the surprising insouciance to be found among social anthropologists on the subject of what is possible in adult language-learning. Professor Fortes exemplifies the problems involved very clearly in his Introduction to *The Dynamics of Clanship among the Tallensi*. He says:

> 'As there is no linguistic literature for the Tallensi we had to learn their dialect from scratch, with the assistance of a semi-literate interpreter and the scanty literature on Mole-Dagbane.'

So far so good.

> 'It took us about six months to learn enough Talni for workaday communication with the people. By the end of the first tour we became proficient enough to dispense with an interpreter. Nevertheless, I know only too well that we reached but a moderate standard in our vocabulary and in our appreciation of the finer shades of thought and feeling that can be expressed in Talni' (1945: xii).

Let us abstract the sense of this statement: for six months the anthropologist had no 'workaday communication' except through a semi-literate interpreter. He finally, after a 'tour' (eighteen months?) dispensed with an interpreter when he still had only 'a moderate standard of vocabulary' and could not fully appreciate the 'finer shades' of Talni. This is the linguistic mesh through which it is purported that Tallensi culture is given to us. To say this is, of course, not to impugn Fortes's fieldwork. One may confidently take this writer as an example, precisely because his technical linguistic ability shows on every page. We are dealing with a mode of expression: in the ideology of that period, which from that point of view can only now be said to be ending, interpreters were always 'dispensed with' as if sucked dry and banished. The notion of the language well and truly learnt belonged with the lean-jawed traveller of the 'I-rapped-out-a-few-words-of-Swahili' type, and had romantic rather than realistic origins. One suspects Malinowski of encouraging this particular brand of naïveté, although the American Boasians were not free from it either. It should be emphasized that anthropological practice was evidently vastly superior to the view of language that purported to direct it. Nevertheless, to regard language as a tool of research presenting very few problems was mistaken, and it is no coincidence that the most delicate work of modern social anthropologists in the fields of myth, belief, and symbolism commonly rests upon firm foundations of sound education outside social anthropology in languages, philosophy, classics, or one of the other rigorous humanities.

Technical courses in linguistics were taken by many fieldworkers, but they did not, despite the mechanistic views current, have the effect of producing general familiarity among social anthropologists with the ordinary jargon of descriptive linguistics. This contrasts with the American case. It is not entirely unadmirable, to be sure. The point is made here merely to emphasize that a technical view of language has not necessarily led to any common familiarity with language technicalities. Indeed, even among graduate students the signs used in ordinary phonological transcription of no great sophistication tend to awaken much the same revulsion as those used in mathematics (or in elementary statistics). This must be due precisely to a mechanistic view of both: the elements of technical linguistics (as, for many, those of statistics) are to be mugged up for special purposes, the principles perhaps only barely understood. They go with travel inoculations, not to be seriously thought about until necessary. The post-Malinowskian view of language worked with an abiding faith in 'fieldworkers' modified Berlitz' – a kind of 'look, listen, and say'. In an important sense Malinowski's 'context of situation' was a theoretical charter for this faith: as if context would tell all if you really had eyes to see. In practice there was commonly recourse to bilinguals or, rather, partial or inadequate bilinguals, as we should expect. It was not that social anthropologists failed to learn the languages, but that they did not accord their achievements the intellectual status they deserved. They clearly learnt something, but they never examined how they did it, or publicly exchanged detailed ideas on it, or built up their experience from one another's mistakes.[1] Even an otherwise excellent and up-to-date fieldwork symposium like Epstein's (1967) has no chapter on language (and no reference to it in the index). Malinowski's own contribution is discussed in this volume; we touch here on the failure of his most representative pupils to regard the study of language, even at that technical level upon which modern fieldwork might be thought implicitly to depend, as more than another subject to remain necessarily naïve about – like psychoanalysis or macro-economics (Gluckman, 1964).

The truly formidable problem of communication between the fieldworking social anthropologist and the members of the other society lies at the heart of traditional social anthropology, although few untutored readers would have guessed this from the blander monographs of the last thirty years. There are exceptions: the classical account of Evans-Pritchard, for example (1940), or, more recently, the linguistically candid statement of Maybury-Lewis (1967). Generally, in the monographs themselves the struggle is over. The contradiction between the scale of the task of interpretation and the supposed linguistic apparatus involved is remarkably great, as we have seen. It may be resolved in this way. Even the most exemplary technical approach to language would not in fact have solved the basic problem of communication. The anthropological 'experience' derives from the apprehension of a critical lack of fit of (at least) two entire world-views, one to another. The crudity of the functionalists' linguistic tools did not therefore impede this insight. On the contrary, the experience of *mis*understanding is crucial to it. Had all social anthropologists been really thoroughly trained in (say) the phonemics of their day, it is even possible that they would in fact have become far less quickly aware that transcriptions are not enough. The problem might have been obscured, as it is in some Western sociology, by an apparently detailed, but really superficial, comprehension. Post-Malinowskians talked as if they used language as a 'tool' for the understanding of societies, but in fact they were forced to attempt this understanding by the imposition upon their material of various 'structures', of which the intuitive and observational bases were only partially open to examination. By the fifties the existential status of such structures had become a worry to the thoughtful. The stage was set for the discussion of 'models', cognitive categories, and the like. The study of language had, of course, a real relevance to social anthropologists concerned with these subjects, not primarily at the technical level but, on the contrary, at the more general levels of linguistic theory and practice.

These remarks are certainly not intended to turn into a virtue a wrong-headed approach to language. French and American social anthropologists arrived at similar ends without detachment from the study of language. They do, however, suggest why the functionalist ethnographic monographs of the postwar period contain few classics, and why on the contrary the most interesting recent work has lain not in traditional ethnography but in the analysis of primitive (and scientific) models of the world.

THE PRAGMATIC LEVEL

The second level of contact between social anthropology and linguistics has been essentially one at the level of 'data'. There was a time when much of the most fruitful interaction between the two disciplines could be placed under this head. It has always been common, for example, for anthropologists, especially in America, to be concerned with the historical implications of linguistic material. Where well-established literary and linguistic specialisms have existed for certain cultures and regions, social anthropologists have turned to them with gratitude (for example: for Indian studies, Dumont and Pocock, 1957–66; for Sinology, Freedman, 1963). The general revival of historical interests in British social anthropology since the fifties (Evans-Pritchard, 1950, 1961a) has also directed attention to linguistic work in more traditional ethnographic areas. Thus, classifications of the languages of Africa which have thrown new and frequently confusing light on the history of the continent (Greenberg, 1963b; and Guthrie, 1948, 1953, 1962) have led to some concern with the nature of the classification of languages and its relation to tribe (cf. Ardener, 1967: 293–299; Chilver and Kaberry, 1968: 9–12). Similarly deriving from problems in the classification of exotic languages there has been awareness of the work of Swadesh and of the theories associated with the names 'lexicostatistics' and 'glottochronology' (Swadesh, 1950; Hymes, 1960). The native tradition for these historico-linguistic interests goes back through administrator-anthropologists like Meek (e.g. 1931), Talbot (e.g. 1912), and

Northcote Thomas (e.g. 1914). Such men were, however, out of fashion for a long time, and were later frequently accorded the reduced style of 'ethnologist'.

At this level, there is a sense in which social anthropology has been able to 'take or leave' the contributions from linguistics. The two kinds of data, social and linguistic, did not always mix well, and it is paradoxically because of some contacts at this level that the dissatisfaction with linguistics characteristic of the majority of postwar functionalists has been confirmed. The workers in the two subjects inevitably build numerous working theories on detailed data which do not necessarily hold much insight for each other. It is at this level also that ideals of 'teamwork' or even of common seminars between working social anthropologists and working linguists sometimes fail to be effective. As we shall see, Lévi-Strauss spent years struggling with linguistic terminology on this level, and did not begin to clarify his notion of the relevance of structural linguistics until he had in effect abandoned the pragmatic level for the level of explanation. The best recent work in sociolinguistics does not restrict itself to one level of operation: it looks for unifying principles within which the specific methods and data of social anthropology and linguistics can be used, each to its own best advantage. Nevertheless, a good modern field in which pragmatic contacts can be made lies in work concerned with the way in which members of societies classify their environment. A discussion here will serve to introduce in a practical way some of the implications to be further considered at the level of explanation.

Classification and category

This field of linguistics abuts squarely upon the concerns of social anthropology. Long ago, Durkheim and Mauss (trans. 1963) drew attention to certain unifying principles linking the social and mental categories of a people. Many well-known names in American linguistic and cultural anthropology (for example, Sapir, 1921; Whorf, 1956; Pike, 1954; Conklin, 1955; Lounsbury, 1956; Goodenough, 1956; Frake, 1961; and others) have made contributions in different ways in this field (sometimes inadequately called 'cognitive'), as well as European social anthropologists like Lévi-Strauss (in much of his vast corpus), Leach (e.g. 1964), Douglas (1966), and Needham (e.g. 1960b). Some of the developments have become very intricate. Broadly speaking, most of this work confirms Saussure's conclusion that language is not simply a labelling device for elements of the 'real' world. Rather, there is some relationship between the categories through which the world is experienced and the language used to express them. Propositions phrased loosely in this way are not a matter of serious conflict of opinion, but the long-standing philosophical and metaphysical questions they raise are far from solved (L. J. Cohen, 1966; Hook, 1969: 3–47). The extreme view that language actually determines the world-view in a quasi-independent manner is usually attributed to Whorf, and this version is commonly rejected (see Hoijer, 1955; L. J. Cohen, 1966: 82–94). In some respects the work of the German semanticists is nowadays more stimulating because of their more truly structural approach, deriving from Saussure. A debt is owed to Ullmann (1951) for making their works more familiar in this country.

For those social anthropologists to whom the general implications of this body of work are still new, they may be best illustrated by taking the usual elementary example: the classical case of colour terminology. That is: the manner in which the physical colour spectrum is divided in different languages. We may take the example, first popularized by Hjelmslev (1943: 48–49; trans. 1963: 52–53), of the different range of reference of certain colour terms in English and Welsh, whose reprinting[2] yet again I justify by adding, for my own purposes, columns for modern colloquial Welsh and for Ibo, and extending the spectrum to include 'black' (*Figure 1*).

How we interpret the relationship between the underlying reality and the 'imposed classification' is controversial. The Newtonian colour labels for the divisions of the spectrum do not provide such a reality, for they classically exemplify the same process. It is recorded that Newton called in a friend to label the colours of his spectrum, because he himself was not skilled at distinguishing hues. He wished that there should be seven colours, and the term 'indigo' was used to make up the number.[3] This quite extraordinary tale reveals much about the category 'seven' in Renaissance scientific thought, and about the importations of indigo dye to Europe in the same period. Work has been done, nevertheless, suggesting that there are certain essential details given in any colour classification which make for universals in the classification of colours at a much deeper level than that revealed by a simple comparison of different systems. There is in none of these respects any true difference in principle between the commonplace, but always striking, example of colour classification and various other

FIGURE 1 *Certain colour categories*

<table>
<tr><th>ENGLISH</th><th>STANDARD WELSH</th><th>MODERN COLLOQUIAL WELSH</th><th>IBO</th></tr>
<tr><td rowspan="2">green</td><td>gwyrdd</td><td rowspan="2">gwyrdd</td><td rowspan="4">ahehea ndu</td></tr>
<tr><td rowspan="3">glas</td></tr>
<tr><td>blue</td><td>glas</td></tr>
<tr><td rowspan="2">grey</td><td rowspan="2">llwyd</td></tr>
<tr><td rowspan="2">llwyd</td><td rowspan="4">ojii</td></tr>
<tr><td rowspan="2">brown</td><td rowspan="2">brown</td></tr>
<tr><td rowspan="2">du</td></tr>
<tr><td>black</td><td>du</td></tr>
</table>

categories imposed upon the social and physical environment by different sociolinguistic communities.

The intuition that a total relativism is unproductive has been supported by the evidence from comparative study, which suggests that a necessary relativism *vis-à-vis* (for example) the categories of English need not lead us to assume a total arbitrariness in all human categorization. I do not intend to enter far into this debate as far as kinship terms are concerned. Lounsbury (1969: 18) has referred to some positions taken by colleagues of mine (e.g. Beattie, 1964b) together with that of, for example, Leach (1958), as examples of the 'extreme relativist view'. These and some apparently similar approaches (Needham, e.g. 1958) in fact avoid his charge since their effect is to attribute to the kinship structure homologies with other symbolic structures (not necessarily genealogical) which are or may be attributed to universals of another sort – those of the human classifying processes. Furthermore, certain classifications at least are likely to be closely calqued upon basic physical and biological realities in the human condition, from which the different sociolinguistic categorizations of various communities may deviate perhaps only in their degree or direction of 'spread'. The 'relativism' in such cases occurs only in the determination of the boundaries. Nevertheless, the demonstration of those classifications which have a 'universal' core, and those which do not, is by no means easy, and cannot be assumed in advance. A degree of relativism must then have the status of a heuristic hypothesis. There seems no pressing need to fear it, although a social anthropologist cannot avoid the comment that, in all societies, any tampering with the boundaries of categories does awaken the fear of anomaly – generating pollution beliefs, inversion phenomena, and taboo (Douglas, 1966). It is the thought categories of our own tradition that are tampered with in such studies. 'Relativism' may then sometimes appear as a fundamental philosophical danger.

In any event, it is generally agreed that the everyday hypothesis that common categories are entirely universal would not (even in the absence of comparative material) survive evidence that changes may occur in such systems. The most striking thing about Hjelmslev's Welsh colour categories is that they are *not* used, for example, in explaining to the Welsh-speaking public certain changes in the colour code for electric cables (*Y Cymro*, 25 March 1970). The modern forms have been lined up with English, as in the third column of *Figure 1*. Furthermore, *gwyrdd*, we learn, was an old loan category from Latin *viridis* (Lewis, 1943: 10). This intruded on the domain of *glas*, which would formerly have had a 'blue-green' range even closer to Ibo *ahehea ndu* (Ardener, 1954). Further comparison with the Ibo system may help to elucidate some of the issues, through which a kind of universalism emerges from anthropological relativism. The basic colour opposition in Ibo is *ocha*:*ojii* (brightness:darkness). In this respect the language falls into a well-recognized class. Beyond that there are terms for 'red' (*obara obara* or *uhye uhye*), 'blue-green' (*ahehea ndu* or *akwukwo ndu*), and 'yellow' (*odo odo*), with concrete referents ('blood' or 'camwood', 'living vegetation' or 'leaves', and 'yellow dye plant'). There is a battery of other descriptive possibilities for specific hues, but except for the addition of 'yellow' the basic system rather resembles Conklin's account of the Hanunóo (1955), a well-known type-case. The single axis of comparison between English and Ibo in *Figure 1* thus completely breaks up the continuum *ocha:ojii*, which lies along the axis of brightness, while *ahehea ndu* lies on the axis of hue (see *Figure 2*).

There is a similar opposition in Welsh *gwyn:du*. The 'grey' term *llwyd* also belongs in the middle of the *bright:dark* axis,

FIGURE 2 *Brightness and hue*

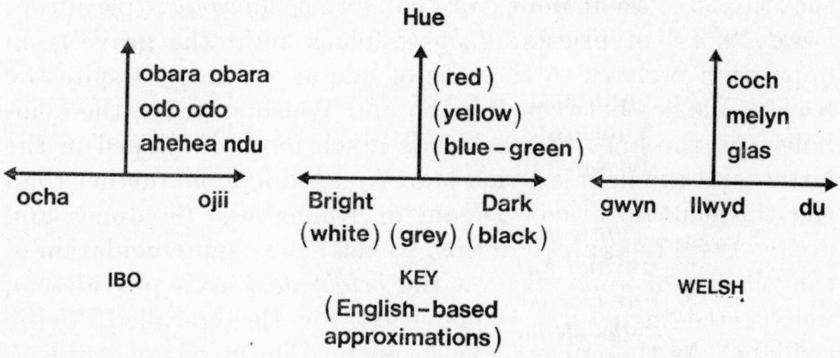

thus making a triadic division, compared with the Ibo dyad. The terms referring to hues: *glas* 'blue-green', *coch* 'red', and *melyn* 'yellow', are similar to the basic Ibo ones. The factitious continuity of the 'spectrum' from 'green' to 'black' in the second column in *Figure 1* is merely dictated by the first column for English. It results from certain documented English discrepancies with Welsh: e.g. 'grey' mares in Welsh are 'blue': *glas* (*caseg las*), while 'brown' paper is 'grey': *llwyd* (*papur llwyd*).[4] In the first case English uses a *bright:dark* term against a Welsh hue term, whereas in the second the situations are reversed. The Welsh colour terms are therefore best elucidated not in terms of 'perceptual grids', arbitrarily placed over the spectrum, but in structural terms, which would see the Welsh historical transition as matching that of other systems towards more and more differentiation of terms along the hue axis without losing the *bright:dark* opposition.[5]

Such structures clearly intertwine 'mental' and 'natural'

phenomena, yet they are linked, through their symbolic expression in language, with the 'social'. Furthermore, such structures are embodied in further meta-levels of symbolism, 'calqued' (to use a linguistic metaphor) upon them. Thus, among the Ibo, the *ocha*:*ojii* opposition is associated with oppositions like *beautiful*:*plain*, *ritual*:*secular*, *female*:*male*, *weak*:*sturdy* (Ardener, 1954), in which the *ocha* category bears the aspect of 'purity and danger', while *ojii* is homely and reassuring. This kind of polarity is of course very familiar in social anthropology. The Welsh usages invite many speculations. For example the *bright*:*dark* axis as a whole (*gwyn*:*llwyd*:*du*) seems to symbolize the 'sacred', 'anomalous', or 'dangerous' (*gwynfa*: 'paradise'; *llwyd*: 'holy' of priests; *dubwll*: 'black pit', 'the grave') – in opposition perhaps to the axis of hue as a whole. Despite the basic analogies between the Ibo and Welsh systems, the symbolism of the hues themselves is much more developed in the latter, and the field is a rich one. We need look no further than the thirteenth-century 'Dream of Rhonabwy' (in Jones and Jones, 1949) to appreciate this. Nevertheless, our elucidation of the placing of anomalies on the *bright*:*dark* axis provides an unexpected structural explanation for the so-called 'Celtic twilight'. As the ancient Welsh poem, 'The Spoils of Annwn', puts it:

ygkaer pedryfan ynys pybyrdor
echwyd amuchyd kymyscetor

(*In the Four-Cornered Fortress* [*of the Otherworld*], *the isle of the strong door,*
Noonday and jet blackness are mingled)

(Loomis, 1956: 136, 165).[6]

In social anthropology the relationship of colour structures to other structural features in society has been analysed by, for example, Turner (1966: 'red', 'white', 'black'), Tambiah (1968: 203–205), and Leach (1970: 21–35: 'red', 'green', 'yellow'); for the psycholinguistic background see e.g. Brown and Lenneberg (1954), Lenneberg and Roberts (1956), and Berlin and Kay (1969).

The great interest of the work of the German linguist von Wartburg for social anthropology lies in his useful demonstration of change in structures of interlocking categories. Where such change occurs we are hard put to determine whether the change is essentially one in 'language' or in 'culture' or 'society'. Any attempt at rigid distinction becomes in fact hair-splitting. This is a field in which linguistics and social anthropology frequently overlap totally in their subject-matter, and one therefore in which the analyses of each will be of interest. Once more a familiar example will help us. Whereas Latin distinguished 'father's brother' from 'mother's brother', and 'father's sister' from 'mother's sister', this distinction has been lost in,

FIGURE 3 *The fates of some Latin kin terms*

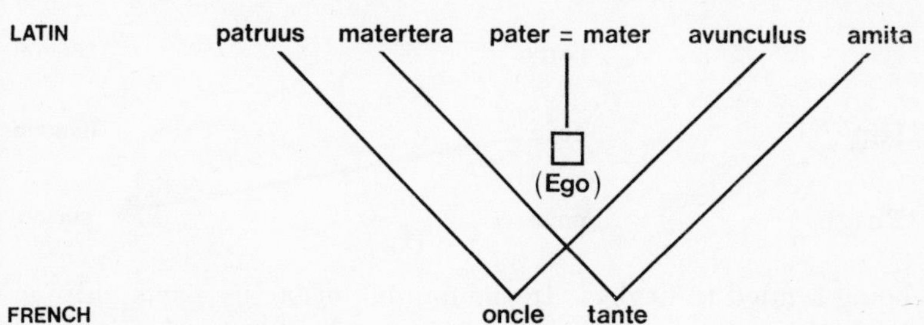

for instance, French (*Figure 3*). Linguistic analysis shows us that 'parent's male sibling' (*oncle*) and 'parent's female sibling' (*tante*) are reflexes of the Latin terms for 'mother's brother' and 'mother's sister' (the latter being more easily seen in our own word 'aunt', which derives from Old French). Linguistic analysis might also suggest reasons why this pair of terms should have been preferred to patrilateral ones. Thus it might be argued, for example, that the reflexes of *matertera* and *patruus* would fall together too closely in French with the reflexes of *mater* and *pater*. This will not do, however, because the empty slots, instead of being filled with new terms (as they were in other systems of classification), were absorbed. Von Wartburg (1969: 156) points out in an essentially anthropological way that we are dealing with a weakening of the difference in legal status of patrilateral and matrilateral relatives in relation to ego, which had been so important in the older Latin system.

In the medieval world the French solution was accepted by other peoples including the Germans, who had retained the patrilateral : matrilateral distinction (FB *Vetter*, FZ *Base*, MB *Oheim*, MZ *Muhme*). Behind all such major category shifts there no doubt lies a social revolution. It is, however, likely that at some period the old and new terminologies coexisted; thus breaking the simple direct calibration between terminology and social organization maintained by Radcliffe-Brown. Furthermore, Malmberg (1964: 130) notes that the distinction is still retained in Swedish despite analogous jural changes.[7]

It is precisely the diachronic aspect of human category systems that even modern social anthropologists have for the time

FIGURE 4 *'Hip' and 'thigh'*

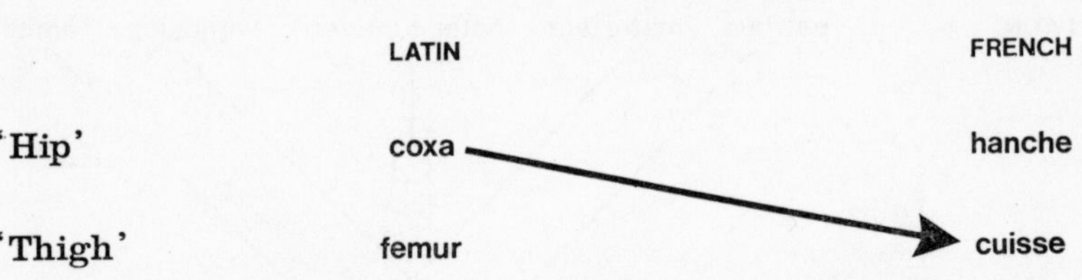

being tended to neglect. In the naming of bodily parts, 'hip' in Latin was *coxa*, and 'thigh' was *femur*. In French the reflex of *coxa* (*la cuisse*) has come to mean 'thigh' and a new term of Germanic provenance, *hanche*, now fills the category once occupied by *coxa* (see *Figure 4*). The situation in Italian, French, and Portuguese is similar. The linguist says:

> 'The explanation lies in the awkward situation which had arisen in Latin: *femur, -oris* had become homonymous with *fimus* 'dung' following the modification of *fĭmus, -i* to *femus, -oris* under the influence of *stercus, -oris*. In order to avoid the now unacceptable *femur*, speakers had recourse to the name for the next nearest part of the body, *coxa*, which henceforward designated the region from the hip to the knee. And as this extension inevitably led to confusion, they turned in case of need to German **hanka*, which they had sometimes heard used by Germanic mercenaries and colonists' (von Wartburg, 1969: 118).

The anthropological problem lies precisely in the last sentence. The acceptance of **hanka* is not a self-evident further step. It had social as well as linguistic aspects and we are in that world of diglossia, idiolect, register, and diatype, which is analysed by the contributors to Part II of this volume.

As von Wartburg himself notes, 'apart from *titta* "female breast", no other name for a part of the body was borrowed from Germanic at this early period' (p. 118). This arouses the suspicion that what appears to be category slip, caused by adventitious homonymy, may be in effect the merging of portions of two different registers pertaining to the body: a 'polite' and a 'sexual'. (Wartburg's 'German wet-nurses' can surely be only part of the story?) *Coxa* was borrowed into Late British, and survives in Welsh (*coes*: Lewis, 1943: 23) for the whole leg. The conservative nature of British Latin (Jackson, 1953: 109–112) tends to confirm the evident politeness of *coxa*, rather like Victorian 'limb'. In C. A. Ferguson's (1959) H:L classification (with Denison's use of diatype), *coxa* belongs to the 'H diatype'. The 'polite' body has many fewer subdivisions than the 'sexual' body. The 'medical' body may have more divisions than either and can be ambiguously polite or sexual. The Romance 'lower leg' took on a Greek veterinary terminology: *camba*, and in French this became 'the whole leg', thus subsuming *coxa*, as *jambe* does *cuisse* to this day. The present French bodily classification contains the debris of all classifications – a veritable *bricolage* (Lévi-Strauss, 1962b), which still continues while the *soutien-gorge* exists (to support a 'throat' which includes 'the breasts'). The linguistics of bodily categories would benefit from links with the social anthropology of bodily symbolism (Douglas, 1966).

At a more complicated cognitive level: there was the division in Middle High German, analysed by Trier (1931) and his pupils, between *wîsheit*, *kunst*, and *list* (which now mean approximately 'wisdom', 'art', and 'artifice'). *Kunst* was at the time, however, used for 'higher' courtly skills, and *list* for 'lower' non-courtly skills (von Wartburg, 1969: 157; Ullmann, 1959: 166). *Wîsheit* covered both, plus all human wisdom. By about 1300, however, *list* had fallen out (having become 'craft' or 'trick'), and *wîsheit* had become restricted to mystical experience. The field was now totally restructured by *kunst* and *wizzen* (a new term), the former now acquiring connotations of 'art' and the latter of 'knowledge' (von Wartburg, 1969: 157–158). The change represented not an autonomous category shift, but 'an abandonment of a social assessment of the field of knowledge' (ibid.: 161), resulting from the collapse of the courtly structure. An abandonment, a social anthropologist would insist, in favour of another.

The notion of the 'linguistic field', the 'semantic field', or the 'conceptual sphere'[8] was expanded by Trier until it has excited criticism:

> 'He postulates that the entire world-picture, which the individual and the linguistic community carry within them, can be completely and organically subdivided, from the whole downwards, into fields of ever-diminishing size. And he believes that, within these fields, the semantic domains of the individual words fit together in the same way to form an unbroken mosaic' (von Wartburg, 1969: 164).

A major defect of Trier's approach is that it does not express the multidimensionality of human category-making. Nevertheless, the independent development by the German semanticists of theories close to those of Sapir and Whorf is of great interest. The former stress vocabulary whereas the latter are also concerned with grammatical determinants. Similarly, culture and language were conceived by Pike (1954) as combining to provide a 'conceptual grid' through which individuals regard the world. Others speak of a 'filter'. Capell (1966) gathers together much useful material in this light. The static implications of these particular analogies are obvious, as is the positivistic assumption of a stable underlying reality.

Whorf, himself a 'total relativist' if ever there was one, had nevertheless a firm grip on reality. His account of his work as a fire insurance assessor is a classic (see Carroll, 1964: 135–137). For him, 'empty gasoline drums' exploded because they were classed as 'empty' (so that people smoked near them) instead of as 'full' (of gasoline fumes). 'Spun limestone', and 'scrap lead' from condensers, burst into flames, neither being as non-flammable as the classes 'stone' and 'lead' would suggest. Whorf's 'reality' was inextricably intertwined with human classifications. Physical explosions were produced by a careless mixture of categories as well as of chemicals. All the foregoing discussion obviously raises important implications for social anthropologists in the interpretation or translation of the categories of one society in terms of another. It is clear, however, that this task is not likely to be effectively tackled even in 'empirical' conditions with a merely 'technical' approach to language.

The way in which various levels of analysis and various disciplines fall together in this field can be exemplified further. The Banyang and Bangwa are two neighbouring peoples of West Cameroon. Among the former the linguistic term *ngo* refers to both 'gun' and 'fire'. Among the latter the word *ŋwo*, borrowed from the former, means 'gun', while *emɔ* means 'fire'. The implication that the Bangwa first received firearms from the Banyang direction is useful, since it was at least possible, on general grounds, that they received them from peoples on the other side. So far, then, linguistic data have suggested a historical implication. However, the Banyang themselves received the gun from the Efik via the Ejagham. In each case the artifact was exchanged without the Efik word. Yet Efik (and Ejagham) also label 'gun' and 'fire' by one term (Efik *ikaŋ*, Ejagham *ngon*). The Banyang accepted *both* the gun *and* (through translation) its identification with fire. This identification did not, as we see, survive the onward transmission to the Bangwa. The problem we now face is the explanation of the different kinds of linguistic contact between Efik (and Ejagham) and Banyang, and Banyang and Bangwa. We may note, however, that physical contact between Banyang and Bangwa is interrupted by a high escarpment. The further analysis of these differences and similarities would lie in both linguistics and social anthropology, and in social anthropology for its own sake – not simply for the assistance (if any) this may yield to linguists.

A more complex problem is touched upon on page 223 below. This is the well-known process whereby loan-words from Norman French produced the parallel terms in English for 'live' and 'slaughtered' farm beasts: sheep/mutton, calf/veal, pig/pork, and cow/beef. Sir Walter Scott drew the conclusion that the split in the English categories reflected the fact that the English knew the product on the hoof, whereas the Normans received it cooked. The perpetuation of the division when the Normans and English became one speech community is less easily explained. It is here that what would appear to be a simple marriage between social anthropology and linguistics through the notion of 'social stratification' appears totally inadequate. Other distinctions on class lines vanished, frequently by the supersession of the cruder English by the politer French. The structuring of this regular series of oppositions is quite other, and is likely to express certain classifying propensities among the speakers of English, through which they turned a fortuitous bilingual treasure to their own ends. The study of such structures has, so far at least, been mostly the work of social anthropologists (Lévi-Strauss, e.g. 1962b and *passim*; Leach, 1964).

THE LEVEL OF EXPLANATION

I have considered the question of classification under the heading of 'pragmatic' contacts between social anthropology and language. In fact, it is clear that these matters raise theoretical issues of some moment. I shall examine here the contacts between the explanatory theory of social anthropology and linguistics mainly under headings relating to Ferdinand de Saussure and Claude Lévi-Strauss. In the time of the former, principles were stated which have come clearly to the fore (as far as social anthropology is concerned) only in the time of the latter. The discussion of these writings will form a framework for the consideration of a number of other theoretical positions and analytical themes in the past and present contacts between the two disciplines. Then, under the heading 'The Present Volume', the relation of the papers gathered here to some of these issues will complete this introductory essay.

Ferdinand de Saussure

The total neglect of Saussure by British social anthropologists for so long is at first sight incredible. It can be explained in part by the intellectual isolation, and preoccupation with ethnography, of the interwar period. In mitigation, however, it should be said that J. R. Firth, the functionalists' own linguist, was not a truly sympathetic interpreter of Saussure, and that Malinowski never understood him. Even in the more enlightened conditions of recent years many social anthropologists seem to have discovered Saussure backwards, as it were, through Roland

Barthes and Lévi-Strauss, both of whom in their different ways insert a barrier between the reader and Saussure. Yet his thought lies behind many of the ideas we have just discussed. Obviously, with over fifty years of debate behind us, the following remarks can be only the merest sketch of even his purely anthropological significance, but in a book primarily addressed to social anthropologists the task is worth undertaking.

Ferdinand de Saussure made great contributions to comparative philology at an early age (1878). He taught Sanskrit in Paris from 1881 to 1891, but he is known chiefly for his lectures on linguistics given at the University of Geneva 1906–11. In 1916, after his death, his pupils Charles Bally and Albert Sechehaye published a remarkable reconstruction of his lectures, by a process which is itself of keen anthropological interest:

> 'All those who had the privilege of participating in his richly rewarding instruction regretted that no book had resulted from it. After his death, we hoped to find in his manuscripts, obligingly made available to us by Mme de Saussure, a faithful or at least an adequate outline of his inspiring lectures. At first we thought that we might simply collate F. de Saussure's personal notes and the notes of his students. We were grossly misled. We found nothing – or almost nothing – that resembled his students' note-books. As soon as they had served their purpose, F. de Saussure destroyed the rough drafts of the outlines used for his lectures. In the drawers of his secretary [read 'secretaire' or 'writing desk'!] we found only older outlines which, although certainly not worthless, could not be integrated into the material of the three courses' (Saussure, 1916, 1922 edn: 7–8; trans. 1964: xiii).[9]

So it was that the notebooks of seven students were pooled, and the courses reconstructed.

> 'The problem of re-creating F. de Saussure's thought was all the more difficult because the re-creation had to be wholly objective. At each point we had to get to the crux of each particular thought by trying to see its definitive form in the light of the whole system. We had first to weed out variations and irregularities characteristic of oral delivery, then to fit the thought into its natural framework and present each part of it in the order intended by the author even when his

intention, not always apparent, had to be surmised' (1922: 9; trans. 1964: xv).

Thus was compiled and published the *Cours de linguistique générale*, and with it was founded the Geneva school of linguistics which Bally and Sechehaye carried on in succession to the master until 1945, dying in 1946 and 1947 respectively. Since then all the sources have been published and critically analysed (Godel, 1957; Engler, 1967, 1968). It is somehow appropriate that the *Cours* and Saussure should coexist like signifier and signified in one of his own linguistic signs!

For anthropologists the significance of Saussure's own approach is that his analytical ideas were 'sociolinguistic' rather than purely linguistic. His central distinction was of course between *la langue* and *la parole* (which may be translated as 'language' and 'speech', or 'speaking' – Engler, 1968: 54). *La langue* for Saussure is the system that is abstracted from the whole body of utterances made by human speakers within a speech community. *La parole* is susceptible of acoustic measurement, of tape-recording, and of other physical tests. *La langue* is not, because this is a system abstracted from, and in turn superimposed upon, *la parole*. This distinction *langue/parole* can provide a master exemplar for other distinctions: such as the colour category versus the physical spectrum, or the kinship category versus the biological relationship measured by the study of genetic structure and mating patterns. Yet *langue/parole* is used by Saussure in several different ways. This basic antinomy between 'form' and 'substance' (where 'form' at one level may become 'substance' at another) has been frequently hardened into typologies: types of *langue*, types of *parole*, intermediate forms (e.g. Sechehaye, 1940). Yet its essential character derives precisely from this supposed source of confusion (Hockett, 1968: 15; Householder, 1970: 130). We can now see that its interest lies for social anthropology in its original intuitive form, and the antinomy deserves a place among those ideas that are part of the 'intellectual capital' of the subject (Evans-Pritchard, introduction to Hertz, 1960: 24; Needham, 1963: xl–xliv).[10]

Also of central interest to us is Saussure's vision of language as a system of signs. His contribution here was to stress that language is not a simple labelling device (*une nomenclature* – 1922: 34): as if there were only objects in the real world waiting to be given 'names'. He did this by talking of a linguistic sign as consisting of two components: the 'signifier' and the 'signified'. The English term *tree* is such a linguistic sign, consisting both of the acoustic chain rendered as /tri:/ and of the range of phenomena that this sequence signifies in English. One could not therefore equate two signs in different languages (say, *tree* in English and *arbre* in French) without taking into account differences in the 'signified' component. Saussure's 'signified' is, however, not reality but a 'concept'. The sign is not a combination of a set of acoustic measurements with a botanical organism (Malmberg, 1964: 44). 'Both parts of the sign are equally psychical' (Saussure, 1922: 32; 1964 trans. 'psychological', p. 15). The 'arbitrariness' of the linguistic sign is a Saussurean notion of some complexity (Benvéniste, 1939). It was clearly designed to answer adherents of the view (supported incidentally by Tylor) that all language had a representational origin – like 'sign' language. The acoustic chain may not in fact be entirely arbitrary in its association with the 'concept' (e.g. Jakobson, 1960; J. R. Firth, 1957a: 192–193). Like Durkheim and Lévi-Strauss (and Chomsky), Saussure wishes to stress the objectivity of his psychical entities:

> 'Linguistic signs, while being essentially psychical, are not abstractions; the associations ratified by *le consentement collectif*, of which the totality makes up language, are realities which have their seat in the brain' (1922: 32; my trans.).

Saussure was aware of the very broad implications of his theory of signs. He thought that there should be a special discipline to take into account all systems of signs (*une science qui étude la vie des signes au sein de la vie sociale*) – under the name 'semiology'.

> 'Semiology would show what constitutes signs, what laws govern them. Since the science does not yet exist, no-one can say what it would be; but it has a right to existence, staked out in advance. Linguistics is only a part of the general science of semiology; the laws discovered by semiology will be applicable to linguistics, and the latter will circumscribe a well-defined area within the mass of human facts' (1922: 33;

trans. 1964: 16 – where *humain* is translated as *anthropological*).

And further:

> 'If we are to discover the true nature of language (*langue*) we must learn what it has in common with all other systems of the same order: certain linguistic factors that might seem very important at first glance (e.g. the role of the vocal apparatus) ought to receive only secondary consideration if they merely serve to set language apart from other systems. In this way, one will do more than clarify the linguistic problem. By studying rites, customs and the like, as signs, I believe these facts will appear in a new light, and one will feel the need to include them in the science of semiology and to explain them by its laws' (1922: 35; trans. 1964: 17, which has been heavily amended here).

These prophetic remarks, published while Malinowski was still in the Trobriands, and no doubt formulated some time before 1911 (thus being blocked off from us by a whole generation of functionalism), are the ultimate source of many of the more general influences, coming from linguistics and the French school, which have penetrated through various cracks in the foundations of empirical social anthropology since 1945 and have gradually become part of the climate of thought. Saussure himself, like Bloomfield, the eminent American linguist of the next generation, was most concerned with the links between his study and psychology. But Saussure does ask the question: 'Must linguistics then be combined with sociology?' (For him *anthropologie* is not yet 'social' anthropology.) 'Language', says Saussure, echoing Durkheim, 'is a social fact' (1922: 21; trans. 1964: 6).

Doroszewski (1933), who clearly demonstrates the Durkheimian nature of Saussure's *langue* (Durkheim's social:individual = Saussure's *langue*:*parole*), makes the interesting point:

> 'F. de Saussure – as I know from an exact source – followed the philosophical debate between Durkheim and Tarde with deep interest. If one takes into consideration not only the idea, essential for Saussure, of *langue* but also the comple-

> mentary one of *parole*, the Saussurean doctrine as a whole then appears as a curious attempt, undertaken by a linguist of genius, to reconcile the opposed doctrines of Durkheim and Tarde. In the opposition of *langue* and *parole* one glimpses the opposition of the idea of Durkheim to that of Tarde' (90–91, my trans.).

French linguists have generally retained a 'sociological' viewpoint since Saussure's day. Vendryes (1921, 1952) and Sechehaye (1933), for example, reaffirmed his aims. Meillet contributed to *L'Année Sociologique*. Marcel Cohen (1948, 1955 edn: 40), while finding Durkheim's school *plutôt idéaliste*, mentions Saussure in the same breath as Marx and Engels (the latter's *Der fränkische Dialekt* was published in Moscow in 1935).

Another parallel between Saussure's thought and that of French sociology, and of the social anthropology of Radcliffe-Brown and Evans-Pritchard following it, is his use of the terms *synchronic* and *diachronic* to describe two basic approaches to his subject-matter. Saussure was concerned to show that the historical study of language, which had dominated linguistics until his day, was not the only mode of investigation. He likened this to the study of a longitudinal section along the stem of a plant (1922: 125). He demonstrated that a cross-section of the stem – his analogy for a synchronic study – would also show a system. The Malinowskian advance in social anthropology, which occurred soon after Saussure's death, took a similar form. The 'structural–functional' position stressed the synchronic *pattern*, in contrast to the historicist approaches – the preoccupation with origins – of the preceding period. Saussure was, however, a more flexible thinker than Malinowski, or, at least, than the latter's immediate successors. He recognized the significance of both synchrony and diachrony, although he argued that the two approaches were to be clearly separated. He speaks of 'laws' for both approaches, but achieves an important insight which leads him far beyond Radcliffe-Brown, another believer in laws, who died only in the fifties. He says: 'The synchronic law is general but not imperative . . . the synchronic law reports a state of affairs.' Synchronic patterns contained no indication of their own stability or lack of it: 'The arrangement that the law defines is precarious, precisely because it is not imperative' (1922: 131; trans. 1964: 92). Sometimes, as we shall see, Saussure loosely uses the term *équilibre* for a synchronic state, but there is here no sideways slip into a view of a self-perpetuating equilibrium of a quasi-organic type, such as has dogged social anthropology into our own days.

It is worth citing directly some other statements of Saussure despite their familiarity to linguists: for example, his likening of language to chess.

> 'But of all comparisons which might be imagined the most fruitful is the one that might be drawn between the functioning of language and the game of chess. In both instances we are confronted with a system of values and their observable modifications' (1922: 125; trans. 1964: 88).

(Not a system of valuations, 'moral values', but a system in which all parts have a certain weighting, a *valency*.) In what follows it may be worth reading 'society' for language':

> 'First: a state of the set of chessmen [i.e. the state of the board at any one time] corresponds closely to a state of language. The respective value of the pieces depends on their position on the chessboard, just as each linguistic term derives its value from its opposition to all the other terms' (1922: 125–126; trans. 1964: 88).

(Note that word 'opposition'. Here we have clearly stated the now fashionable anthropological view that elements in the system define themselves in opposition to all other elements in the system.)

> 'In the second place, the system is always momentary: it varies from one position to the next. It is also true that values depend above all else on an unchangeable convention: the set of rules that exists before a game begins and persists after each move. Rules that are agreed upon once and for all exist in language too; they are the constant principles of semiology.'

(We may note here the insight that the very positions of the pieces, and their values, embody the operation of rules.)

> 'Finally to pass from one state of equilibrium to the next, or – according to our terminology – from one synchrony to the

> next, only one chess piece has to be moved: there is no general rummage. Here we have the counterpart of the diachronic phenomenon with all its peculiarities' (1922: 126; trans. 1964: 88).

In particular, Saussure notes that changes affecting single elements (as with the movement of only one chess piece) have repercussions on the whole system:

> 'Resulting changes of value will be, according to the circumstances, either nil, very serious, or of moderate importance. A certain move can revolutionize the game, and even affect pieces that are not immediately involved' (1922: 126; trans. 1964: 89).

Saussure had in mind linguistic phenomena of the type (say) of the loss of Indo-European *p* in Common Celtic. All modern Celtic languages do have *p*. Sommerfelt and others said, in effect, that the whole phonological system shuddered, as it were, and rebuilt itself (Hamp, 1958: 209–210). The *p* in Welsh, for example, is frequently a reflex of Indo-European **qu* (Jackson, 1953: 413). But we may extend this to those socially more significant sections of language that we have already noted, as when a term drops out from a slot of a system of classification. Diachronically, two of the pieces in the Latin kinship set *avunculus* (MB), *amita* (MZ), *patruus* (FB), *matertera* (FZ), disappeared. The synchronic values of *tante* (MZ, FZ) and *oncle* (MB, FB) as members of a two-piece set are quite different from those of their diachronic 'sames' *amita* and *avunculus* which existed in a four-piece set. So also with the loss of *femur*, in our other example, with its bilingual repercussions.

Saussure says, further: 'In chess each move is absolutely distinct from the preceding and the subsequent equilibrium. The change if effected belongs to neither state: only states matter.' This last is an aphoristic remark which is expanded as follows:

> 'In a game of chess any particular position has a unique characteristic of being freed from all antecedent positions: the route used in arriving there makes absolutely no difference; one who has followed the entire match has no advantage over the curious party who comes up at a critical moment to inspect the state of the game . . .' (1922: 126; trans. 1964: 89).

We come now to a feature of Saussure's thinking that many have found unnecessarily rigid. He insists not only that a *synchronic* study of phenomena must be conceptually distinguished from a *diachronic* study, but that the 'facts' elicited belong in effect to two different universes. Diachronic formulations cannot be reduced to synchronic ones. There is an 'opposition' between the two modes, which derives from his conviction that the methodologies of the two modes are not interchangeable. Saussure has been criticized for this by some who wrongly think that they are making a stand for linguistic holism by denying that the synchronic and the diachronic can be separated.[11] We are, of course, concerned here with models drawn upon different selections of data, and Saussure's instinct was sound in recognizing that rigour demanded that they be not confused.

Saussure states the intuitive problem of such critics much more effectively when he envisages (as a purely speculative hypothesis) the possibility of a 'panchronic' viewpoint. In this he is particularly advanced. 'In linguistics,' he says, 'as in chess, there are rules that outlive all events' (1922: 135; trans. 1964: 95). The way in which a panchronic view might be developed may be clarified as follows: We say that synchrony equals a state of the chessboard. The observer will deduce some of the rules, even most of the rules, of chess from sequential states of the board, the 'values' of the elements (the pieces) embodying in their positions the rules. But certain of the rules can never be deduced from either the game so far, or the present state of the game, e.g. the rule for mate. It is the rules in this total sense that Saussure would exclude from synchrony and diachrony and assign to the panchronic field. Saussure's refusal to build these rules into the linguistic phenomena themselves is an index of his determination to maintain a distance between language and the *study of* language. We have seen that the diachronic model for him depends upon the 'opposition', the contrast, of each element with another in a series; while the synchronic model depends upon the opposition of each element to each other in a system at a single state in time. The rules that link the two analytical modes of opposition do not appear in either mode separately. He correctly perceived, despite the obscurities of his expression, that their methodological opposition was resolved not *in* language, but in what is now commonly termed metalanguage.

Whatever criticisms may be advanced against Saussure (Collinder, 1968, makes a spirited attack on Saussure's 'polemic' claims)[12] it is now the essential 'modernity' of his propositions that comes through the lecture-notes of his students. It is all there, not only synchrony and diachrony, but the idea of opposition, later to be further developed by Trubetzkoy, Jakobson, and the Prague School, and thence bequeathed to Lévi-Strauss. Much modern toying with games theory is made to look jejune before Saussure's early-twentieth-century analogy. (He was always aware of its pitfalls: 'In order to make the game of chess seem at every point like the functioning of language, we should have to imagine an unconscious or unintelligent player' – 1922: 127; trans. 1964: 89.) His chess analogy, of course, reappears in Wittgenstein (for example, 1963: 15),[13] in the jurist Hart (1961), and in Ross (1958); see also below, pp. 215–217. If Saussure is the true father of structuralism, we must, however, pay tribute to the influence of the French school of sociology in stimulating his thought. Saussure, as it were, channelled into linguistics parts of the new *sociologie* which lacked concrete application, given the paucity of systematically collected social data available at the time. The more copious linguistic data served as a testing-field from which the analytical concepts were returned to Durkheim's successors in a later generation, added to and enriched. Lévi-Strauss frequently speaks with Saussure's words:

> 'Anthropology aims to be a *semiological* science . . . This is yet another reason (in addition to many others) why anthropology should maintain close contact with linguistics, where, with regard to the social fact of speech there is the same concern to avoid separating the objective basis of language (sound) from its signifying functions (meaning)' (Lévi-Strauss, 1963a: 364).

Hjelmslev of Copenhagen now seems to us, as he did years ago to Bally (Hjelmslev, 1959: 31), to be the most clear exponent of the Saussurean vision. He cites (1943 and trans. 1963: 107–108) Czechoslovak 'semiological' work of the thirties on folk costume, art, and literature which is not easily accessible,[14] as well as Buyssens (1943). He is aware of the relevance of logicians like Carnap, and sees sign systems as 'abstract transformation systems' (p. 108), bringing us, in 1943, into the world of modern social anthropology, and, as elsewhere (see below, p. 228), using the terminology of generativeness fourteen years before its American incarnation. He remarked in 1948 (in Hjelmslev, 1959: 34) that semiology did 'not appeal to linguists'. Even he did not seem prepared to pursue further the fact that 'in Saussure's *Cours* this general discipline is thought of as erected on an essentially sociological and psychological basis' (Hjelmslev, 1943: 96; trans. 1963: 108). Yet his system does not close in upon itself to subsume only linguistic data: 'In practice a language is a semiotic into which all other semiotics may be translated – both all other languages, and all other conceivable semiotic structures' (1943: 97; trans. 1963: 109). Of which, more later.

This is different from Barthes (1967: 9), who says that, contrary to Saussure's expectation, semiology must form part of linguistics because: 'It is far from certain that in the social life of today there are to be found any extensive systems of signs outside human language.' This remarkable misapprehension derives from Barthes's concern with the semiology of minor systems (the Highway Code, fashion). His basic problem, however, going back to Hjelmslev's observation, is that linguists could not actually see in the sociology or anthropology they were offered in the generation after Saussure any real evidence of what Saussure meant. The sociology of Durkheim had, as it were, gone underground. Only now, through Lévi-Strauss, has a semiotic of wide social relevance begun to emerge. Barthes's semiology, like that of Buyssens (1943), is much too closely calqued on detailed linguistic example to fill the role. It is a *semiologia minor* of small iconic systems. To understand Saussure's semiology aright we must see that its principles will be only partially derivable from language; a semiotic of society will derive its own principles which would be conjoined with those of other systems. Barthes's difficulty is akin to that of anthropologists who attempt to apply the pragmatic operational concepts (data-laden) of another discipline to their own.

Saussure's panchronic (or panchronistic) approach, on the other hand, which for him remained merely a programme, because he could see no model or method to do justice to it, has passed as far as language is concerned into the hands of the transformational generative grammarians. Chomsky states that rules can be deduced from the study of language in a given state, such that, for him, a grammar can predict all well-formed sentences in a language, including those that no one has uttered. It has been frequently said that the 'competence' and 'performance' of the generative grammarians is analogous to the opposition *langue*:*parole*, although Chomsky's own view has not remained consistent on the matter (1968). It has been further recognized (King, 1969: 11) that the strict Saussurean principles make comparison between two dialects impossible: for the 'values' of elements in the two systems are not the same. Thus *o* in a dialect with a five-vowel system is not comparable in value with *o* in a dialect with a seven-vowel system. This problem is not unlike that presented by diachronic linguistics: in what sense does /ai/ in the Modern English vowel system 'correspond' to Middle English /i:/? The transformationalist solution is, nevertheless, implicit in Saussure's rigorous perception of the use of models. The evident connections between the values in two systems can be described only at the level of oppositions between rules themselves in a system of rules. This is what transformationalist treatment in terms of 'rule-loss' and 'rule-acquisition' really means (Chomsky, 1968, and see below, p. 232). The 'grammars' of the transformationalists are models of 'competence'. They are seeking in effect transformational 'meta-rules' for the linking of Saussurean 'states'. Just as Saussureans (and Saussure) frequently mistake the model *langue* for a reality greater than the model, so too do many transformationalists speak as if their programmes for a model of 'competence' are already achieved. The panchronic approach may, then, be said to be in process of formulation – in principle at least. We shall not be surprised if its practice presents great difficulties.[15]

Semiotic and society[16]

Why should social anthropologists think again about Saussure? Apart from his significance in having anticipated the discussion of diachrony and synchrony, and having shown the way to the notion of system and opposition, and the rest, his ideas contain a generality that simplifies the task of even the most empirically minded. I will take one example. We commonly find that ritual signs have contradictory poles of meaning. Turner (1964: 30–31) expresses this distinction in different ways. Thus a symbol may refer to 'emotions, blood, genitalia' (at the 'sensory' pole), and at the same time to 'unity, continuity of groups' (at the 'ideological' pole). Sapir's division of symbols into 'condensation' symbols (with unconscious roots) and 'referential' symbols (signals, flags) corresponds, in Turner's view, to these two poles – save that ritual symbols combine both. Some social anthropologists restrict the term 'sign' to Sapir's referential symbols, and 'symbol' to Sapir's condensation symbols. These distinctions are not too easy to defend from a Saussurean point of view. Take a Ndembu linguistic sign, the *signifier* – *mudyi* (an 'acoustic image'); the *signified* – 'a tree with milky-white sap' ('the concept'). Now, the association of 'milky-white sap' with 'mother's milk' is so salient that the equation might even qualify for immediate inclusion in the Ndembu dictionary as part of the 'concept' (ibid.: 21–27). The more 'biological' or 'sensory' aspect may thus qualify by a lexicographical definition as 'conscious'. The 'unity of the matrilineage' or the like might well be shown to be, on the contrary, unconscious. The emotional, biological ('sensory') pole may then possibly appear more clearly part of the linguistic sign than the 'ideological' pole.

It would seem more useful to turn to the distinction between a linguistic sign and a ritual sign. Now a ritual sign is not expressed *as such* in language. The '*mudyi* tree', as a member of a set of ritual signs, forms part of a semiology distinct from the lexical element *mudyi*, as a linguistic sign in the Ndembu language. The ritual tree is, however, no less a 'concept' than the signified of *mudyi*. The botanical tree thus generates two 'concepts'. One is tied to the acoustic chain *mudyi* and is a linguistic sign. The other is tied to ritual images, and is a ritual signifier, in a ritual sign (see *Figure 5*).

In principle, such a sign exists without any 'label': its label (that by which it is known) is its 'value' as an element in a system of like elements. In practice, ritual signifieds overlap linguistic signifieds. Elements termed 'sensory' and 'ideological' can fall into either field. The linguistic signifieds can nevertheless be consciously 'unpacked' in language. The ritual signifieds by definition contain elements that no one has as yet unpacked into the semiotic of linguistic signs. We may translate the ritual semiotic into language, but if we are not careful we end up with the heaps of polarities in which Turner's many valuable treatments leave us knee-deep. A 'metasemiotic' which will deal with the structure of all signs must make for a greater simplicity than does the laborious rendering of ritual signifieds into natural

FIGURE 5 *Linguistic and ritual signs*

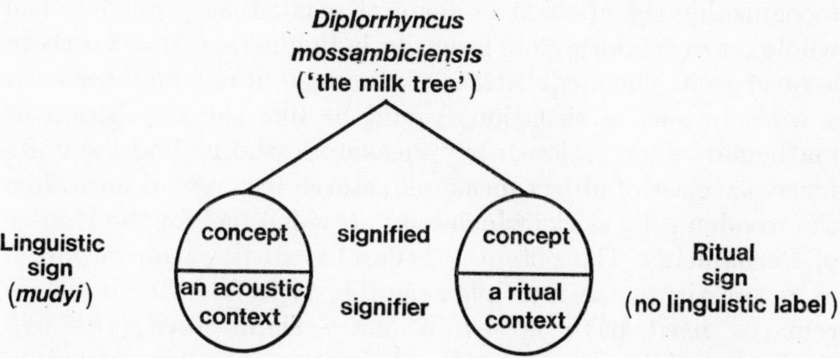

language. The polarities within symbols may be at least provisionally understood by placing their elements in different sign systems. What has been said about ritual semiotic in relation to linguistic semiotic is applicable to all semiotics we may define. We may agree so far with Barthes that language will often provide an index to some of these systems, as in his own study of fashion – but, interestingly enough, this is just where language as a semiotic is most obscure. These hints of other systems often subsist as 'redundancies' in language. The semiotic of the human body has already been mentioned here. Its continual 'interference' with the linguistic classification of the body is one of the daily problems of ordered social existence, although it has been illustrated above from traditional linguistic material.

Blank banners

We might visualize a semiotic system that depended, in the absence of the power of speech, upon the apperception by the human participants of contextually defined logical relations among themselves in space. Let us say: the relative position of each participant to another in a gathering, and to items in a fixed environment. The 'elements' of the semiotic would be stated by their existential presence and would acquire 'meaning' ('value') through the 'relations', which would themselves be apperceptible as some kind of syntax. The possible range of such separate semiotics without speech is great. Careful structuring of the bio-physical environment would be required, for the actors themselves are symbols in the semiotic, and a recognizable set of theatres for action must be provided. The whole set of semiotic slots is empty in linguistic terms, for there is no speech. The 'acquisition' of language (if one may use such a word in such a situation) would be like the acquisition of mathematics for zealous early measurers who had *ad hoc* units for every class of object measured, stored in physical form (like the wooden tally sticks which long provided fuel for the Houses of Parliament). The potential generality of the acoustic image as a substitute for multiplex signifier-types is evident. These remarks need have no evolutionary significance (although William Golding's novel, *The Inheritors*, has his retreating Neanderthalers using the new acoustic semiotic with only partial skill – for quick and accurate communication they show each other 'pictures'). If they *were* to have such significance, it would undoubtedly be to tell us (*pace* Chomsky) that non-linguistic semiotics had reached a high degree of sophistication before language more and more codified their realm.

The similarity of my hypothetical case to 'primitive' semiotics, which actually coexist with language, suggests that the need for careful structuring of the environment is the greater where language does not purport to translate all semiotics. The chief feature of archaic, folk, 'minority', and certain other forms of society – a factitious conformity – thus acquires the aspect of a 'channel-holding' mechanism. Furthermore, if new movements occur even in highly 'linguistic' societies they may, perhaps can only, be expressed at first in a non-linguistic semiotic. To that extent the political movements of the seventies are demonstrations with blank banners, whatever may, for the nonce, be inscribed upon them. At a more detailed level: the supposed 'restricted codes' of Bernstein's working-class dropouts are best understood as a local variant of the 'primitive' case.

Finally, the ancient and still flourishing human apperception of non-linguistic semiotics, through the structuring of the bio-social environment at all levels, provides a suitably non-mystical 'locus' for Durkheimian collective representations, and other 'cosmological' entities, which long ago roused the revulsion of Malinowski, as they still do of others in those departments of social anthropology where his orthodox tradition was transmitted unbroken. It must be admitted that Durkheim himself (1898, trans. 1951) struggles with the relationship between individual and collective representations. He is reduced to a declaration of faith, and some hopes for telepathy! (1951: 18–23.)

The French school bases itself upon the notions of *extériorité* and *extériorisation* – terms that English-speaking commentators do not always comprehend. For Saussure, *extériorité* was a feature of *langue* (Doroszewski, 1933: 89). Sechehaye (1933: 63), his pupil, saw language as 'like' customs, beliefs, political organization: 'Comme toutes ces choses, elle constitue un objet extérieur à l'individu. . . .' How appropriate that Cassirer should, in the same journal in the same year, speak of the linguistic construction of the world of objects as 'l'extériorisation des simples états du moi' (1933: 30). That Simonis should speak of Lévi-Strauss's work as expressing the 'exteriorisation of man' (1968: 335) is thus natural and expected. It is not just that Saussuro-Durkheimians see collective representations as 'outside' the individual: the individual is somehow part of them. It is of interest that McLuhan (1970: 37–40) reproduces the essential notion of *extériorisation* as 'outering' – although I am not aware of the process by which he thus incorporated seventy years of French thought.[17]

The terminology of semiotic can be expressed more mechanistically through communication theory. We have to visualize that the message on one channel becomes itself the channel for meta-messages. Lévi-Strauss (1963a: 61) implicitly states the general case, from the particular case of women: *human beings speak, but they are themselves also symbolic elements in a communication system* (see also Ardener, in press). When language fails or lags in its task, as is clearly to some extent the case in social life today, we shall be glad of our attempts to unravel the general semiological principles, to which Saussure so long ago directed our attention.

Claude Lévi-Strauss and the phoneme

The original essays in which Lévi-Strauss set out his inspiration from linguistics are far from uniform in their view of the subject. The first statement was published as long ago as August 1945, in the opening issue of *Word*. His introductory remarks gain additional interest in view of the time of their publication:

> 'Linguistics occupies a special place among the social sciences, to whose ranks it unquestionably belongs. It is not merely a social science like the others, but, rather, the one in which by far the greatest progress has been made. It is probably the only one which can truly claim to be a science and which has achieved both the formulation of an empirical method and an understanding of the nature of the data submitted to its analysis' (1963a: 31).

He speaks of its 'privileged position' and of psychologists, sociologists, and anthropologists 'eager to learn from modern linguistics the road which leads to the empirical knowledge of social phenomena' (ibid.). The praise of linguistics is, at least in part, a conventional praise of one's hosts in a new journal, and a certain disarming of criticism of trespass. Nevertheless, 1945 was early days indeed for a vision that is hardly fully accepted by the majority of functionalist social anthropologists after a quarter of a century. One might, of course, say 'old days indeed', for Lévi-Strauss refers to an article of Mauss (1924) for the statement: 'Sociology would certainly have progressed much further if it had everywhere followed the lead of the linguists . . .' (in Mauss, 1950, 1966 edn: 299). Lévi-Strauss believed that the position had changed in degree: linguists and social anthropologists had kept an eye on one another, but if the latter had not followed the linguistic example as far as they might, 'after all anthropology and sociology were looking to linguistics only for insights; nothing foretold a revelation' (1963a: 33).

What was this revelation, in 1945? He says: 'The advent of

structural linguistics completely changed this situation' and goes on to the apocalyptic:

> 'Structural linguistics will certainly play the same renovating role with respect to the social sciences that nuclear physics, for example, has played for the physical sciences' (ibid.).

A statement published in the month of the explosion of the Hiroshima and Nagasaki atomic bombs would reach an audience that would not underestimate the contribution of nuclear physics: nuclear physics was not then old hat. The revelation referred, in fact, to Prague School linguistics (then emigrated to the United States) to which Lévi-Strauss had been introduced by Roman Jakobson. The statement is curious, and shares the quality of so many programmatic utterances by men of genius – so apparently inadequate and undocumented at the time; and yet brought eventually to a kind of realization.[18]

The generation after Saussure had led to a new phase of consolidation of linguistic theory (broadly in the period 1920–1950), during which many of the developments loosely describable as 'structural linguistics' of different schools came into existence. This period is marked by the achievement for Saussure's synchronic linguistics of a *method* which offered the same rigour as that of 'comparative philology' (Trubetzkoy, 1933: 242–243). The method and the period are marked by the discussion of the so-called *phoneme*, an essentially common-sense idea which awoke a great deal of discussion while enabling a mass of detailed linguistic work to be produced. It was broadly contemporary with the high Malinowskian period in social anthropology, and it showed much of the same productive endeavour. It was, however, basically the least 'anthropological' of the linguistic movements. Looked at from the Saussurean view (which had a message for diachronic as well as synchronic linguists, and for the study of all signs, not merely of linguistic signs), it was an inward movement.

The structuralists concentrated most characteristically on one of the essential elements: synchronic linguistics (cf. Wells, 1947). The phoneme was at home only in the detailed data of linguistic description. To see the early Lévi-Strauss and even Pike (who was a linguist and an anthropologist) struggling with it – Laocoön-like figures coiled up in serpents – to apply it to social phenomena is quite astonishing. The relation of the phoneme to Saussurean principles is like that of the roller-skate to the concept of the wheel – a particular and specialized application. To those ignorant of the wheel the roller-skate may appear to be a beautiful object, as no doubt it is. We should look very foolish if we built a carriage in the form of a roller-skate. To some extent this is what our anthropologists have been up to, even demonstrating it with simple pride to linguists. In short, it was the Saussureanism of the phoneme that was transferable – not the terminology. By its 'Saussureanism' I mean its relationship to the opposition *langue*:*parole*, and to the notions of 'system', 'opposition' itself, 'value', and the like.

The common-sense aspect of the matter is best approached by our most characteristically British contribution to linguistics: the almost single-handed development of the study of phonetics during the lifetime of Henry Sweet (1845–1912). Phonetics could be very simply defined for a long time as the study of *the acoustic features of speech and modes of their accurate transcription*. The rub lies in the second part. For, to some extent, the study of phonetics derives from an interest in the discrepancy between the spoken and written forms of language, and the assumption originally was that acoustic features = 'sounds' = letters in an alphabet. It is no coincidence that phonetics in this country developed when it did. The situation with English in England exemplified, and still exemplifies, some of the best stimuli for such a study: (a) a discrepancy between the orthography of the written language and its received pronunciation; (b) a discrepancy between the received pronunciation in its turn and the dialects of English; (c) a discrepancy between the social statuses of different forms of speech, including received pronunciation and the dialects. British phonetics, so often scorned as old-fashioned by American linguists (Gleason, 1955a), was a true exercise in sociolinguistics. Henry Sweet was dramatized as Professor Higgins by Bernard Shaw in *Pygmalion* (and set to music in *My Fair Lady*), and Higgins's problem is essentially that of Bernstein (1958, 1960, 1961, 1965): one of social engineering.[19]

By the 1880s there was also a strong international interest in phonetics. In 1886 the International Phonetic Association was born (at first under the name of the Phonetic Teachers' Association) with the early and admitted aim of producing a phonetic alphabet capable of writing any 'sound' in any language, an aim that turned out to be, in its narrowest sense, either impossible or misguided (IPA, 1949; J. R. Firth, 1957a: 92–120). Nevertheless this search for a complete alphabet of sounds led the phoneticians by a meticulous and highly empirical route to the same conclusions as Saussure. They started off by thinking that there was only a difference between 'writing' or 'spelling' and the sounds of speech, and that if more 'sounds' could be written orthography would be more correct. In fact they discovered, when they precisely analysed 'sounds', that speakers acted linguistically as if only a certain number of sounds existed. The rest they classed together with these few. Each language classed them differently. Here, then, came the first perception of linguists working at the level of *parole* that the *langue* structure extended into the 'phonetic' sphere. Thus the category we may mark /r/ in Japanese has an acoustic spread that covers a particular 'band'. This overlaps with the conventional /r/ of English (just as the terms for colours in the two languages overlap in their subdivisions of the visual spectrum), but part of the realization of /r/ in Japanese also overlaps with the realization of /l/ in English. All that remained was to give a name to the 'conventional sounds' of a language to distinguish them from the 'real sounds': discovered by the phoneticians. Sweet was quick off the mark. The 'real sounds' were recorded in 'narrow' transcription and the conventional ones that speakers recognized were those recorded in 'broad' transcription (Jacobson, 1966). Had the matter remained there we should have realized sooner that the supposed 'real' sounds were as much an abstraction as were the conventional ones.

But the term needed was supplied as we know: the 'native phonological categories', the conventional sounds that the speakers recognized, came to be called *phonemes*. In the terminology that was later accepted, speech sounds were called *phones*. The acoustic phones, which a language's speakers called 'the same', were called *allophones* of the *phoneme*. The basic term itself was later the subject of dispute. It was claimed as having been invented, or first used, or first 'properly' used, by numerous schools. Most workers in general linguistics in the period from 1870 to 1912 had, however, come to see the need for the distinction between the 'significant' sounds and the 'insignificant' sounds used in speaking a language. Trubetzkoy (1933: 227) attributes the basic distinction to J. Winteler in 1876. As for the term: it was used at least as early as 1876 in France (*phonème*) by Havet, although only in the meaning of 'speech-sound', i.e. just what it is not. The first person to use it in print in the sense it has today (as *fonema*) was Kruszewski, a student of the University of Kazan in 1879, who derived the idea from the Russo-Polish linguist Baudouin de Courtenay who had been working on it since 1868. Sweet never used the term, but by 1915 de Courtenay's term was in use with the students of Sweet in London (D. Jones, 1964: 4). Sapir, the American linguist, did not use it consistently until the thirties. It fully entered American usage with Bloomfield's book *Language* (1933). On the continent, Trubetzkoy, Karcevskij, and Jakobson received the phoneme concept from Baudouin de Courtenay, although none, as it happens, was his pupil (Trubetzkoy, 1933: 229).

The story of the phoneme is thus two separate stories: the story of an idea and the story of a term. The term for some time overwhelmed the idea. Broadly, two main approaches developed:

1. The Bloomfieldian or American view. According to this: the phoneme could be abstracted from a language by a careful methodology, if you had enough actual utterances, by merely noting which sounds actually distinguished one meaningful unit from another. There were numerous 'discovery procedures' purporting to achieve this. They were so apparently good that bigger and better units were attempted. After *phonemes* came *morphemes*, and so on to a large number of other *emes*. Structural linguistics of the post-Bloomfieldian school had become a pseudo-observational science. Suffice it to say, as I said earlier, that there could hardly be a term more firmly tied to linguistic data than the post-Bloomfieldian phoneme.

2. The Prague version developed the theme differently. Its adherents attempted to go to more universal principles through which the phonemes themselves were to be constructed. They did this by developing the concept of oppositions at the phonological level: the so-called 'distinctive features'. Trubetzkoy (1933: 227) saw that Saussure's theory remained incomplete

until phonology made this advance, and that the 'phoneme' linked Saussure's (and de Courtenay's) programme to the facts. He nevertheless remained clear that the definition of a phoneme was its *place* in a system. With this we find the phonemic idea breaking into Saussurean generality again. After all, the 'value' of a phoneme derived from its position in a phonological system (as Hjelmslev always saw). The universals that lay behind the phonemes were the universal rules of opposition: those rules whereby the 'values' of single elements in systems of elements are determined.

The 'distinctive features' of Trubetzkoy and Jakobson were of an acoustic or articulatory type ('*tense*:*lax*', '*grave*:*acute*', and the like). The binary mode of distinction and its notation could be applied to the precise determination of the values of elements in other systems – not only those of language. To perceive this was, as I have said, laboriously to re-create the generality from which the Prague phoneme derived its distinctive features. It was Prague's and especially Jakobson's phonemes that stimulated Lévi-Strauss (for a later statement: Jakobson and Halle, 1956; for the stimulation: Simonis, 1968: 163–166).

Linguists spent a long time looking at phonemes, and there was much controversy as to whether they were 'real'. They had reached the stage the comparativists had reached in the nineteenth century. Their phonemic reconstructions were as rigorous (and often as outlandish to the eye) as those of comparative philology, but their principles and problems were alike (below, p. 226). Since Bloomfieldians had supposedly 'objective' ways of discovering phonemes, they usually thought that they were there ('God's Truth'). The counter-view was that they were in the mind ('Hocus Pocus'). These were Householder's terms (1952). The confusion between model and reality represented by this debate is now obvious. Essentially, phonemes were formulaic statements for the abstraction of significant units of speech. The analyst simplified the initial 'phonetic' data by using fewer terms but at the expense of requiring a book of rules to interpret them. We may put it: *emic* + rules → the *etic*; or, at a different level: model + reality conventions → the corpus of data. The English phoneticians must be admired for their refusal to become mixed up with the metaphysics of the phoneme (D. Jones, 1962; 1964: 15). In the imagery of formal systems: their theory was restricted to the generation of 'adequate' systems of transcription.

It is an irony perhaps that the phoneme debate accounts in part for some of the revulsion of postwar British social anthropologists from linguistics. To many of them it seemed alien, and fraught with transcription symbols. Somewhat similarly did the kinship debates of social anthropology strike members of other disciplines. In 1945, then, Lévi-Strauss's act of will was remarkable: the wedding of the phoneme to kinship. The paper in *Word* shows the process of his thought as he tried to map a Prague School view of system upon kinship. His well-known *élément* or 'atom' of kinship (1963a: 48) was the result. The symbols (+) and (−) derive by direct analogy from the marking of 'presence' or 'absence' of distinctive features by which Prague School phonemes were analysed. To appreciate the unexpectedness of the endeavour, we should place ourselves in the United States at the date. Linguistics was still in the full post-Bloomfieldian phase, now highly empirical and 'behaviourist'. For another ten or fifteen years, the introductory literature will still be full of references to 'discovery procedures' and the like (Gleason, 1955a and b; Hockett, 1958). When Zellig Harris *will* write his *Methods in Structural Linguistics* (1951, preface signed in 1947), the highwater of those trends, Noam Chomsky will merely be acknowledged as having given 'much-needed assistance with the manuscript'. We are three years before the publication of the crucial papers in communication theory (Shannon, 1948; Shannon and Weaver, 1949) which gave the later Jakobsonian linguistics its special form.

Lévi-Strauss was not even looking to American anthropological linguistics, which was also essentially Bloomfieldian, although the influence of Sapir was strong. Voegelin and Harris (1945) referred to Lévi-Strauss's article in their contemporary paper 'Linguistics in Ethnology', but its approach was totally different. Although unexceptionable ('talk and non-vocal behaviour together constitute an ethnolinguistic situation', p. 457), the spirit was resolutely pragmatic. Their later paper (1947 – 'the data of linguistic and cultural anthropology are largely the same', p. 588) is similar in drift. The immigrant Prague School structuralism, like European linguistics as a whole, was certainly not then over-valued by Americans (Householder, 1957: 156, notes that 'European' was equivalent to 'pre-scientific'). All this was changing, and extremely rapidly, but Lévi-Strauss's declaration for Prague was not along the grain of the relationship between the fieldwork-oriented anthropology and the descriptive linguistics of the date. No wonder he had difficulty in expressing the exact nature of the revelation. He quotes Trubetzkoy's view of the aims of structural linguistics ('discovering general laws either by induction "or . . . by logical deduction, which would give them an absolute character" '), and of its demonstration of the concept of system. Lévi-Strauss shows no sign of being really at home with the Prague concepts. He says: 'Thus for the first time, a social science is able to formulate necessary relationships. This is the meaning of Trubetzkoy's last point.' All this is very jejunely expressed in view of the previous statements about nuclear physics – and in the light of what follows:

> 'But when an event of this importance takes place in one of the sciences of man, it is not only permissible for, but required of, representatives of related disciplines immediately to examine its consequences and its possible application to phenomena of another order' (1963a: 33–34).

The direct application, when it comes, illustrates Lévi-Strauss's major problem: what he wanted from Prague was the notion of 'opposition' which he intuitively grasped to be of great importance. Unfortunately, the principle was obscured by its expression in the garb of the phoneme. As we have seen, it was an operational concept in linguistics: one that made it possible to link Saussure's *langue* and *parole* – the principle of the wheel realized in the specialized roller-skate. The idea of the (+ –) notation was the technical contribution deriving from Lévi-Strauss's 1945 contacts with Prague linguistics. It is, however, interesting to note that in so far as his (+ –) analyses bore any relationship to the phoneme at all, his usage implied that the infrastructure of kinship relations (the source of oppositions equivalent to the acoustic and articulatory ones in Prague analysis) was largely affective in nature. This was in some ways rather unexpected, given the general views of the

French school. Simonis (1968) shows that his concern then with the 'unconsciousness' of underlying systems owed much to Freud. Mauss had, however, long ago asked of psychology: 'Donnez-nous donc une théorie des rapports qui existent entre les divers compartiments de la mentalité . . .' (1950, 1966 edn: 305).

I have discussed the implications of this first paper of Lévi-Strauss's at some length, to show that the 'linguistic' nature of it was ambiguous. The difference between my treatment of the paper and that of Simonis (1968: 12–32) is obvious. *Later*, Lévi-Strauss did express himself more clearly on the subject, but in relation to a rather different linguistics. Simonis reads back the essential Lévi-Strauss into the first paper, justifiably in one sense, for it is truly Lévi-Strauss and not linguistics that speaks there. But as Simonis himself admits, 'Certes, les détails manquent' (p. 19), and his own excellent 'Annexe' on 'Le modèle linguistique' has to be placed much later in his book (pp. 159–168). He shows us that the answer to the implied question, 'Why did Lévi-Strauss see social anthropology and linguistics as related in that way, so early?' is that Lévi-Strauss was already thinking in that way. The publication of *Les Structures élémentaires* in 1949 showed more clearly his assimilation of the notion of a structure as a formal system. This, however, derived from Mauss as much as from linguistics.

By 1951 the scene had changed: in that year Lévi-Strauss published 'Language and the Analysis of Social Laws' in the *American Anthropologist* (Vol. 53 (2): 155–163; 1958 and 1963a, Chapter III). In the interval the communication theorists had come into notice, and this time the phrase: 'a recent work, whose importance from the point of view of the future of the social sciences can hardly be overestimated' turns out to refer to Wiener's *Cybernetics* (1948). The paper is a similar exercise to the first: the working-out through a welter of suggested analogies of some way of applying a stimulating idea. One of Wiener's points was that social studies, being made by beings on the same scale as the phenomena studied, could not be treated usefully by the methods of natural science. This is related to the 'Maxwell's Demon' question: whether a being of the size of a molecule might be able to reverse entropy (Maxwell, 1871, 1872 edn: 308–309; Wiener, 1948: 57–58). Lévi-Strauss suggests, on the contrary, that the facts of language are distantiated from the observer. It 'lives and develops as a collective construct' (1963a: 57). Further, the 'long runs' that Wiener thought inaccessible to social studies were available to students of the historical linguistic families (Indo-European and the like):

> 'We thus find in language a social phenomenon that manifests both independence of the observer and long statistical runs, which would seem to indicate that language is a phenomenon fully qualified to satisfy the demands of mathematicians . . .' (ibid.).

For similar cases in anthropology, Lévi-Strauss cites Kroeber's work on fashion and his own on the interpretation of kinship systems through the circulation of women. It is here that he achieves the essential insight of the paper: that Maussian systems of exchange and reciprocity are analogous to systems of communication, of which language is also one. The subsequent importance of this insight for social anthropology has obscured the fact that, in the original paper, it is overwhelmed by a premature and misguided attempt to correlate kinship structures with structural features of the languages of families established by comparative philologists. He takes the Indo-European and Sino-Tibetan families, as well as 'African', 'Oceanic' (both unattested), and 'American Indian'. At this grand level the attempt collapses. Possibly he was influenced by unacknowledged echoes of Saussure, whose tentative correlations between language families and social and psychological factors are more soundly documented (*Cours*, 1922: 304–317; trans. 1964: 222–231). Lévi-Strauss's reading of Wiener at this time is the source of his distinction between 'mechanical' and 'statistical' models, one that has not always been clearly understood by social anthropologists (see below, p. 233). This rather uncertain paper was criticized, although not always perceptively, by Moore and Olmsted (1952).

In 1952 he presented, at a Conference of Anthropologists and Linguists at Bloomington, Indiana, a paper entitled 'Linguistics and Anthropology' which was first published in 1953 (appearing later as Chapter IV of Lévi-Strauss, 1958 and 1963a). By now the communication engineers had fully made their mark and this stirred him to say, about the relationship of anthropologists to linguists:

> 'For many years they have been working very closely with the linguists, and all of a sudden the linguists are playing their former companions this very nasty trick of doing things as well and with the same rigorous approach [as] was long believed to be the privilege of the exact and natural sciences. Then on the side of the anthropologist there is some, let us say, melancholy, and a great deal of envy' (1963a: 69).

Once more, then, a revelation. In 1945 it was the Prague phoneme, in 1951 it was Wiener, in 1952 communication theory proper. Like the conductor of a circus orchestra, signalling loud chords for the acrobat to appear, he may well be relieved when on the third crash the acrobat actually does so.

> 'Now what connexions are possible with linguistics? I cannot see any whatsoever, except only one, that when the anthropologist is working in this way he is working more or less parallel to that of the linguist. They are both trying to build a structure with constituent units. But, nevertheless, no conclusions can be drawn from the repetition of the signs in the field of behaviour and the repetition, let us say, of the phonemes of the language, or the grammatical structure of the language; nothing of the kind – it is perfectly hopeless' (1963a: 70).

This rather surprising recantation of the 1945 and 1951 papers occurs on the very eve of Lévi-Strauss's achievement of a homology between social anthropology and language. The views expressed in the body of this paper are indeed already clearer. He sets out his three levels of relationship between anthropology and linguistics, which (although they have been departed from here) contain useful insights. He looks ahead to *La Pensée sauvage* when he refers to 'this uninvited guest which has been seated during this Conference beside us and which is the human mind' (ibid.: 71).

Finally, in *Anthropologie structurale* (1958), in which Lévi-Strauss reprinted the 1945, 1951, and 1952 papers, he inserted a 'Postscript' (1958 and 1963a, Chapter V) which presents at length analogies with Jakobsonian linguistics in anthropological terms. In particular, the publication of Jakobson and Halle (1956), in which the implications of communication concepts ('code', 'message') had been assimilated into the Prague system, now shows its influence. Lévi-Strauss, through Benvéniste's discussion of the linguistic sign (1939), also returns to broad Saussurean principles. The Prague-type method is now used to distinguish ideological oppositions, not affective or kin-based ones. His approach to symbolism as pervading all domains (foreshadowed in his Introduction to Mauss, 1950) leads to his remarkable citation of Marx ('who cannot be suspected of idealism') on the symbolism of gold and silver. After this the elements for the structural study of myth and symbolism are all present, to be fully developed in *La Pensée sauvage* (1962b) and afterwards. The return to Saussure was finally expressed in its most unequivocal form in the *Leçon inaugurale* (trans. 1967: 16–17):

> 'What then is social anthropology? No one it seems to me was closer to defining it – if only by virtually disregarding its existence – than Ferdinand de Saussure, when, introducing linguistics as part of a science yet to be born, he reserved for this science the name *semiology* and attributed to it as its object of study the life of signs at the heart of social life . . . I conceive, then, of anthropology as the bona fide occupant of that domain of semiology which linguistics has not already claimed for its own . . .'

Evans-Pritchard

We had had by 1958 a mental Odyssey, thirteen years of Lévi-Strauss reflecting upon linguistics. The ideas are those of the great Saussurean development, inspired with Durkheim's *sociologie*, passed through Baudouin de Courtenay's phoneme, rendered linguistic flesh by the Prague School and post-Bloomfieldian structuralists, scientized by the communication engineers, perceived intuitively by Lévi-Strauss, and reunited with Durkheim through Mauss. In this extraordinary personal achievement, linguistics, as a discipline, became, as his frequent admiring statements express, an ideal type. He was nevertheless the only social anthropologist equipped to perceive intuitively the analytical and explanatory, rather than the pragmatic, implications of linguistics in the period 1945–1955. The American anthropological linguists failed to do this, perhaps because of their empiricist, even behaviourist, preoccupations. In 1948 Greenberg was brilliantly aware of the significance of semiotics from the work of Morris (1946). Goodenough too (1957) reacted against the Bloomfieldian structural linguistics, through Morris. Yet both wrote of sign 'behaviour'. So, too, Pike's comprehensive approach (1954, 1955, 1960 – see also 1956) to the notion of *emic* and *etic* was a theory of 'behaviour'. And so, as Casagrande (1963 : 294–295) says:

> 'It is a paradox that the anthropological approach most closely approximating the methods of present-day structural linguistics, that of French-British social anthropology, was developed abroad rather than in the United States, where linguistics and anthropology have had such close relations over the years.'

The French part of this paradox we have considered. He rightly adds: 'It is further remarkable that, except for Malinowski, British social anthropologists have shown so little interest in linguistics' (ibid.).

It may be appropriate here to pay more attention to this latter question, which has been alluded to earlier. For its answer we must look towards a British social anthropologist who, without being a linguist, did encourage a fruitful interest in language at all levels, and in those subjects and writers now of great interest to both social anthropology and linguistics: that is E. E. Evans-Pritchard. It is true that many of his writings have had an explicit linguistic basis (e.g. 1934, 1948, 1954b, 1956b, 1961b, 1962c, 1963b, together with the large number of Zande texts: 1954a, 1955, 1956a, 1957, 1962a, 1962b, 1963a, 1963c, and others). This is not, however, so much the point. His social anthropology has itself tended to be informed with an approach that was consonant with that of the continental schools of linguistics. His famous phrase about 'relations between relations' independently echoes Hjelmslev. His notion of 'opposition', as originally developed in *The Nuer* (1940), was Saussurean in type. No doubt his readings in French sociology prepared him for this realization (cf. Evans-Pritchard, 1962d: 61). Nothing could be further from the later euhemerization of the idea as 'conflict' in the works of Gluckman. Pocock (1961: 78) cites Adam Ferguson as an intellectual ancestor, who wrote, for example: 'The titles of *fellow citizen* and *countryman* unopposed to those of *alien* and *foreigner*, to which they refer, would fall into disuse, and lose their meaning' (A. Ferguson, 1767: 31). In the Oxford period we may also note the influence of Dumont upon his department.

With Evans-Pritchard's encouragement, several of his pupils and colleagues continuously engaged themselves in translations of mounting and daunting complexity from the French sociological school (Pocock: Durkheim, 1951; Cunnison: Mauss, 1954; Needham (with C. Needham): Hertz, 1960; Needham: Durkheim and Mauss, 1963; Needham: Lévi-Strauss 1963b; Needham (with Bell and von Sturmer): Lévi-Strauss, 1969a). This technical linguistic task was accompanied by the important exegesis and creative interpretation of the works themselves that characterized Oxford-trained social anthropologists. In addition, original works of the first importance reflected aspects of this tradition, for example: Lienhardt, 1961; Needham, 1962; and Douglas, 1966. Evans-Pritchard's interest in orally derived texts found further expression in the volumes edited by himself, Lienhardt, and Whiteley (1964: series), an interest which was also exemplified by Finnegan (1969a, 1970) and other recent students. For further concern with themes of linguistic relevance from the same milieu, one may cite Beattie (1957, 1960, 1964b), Needham (1954, 1960a), Beidelman (1964), Ardener (1968), Beck (1969), to name a selective but representative range. Finally, in his own department Evans-Pritchard encouraged his colleagues to teach in the field of social anthropology and language.

It was Evans-Pritchard, then, rather than Malinowski, who provided the secure pedagogical conditions for a serious if belated participation of British social anthropology in the problems of language – a participation that by-passes the Malinowskian tradition. Only Leach among Malinowski's students followed a similar path, and still maintains an innovating position, with contributions bearing on the linguistic field (1957, 1958, 1964, 1970; see also Tambiah, 1968, and Humphrey, below, in the new Cambridge tradition). Pocock perceptively said as long ago as 1961 that Evans-Pritchard's work effected for British social anthropology 'a shift from function to meaning' (p. 72), and added: 'there is some indication that the full implications of this movement . . . were not drawn by all social anthropologists in the post-war period' (p. 77).

In one respect Pocock was perhaps over-optimistic in his appraisal:

> '[Evans-Pritchard's] refusal to make explicit the shift in emphasis had certain tactical advantages. No storm blew up which might have obscured the presentation under a cloud of dust, a sense of continuity was preserved and many younger anthropologists were able to see the deeper relevance of language to their studies' (p. 79).

It may well be that it had strategic disadvantages: a reviewer (Blacking, 1963: 194–195) wrote of Pocock's book:

> 'It is too easily within the reach of young and enthusiastic minds in search of new information about the human condition; and as such it can do irreparable harm . . . the book is very narrow and parochial . . . it does a grave disservice to Social Anthropology.'

The same reviewer believed that Malinowski's *Coral Gardens* 'implicitly' achieved the shift from function to meaning. This was, of course, the point: it might have done, even should have done, but did not – and there were thirty years of tedium in the homes of orthodox functionalism to prove it. It may be noted that Evans-Pritchard never practised that brutal suppression of contrary opinion that biographers, with surprising tolerance, cite so often of Malinowski (R. Firth, 1957: 1; Kardiner and Preble, 1961: 167–168). Malinowski's position as the great linguistic anthropologist of the functionalist school is touched on further below. The slightly less favourable view than usual that I express may easily be balanced without seeking far in the literature. I have, however, come reluctantly to the conviction that it was exactly because of Malinowski's personal influence on social anthropology that the functionalist interest in language withered, together with much else, in the climate of rather provincial anti-intellectualism that fell like a drought upon his empire at his death.[20]

'Structural' or 'transformational'?

Anthropologie structurale (1958) appeared a year after *Syntactic Structures* (1957) by Noam Chomsky, in total independence. In the next ten years the mature system of Lévi-Strauss, applied to the detailed material of myth, was directed towards the generation of models reflecting 'fundamental structures of the human mind'. Chomsky's linguistics set out to generate models (grammars) mapped upon human linguistic 'competence', which was likewise firmly seated in the human mind. Lévi-Strauss's corpus of data, 'myth', was all versions of the myth, including, it is implied, versions yet to be formulated (1963a: 216–217). Chomskyan grammars set out to generate all well-formed utterances in a language. Both systems used notations inspired by the mathematics of formal systems. Both advanced old problems by the application of the notion of 'transformation'. In this respect Lévi-Strauss's final message was, ironically enough in linguistic terms, not 'structural' but 'transformational': as if by seeking St Brendan's Isle he had truly discovered America.

There are considerable differences, of course. The two approaches are authentically of their own disciplines, but Lévi-Strauss is much less rigorous, as well as less lucid, in his expression than is Chomsky. The latter concludes from a reading of *La Pensée sauvage* only 'that the savage mind attempts to impose some organization on the physical world – that humans classify, if they perform any mental acts at all' (1968: 65). Chomsky is also, more justly, sceptical about Lévi-Strauss's Prague School model:

> 'The significance of structuralist phonology, as developed by Trubetzkoy, Jakobson, and others, lies not in the formal properties of phonemic systems but in the fact that a fairly small number of features that can be specified in absolute, language-independent terms appear to provide the basis for the organization of all phonological systems . . . But if we abstract away from the specific universal set of features and the rule systems in which they function, little of any significance remains' (ibid.).

Chomsky makes the telling point that linguistic structures are the 'epiphenomenon' of 'intricate systems of rules'. He speaks of 'systems of rules with infinite generative capacity' (ibid.: 66). Finally: 'If this is correct, then one cannot expect structuralist phonology, in itself, to provide a useful model for investigation of other cultural and social systems' (ibid.). Just so. Yet, as we have seen, the improbable was achieved by Lévi-Strauss – by intuition more than by logic. Chomsky's strong drive in favour of a distinction between human systems and non-human systems, and between language and other semiotics, makes him loth to open his system to the possibility of a general semiological anthropology. He would not support the hypothesis of a prior non-linguistic semiotic (cf. Chomsky, 1968: 60 and 70–72) if it were to encroach on the privileged position of language. It may be the prejudice of an anthropologist, but it seems that in this, and in some other respects, Lévi-Strauss has more to say to humanity as a whole than has Chomsky. Their different modes of approach to contemporary problems are also instructive: the one providing what Simonis calls a model of the 'exteriorization of man', and, as I believe, a method of interpreting the inarticulate, even anti-articulate, movements of our time; the other more limited, even (behind the social criticism) less revolutionary. This would be natural, perhaps, for anthropology is still the study of man, while linguistics, even transformational generative grammar, is still the study of language.

Similarity of terminology can, however, bring confusion. The Chomskyan system is characterized by precision of expression, where Lévi-Strauss is programmatic. Detailed point-by-point comparisons are not to be recommended. Thus, the antimony between 'deep' and 'surface' structure occurs in Lévi-Strauss, as in Chomsky ('Ainsi l'analyse structural se heurte à une situation paradoxale, bien connue du linguiste: plus nette est la structure apparente, plus difficile devient-il de saisir la structure profonde . . .' – 1958). The 'deep structure' of Chomsky, as applied, for example, to sentences with ambiguous surface structures, is revealed through clearly stated sequences of transformations within one model, say that of English (see Hymes, below, p. 53). The 'competence' of the transformationalists can, of course, be seen as a kind of generalized 'deep structure', or a generalization of the base rules for the set of all deep structures of a language. The semantic component of the language is tied to the deep structures. Lévi-Strauss's deep structures in the analysis of myth, on the contrary, are derived from units already ascribed a conventional meaning. The transformations of inversion, sign reversal, and the like, operate to demonstrate, through the differences or contradictions in surface meaning between related myths, the nature of the myth-logic itself (1964, 1966b, 1968).

Compared with Lévi-Strauss, Chomsky is (paradoxically for a proclaimed 'rationalist') more 'empiricist' in style. There is generally recognized to be a difference in tone and aims between the Chomsky of before *Aspects of the Theory of Syntax* (1965) and the subsequent Chomsky. Pre-*Aspects* Chomsky still shows signs of his explicit concern with exact models: as his system was received at the time, it appeared as a rebuttal of simple 'left-to-right' generated models of language, of a 'finite-state' type. Such models derived ultimately from the original work of Shannon in communication theory (1948), and with Chomsky the main wave of direct application of that theory to language subsides. The finite-state model is expressed in 'box-and-arrow' form as in computer studies: so are the alternative, more powerful models of *Syntactic Structures* (1957) and of *Current Issues* (1964). Post-*Aspects* Chomsky has turned from prime and only concern with the output of his model – the corpus of utterances – to a more difficult problem, which in a sense was left over from the destruction of the finite-state model with its implied statistical probabilities. This was: how does a child acquire the model of competence (the generative grammar) for his language?

> 'From this point of view, one can describe the child's activities as a kind of theory construction. Presented with highly restricted data, he constructs a theory of the language of which this data is a sample (and, in fact, a highly degenerate sample, in the sense that much of it must be excluded as irrelevant and incorrect – thus the child learns rules of grammar that identify much of what he has heard as ill-formed, inaccurate and inappropriate). The child's ultimate knowledge of language obviously extends far beyond the data presented to him. In other words, the theory he has in some way developed has a predictive scope of which the data on which it is based constitute a negligible part' (1969: 63).

Chomsky maintains, therefore, that the organism has 'as an innate property' a structure that will account for this mode of acquisition – put frivolously by McNeill (in Lyons and Wales, 1966: 116): 'Metaphorically speaking, a child is now born with a copy of *Aspects of the Theory of Syntax* tucked away somewhere inside.' Chomsky has turned to Descartes, Leibnitz, and the rationalist philosophers of innate ideas for a philosophical charter for his approach; these thinkers being opposed to Locke and the empiricists, whose most extreme descendants are taken to be the psychological behaviourists. The philosophical basis of Chomskyan mentalism is a subject of disputation. In effect he gives an ontological status to what behaviourists see as a 'capacity' or a 'capability' for language. It would be out of place here to attempt a detailed discussion (see, for example, Cohen, 1966: 47–56; Hook, 1969; Lyons and Wales, 1966; Lyons, 1970). It is sufficient to note for our purposes that the Chomskyan system began with a transformational generative grammar, with the characteristics of a well-defined system. It has now at least two other systems hooked on to it: a language acquisition model genetically located in the organism, and a phonological model that commands the chains of phonemes. The mental status of the competence model itself has occasioned disagreement. Is it 'present' as an analogue of a full write-out of a transformational analysis, or is it expressed in some other form – in the way that, for example, the cogs of a clock only indirectly enact what we know about the movements of the sun and earth from the Newtonian laws of motion? (L. J. Cohen, in Lyons and Wales, 1966: 164.)

The Chomskyan movement as a historical phenomenon is of great anthropological interest. Intellectually, the inevitable and even praiseworthy arbitrariness of the first Chomskyan models has been succeeded by an accretion of partial models loosely articulated to the original; or at best, to cite the analogy so frequently used (Wiener, 1948: viii; Leach, 1961: 26), 'epicycles' are added. The imperialism of the Chomskyan system, which once lay firmly within the domain of *langue* ('all well-formed utterances'), now takes its seat in the brain, and seems at times to wish to break right through the domain of *parole* itself, and to require the generation of the very acoustic wave-forms. This Faustian aim is beyond the competence of any single model; with the computer engineers, we should remember that ultimately the only effective store of the natural order is the natural order. The original notion of formal generativeness is submerged, as of too limited a range, and the originally rigorous terminology with its new philosophical outriders begins to take on the appearance of a set of procedures to distinguish the orthodox from the unorthodox. Lévi-Strauss throws light on this process: the Chomskyan movement as a whole is now beginning to work as a mythical system with its own (anthropological) transformational rules. In due course, no doubt, these will become explicitly recognized ('unpacked', as the philosophers say), the system as we know it will be 'exploded', and a new system will be set up by others by *bricolage* from the remains, starting another cycle with similar consequences. Thus it is not truly a criticism, and certainly not an exaggeration, to say that it contains mythical elements; this is the power of all great human systems: the models are, at least in part, *ex post facto* justifications. It is, however, an index of the richer quality of Lévi-Strauss's structuralism that it is able to become conscious of this very process. 'That is why', he says, 'it would not be wrong to consider this book itself as a myth: it is the myth of mythology' (1964; trans. 1969b: 12).

We can transpose these remarks in terms of Hockett's (1968) critical review of Chomsky's theory. He sets up a summary formulation of Chomsky's system (at 1965) in nineteen points, which were largely endorsed by Chomsky himself. The case is then argued with considerable skill and documentation through the volume that *no physical system, and in particular language, is well defined*. His attack is upon the original programme, therefore, for its *arbitrariness*. But it is by now self-evident that a model of a formal system (which is well defined) says nothing of the 'well definition' of the natural order. Truly generative models *are* models: they are, of course, less than the phenomena they help to explain. Nevertheless, Hockett's criticisms confirm in a different way our awareness of the ambiguity of the Chomskyist movement. We have said that what seems to have begun in 1957 as a conscious application of model-building to postwar structural linguistics – its 'generative' and 'transformational' terminology is quite clear on this point – has now outgrown its early phases. The well-known capacity of Chomsky for fresh and creative development has disguised the fact that his total system is no longer itself well defined.

Hockett's critique thus paradoxically falls on two contradictory grounds: If Chomsky's model of a system were formal and thus well defined, it would not be a counter to the system to say that language as a natural phenomenon is not well defined; and, in so far as Chomsky's system is *not* well defined, Hockett has no criticism. In fact, Hockett's discomfort probably derives from an intuition of the contradiction between the formalism of the transformationalist terminology and the lively and speculative accretions of the transformationalist world-view. In my paper below I suggest that the Neogrammarian model of comparative philology was totally generative. Its basic 'inextensibility' should illuminate both the power of truly generative models and the dangers of forgetting their functions. The dissatisfaction of Chomsky with his earlier aim, and the extension of the search to meaning and beyond, have been highly productive, but no total formal system has yet been set up for this. Chomsky is both Bopp in level of achievement of his programme, and Brugmann in his search for precision. It is this desire for a totally formalistic presence that falsely sets him apart from Lévi-Strauss, who disguises his own formalism in literary metaphor.

These are presumptuous remarks coming from a social anthropologist. The reason why I feel impelled to make them is precisely because the generous aims of the transformationalists and those of the new social anthropology are, within their disciplines, rather similar. It is interesting that their thinking covers some of the same ground. It seems sometimes that the transformationalist approach would benefit from a more careful consideration of non-behaviourist social anthropology, which would in turn no doubt gain much from the encounter. The kinds of criticism made of the latter by the survivors of Malinowski (who occur in all age-groups) resemble those made by the American post-Bloomfieldians of the transformationalists. The older social anthropology finds the newer variety 'incredible', precisely for its apparent indifference to a particular positivist view of the natural order. The neo-anthropologists are also asked to provide the equivalent of 'discovery procedures', and they too seem to regard the aim as only of subsidiary interest, although in fact large amounts of 'empirical' data have been analysed (I refer specifically to their work in kinship and symbolism). They too began with the establishment of elegant and simple models of formal systems. They too have grown out of these earlier aims in the direction of theories of wide-ranging scope. They too are prepared to consider the existence of universals, beyond the scope of ethnographic solipsism.

The relationship between aspects of the transformationalist approach and the broadly 'structural' trends in social anthropology, both in their rigorous phases and in their creative expansion, is the more interesting since, as we have seen, the two movements are only very indirectly linked. There is no certainty that they will not turn in very different directions; they are in no way dependent upon each other. Hockett's critique of Chomsky far outshines any critique in social anthropology directed against the newer movements,[21] but the message is the same: the models are too rigid and are imposed on reality; the 'facts' are twisted to fit. But, as we have seen, the nature of a model is to define out and to establish rules of relevance. All new models thus appear supremely open to such charges. As I have shown (below), the generativeness of the Neogrammarian model was preserved by three rules, of which one was that of 'analogy'. The criticism made of this rule by the earlier comparativists was exactly that 'analogy' was a fact-twister, and Osthoff and Brugmann had to answer the charge of 'arbitrariness' as early as 1878. Their critics were of course trivially 'right', as Hockett is 'right', and as the functionalist and neo-functionalist charges in our own subject are also 'right'. No answer could be made to the critics save that the power of the new model finally developed was a guarantee of the status of the new protective rule. None now will doubt the productiveness of the approach. The shears that protect a model are not 'arbitrary' in the common-sense usage, but in a particular technical sense. It would have been no compensation to the nineteenth-century critics, had they lived, to learn that we agree with them.

Reflection on the situation with British post-functionalist 'neo-anthropology', however, shows how relatively weakly placed it is compared with the newer movements in linguistics. We must note the relatively small number of its practitioners, and their relative isolation. The voluminous work of Lévi-Strauss was, it seems, not enough to establish it on the one hand, nor was the detailed research of its native exemplifiers and developers on the other.[22] As late as 1970, most senior anthropological posts were filled by continuators of Malinowski. The latter nevertheless showed a sad lack of confidence in their own discipline.[23] Even while, one after another in the sixties, practitioners of the older social anthropology declared the death of the subject, the new one already existed at both the programmatic and the empirical level. Of many a rider then lamenting the death of his horse, it could perhaps more justly be said: ''Twas not the horse that died.'

THE PRESENT VOLUME

I have written at some length on the general theme of this volume in order to show that the relation between social anthropology and the study of language is a genuinely fruitful one at all levels. They are subjects that abut together on the frontiers of important fields which have too long been neglected by the empiricist tradition. In now presenting the papers in this volume to a general anthropological audience it seems best to do so by continuing to pursue and exemplify the line of thought developed here. If this cannot do full justice to the skill and varied content of the contributions (an insuperable editorial problem in volumes of this kind), it may at least do them the credit of demonstrating the argumentative stimulation they arouse.

Part I of the present volume begins with Miss Henson's account (to which some allusion has already been made) of the long-standing nature of the British anthropological detachment from linguistics. For her period, 1850–1920, she has in part defined her group as the contributors to, and readership of, the journals of the Ethnological Society and of the Royal Anthropological Institute. Although not all the former were necessarily British or anthropologists, the mainstream attitudes are quite clear. As we have seen, the comparative linguists had their chief effect through the German-born Max Müller at

Oxford. He developed his views in the more speculative phase of linguistic studies of the age of Bopp and Schleicher, before the rise of the Neogrammarians. Müller remains, however, the only theorist with anything remotely like a modern approach to myth. Tylor's interest in deaf-and-dumb and sign languages prefigures some of the proposed semiology of Saussure, but he held firmly to an evolutionist view that early linguistic signs were 'motivated'. The use of 'native' categories like *mana*, *totem*, and *taboo* did not at this earlier period (nor, indeed, much later) lead on to a consideration of the relation of category to language. Nevertheless, the collection of 'comparative' material under these heads did lead to important advances in the hands of other theorists (*totemism*: Lévi-Strauss, 1962a; *taboo*: Freud, 1913; Steiner, 1956; Firth, R., 1966: 109–113; *mana*: Mauss, 1950: 101–115; Firth, R., 1940; Milner, 1966).

If German comparative philology was not a good exemplar for anthropologists of the day, British phonetics was not in a position to be very helpful. Henry Sweet, the phonetician, who was at that time at Oxford, had to fight (as did many of his successors) for a place for a version of linguistics other than that enshrined in the humanities syllabus. His polemical reputation may have convinced our grandfathers that the synchronic problem of language was essentially a technical matter of transcription. Nevertheless, the early anthropologists, with few exceptions, were hardly aware even of the 'phonetic' problems. It may well be that the native genius for the exotic expressed through deep linguistic study was almost totally absorbed in the study of the classics, on the one hand, and in imperial duties, on the other. There is every reason indeed to look back past the early pre-emptors of the name 'anthropology' to Sir William Jones, sometime President of the Asiatic Society. His famous *Discourse* of 1786, delivered in Calcutta, which by common consent first clearly asserted the relationship of Sanskrit to the Classical languages and Gothic and Celtic, is otherwise more of an ethnographical disquisition than a linguistic one (Jones, 1799; now in Lehmann, 1967: 10–20). Like Sweet he was a polemical figure:

> 'In the parliamentary election of 1780, as a candidate for the University of Oxford, his detestation of the American

War and of the slave trade were too strongly expressed to be agreeable to the voters, and he was forced to withdraw from the contest. In the same year he failed to secure election as Professor of Arabic in the University for similar reasons' (J. R. Firth, 1957a: 161).

Certain precursors of Koelle (1854) in Africa might be mentioned for their ethnographic as well as their linguistic contributions. Latham has been mentioned by Hymes (1964: 3), to whom may be added Clarke (1848).

Malinowski's role in introducing language to social anthropology was ambiguous and disappointing, as we have indicated, as far as his own subject was concerned. Professor Robins discusses the present status of the concern with 'context of situation' which the London School of Linguistics has shared with him. From being largely neglected by transatlantic theorists, this able group of scholars has recently been the subject of 'positive vetting' by transformationalist emissaries (Langendoen, 1968), to which Professor Robins responds. To a social anthropologist, however, it sometimes appears that our linguistic colleagues (Berry, 1966, is an exception) are very generous in apportioning the credit for their present renown, the major part of which must surely go to J. R. Firth, who trained linguistic successors who looked for long in vain for any sign of interest among their anthropological coevals. With the exception of Whiteley, no postwar social anthropologist for many years was trained in this tradition. Such persons were usually referred to by Malinowski's successors as having 'gone over to linguistics'. Firth's (1957b) excellent account of Malinowski's views (in R. Firth, 1957, and Palmer, 1968) is a tribute more often to the insight of the author than to that of his human subject. Many social anthropologists remember clearly ideas of Firth's in his lectures which are now in current fashion. For example, his account of the 'myth' of 'the lion' in Luganda compared with that of the English ('the lion-house', 'Red Lion', 'lions in Trafalgar Square', 'social lion'). His long interest in possible phonological correlates of meaning (in J. R. Firth, 1957a: 43–45, 192–193) became respectable with Jakobson and Halle (1956), Jakobson (1960), and other writings. Although he, and also Ullmann (1963: 226), cited the countervailing examples, certain distinctive features ('lax'/'tense', 'grave'/'acute', and the like) clearly have correlates with other sensory patterns (e.g. Firth's classic *oombooloo* and *kikiriki* drawings – rotund and spiky respectively).[24]

Firth says:

> 'I know from personal association with Malinowski that those parts of de Saussure's general linguistic theory which led [in the direction of French sociology] he found not only unattractive but of little practical value in the study of meaning, which was his principal interest' (p. 95).

Firth sees Malinowski as fulfilling certain views of Sweet's, who said: 'Our aim ought to be, while assimilating the methods and results of German work, to concentrate our energies mainly on what may be called "living philology"' (J. R. Firth, 1957b: 100). It is significant that J. R. Firth himself refers to the Bloomington Conference of 1952 and remarks that it did not 'face the problems stated by Lévi-Strauss' (ibid.: 116, referring to Lévi-Strauss's paper there: see Lévi-Strauss 1963a, Chapter IV). The move back from phonemics to meaning, which was asked for by the Conference, was squarely in line with Firth's interests. Malinowski's concern with 'meaning' was, of course, his great contribution at a time when only the German school of linguists was still actively concerned with the subject (it is unlikely, however, that the work of Trier and von Wartburg would have appealed to him).

As Leach points out (1957: 130; 1958), Malinowski totally rejected any attempt to relate terminological labels to systems of categories, and some of his denials border upon the absurd. Malinowski thought he was defending the Trobrianders from imputations of 'pre-logical' inferiority, a magnanimous error, rooted however in his own ethnocentric assumption that Western 'reasonableness' provided the only possible 'rationality'. Malinowski believed in 'homonyms', established by accidental coincidences. The historical falling together of 'different' words in the documented languages may well have been in his mind. He would not have understood, however, as von Wartburg did, the way in which homonyms produced by phonemic change may *fail* to survive when they cross an important category boundary (cf. above, *femur* 'thigh', *fimus* 'faeces' → **femor-*).

Malinowski's extreme statements are, of course, a useful reminder against equally extreme views of 'category'. His view of context, properly argued, would even provide a structural basis for certain sub-category boundaries within 'homonymous' categories. This is best achieved by a Saussurean view of 'value' and 'system'. Thus the systematic 'values' of Trobriand *tabu* 'grandmother', *tabu* 'grandfather', *tabu* 'father's sister', and the like (Malinowski, 1935, II: 28, 113) *might* be argued to differ from each other because of the disparate linguistic and non-linguistic elements present in the 'context of use', in each case. But, of course, we cannot prejudge the nature of any such contexts simply on the basis of these prior English glosses chosen by Malinowski. He was not really a kind of componential analyst (Lounsbury, 1965). Leach's re-analysis of the *tabu* term (1958) is in fact ethnographic 'context of situation' raised to professional levels. The term is shown to refer to a category of marginal relationships, and one that is not exhausted by the 'homonyms' Malinowski himself cites (Leach, 1958: 121, 144). Lounsbury (1969: 18) has asserted that Leach's analysis is one of extreme relativism. I have touched upon this earlier (p. xxi). In fact the underlying 'universal' is transferred from an ethnocentric notion of kinship to a category of 'marginality' or 'liminality' inherent in the relations of human beings to each other, here mapped upon a set of genealogical references.

Hocart (1937, ed. Needham, 1970: 173–184) effectively demolished Malinowski's approach in his own time. The recent demonstration that Trobriand *tabu*, 'taboo', falls into a different etymological set, by the rules of proto-Austronesian, from the *tabu* kin term (Chowning, 1970) does not restore Malinowski's own argument. It does, of course, raise the largely ignored question of the diachronic aspect of cognitive categories (above). Furthermore, as far as the contemporary valuation of the Trobriand term *tabu* is concerned, the problem presented by the confrontation of 'Neogrammarian' etymologies with the folk-etymologizing propensity (Ardener, below) is brought into focus. In oral cultures there are no privileged historical etymologies. When Hocart asks, 'How can we make any progress in the understanding of cultures, ancient or modern, if we persist in dividing what the people join and in joining what they keep apart?' (1970: 23), we must apply this principle equally to the effects of phonetic change – provided such changes are in fact assimilated, for (as we have seen) they are capable of being by-passed if they prove to be semantically unacceptable to 'the people'.

If we are to accept such a view, however, we should not forget its corollary that a people's own linguistic glosses provide a significant mode of analysing a lexical category. What the people keep apart we should also not join. For example: the 'risible' features of the 'strange' must once have been evident enough to make the ambiguity of English *funny* of no folk interest in one period of colloquial English. It was then a unit category. The social conscience of the middle classes later created the (now whimsically old-fashioned?) division 'funny-peculiar, funny-haha', thus creating a conscious semantic taxonomy (how shall we unravel the recent 'not queer-*queer*, but queer-funny'?). A careful study of sociolinguistic categories must take into account popular semantic and etymological exegesis. This would be a true 'ethnolinguistics' (that is, a linguistics produced by 'the people', parallel in formation with 'ethno-medicine') – or even an 'ethno-metalinguistics'.

At his best Malinowski did perhaps strive after something like this. In general, however, he bequeathed, on the one hand, a behaviouristic view of context (which even the well-disposed Firthian linguists had to shrug off) combined, on the other, with an intellectually ethnocentric mode of analysis. In so far as Malinowski contributed to the vitality of the London School of Linguistics, whose creativity (as Professor Robins shows) is undiminished, he must be accorded full recognition for it. On pedagogic grounds I have already suggested that his contribution (in contrast with that of J. R. Firth) may nowadays be viewed with a more muted enthusiasm.[25] Langendoen (1968) separates the Malinowski of the early twenties from the Malinowski of *Coral Gardens* (1935). Early Malinowski holds (for him) views such as: 'that social structure is a psychological and, hence, not a directly observable reality, and that behaviour can only be understood in terms of it'; and that: 'categories of universal grammar must underlie categories implicit in non-linguistic human behaviour' (pp. 35–36). This is to do much more than justice to a rather unreflective psychologism, and a school-book view of grammar. The picture of Malinowski as a proto-Chomskyan 'rationalist', whose later views were distorted by contact with J. R. Firth, would have its attractions were it not in contrast with all we know of Malinowski the 'empiricist' anthropologist.

Professor Hymes shows, in his comprehensive review, what is meant in sheer scope and method when we refer to American anthropological linguistics. His essentially undoctrinaire writings provide a mine of varied material, to which all interested in 'sociolinguistics' from a wide range of disciplines are indebted. His book of readings alone (1964) is in itself, because of his commentaries and scholarship, an original work. There is, nevertheless, a special consistency of view that emerges in his contribution below, as in other writings (1962; Gumperz and Hymes, 1964), which derives from his firm hold upon the 'ethnography of speaking'. The idea is effectively a realization of the social anthropology of *la parole*. Hymes's encyclopaedic approach may superficially appear to be irreconcilable with those deriving from the continental linguistic schools, for which this Introduction has argued equally consistently. This impression would be mistaken. Hymes directs our attention to the plane at which language is generated in society – in this respect he is close to what many working linguists and anthropologists ideally demand of a 'sociolinguist'. Any analysis of material acquired from this standpoint has, however, to be organized through models, and through less conscious organizing systems, set up by speakers and actors, by social anthropologists and linguists and sociolinguists – or by ethnographers of speaking.

The fecundity of Professor Hymes's insights comes from the fact that so many structural statements made from different logical premisses must meet at the 'plane of articulation'. Whether it be Chomsky's 'performance:competence', or Bernstein's 'restricted:elaborated codes', they are all open to revision, illustration, confirmation, or comment at this meeting-place. The plane of the ethnography of speaking may thus be placed diagrammatically at right angles to their plane, in the same conceptual relationship as *syntagm* to *paradigm*. As there is a choice of 'paradigms', so there is a choice of 'syntagms',[26] although this is commonly less clearly realized. Professor Hymes exercises this choice with great freedom. There is hardly a branch of linguistics and social anthropology in which the ethnographer of speaking may not appear. Thus Colson and Gluckman write on gossip, but where is the gossip delineated? 'Ethnographic accounts are rife with terms that in fact denote ways of speaking, though they are not always recognized to be such' (below, p. 71). Hymes's basic approach is formally consistent, despite the variety of paradigmatic systems it cross-cuts, which makes his paper in itself an introduction to sociolinguistic writings. Had postwar functionalism developed Malinowski's own linguistic insights, it might well have extended ethnographically in the plane of Hymes's interest. 'Context of situation' itself belongs to that syntagmatic plane.

On these grounds Professor Pride's rejection of the view that contexts of situation are *necessarily* 'below the level of a general abstract theory' (p. 96) seems particularly convincing. As a sociolinguist coming from the direction of linguistics, he places himself at the plane of linguistic transactions: thus linking it with Barth's model of social anthropological analysis. The interest of Barth's model is that it too falls in the syntagmatic plane, with a clear definition of the elements of the model: the notional 'transactions'. In social anthropology it is sometimes complained of as 'rigid', 'partial', 'mechanistic' – all, as we shall agree by now, the honourable stigmata of a model of a formal system. If fully articulated it could probably be shown to be truly 'generative' in the formal rather than the metaphorical sense. Gluckman's interchange with Paine on gossip (Paine, 1967, 1968; Gluckman, 1968), where Paine takes a 'transactional' view, is based in part on a failure to see that syntagmatic models are not in the same plane as paradigmatic models (Gluckman's 'transactions between individual persons cannot explain institutional structures', 1968: 30, is thus a truism).

In social anthropology, 'transactional' imagery may be described as a part of the 'highest stage of functionalism'. That is: a functionalism become aware (or about to become aware) that the field of behaviour or action, even when arbitrarily isolated from the ideological programme that determines its meaning, must itself be structured by the observer before it can be 'observed'. The interest to the sociolinguist of this approach pinpoints certain differences in the histories of anthropological and linguistic inquiry. Functionalist anthropology was (in loosely Saussurean terms) concerned with the social as *parole*. The most recent developments have led social anthropology to be concerned with the social as *langue*. During the same period, linguistics has been mainly concerned with *langue* (the diachronic and synchronic versions, as well as the 'structural' and 'transformational' views, differed until very recently only in emphasis in this particular respect). It is natural that now sociolinguists, in seeking to study language as *parole*, should either use functionalist approaches or find those of functionalist social anthropology converging on the same area.

The relative lack of formalism in the old functionalist world-view will undoubtedly be amended by this, but there is still an uncertainty in the newer developments. 'Theory', to the functionalist, has long meant the confusion of statements based on models of a syntagmatic type (to which the stress on observation binds him) with paradigmatic statements. The confusion became the worse confounded because the truly paradigmatic statements of writers like Evans-Pritchard were interpreted as syntagmatic ones. I have already referred to the notion of 'opposition' in *The Nuer* (paradigmatic) being reinterpreted as 'conflict' (syntagmatic). Douglas (1970a: xiv–xxii) now shows how *Witchcraft, Oracles and Magic*, which was about 'cognitive structure' (paradigmatic), was reinterpreted as about 'social control' (syntagmatic). I have developed some of these points elsewhere (1971). It is necessary to touch on them lightly here, however, in order to suggest that there are two approaches to sociolinguistics which parallel those of functionalist and post-functionalist ('neo-anthropological') social anthropology. They may be expressed diagrammatically as follows:

Paradigmatic	Social Anthropology A ('structuralist' of Lévi-Strauss; 'neo-anthropological' of Needham, Leach, Douglas)	Sociolinguistics A
Syntagmatic	Social Anthropology B ('functionalist', 'neo-functionalist': transactions, networks, etc.)	Sociolinguistics B

Sociolinguistics as generally described is essentially a Sociolinguistics B. It is that of Malinowski, of Hymes in his most characteristic phases, and of Pride at his most analytical, as well as of Whiteley, Denison, and others. Sociolinguistics A is essentially the approach developed in this Introduction: which some may possibly consider only an epistemological raid from Social Anthropology A, for the writers who have set it out from the linguistic side are not normally thought of as *socio*linguists. The names that would be cited (Saussure, Jakobson, Hjelmslev, the later Firth, the German semanticists, Sapir, Whorf, and their American exemplifiers) are leading names in general linguistics. Furthermore, the transformationalist approach (for some the very antithesis of a sociolinguistics) has its nearest anthropological congener in Social Anthropology A. At our Conference much debate was generated between A-type and B-type social anthropologists, as well as between A-type social anthropologists and B-type linguists and sociolinguists. Some B-type social anthropologists rejected linguists of any type. In such circumstances of confusion it is wisest not to give hostages to new labels, and certainly not to new 'disciplines', built on any outmoded nineteenth-century style: with their nation-state apparatus of buildings, professorships, and degree structures. It looks likely that Sociolinguistics B will for some time to come appear to be the major bearer of the label 'sociolinguistics', while Sociolinguistics A will be apprehended as a kind of social anthropology, a kind of linguistics, or a kind of philosophy, according to the point of view of the practitioner.

Part II of this volume is concerned with some of the subject-matter of joint inquiry between social anthropology and linguistics. The existence of multilingual situations has long provided a field for the comparison of models of language and of society. The loosening of rigid terminological distinctions between 'language', 'dialect', 'register', 'code', and the like has greatly extended the range of relevance of such studies. We now see that the problems presented by the coexistence of several varieties of 'one language' are not different in kind from those presented by the coexistence of 'different languages' in a multilingual speech community. This makes it possible to include Dr Crystal's survey of the minuter differences of variety in monolingual speech. We are in the realm of 'code-switching' (although many linguists would restrict this term to switching between languages – see Whiteley, 1971: 13–14). Professor Whiteley's introduction to this Part shows that these studies bear very closely upon the Chomskyan model of 'competence: performance' (as well as, we may add, upon Lévi-Strauss's 'fundamental structures of the human mind'). 'Multilingual' situations thus provide a genuine field for empirical work in which both syntagmatic and paradigmatic approaches may be brought to bear. So far most of the work that has been carried out has been of a syntagmatic type, but there is no lack of hints for 'paradigmatists'.

Dr Tonkin's paper attempts 'a social history' of the succession of pidgins, ending in Pidgin English, on the Guinea Coast. This is a 'diachrony' of the *social* situation not of the *linguistic* situation – for which there is only scattered phonological or other documentation. Yet such studies bring into doubt certain supposedly 'linguistic' typologies, by revealing the sociological assumptions that lie behind them. In particular, the distinction creole : pidgin disappears. The supposed difference lay essentially in the presence (in creoles) or absence (in pidgins) of monolinguals in the language type, and of transmission between generations. More deeply, perhaps, it derived from conflicting analytical reluctances: on the one hand, from a reluctance to award the full status of 'a language' to what might be thought to be 'invented', or 'limited', jargons; and, on the other, from a reluctance to deny it to forms of speech which had become mother tongues to some, if not all, of their speakers.

Pidgins have been a stumbling-block to all the great schools of linguistics. Both pre-Saussurean and post-Saussurean linguistics have usefully operated with models in which the basis of the diachronic or synchronic system was the single language. We have seen that the treatment of languages as if they were well-formed systems has led to great advances. An unsatisfactory treatment of pidgins was part of the price paid for those advances, for most of the efficient models of language have 'snipped out' pidgin phenomena, with the very shears that demarcated their field of operation (below, p. 222). We may note, further, that West African Pidgin English has in reality always been a part of a multilingual or plurilingual context in combination with English or with one or more African languages. Where it has become supposedly 'creolized' it has become in fact diglossic – primarily with forms of standard English. 'Available evidence suggests that most of Africa has been multilingual for a long time, even if the domains of such behaviour were characteristically restricted, e.g. to trade or hostility' (Whiteley, 1971: 22). Dr Denison's detailed analysis of the linguistic diatypes of Sauris – a 'trilingual' community in the Carnian Alps, in which a variety of German coexists with Friulian and Italian – is thus concerned with a situation that is also common in Africa, and throws light on other possibilities in the past of Europe.

In considering the papers in Part II, and those sections of the papers of Hymes and Pride that bear upon the topic, one may perhaps note in sociolinguistic thought so far a certain prejudgement in the attribution of a 'social status' to certain varieties of language. We should not lose sight of the fact that much work in this field is still in the classifying phase. To simplify a little: at the first stage it may well appear intuitively (or from statements and observations) that certain diatypes have 'high' or 'low' status. From there we may proceed with C. A. Ferguson (1959) and Fishman (1968b) to 'H' and 'L' divisions of diatypes. We may then appear to discover that H diatypes are being used in L social contexts, or the like. Theory here is now at the dangerous phase: the original source of the differentiation (which was an *ad hoc* assessment of the status of contexts of use) begins to pass out of recognition, and we are all set for many comfortable years of exemplification of 'H-ness' and 'L-ness', until the basis of the typology is again revised.

As Dr Denison rightly points out, the Sauris situation, in any event, appears to require an 'M' diatype (for 'middle'). The various diatypes are in effect in opposition to each other. We first need a model of the structure of these oppositions in the whole linguistic context. We require, likewise, a model of the structural oppositions within the society at large. We may attempt to map these two models (or sets of models) upon each other; it may be, as we hope, that there will be some transformational links between them. Thus we avoid prejudging the basis of the mapping; for the term 'status' itself ceases to have any particular privileges in such an analysis. Furthermore, the possibility of negative and inverse transformations (perceived as 'contradictions' or 'exceptions') becomes a normal expectation and can be examined as such. The language of paradox and of incipient nominalism (*some H settings have L diatypes*) gives way to the language of structure – here derived from social anthropology, despite its resemblance to that of transformational linguistics. Denison's material illustrates this well with the oppositions Italian : Friulian, Italian : German, Friulian : German, Friulian of Sauris : Friulian of Udine, German of Sauris : standard German, on the linguistic side, together with the no doubt more delicate ones that he is able to observe. On the social anthropological side one can already detect some crude relevant oppositions – Udine : Sauris, rural : urban, home : school, adult : child, architect : foreman, foreman : workman, and so on. The rich material in Denison, 1968 (e.g. pp. 584–585), would suggest many more.

One might suspect a temporal structure also, cyclical perhaps, in which the tourist season (more Italian spoken?) may be opposed to the rest of the year. It is also possible that the young, who speak more Italian, will not retain this tendency when their social prospects are firmly assured. This point is worth making because of the question of prediction. Is Sauris German dying out (Denison, 1968: 589)? To take an example: it has been said through most of our lives that congregations in Soviet churches consist of persons over the age of fifty, and thus that organized religion is 'dying out'. It is clear, however, that the fifty-year-olds of today were adolescents in the thirties. The congregations seem to have acquired a pattern of recruitment by age. The *possibility* of such a structure over time means that the opposition *youth*:*age* may outlive the present occupants of the 'age-slots' concerned. All of these comments are highly speculative, and take the excellently documented case merely as a convenient example. A full social anthropological study would start from hints such as these, and *even if not expressed in this terminology* would proceed to the further finer distinctions that a field-study would yield. The division H and L would be subsumed in such an analysis, while the middle term M could be dispensed with. The results might not turn out to look very different but we should have avoided an *ad hoc* terminology (an avoidance that is, indeed, part of the spirit of Ferguson's original analysis – see Hymes, 1964: 431).[27]

These remarks are relevant to some social anthropologists who find it difficult to visualize how a structural analysis in the newer sense can be the subject of 'empirical' study (I am referring, of course, to a social anthropological study without overt linguistic aims). The Sauris-type situation could never, however, be easily handled by a social anthropologist without Dr Denison's linguistic skill. It would be possible to imagine a social anthropological study, nevertheless, which produced models of Sauris society that would assist the linguist. The 'diatypes' are, we may guess, symbolically realized at more levels than one.

Dr Crystal's paper examines in a comprehensive manner some varieties of 'colouring' given to utterances (prosodic, non-segmental features) by speakers of a language, which, consciously or unconsciously, signal social categories. He singles out sex, age, status, occupation, and 'genres' of speech. This kind of work is of great theoretical interest: for it demonstrates a semiotic in language, still at the phonological level, which coexists with the main semiotic in the form of 'redundancies to the code' (cf. Jakobson and Halle, 1956). The most delicate linguistic techniques must be combined with fairly delicate social anthropological knowledge of a society, for the problems of observation and transcription are relatively difficult for both specialists. Dr Crystal's description of the modalities concerned is most valuable. The various levels at which communication may occur produce the possibility of structures that may escape ordinary analysis. Of course, the destructive implications for some simple views of the 'accuracy' of social anthropology are great, especially where genres are particularly susceptible to non-segmental semiotic structuring: for example, the case of myth itself, which may be marked in its oral transmission by special modes of articulation, contrapuntal to the 'text'. As for the notion of 'the-language-well-and-truly-learnt', so characteristic (as we have seen) of the post-Malinowskian functionalism – that recedes even further over the horizon. Not surprisingly, a resolutely structural approach leaves the social anthropologist immune. The failure of models to generate the natural order, and *a fortiori* their failure to generate all of the natural order, is only in the nature of models, so that a further blow to the faded vision of ethnographical omniscience can only be welcome; while, on the other hand, the common evidence of a close articulation between levels of meaning in society makes it possible that some of the message of the inadequately delineated semiotic may be revealed through other semiotics. Dr Crystal's work shares the characteristic of the works of the great English phoneticians: an apparently technical linguistic apparatus is concerned with the most critical sociolinguistic facts.

Part III takes up themes that are implicit in this Introduction. My own paper deals with the question of what models generate. Dr Milner's analysis of the structure of traditional sayings, and Mrs Humphrey's exposition of the symbolism of the Buryat Mongol ongon, are both excellent examples of what Saussure's semiology should embrace. Elsewhere Milner (1969) attempts a structural analysis of the logic of Samoan tattooing, without direct treatment of the iconic elements. The isolation by Barthes of the 'iconic' systems as the main non-linguistic structures is to limit the insights of Saussure, as well as the practice of Lévi-Strauss.

In analyses of this type, the question of where the structures are *located* is still raised by 'positivist' social anthropologists, as it was in the original oral discussion of this paper. It is the old 'God's Truth' or 'Hocus Pocus' argument raised about the phoneme (Householder, 1952), as well as about componential analysis (Burling, 1964) and the 'grammatical' rules of household composition (Burling, 1969), all over again. Once more the question is not a real one, as we saw above. The chiastic square of Dr Milner is excellent as the frame for structural patterns: of which the semantic are only a class. Human minds can use, as comparative experience shows, any evident structural regularity upon which to build the most unexpected and varied semiotics (e.g. left:right, male:female – Hertz, 1960; Needham 1960b, 1967). The logical sums discovered by Dr Milner need not even be totally consistent. They form a kind of indexing device, and provide a stylistic which can even dress up irregular forms: like *Cold Comfort Farm* pseudo-wisdom ('If sukebind do blow: we shall have snow'), in which the logical sum, if any, is vacuous. These are the imaginary games that have never been played (p. 226 below), which defeat attempts to generate all the human order from single models. The *bricoleur* is always at work.

In Mrs Humphrey's analysis, useful light is thrown upon the nature of the semiological sign. She is also able, from her general study of Buryat social anthropology, to place the semiotic of myth in relation to the semiotic of the ongon. Unresolved contradictions at one level (or some of them) are resolved at the other. The relating of one semiotic to another in the manner of one model of a formal system to another, through transformations, provides that check upon interpretation which worries well-disposed social anthropologists of an empirical bent. It reminds us, and them also, that the empirical or observational system upon which they rested so happily in the past for verification is itself one set of linked models, consciously or unconsciously formulated. Tests of fit have been therefore the demonstration of connections between this 'base' set and all other models. The great development of the positivist set obscures this situation. Symbolic phenomena have not been 'correlatable' or 'calibratable' directly with 'behaviour' or the like, because 'behaviour' is already symbolic. There are always paradoxes and inconsistencies because, instead of distinctly separated 'observable' and 'symbolic' orders, there is a range of structures: some conscious, some unconscious. The analyst is attempting to bring more and more of them to awareness. He is hampered by the 'unaware' elements in his own procedures.

The Maxwell's Demon problem in social anthropology is less that of the scale of the observer (Wiener, 1948: 57; Lévi-Strauss, 1963a: 56) than that of the equivalence of his method of structuring the natural order with that of the actors he hopes to observe. They continually restructure his material; they are living chessmen. The necessary recognition of this does not lead us into solipsism: the natural order is still 'there' even in society, as the continual source of unprogrammed events, which demand incorporation, or as providing certain basic structural givens. The social anthropologist, with the help of the linguist, may be just beginning to get the hang of handling some of this. For that reason the delineation of the symbolic and semiotic structures of society and culture is likely for some time to look more 'real' in human terms, and in the end is even likely to 'predict' more, than are the hundreds of social surveys daily undertaken.[28] For social anthropology the challenge is that of the 'demonstration with blank banners' to which I have referred. It is the continuation of the work (begun by Durkheim, Mauss, Lévy-Bruhl, and Evans-Pritchard) of eliciting the inarticulate as well as the articulate rationalities of human beings. A Mongolian ongon thus serves as an appropriate frontispiece to this volume.

NOTES

1. If not never, then hardly ever. The correspondence involving Bohannan (1956, 1958a, 1958b) with Beals (1957) and Taylor (1958), for example, is curiously muffled on the subject. Bohannan seems to argue that linguistics does not help in the learning of languages. This brief interchange comes from a milieu that was nevertheless exceptional in retaining an interest in language (p. lvix).

2. See also Hjelmslev, 1943: 49; trans. 1963: 53; Malmberg, 1964: 128; Capell, 1966: 39 (where it is not correctly demarcated). Hjelmslev also alludes to other systems: differentiation of siblings by sex and age as between Magyar, French, and Malay (see Hjelmslev, 1957: 104); differentiation of 'tree–wood–forest' between French, German, and Danish (1957: 106; 1943: 50; trans. 1963: 54). See also Ullman (1951).

3. Newton (December 1675) thought the seven colours would correspond to the seven intervals in our octave:

> 'For some years past, the prismatic colours being in a well darkened room cast perpendicularly upon a paper about two and twenty foot distant from the prism, I desired a friend to draw with a pencil lines cross the image, or pillar of colours, where every one of the seven aforenamed colours was most full and brisk, and also where he judged the truest confines of them to be, whilst I held the paper so, that the said image might fall within a certain compass marked on it. And this I did, partly because my own eyes are not very critical in distinguishing colours, partly because another to whom I had not communicated my thoughts about this matter, could have nothing but his eyes to determine his fancy in making those marks' (correspondence in I. B. Cohen, 1958: 192; Turnbull, 1959: 376–377).

Berchenshaw wrote of Newton's system (10 February 1676):

> 'That the natural genuine, and true reason of the excellency and fullness of the harmony of three, four, five, six and seven parts, may clearly be discerned by the system of seven parts' (Cohen, op. cit.: 226).

4. *GPC* (1968), s.v. *glas*, divides the colour referents into (1) blue, azure, sky-blue, greenish-blue, sea-green; (2) green, grass-coloured, bluish-green, light-blue, pale-blue or pale-green, greyish-blue, slate-coloured, livid, pallid, pale, crystal-grey, grey; (3) silver-coloured; (4) greyish-white, steel-coloured, iron-grey. A further puzzle could not be elucidated without the structural diagram in *Figure 2*: *glas*, finally, can sometimes have the same referent as *llwyd*, 'grey', 'holy of clerics', which is explicable because of their neighbouring positions at the point where the Welsh axes of hue and brightness join.

5. Ardener (1954). It was Miss M. M. Green (a linguist and anthropologist) who first mentioned the characteristics of *ocha* to me. In the functionalist terms of the day I expressed the *ocha*:*ojii* antinomy in terms of 'attitudes'. A simplified orthography has been used here. The 'Africa Alphabet' renderings, where they differ from those in the text, are as follows: *ɔcha*, *ɔbara ɔbara*, *uhyɛ uhyɛ*, *ahehea ndɘ*, *akwɘkwɔ ndɘ*. The theory of a historical order in the succession of

types of colour classification comes from Berlin and Kay (1969). In their view, systems may contain (1) 'black' and 'white' only; (2) 'black' plus 'white' plus 'red'; (3) 'black' plus 'white' plus 'red' plus 'yellow' *or* 'green'; (4) 'black' plus 'white' plus 'red' plus 'yellow' *and* 'green'; (5) 'black' plus 'white' plus 'red' plus 'yellow' plus 'green' plus 'blue'; (6) 'black' plus 'white' plus 'red' plus 'yellow' plus 'green' plus 'blue' plus 'brown'; and so on. Thus Hanunóo would be in phase 3, Ibo and early Welsh in phase 4.

6. The translation presents some difficulties, but 'The crepuscular light' is attested in other Celtic sources: 'terram pulcherriman . . . obscuram tamen et aperto solari lumine non illustratam' (Loomis, 1956: 165).

7. These cases support Kroeber (1909) and what I take to be the present position of Needham (see Needham, 1971).

8. Von Humboldt (1836/1967) is the intellectual ancestor of the field theory, although his 'mother tongue mysticism' is not always attractive. It dates in its modern form from 1910 with R. Meyer's analysis of military terminology. Weisgerber, Trier, Porzig, Jolles, and Ipsen (who first used the term 'field') are the chief names (full references in Ullmann, 1951: 152–170; see also Ullmann, 1963: 250).

9. I give the page references both of the *Cours* (1922 pagination) and of the translation (1964 edn), but generally quote the latter, despite its detailed inadequacies, so that the flow of the English text may not be broken up by frequent passages in French. Nevertheless, I have amended the translation in various places where noted, since sometimes it is seriously misleading, and at least once unintentionally comic.

10. 'Social anthropology in Britain (to speak only of that country where it has acquired most renown in recent decades) has been inspired by certain general ideas, subtly derived from the early French sociologists, which have had a singular theoretical influence, and much of the progress is to be attributed to them.

'They are analytical notions such as "transition", "polarity" (opposition), "exchange", "solidarity", "total", "structure", "classification". Now these are not theories but highly general concepts; they are vague, they state nothing. At first sight there is nothing to be done with them, and certainly they cannot be taught as elementary postulates in introductory courses of social anthropology. Indeed, their significance is only apprehended after arduous application to the task of understanding social phenomena; the less one knows about human society and collective representations the less they appear to mean. Yet they have proved to possess a great and perennial analytical value, such that it may be claimed that it is they which are essentially the "theoretical capital" of social anthropology' (Needham, 1963: xlii–xliii).

11. Thus, von Wartburg (1969: 194).

12. Collinder (1968: 183) says that Schuchardt expressed the notion of *la coupe verticale* and *la coupe horizontale* of language in 1874. For Collinder (p. 210):

> 'Das Panorama, das im Cours de linguistique générale aufgerollt wird, ist kein getreues Bild der wirklichen Sprachwelt. Dieses *système où tout se tient* ist nicht einer urwüchsigen Landschaft ähnlich; es gleicht viehmehr einem altmodischen zugestutzten französischen Schlosspark.'

We see here the wrong-headed but common complaint that a formal model does not generate 'reality'.

13. With reference to Wittgenstein's *Philosophical Investigations* (1953), Ullmann says (1959: 303):

> 'There is an unmistakable affinity between some of his ideas and contemporary linguistic thought – an affinity all the more remarkable as Wittgenstein does not appear to have been familiar with books on linguistics.'

We may note this also in Waismann (1968).

14. For example: Bogatyrev, 1931 (which I have been unable to consult), and 1935.

15. I am aware that a 'panchronistic linguistics' has been several times previously announced (Ullmann, 1951: 258–299). It is no coincidence that it should have had an important part in a vision of semantics. Nevertheless, in discussing the diachrony:synchrony distinction of Saussure, we must recognize that this exists at the level of models of formal systems (see my paper in this volume). Similarly, the 'panchrony' of Saussure must be realizable at the model level: so far only the transformationalists have credibly demonstrated, if only partially, the possibility of such a model. It is interesting that 'panchrony' was generally ignored in exegesis of Saussure by structural linguists, for whom his message was a charter for synchrony, and for whom even diachrony was of lesser import (e.g. see Wells, 1947, in Joos, 1957).

16. The term *semiotic* goes back to Locke, as 'the doctrine of signs'. Its use was developed by C. S. Peirce. Morris, Carnap, and Hjelmslev helped its modern vogue. Margaret Mead coined the term *semiotics* for the study of 'patterned communications in all modalities' during a discussion at the Indiana Conference of 1962, which is reported in Sebeok, Hayes, and Bateson (1964, see pp. 1–7, 275–276). *Semiotics* thus lies close to Saussure's *sémiologie* (closer indeed than does Barthes's *sémiologie*). It may be useful to retain *semiology* to describe the study of *semiotics*, used as the plural of *semiotic*. In its turn, a *semiotic* is a sign system. The coexistence in society of large numbers of semiotics means that any useful description must be made through models of systems, abstractions, ideal systems.

17. McLuhan (1970: 39) speaks of chairs 'outering' the human body, leading then to tables, and a restructuring of the human environment. His 'pop' usages sometimes curiously, but inadequately, reflect modern 'structuralist' trends.

18. The brief discussion of the phoneme included here is obviously selective, and might be omitted were it not that the term as discussed by Lévi-Strauss still has a mysterious aspect for some of his readers. Their questions are not necessarily directly answered by turning to standard works on linguistics. I include the section, aware of its European bias. This may be balanced by consulting Fries (1963) on the Bloomfieldians. He notes that 'the strong stress upon the procedures and techniques of analysis . . . did not stem directly from Bloomfield' (p. 22). In general, see Mohrmann, Norman, and Sommerfelt (1963); Mohrmann, Sommerfelt, and Whatmough (1963); and Hockett (1968: 9–37).

19. Shaw says of Sweet's polemic Oxford reputation:

> 'With Higgins's physique and temperament Sweet might have set the Thames on fire. As it was, he impressed himself professionally on Europe to an extent that made his comparative personal obscurity, and the failure of Oxford to do justice to his eminence, a puzzle to foreign specialists in his subject . . . although I well know how hard it is for a man of genius with a seriously underrated subject to maintain serene and kindly relations with the men who underrate it, and who keep all the best places for less impor-

tant subjects which they profess without originality and sometimes without much capacity for them, still, if he overwhelms them with wrath and disdain, he cannot expect them to heap honours on him' (*Pygmalion*, Preface, 1941 edn: 8–9).

See also Jakobson, 1966.

20. Jarvie (1963) no doubt was justifiably reacting against this. The present writer reviewed Jarvie's book in a critical vein (Ardener, 1965) because it seemed unaware of the important developments outside the Malinowski tradition, to which I refer. My own concern is with the excessively long time that recognition of the obvious changes in the climate of thought in the subject, and in the skills required, has taken to percolate through. We are virtually forced to fall back on *ad hominem* explanations, in a small subject like social anthropology. Malinowski's impatience with contrary opinion was accepted as fair exchange for scientific advance. His failure to recruit and keep many students of a sceptical bent from the mainstream of the European tradition must surely account for his neutral intellectual legacy. The death of Nadel (in Australia) was a loss. Whatever Radcliffe-Brown's faults, the existence of his works enabled the dissidents from Malinowskian anti-intellectualism to find a temporary alternative stimulus, if only through attack (e.g. Evans-Pritchard and Leach). For some reason, women anthropologists in the Malinowski tradition also maintained a lively presence, and continue to do so.

21. The only critique of stylistic interest comes indeed from the American Marvin Harris (1969), a 'plague-on-all-your-houses' cultural materialist. He speaks with reluctant if ironical admiration of 'professional idealists, as distinct from eclectic American amateurs who have rubbed shoulders with logical positivism and behaviourism too long to know how to really get off the ground' (p. 505).

22. See also below, p. lxxvi, and Ardener, 1971. I use the nonce-term 'neo-anthropology' to cover post-functionalist movements of a creative type, not all of which would accept the term 'structuralist'. Some of them clearly have a good deal in common in subject-matter with the so-called 'new ethnography' of the United States (Sturtevant, 1964). Leach, a senior exponent, still ambiguously claims to be a 'functionalist'. The neo-anthropologists are recognizably different in interests and style from the majority of the British profession in characteristic ways, but since they do not necessarily agree even with each other (and may refuse to be linked together) they lack the earmarks of a school. In this respect they have remained isolated and divided *vis-à-vis* the relatively united 'Palaeo' group.

23. Barnes (1963), Freedman (1963), Goody (1966), Maquet (1964), Worsley (1966) made valuable points. Leach may have inadvertently set off the fashion (1961), but his language was not properly understood. As long ago as 1954 (pp. 92–93) Leach wrote, in reviewing Pocock's translation of Durkheim (1951), of a 'general revival of interest in ideas and ideals for their own sake, in contrast, for example, to the extreme empiricism of Malinowski'. In the 1960s hardly an issue of the main international professional journals failed to contain some discussion of the views of Needham and his pupils. Hardly a literary journal lacked some exegesis of Lévi-Strauss. Douglas (1966) did much to draw the attention of social anthropologists in general to some of the important themes. The activity of Evans-Pritchard's colleagues and pupils (other than Needham) has been mentioned. Yet the significance of none of this was truly taken note of until the end of the decade by the representative professors of the subject. For a *justified* pessimism, see now Needham (1970).

24. See now Leach's paper in Needham (1971).

25. I accept Tambiah's point (1968: 203) that Malinowski's views were at times closer to those of Evans-Pritchard than we might expect.

26. The terms *paradigm* : *syntagm* – from later restatements of Suassure's opposition of *série associative* to *syntagme* (1922: 170–184) – represent, however, a more basic relation, not restricted to language. Dr Milner uses the opposition in a closely linguistic context (p. 254 below). The linguistic uses apply to 'linear chains'. In the anthropological language of structure, *syntagmatic structures* are apperceptions of relations between events as they are generated; *paradigmatic structures* specify the *kinds* of event that are generated. It may not at first be clear that the relationship *paradigmatic* : *syntagmatic* does not yield its significance through a model that is (a) static, (b) of two dimensions. If we take a model of the continuous generation of events, the syntagmatic axis must correspond in reality to a four-dimensional continuum (the three dimensions of space and one of time). The paradigmatic 'axis' then becomes a fifth logical dimension of interesting properties. It is homologous with the expression in physics of the mode of specification of the moving 'present' (a 'time-like' displacement) in a four-dimensional continuum – for which a further conceptual dimension is required. I have not gone into these matters in the text, but they appear in Ardener (1971). I allude to them here (a) because Lefebvre (1966: 227, 247) by adding a supposed 'third' dimension to the *paradigmatic* : *syntagmatic* relation confuses several important distinctions, (b) because the problem of models of 'historicity' in social anthropology raised below ('games that have never been played', pp. 226–227) is essentially an artifact of *syntagmatic* analysis.

27. The social anthropology of Africa had its 'A' and 'B' types of town (Southall, 1961: 6 ff), for an examination of which see Krapf-Askari, (1969: 17–19, 157–163). Terminological labels obscure such matters further (e.g. 'statelike' and 'stateless' political systems). A more precise parallel with the particular interdisciplinary circularity of 'H' and 'L' is the use of terms like 'rank', 'greeting', by ethologists. For the application of this criticism see Callan (1970).

28. To contrast a statistical study with a symbolic study of the same ethnographic phenomena: see Ardener, 1962 (marital instability) and in press (symbolism and women); and Ardener *et al.*, 1960 (economics), and Ardener, 1970 (belief).

REFERENCES

ARDENER, E. W. 1954. Some Ibo Attitudes to Skin Pigmentation. *Man* **54**: 101.

—— 1962. *Divorce and Fertility: An African Study*. London: Oxford University Press.

—— 1965. Review of Jarvie, 1963. *Man* **65**: 57.

—— 1967. The Nature of the Reunification of Cameroon. In A. Hazlewood (ed.), *African Integration and Disintegration*. London: Oxford University Press.

—— 1968. Documentary and Linguistic Evidence for the Rise of the Trading Polities between Rio del Rey and Cameroons 1500–1650.

In I. Lewis (ed.), *History and Social Anthropology*. ASA Monograph 7. London: Tavistock.
— 1970. Witchcraft, Economics and the Continuity of Belief. In Douglas (ed.), 1970a.
— 1971. The New Anthropology and its Critics. (Malinowski Lecture.) *Man* (n.s.) **6.**
— in press. Belief and the Problem of Women. In J. La Fontaine (ed.), *The Interpretation of Ritual*. London: Tavistock.
— ARDENER, S. G., and WARMINGTON, W. A. 1960. *Plantation and Village in the Cameroons*. London: Oxford University Press.
BARNES, J. 1963. Some Ethical Problems in Modern Fieldwork. *British Journal of Sociology* **14** (2): 118–134.
BARTH, F. 1966. *Models of Social Organization*. Occasional Paper No. 23. London: Royal Anthropological Institute.
BARTHES, R. 1964. *Eléments de sémiologie*. Paris: Le Seuil.
— 1967. *Elements of Semiology*. Trans. of Barthes, 1964. London: Cape.
BAZELL, C. E., CATFORD, J. C., HALLIDAY, M. A. K., and ROBINS, R. H. (eds.). 1966. *In Memory of J. R. Firth*. London: Longmans.
BEALS, R. L. 1957. Native Terms and Anthropological Methods. *American Anthropologist* **59**: 716–717.
BEATTIE, J. 1957. Nyoro Personal Names. *Uganda Journal* **21**: 99–106.
— 1960. On the Nyoro Concept of *Mahano*. *African Studies* **19**: 145–150.
— 1964a. *Other Cultures*. London: Cohen & West; New York: Free Press. Paperback edn, London : Routledge & Kegan Paul, 1966.
— 1964b. Kinship and Social Anthropology. *Man* **64**: 101–103.
— 1968. Aspects of Nyoro Symbolism. *Africa* **38** (4): 413–442.
— 1970. On Understanding Ritual. In B. Wilson (ed.), *Rationality*. Oxford: Blackwell.
BECK, B. E. F. 1969. Colour and Heat in South Indian Ritual. *Man* (n.s.) **4** (4): 553–572.
BEIDELMAN, T. O. 1964. Pig (Guluwe): An Essay on Ngulu Sexual Symbolism and Ceremony. *Southwestern Journal of Anthropology* **20**: 359–392.
BENVÉNISTE, E. 1939. La Nature du signe linguistique. *Acta Linguistica* **1**: 23–29. Reprinted in Benvéniste, 1966, pp. 49–55.
— 1966. *Problèmes de linguistique générale*. Paris: Gallimard.
BERLIN, B., and KAY, P. 1969. *Basic Color Terms, their Universality and Evolution*. Berkeley and Los Angeles: University of California Press.

BERNSTEIN, B. 1958. Some Sociological Determinants of Perception: An Inquiry into Sub-cultural Differences. *British Journal of Sociology* **9**: 159–174. Reprinted in Fishman (ed.), 1968a.

—— 1960. Language and Social Class. *British Journal of Sociology* **11**: 271–276.

—— 1961. Aspects of Language and Learning in the Genesis of the Social Process. *Journal of Child Psychology and Psychiatry* **1**: 313–324. Reprinted in Hymes (ed.), 1964.

—— 1964. Elaborated and Restricted Codes: Their Social Origins and Some Consequences. In Gumperz and Hymes (eds.), 1964, pp. 55–69; and in Smith (ed.), 1966, pp. 427–441.

—— 1965. A Socio-linguistic Approach to Social Learning. In J. Gould (ed.), *Penguin Survey of the Social Sciences 1965*, pp. 144–168. Harmondsworth: Penguin.

BERRY, J. 1966. Introduction to second edition of Malinowski, 1935, Vol. II, pp. vii–xvii. London: Allen & Unwin.

BLACKING, J. 1963. Review of Pocock, 1961. *African Studies* **22** (4): 194–195.

BLOOMFIELD, L. 1933. *Language*. New York: Holt, Rinehart & Winston; London: Allen & Unwin, 1935.

BOGATYREV, P. 1931. Příspěvek k strukturální etnografii. *Slovenska miscellanea*. Bratislava.

—— 1935. Funkčno-štrukturálna metoda a iné metody etnografie a folkloristiky. *Slovenské Pohľady* **51**: 550–558.

BOHANNAN, P. 1956. On the Use of Native Language Categories in Ethnology. *American Anthropologist* **58**: 557.

—— 1958a. On Anthropologists' Use of Language. *American Anthropologist* **60**: 161–162.

—— 1958b. Rejoinder to Taylor, 1958. *American Anthropologist* **60**: 941–942.

BROWN, R. W., and LENNEBERG, E. H. 1954. A Study in Language and Cognition. *Journal of Abnormal and Social Psychology* **49**: 454–462. Reprinted in Saporta (ed.), 1961.

BURLING, R. 1964. Cognition and Componential Analysis: God's Truth or Hocus Pocus. *American Anthropologist* **66**: 20–28.

—— 1969. Linguistics and Ethnographic Description. *American Anthropologist* **71** (5): 817–827.

BUYSSENS, E. 1943. *Les Langues et le discours: essais de linguistique fonctionelle dans le cadre de la sémiologie*. Brussels: Lebègue.

CALLAN, H. 1970. *Ethology and Society: Towards an Anthropological View*. Oxford: Clarendon Press.

CAPELL, A. 1966. *Studies in Sociolinguistics*. The Hague: Mouton.

CARNAP, R. 1937. *The Logical Syntax of Language*. London: Kegan Paul, Trench, Trubner.

CARROLL, J. B. (ed.). 1964. *Language, Thought and Reality: Selected Writings of Benjamin Lee Whorf*. Cambridge, Mass.: MIT Press.

CASAGRANDE, J. B. 1963. Language Universals and Anthropology. In Greenberg (ed.), 1963a, pp. 279–298.

CASSIRER, E. 1933. La Langue et la construction du monde des objets. *Journal de Psychologie* (Numéro exceptionnel) **30** (1): 18–44.

—— 1953. *Philosophy of Symbolic Forms*, Vol. I. New Haven: Yale University Press.

—— 1954. *An Essay on Man*. New York: Doubleday.

CHILVER, E. M., and KABERRY, P. M. 1968. *Traditional Bamenda*. Buea, Cameroon: Government Press.

CHOMSKY, N. 1957. *Syntactic Structures*. The Hague: Mouton.

—— 1964. *Current Issues in Linguistic Theory*. The Hague: Mouton.

—— 1965. *Aspects of the Theory of Syntax*. Cambridge, Mass.: MIT Press.

—— 1968. *Language and Mind*. New York: Harcourt, Brace & World.

—— 1969. Linguistics and Philosophy. In Hook (ed.), 1969, pp. 51–94.

CHOWNING, A. 1970. Taboo. *Man* (n.s.) **5**: 309–310.

CLARKE, J. 1848. *Specimens of Languages*. Berwick-on-Tweed.

COHEN, I. B. (ed.). 1958. *Isaac Newton's Papers and Letters on Natural Philosophy and Related Documents*. Cambridge: Cambridge University Press.

COHEN, L. J. 1966. *The Diversity of Meaning*. Second revised edition. London: Methuen. (First edition, 1962.)

COHEN, M. 1948. *Linguistique et matérialisme dialectique*. Paris: Perches. Also in *Cinquante années de recherches linguistiques, ethnographiques, sociologiques, critiques et pédagogiques*, 1955, pp. 38–52. Paris: Klincksieck.

COLLINDER, B. 1968. *Kritische Bemerkungen zum Saussure'schen Cours de Linguistique Générale*. Uppsala: Acta Societatis Linguisticae Upsaliensis: Almqvist & Wiksell.

CONKLIN, H. C. 1955. Hanunóo Color Categories. *Southwestern Journal of Anthropology* **11**: 339–344. Reprinted in Hymes (ed.), 1964.

DENISON, N. 1968. Sauris: A Trilingual Community in Diatypic Perspective. *Man* (n.s.) **3** (4): 578–592.

DOROSZEWSKI, W. 1933. Quelques remarques sur les rapports de la sociologie et de la linguistique: Durkheim et F. de Saussure. *Journal de Psychologie* (Numéro exceptionnel) **30** (1): 82–91.

DOUGLAS, M. 1966. *Purity and Danger*. London: Routledge & Kegan Paul.

DOUGLAS, M. 1968. The Social Control of Cognition: Some Factors in Joke Perception. *Man* (n.s.) **3**: 361–376.

—— (ed.). 1970a. *Witchcraft Confessions and Accusations.* ASA Monograph 9. London: Tavistock.

—— 1970b. *Natural Symbols.* London: Cresset.

DUMONT, L., and POCOCK, D. F. 1957–66. Contributions to Indian Sociology Series. The Hague: Mouton.

DURKHEIM, E. 1951. *Sociology and Philosophy.* Translated by D. F. Pocock from French edition of 1898. London: Cohen & West.

—— and MAUSS, M. 1963. *Primitive Classification.* Translated with an Introduction by R. Needham. London: Routledge & Kegan Paul; Chicago: Chicago University Press.

ENGLER, R. 1967. *Édition critique* of Saussure 1916. Wiesbaden: Harrassowitz.

—— 1968. *Lexique de la terminologie Saussurienne.* Utrecht/Antwerp: Spectrum.

EPSTEIN, A. L. (ed.). 1967. *The Craft of Social Anthropology.* London: Tavistock.

EVANS-PRITCHARD, E. E. 1934. Imagery in Ngok Cattle Names. *Bulletin of the School of Oriental and African Studies* **7** (3): 623–628.

—— 1940. *The Nuer.* Oxford: Clarendon Press.

—— 1948. Nuer Modes of Address. *Uganda Journal* **12** (2): 166–171. Also in Hymes (ed)., 1964.

—— 1950. Social Anthropology: Past and Present. (The Marett Lecture.) *Man* **50**: 118–124.

—— 1954a. Zande Texts. *Man* **54**: 164.

—— 1954b. A Zande Slang Language. *Man* **54**: 185–186.

—— 1955. Zande Historical Texts I. *Sudan Notes and Records* **36**: 123–145.

—— 1956a. Zande Historical Texts II. *Sudan Notes and Records* **37**: 20–47.

—— 1956b. *Sanza,* a Characteristic Feature of Zande Language and Thought. *Bulletin of the School of Oriental and African Languages* **18**: 161–180.

—— 1957. Zande Historical Texts III. *Sudan Notes and Records* **38**: 74–99.

—— 1960. Preface to Hertz, 1960.

—— 1961a. *Anthropology and History.* Manchester: Manchester University Press.

—— 1961b. A Note on Bird Cries and Other Sounds in Zande. *Man* **61**: 19–20.

—— 1962a. Three Zande Texts. *Man* **62**: 149–152.

—— 1962b. Some Zande Texts, Pt I. *Kush* **10**: 289–314.

—— 1962c. Ideophones in Zande. *Sudan Notes and Records* **63**: 143–146.
—— 1962d. *Essays in Social Anthropology*. London: Faber.
—— 1963a. Some Zande Texts, Pt II. *Kush* **11**: 273–307.
—— 1963b. Meaning in Zande Proverbs. *Man* **63**: 4–7.
—— 1963c. Sixty-one Zande Proverbs. *Man* **63**: 109–112.
—— 1964. The Oxford Library of African Literature Series (co-editor with W. Whiteley and R. G. Lienhardt). Oxford: Clarendon Press.
—— 1965. *Theories of Primitive Religion*. Oxford: Clarendon Press.
FERGUSON, A. 1767. *An Essay in the History of Civil Society*. London.
FERGUSON, C. A. 1959. Diglossia. *Word* **15**: 325–340. Also in Hymes (ed.), 1964.
FINNEGAN, R. 1969a. Attitudes to the Study of Oral Literature. *Man* (n.s.) **4** (1): 59–69.
—— 1969b. How to do Things with Words. *Man* (n.s.) **4** (4): 537–552.
—— 1970. Oral Literature in Africa. Oxford: Clarendon Press.
FIRTH, J. R. 1934. Linguistics and the Functional Point of View. *English Studies* **16** (1): 18–24.
—— 1957a. *Papers in Linguistics, 1934–1951*. London: Oxford University Press.
—— 1957b. Ethnographic Analysis and Language with reference to Malinowski's Views. In R. Firth (ed.), 1957, and Palmer (ed.), 1968.
—— 1957c. A Synopsis of Linguistic Theory, 1930–1955. In *Studies in Linguistic Analysis*, pp. 1–32. Oxford: Blackwell.
FIRTH, R. 1940. The Analysis of *Mana:* An Empirical Approach. *Journal of Polynesian Society* **49**: 483–510.
—— 1951. Contemporary British Social Anthropology. *American Anthropologist* **53** (4): 474–489.
—— (ed.). 1957. *Man and Culture*. London: Routledge & Kegan Paul.
—— 1966. The Meaning of Pali in Tikopia. In Bazell *et al.*, 1966, pp. 96–115.
FISHMAN, J. A. (ed.). 1968a. *Readings in the Sociology of Language*. The Hague: Mouton.
—— 1968b. Sociolinguistic Perspective on the Study of Bilingualism. *Linguistics* **39**: 21–49.
FORTES, M. 1945. *The Dynamics of Clanship among the Tallensi*. London: Oxford University Press.
—— 1970. *Time and Social Structure*. London: Athlone Press, University of London.
FRAKE, C. O. 1961. The Diagnosis of Disease among the Subanun of Mindanao. *American Anthropologist* **63**: 113–132.

FREEDMAN, M. 1963. A Chinese Phase in Social Anthropology. *British Journal of Sociology* **14** (1): 1–19.

FREUD, S. 1913. *Totem and Taboo*. London: Routledge & Kegan Paul, 1950. Standard Edition, Vol. 13. London: Hogarth.

FRIES, C. C. 1963. The Bloomfield 'School'. In Mohrmann, Sommerfelt, and Whatmough (eds.), 1963, pp. 196–224.

GARVIN, P. L. (ed.). 1957. *Report of the Seventh Annual Round Table Meeting on Linguistics and Language Study*. Washington: Georgetown University.

GLEASON, H. A. 1955a. *An Introduction to Descriptive Linguistics*. New York: Holt, Rinehart & Winston.

—— 1955b. *Workbook in Descriptive Linguistics*. New York: Holt, Rinehart & Winston.

GLUCKMAN, M. (ed.). 1964. *Closed Systems and Open Minds*. Edinburgh and London: Oliver & Boyd.

—— 1968. Psychological, Sociological and Anthropological Explanations of Witchcraft and Gossip: A Clarification. *Man* (n.s.) **3**: 20–24.

GODEL, R. 1957. *Les Sources manuscrites du Cours de linguistique générale de F. de Saussure*. Paris: Droz.

—— (ed.). 1969. *A Geneva School Reader in Linguistics*. Bloomington: Indiana University.

GOLDING, W. 1955. *The Inheritors*. London: Faber.

GOODENOUGH, W. H. 1956. Componential Analysis and the Study of Meaning. *Language* **32**: 195–216.

—— 1957. Cultural Anthropology and Linguistics. In P. L. Garvin (ed.), 1957.

GOODY, J. 1966. The Prospects for Social Anthropology. *New Society*, 13 October: 574–576.

GPC 1964. *Geiriadur Prifysgol Cymru*, Part XVIII. Cardiff: Gwasg Prifysgol Cymru.

—— 1968. ibid., Part XXII. Cardiff: Gwasg Prifysgol Cymru.

GREENBERG, J. H. 1948. Linguistics and Ethnology. *Southwestern Journal of Anthropology* **4**: 140–147.

—— 1955. *Studies in African Linguistic Classification*. Connecticut: Compass.

—— (ed.). 1963a. *Universals of Language*. Cambridge, Mass.: MIT Press. Paperback edition, 1966.

—— 1963b. *The Languages of Africa*. The Hague: Mouton.

GUMPERZ, J. J., and HYMES, D. (eds.). 1964. *The Ethnography of Communication*. Menasha, Wis.: American Anthropological Association.

GUTHRIE, M. 1948. *The Classification of the Bantu Languages*. London: International African Institute.

—— 1953. *The Bantu Languages of Western Equatorial Africa.* London: International African Institute.

—— 1962. Some Developments in the Pre-history of the Bantu Languages. *Journal of African History* **3**: 273–282.

HAMP, E. P. 1958. Consonant Allophones in Proto-Keltic. In *Lochlann*, Vol. I, pp. 209–217. Oslo: Oslo University Press.

HARRIS, M. 1969. *The Rise of Anthropological Theory: A History of Theories of Culture.* London: Routledge & Kegan Paul.

HARRIS, Z. S. 1951. *Methods in Structural Linguistics.* Chicago: Chicago University Press.

HART, H. L. A. 1961. *The Concept of Law.* Oxford: Clarendon Press.

HERTZ, R. 1960. *Death and the Right Hand.* Translated by R. and C. Needham. London: Cohen & West.

HJELMSLEV, L. 1943. *Omkring sprogteoriens grundlaeggelse.* Copenhagen: Munksgaard.

—— 1957. Pour une sémantique structurale. In Hjelmslev (ed.), 1959, pp. 96–112.

—— (ed.). 1959. *Essais linguistiques.* Copenhagen: Nordisk Sprog- og Kulturforlag.

—— 1963. *Prolegomena to a Theory of Language.* (Translation by F. J. Whitfield of Hjelmslev, 1943.) Second edition. Madison, Wis.: University of Wisconsin Press. (First edition, 1961.)

HOCART, A. M. 1937. Kinship Systems. *Anthropos* **22**: 345–351. Reprinted in Hocart, *The Life-giving Myth*, second edition, edited by R. Needham. London: Methuen, 1970.

HOCKETT, C. F. 1958. *A Course in Modern Linguistics.* New York: Macmillan.

—— 1968. *The State of the Art.* The Hague: Mouton.

HOIJER, H. (ed.). 1955. *Language and Culture.* Chicago: Chicago University Press.

HOOK, S. (ed.). 1969. *Language and Philosophy.* New York: New York University Press.

HOUSEHOLDER, F. W. 1952. Review of D. Jones, *The Phoneme. International Journal of American Linguistics* **18**: 99–105.

—— 1957. Rough Justice in Linguistics. In Garvin (ed.), 1957, pp. 153–165.

—— 1970. Review of Hockett, 1968. *Journal of Linguistics* **6** (1): 129–134.

HUMBOLDT, W. VON. 1836. *Über die Verschiedenheit des menschlichen Sprachbaues und ihren Einfluss auf die geistige Entwickelung des Menschengeschlechts.* Berlin: Königliche Akademie der Wissenschaften. Photo-reprint, Bonn: Dummlers Verlag, 1967.

—— 1969. *De l'origine des formes grammaticales suivi de Lettre à M. Abel Rémusal.* Bordeaux: Ducros.

HYMES, D. 1960. Lexicostatistics so far. *Current Anthropology* **1**: 3–44.

—— 1962. The Ethnography of Speaking. In T. Gladwin and W. C. Sturtevant (eds.), *Anthropology and Human Behavior*. Washington: Anthropological Society of Washington.

—— (ed.). 1964. *Language in Culture and Society*. New York: Harper & Row.

IPA 1949. *The Principles of the International Phonetic Association*. London: International Phonetic Association.

JACKSON, K. H. 1953. *Language and History in Early Britain*. Edinburgh: Edinburgh University Press.

JAKOBSON, R. 1960. Why 'Mama' and 'Papa'? In B. Kaplan and S. Wapner (eds.), *Perspectives in Psychological Theory*. New York: International Universities Press.

—— 1966. Henry Sweet's Paths towards Phonemics. In Bazell *et al.*, 1966, pp. 242–254.

—— and HALLE, M. 1956. *Fundamentals of Language*. The Hague: Mouton.

JARVIE, I. C. 1963. *The Revolution in Anthropology*. London: Routledge & Kegan Paul.

JONES, D. 1962. *The Phoneme: Its Nature and Use*. Revised edition. Cambridge: Heffer.

—— 1964. *The History and Meaning of the Term 'Phoneme'*. London: International Phonetic Association.

JONES, G., and JONES, T. J. 1949. *The Mabinogion*. London: Dent.

JONES, SIR W. 1799. The Third Anniversary Discourse on the Hindus. *The Works of Sir William Jones*. Six volumes. London: Robinson & Evans. Reprinted in Lehman (ed.), 1967.

JOOS, M. (ed.). 1957. *Readings in Linguistics I: The Development of Descriptive Linguistics in America 1925–1956*. (Reprinted 1967.) Chicago: Chicago University Press.

KARDINER, A., and PREBLE, E. 1961. *They Studied Man*. London: Secker & Warburg.

KING, R. 1969. *Historical Linguistics and Generative Grammar*. Englewood Cliffs, New Jersey: Prentice Hall.

KOELLE, S. W. 1854. *Polyglotta Africana*. London: Church Missionary Society.

KRAPF-ASKARI, E. 1969. *Yoruba Towns and Cities*. Oxford: Clarendon Press.

KROEBER, A. L. 1909. Classificatory Systems of Relationship. *Journal of the Royal Anthropological Institute*. **39**: 74–84.

LANGENDOEN, D. T. 1968. *The London School of Linguistics: A Study of the Linguistic Theories of B. Malinowski and J. R. Firth*. Cambridge, Mass.: MIT Press.

LEACH, E. R. 1954. Review of Durkheim, 1951. *Man* **54**: 92–93.
— 1957. The Epistemological Background to Malinowski's Empiricism. In R. Firth (ed.), 1957.
— 1958. Concerning Trobriand Clans and the Kinship Category *Tabu*. In J. Goody (ed.), *The Development Cycle in Domestic Groups*. Cambridge: Cambridge University Press.
— 1961. *Rethinking Anthropology*. London: Athlone Press, University of London.
— 1964. Anthropological Aspects of Language: Animal Categories and Verbal Abuse. In E. H. Lenneberg (ed.), *New Directions in the Study of Language*. Cambridge, Mass.: MIT Press.
— 1965. Frazer and Malinowski: On the Founding Fathers. *Encounter*, October. Also in *Current Anthropology* (1966) **7** (5): 560–576.
— 1970. *Lévi-Strauss*. London: Fontana/Collins.
— 1971. More about 'Mama' and 'Papa'. In Needham (ed.), 1971.
LEFEBVRE, H. 1966. *Le Langage et la société*. Paris: Gallimard.
LEHMANN, W. P. (ed. and trans.). 1967. *A Reader in Nineteenth Century Historical Indo-European Linguistics*. Bloomington: Indiana University Press.
— and MALKIEL, Y. (eds.). 1968. *Directions for Historical Linguistics*. Austin, Texas, and London: University of Texas Press.
LEITNER, G. W. 1874. Discussion in *Journal of the Royal Anthropological Institute* **4**: 212–214.
LENNEBERG, E. H., and ROBERTS, J. M. 1956. *The Language of Experience*. Baltimore, Md: Waverly Press. Indiana University Publications in Anthropology and Linguistics 13. Reprinted in Saporta (ed.), 1961.
LEROY, M. 1967. *The Main Trends in Modern Linguistics*. Oxford: Blackwell.
LÉVI-STRAUSS, C. 1949. *Les Structures élémentaires de la parenté*. Paris: Presses Universitaires de France.
— 1958. *Anthropologie structurale*. Paris: Plon.
— 1962a. *Le Totémisme aujourd'hui*. Paris: Presses Universitaires de France.
— 1962b. *La Pensée sauvage*. Paris: Plon.
— 1963a. *Structural Anthropology*. (Translation of Lévi-Strauss, 1958.) New York: Basic Books.
— 1963b. *Totemism*. (Translation by R. Needham of Lévi-Strauss, 1962a.) Boston: Beacon Press.
— 1964. *Mythologiques I: Le Cru et le cuit*. Paris: Plon.
— 1966a. *The Savage Mind*. (Translation of Lévi-Strauss, 1962b.) London: Weidenfeld & Nicolson; Chicago: Chicago University Press.

LÉVI-STRAUSS, C. 1966b. *Mythologiques II: Du Miel aux cendres.* Paris: Plon.

— 1966c. Introduction to third edition of Mauss, 1950. Paris: Presses Universitaires de France.

— 1967. *The Scope of Anthropology.* (Translation of *Leçon inaugurale faite le mardi 5 janvier 1960.*) London: Cape.

— 1968. *Mythologiques III: L'Origine des manières de table.* Paris: Plon.

— 1969a. *The Elementary Structures of Kinship*, edited by R. Needham. (Translated from revised edition (1967) of Lévi-Strauss, 1949.) Boston: Beacon Press; London: Eyre & Spottiswoode. Social Science Paperback edition, 1970.

— 1969b. *The Raw and the Cooked.* (Translation of Lévi-Strauss, 1964.) New York: Harper & Row.

LEWIS, H. 1943. *Yr Elfen Ladin yn yr Iaith Gymraeg.* Cardiff: Gwasg Prifysgol Cymru.

LIENHARDT, R. G. 1961. *Divinity and Experience.* Oxford: Clarendon Press.

LOOMIS, R. S. 1956. The Spoils of Annwn: An Early Welsh Poem. In *Wales and the Arthurian Legend.* Cardiff: University of Wales Press.

LOUNSBURY, F. G. 1956. A Semantic Analysis of the Pawnee Kinship Usage. *Language* **32**: 158–194.

— 1965. Another View of Trobriand Kinship Categories. In E. A. Hammel (ed.), Formal Semantic Analysis. Special Publication of *American Anthropologist* **67** (5), part 2: 1–316.

— 1969. Language and Culture. In Hook (ed.), 1969.

LYONS, J. 1968. *Introduction to Theoretical Linguistics.* Cambridge: Cambridge University Press.

— 1970. *Chomsky.* London: Fontana/Collins.

— and WALES, R. J. (eds.). 1966. *Psycholinguistic Papers.* Edinburgh: Edinburgh University Press.

MALINOWSKI, B. 1935. *Coral Gardens and their Magic,* Vol. II. Second edition, 1966, with Introduction by J. Berry. London: Allen & Unwin.

MALMBERG, B. 1964. *New Trends in Linguistics.* Stockholm: Lund.

MAQUET, J. J. 1964. Objectivity in Anthropology. *Current Anthropology* **5** (1): 47–55.

MAUSS, M. 1950. *Sociologie et Anthropologie.* Third edition, 1966. Paris: Presses Universitaires de France.

— 1954. *The Gift.* Translated by I. Cunnison, with an Introduction by E. E. Evans-Pritchard. (Corrected edition, 1969.) London: Cohen & West.

MAXWELL, J. C. 1871. *Theory of Heat.* Third edition, 1872. London.

MAYBURY-LEWIS, D. 1967. *Akwe-Shavante Society.* Oxford: Clarendon Press.

MCLUHAN, M. 1970. *Counterblast.* London: Rapp & Whiting.

MEEK, C. K. 1931. *Tribal Studies in Northern Nigeria.* London: Kegan Paul, Trench, Trubner.

MEYER, R. 1910. Bedeutungssysteme. *Kuhns Zeitschrift für Vergleichende Sprachforschung* **43**: 352–368.

MILNER, G. B. 1954. Review of J. Perrot, *La Linguistique. Man* **54**: 172.

—— 1966. Hypostatization. In Bazell *et al.*, 1966, pp. 321–334.

—— 1969. Siamese Twins, Birds and the Double Helix. *Man* (n.s.) **4**: 5–23.

MOHRMANN, C., NORMAN, F., and SOMMERFELT, A. 1963. *Trends in Modern Linguistics.* Utrecht/Antwerp: Spectrum.

—— SOMMERFELT, A., and WHATMOUGH, J. (eds.). 1963. *Trends in European and American Linguistics 1930–1960.* Utrecht/Antwerp: Spectrum.

MOORE, O. K., and OLMSTED, D. L. 1952. Language and Professor Lévi-Strauss. *American Anthropologist* **54** (1): 116–119.

MORRIS, C. 1946. *Signs, Language and Behavior.* Englewood Cliffs, N.J.: Prentice Hall.

MURDOCK, G. P. 1951. British Social Anthropology. *American Anthropologist* **53** (4): 465–473.

NEEDHAM, R. 1954. The System of Teknonyms and Death-Names of the Penan. *Southwestern Journal of Anthropology* **10**: 416–431.

—— 1958. A Structural Analysis of Purum Society. *American Anthropologist* **60**: 75–101.

—— 1960a. Descent Systems and Ideal Language. *Philosophy of Science* **27**: 96–101.

—— 1960b. The Left Hand of the Mugwe: An Analytical Note on the Structure of Meru Symbolism. *Africa* **30**: 20–33.

—— 1962. *Structure and Sentiment.* Chicago: Chicago University Press.

—— 1963. Introduction to Durkheim and Mauss, 1963.

—— 1967. Right and Left in Nyoro Symbolic Classification. *Africa* **37**: 425–451.

—— 1970. The Future of Social Anthropology: Disintegration or Metamorphosis? *Anniversary Contributions to Anthropology.* Leiden: Brill.

—— 1971. Introduction to *Rethinking Kinship and Marriage.* ASA Monograph 11. London: Tavistock.

PAINE, R. 1967. What is Gossip about? An Alternative Hypothesis. *Man* (n.s.) **2**: 278–285.

—— 1968. Gossip Transaction. *Man* (n.s.) **3**: 305–308.

PALMER, F. R. (ed.). 1968. *Selected Papers of J. R. Firth 1952–1959.* London: Longmans Green.

PIKE, K. L. 1954, 1955, 1960. *Language in relation to a Unified Theory of the Structure of Human Behaviour*. Three volumes. Glendale Summer Institute of Linguistics.

—— 1956. Towards a Theory of the Structure of Human Behaviour. Reprinted in Hymes (ed.), 1964.

POCOCK, D. F. 1961. *Social Anthropology*. London and New York: Sheed & Ward.

ROBINS, R. H. 1967. *A Short History of Linguistics*. London: Longmans Green.

ROSS, A. 1958. *On Law and Justice*. London: Stevens.

SAPIR, E. 1921. *Language*. New York: Harcourt, Brace & World.

SAPORTA, S. (ed.). 1961. *Psycholinguistics*. New York: Holt, Rinehart & Winston.

SAUSSURE, F. DE. 1878. *Mémoire sur le système primitif des voyelles dans les langues indo-européennes*. Geneva. Now translated in Lehman (ed.), 1967.

—— 1916. *Cours de linguistique générale*. Published by C. Bally, A. Sechehaye, with Albert Riedlinger. Paris/Geneva: Payot. Second edition 1922. Translated by W. Baskin, New York: Philosophical Library, 1959; London: Peter Owen, 1960 (reprinted 1964).

SEBEOK, T. A., HAYES, A. S., and BATESON, M. C. 1964. *Approaches to Semiotics*. The Hague: Mouton.

SECHEHAYE, A. 1933. La Pensée et la langue ou: Comment concevoir le rapport organique de l'individuel et du social dans le langage? *Journal de Psychologie* (Numéro exceptionnel) **30** (1): 57–81.

—— 1940. Les Trois linguistiques Saussuriennes. *Vox Romanica* **V**: 1–48. Zurich. Reprinted in Godel (ed.), 1969.

SHANNON, C. E. 1948. A Mathematical Theory of Communication. *Bell System Technical Journal* **27**: 379–423. Also in Shannon and Weaver, 1949.

—— and WEAVER, W. 1949. *The Mathematical Theory of Communication*. Urbana: University of Illinois.

SHAW, G. B. 1916. *Pygmalion*. Harmondsworth: Penguin Books, 1941.

SIMONIS, Y. 1968. *Claude Lévi-Strauss, ou la 'Passion de l'inceste'*. Paris: Montaigne.

SMITH, A. G. (ed.). 1966. *Communication and Culture*. New York: Holt, Rinehart & Winston.

SOUTHALL, A. W. (ed.). 1961. *Social Change in Modern Africa*. London: Oxford University Press.

STEINER, F. 1956. *Taboo*. London: Cohen & West.

STURTEVANT, W. 1964. Studies in Ethnoscience. *American Anthropologist* **66** (2): 99–131.

SWADESH, M. 1950. Salish Internal Relationships. *International Journal of American Linguistics* **16**: 157–167.

TALBOT, P. A. 1912. *In the Shadow of the Bush*. London: Heinemann.

TAMBIAH, S. J. 1968. The Magical Power of Words. *Man* (n.s.) **3** (2): 175–208.

TAYLOR, D. 1958. On Anthropologists' Use of Linguistics. *American Anthropologist* **60**: 940.

THOMAS, N. W. 1910. *Anthropological Report on the Edo-Speaking Peoples of Nigeria*, Part I. London: Harrison.

—— 1914. *Specimens of Languages from Southern Nigeria*. London: Harrison.

THOMPSON, D'ARCY, W. 1966. *On Growth and Form*. Cambridge: Cambridge University Press.

TRIER, J. 1931. *Der deutsche Wortschatz im Sinnbezirk des Verstandes*. Heidelberg: Carl Winter.

TRUBETZKOY, N. 1933. La Phonologie actuelle. *Journal de Psychologie* (Numéro exceptionnel) **30** (1): 227–246.

—— 1968. *Introduction to the Principles of Phonological Descriptions*. The Hague: Nijhoff.

TURNBULL, H. W. 1959. *The Correspondence of Isaac Newton*, Vol. I. Cambridge: Cambridge University Press.

TURNER, V. W. 1964. Symbols in Ndembu Ritual. In Gluckman (ed.), 1964.

—— 1965. Ritual Symbolism, Morality and Social Structure among the Ndembu. In M. Fortes and G. Dieterlen (eds.), *African Systems of Thought*. London: Oxford University Press.

—— 1966. Colour Classification in Ndembu Ritual. In M. Banton (ed.), *Anthropological Approaches to the Study of Religion*. ASA Monograph 3. London: Tavistock.

—— 1967. *The Forest of Symbols: Aspects of Ndembu Ritual*. Ithaca, NY: Cornell University Press.

ULLMANN, S. 1951. *The Principles of Semantics*. Glasgow: Jackson.

—— 1959. *The Principles of Semantics*. Second edition, with additions. Oxford: Blackwell.

—— 1963. Semantic Universals. In Greenberg (ed.), 1963a.

VENDRYES, J. 1921. Le Caractère social du langage et la doctrine de F. de Saussure. *Journal de Psychologie* **18**: 617–624. Also in Vendryes, 1952, pp. 18–25.

—— 1952. *Choix d'études linguistiques et celtiques*. Paris: Klincksieck.

VOEGELIN, C. F., and HARRIS, Z. S. 1945. Linguistics in Ethnology. *Southwestern Journal of Anthropology* **1** (4): 455–465.

VOEGELIN, C. F., and HARRIS, Z. S. 1947. The Scope of Linguistics. *American Anthropologist* **49** (4): 588–600.

WAISMANN, F. 1968. *The Principles of Linguistic Philosophy* (ed. R. Harré). London: Macmillan.

WARTBURG, W. VON. 1943. *Einführung in Problematik und Methodik der Sprachwissenschaft*. Tübingen: Max Niemeyer.

— 1969. *Problems and Methods in Linguistics*. (Translation of von Wartburg, 1943.) Oxford: Blackwell.

WELLS, R. S. 1947. De Saussure's System of Linguistics. *Word* **3** (1): 1–31. Reprinted in Joos (ed.), 1957.

WHITELEY, W. F. 1966. Social Anthropology, Meaning and Linguistics. *Man* (n.s.) **1** (2): 139–157.

— (ed.). 1971. *Language Use and Social Change*. London: Oxford University Press.

WHORF, B. L. 1956. *Language, Thought and Reality* (ed. J. Carroll). Cambridge, Mass.: MIT Press. Paperback edition, 1964.

WIENER, N. 1948. *Cybernetics*. Cambridge, Mass.: MIT Press. Second edition, 1961.

WITTGENSTEIN, L. 1963. *Philosophical Investigations*. Oxford: Blackwell. (First English edition, 1953.)

WORSLEY, P. 1966. The End of Anthropology? Paper for 6th World Congress of Sociology. (Mimeo.)

Y Cymro, 1970. March 25.

PART I

Social Anthropology, Language, and Sociolinguistics

Hilary Henson

Early British Anthropologists and Language

Bronislaw Malinowski asserted as early as 1920 that: 'Linguistics without ethnography would fare as badly as ethnography would without the light thrown on it by language' (1920: 78). It is only recently, however, that the full implications of such a statement have begun to be appreciated by British social anthropologists, and any explanation of this must take account of the distinctive British attitude towards the relationship between linguistics and anthropology during the formative years of the subject.

In contrast to the American or the French approach, very few British anthropologists considered that language required study in its own right within the bounds of their discipline. With the exception of Müller, who from his half-century of teaching in Oxford falls here into the British context, they merely used it as supplementary evidence to support and extend theories developed within anthropology.[1] Language was indeed such a peripheral interest that very few ideas had evolved any further at the end of the period considered in this paper than at the beginning. For this reason, the material below is grouped according to topic rather than date. The dates chosen for the period as a whole, 1850 to 1920, cover the history of social anthropology from the time at which there was an upsurge of interest in other cultures, both for their own sakes and for the light they could throw on Western society and its origins, until the time when, with the development of fieldwork techniques, increasing emphasis was laid on the use of native categories, and the pragmatic application of linguistics to anthropology.

LANGUAGE AND RACE

One important area of nineteenth-century anthropology in which appeal was early made to linguistic evidence was that of racial distribution and differentiation. Anthropologists were concerned not so much with contemporary racial distributions as with giving them a history, and most of their attempts were dependent on the implicit assumption that linguistic distributions and interrelations exactly paralleled those of race and could thus be used as a substitute proof. The example for such reconstructions came from the early comparative linguists themselves, who assumed that they had deduced elements of a real language that had once been spoken by a people whose descendants were now scattered throughout Europe and Asia. Max Müller, for example, wrote:

> 'It is hardly possible to look at the evidence hitherto collected . . . without feeling that these words are the fragments of a real language, once spoken by a united race at a time which the historian has till lately hardly ventured to realise' (1856: 351).

Anthropologists accepted the linguists' claim that their subject was a historical one, and that their hypothetical Indo-European forms could be used to reach back into man's past ('This method of making language itself tell the history of ancient times' – Müller, 1856: 320). Many of them further accepted the implicit assumption that language could be equated with race. John Kennedy, for example, wishing to prove that the American Indians were all immigrants from other continents, and thus not the result of a separate Creation, used the vague resemblance between fourteen Carib words and certain West African equivalents to prove that the Caribs, at least, had come from Africa (Kennedy, 1856). Hyde Clarke made a more ambitious use of comparative linguistics. He classified all the languages of the world according to certain characteristics he claimed to find in them, assigned them to races which he assessed on a scale of progressive civilization, and produced from this a chronology of world colonization (Clarke, 1874).[2]

Some anthropologists did, however, recognize that such an application of linguistic evidence was merely an attempt to use the prestige of the linguists' apparent success in uncovering history to provide anthropology with a history where it had none before. Tylor (1881) pointed out that the equation of language with race was false, since there were many cases both of different races sharing one language and of races changing from one language to another. The Rev. A. H. Sayce replied to Clarke in the year following the publication of his paper: 'Society implies language, race does not' (Sayce, 1875: 213). In the discussion that followed, Professor Whitney made a neat statement of the way in which language is culturally and not physically determined:

> 'One's language is learned, not made by him. . . . It is virtually an institution, a part of the acquired culture of the people to whom it belongs; and, like every other part of culture, it is capable of transference' (Whitney, 1875: 216–217).

But in spite of such arguments to the contrary, some anthropologists continued to maintain that there was an observable connection between the distinctive characteristics of a language and the mentality of the race that created it. As late as 1883, Gustav Oppert, a professor of Sanskrit, defended this theory in the *Journal of the Royal Anthropological Institute*:

> 'A language preserves, as it were instinctively, its peculiar construction, and if it does not always coincide, either with the particular nation or person who speaks it, it certainly indicates the race of those who spoke it first, and this, in spite of all apparent change, and it retains the mode of thought of those among whom it first sprung up as their natural means of communication, though that race itself might exist no longer' (Oppert, 1883: 33).

It certainly appears that it was the Sanskrit linguists who were most responsible for such arguments. John Crawfurd, in an attack on the theory that Indo-European was ever spoken by such a thing as an Aryan race, claimed that: 'The theory in its ripest state is most fully described by the learned and ingenious Orientalist Professor Max Müller' (1861: 268). In his early writing, Müller certainly did assume that the Aryan language could be used to discover the Aryan race (e.g. 1856), but by 1872 he attacked uncompromisingly any approach that did not differentiate between language and racial characteristics, although he was still prepared to deduce certain cultural patterns from linguistic evidence:

> 'It is but too easily forgotten that if we speak of Aryan and Semitic families, the ground of classification is language, and

language only. There are Aryan and Semitic languages, but it is against all rules of logic to speak, without an expressed or implied qualification, of an Aryan race, of Aryan blood, of Aryan skulls, and to attempt ethnological classification on purely linguistic grounds. These two sciences, the Science of language and the Science of man, cannot, at least for the present, be kept too much asunder; and many misunderstandings, many controversies, would have been avoided, if scholars had not attempted to draw conclusions from language to blood, or from blood to language. When each of these sciences shall have carried out independently its own classification of men and of languages, then, and then only, will it be time to compare their results' (1872: 187).

THE IDEA OF THE PRIMITIVE LANGUAGE

The received idea that languages were linked to the mental capacity of the races that used them assumed in effect that language was physically determined. This was consistent with the general evolutionary bias of nineteenth-century anthropology, which was itself dependent on a biological analogy. It was an axiom that just as certain races were primitive, so the languages that they spoke were similarly simple and undeveloped. Those anthropologists who used comparative linguistic material classified it according to broad structural resemblances between languages, but the ordering of these classifications into stages of evolution was essentially dependent on the initial anthropological assumption that cultures could be so classified. An example is to be found as late as 1901 in the *JRAI*: 'Compared with an Aryan language, Tagalo is deficient in many qualities which have made European tongues the vehicle of civilisation' (Mackinlay, 1901: 214). One of the 'qualities' of Aryan languages quoted by the writer is the possession of grammatical gender. The ethnocentric approach to language was common to almost all the anthropologists of the period, and it was largely this which prevented them from seeing that there was no such thing as a 'primitive' language. The non-Indo-European languages were judged by their exotic nature, and their primitiveness was determined by the extent to which they differed from the European languages.

In any discussions of primitive languages there were two common assumptions about their inadequacy. The first was that the languages, and hence the speakers of the languages, were incapable of anything beyond a minimal generalization and abstraction:

> 'Savages will have twenty independent words each expressing the act of cutting some particular thing, without having any name for the act of cutting in general; they will have as many to describe birds, fish and trees of different kinds, but no general equivalents for the terms "bird", "fish", or "tree"' (Payne, 1899: 103).[3]

The second assumption was that, conversely, primitive languages were incapable of precision and specification, because their vocabularies were extremely small and limited, this failure being exacerbated by their harsh and indeterminate pronunciation: 'By means of more or less significant sounds, then, Fuegian society compounds impressions, and that somewhat imperfectly' (Marett, 1912: 139). Marett's example of extreme primitiveness in language is taken from the same society that first prompted Darwin to speculate on the origins of man.

A further commonly held belief about primitive languages was that they were subject to rapid change:

> 'Indeed, anyone who will attend to how English words run together in talking may satisfy himself that his own language would undergo rapid changes like those of barbaric tongues, were it not for the schoolmaster and the printer, who insist on keeping our words fixed and separate' (Tylor, 1881: 142).

E. J. Payne, who poetically described the rapidly changing vocabulary of savages as 'slippery and unstable as a dream' (1899: 89), gave as evidence for this belief two versions of the Catechism translated into the Mosetena language for the Collegio de Propaganda Fide, the first dating from 1834 and the second thirty years later. It is true that the forms of the words in the two lists show a considerable difference, but it does not appear to have occurred to Payne that perhaps both lists merely represented the faulty transcriptions of untrained recorders.

An inspection of the evidence on unwritten languages which

was available to anthropologists, at least during the earlier part of this period, makes it easier to understand their belief in the existence of 'primitive' languages. Admittedly, the inadequacy of the material in use affected the whole of anthropological research during this period, but certain areas of ethnographic data were at least partially open to observation and interpretation by the untrained traveller. The recording of exotic languages, on the other hand, could avoid ethnocentricity only by a conscious development of techniques, and this was never achieved during the period.

The recorders of these languages used a phonetic notation adapted from that used for the European languages that they knew. This explains the frequent tales of indeterminate and wavering pronunciations, where the phonemic system of a language did not overlap with the one used by the investigator. To give an example, a Scottish missionary, the Rev. Hugh Goldie, wrote of the Efik language:

> '*B* is frequently interchanged with *p*; or rather, a sound between the two, is very frequently employed. *D* has often *r* as a substitute, or rather, through imperfect enunciation, has the sound of *r* given to it. It is occasionally substituted for *F*' (1868: 5–6).

The recorders applied unquestioningly to their material the semantic and grammatical categories of the main European languages, once again explaining the lack of correspondence by a failing on the part of the primitive languages. Accounts of primitive languages generally consisted of brief word-lists elicited from interpreters, or from sessions of pointing and asking for names. In addition there was generally a short grammar based on the traditional categories of Latin and Greek, together with remarks on the more unusual constructions. In the early volumes of the *JRAI* there are many such descriptions. (On the Australian languages alone, there are Taplin, 1871; Barlow, 1872; and Mackenzie, 1873.) The anthropologists themselves never developed techniques that would have permitted them to describe language in its own terms.

PRIMITIVE LANGUAGES AND THE ORIGIN OF LANGUAGE

The assumption that the languages spoken by the small-scale, technologically simple societies of the world were primitive, and lower on the evolutionary scale, was relied on by several anthropologists interested in finding the origins of language. This was by no means the exclusive interest of anthropology alone, having been discussed by philosophers and linguists for centuries, yet it was peculiarly relevant to nineteenth-century anthropology, with its conviction that: 'To know what *Man is*, we ought to know what *Man has been*' (Müller, 1856: 302), since it was clear that: 'The grand characteristic which distinguishes man from all other mundane beings is articulate speech' (Hale, 1891: 414). Because of this, Horatio Hale continued: 'It is language alone which entitles anthropology to its claim to be deemed a distinct department of science' (1891: 414).

Although Hale can be assumed to have been closely associated with British anthropology, in spite of his Canadian affiliations, as is shown by his contributions to the *JRAI*, and by his donation of a copy of his book on the Chinook Jargon to Tylor, it must be admitted that the number of anthropologists in this country who would have agreed with his assessment of the importance of language was small. But of those who held the same opinion, it was the concern of many to find the origin of language. That Hale himself was more interested in the origins of the differentiation between language groups can be seen in his ingenious orphan theory.[4]

Many of those who were most influenced by the work of the comparative linguists once more took as their model of early language the linguists' hypothetical Proto-Indo-European, since this was thought to be of greater antiquity than any recorded language. The 'words' of Indo-European were then believed to be built on monosyllables, called by the linguists 'roots', and these could be used to support the argument that language had developed from a set of undifferentiated animal noises, the monosyllabic roots representing early elaborations of grunts and cries. This was suggested by, for example, Oppert (1883). This particular theory was well suited to the evolutionary analogy, since it did not require a sudden creation of language, but instead suggested a gradual development.[5]

It was, however, in the use of non-Indo-European linguistic evidence as the model of early language that anthropology made its distinctive contribution. E. J. Payne also thought that language had evolved from animal cries, but he believed that the most primitive languages available to the scholar were those of the American continent, and these were very different in nature from the linguists' Indo-European. This led him to a perceptive attack on the historical validity of the monosyllabic roots of Indo-European:

> 'It is objected to the "radicarian" theory which proposes what are notoriously the last products of philological analysis as the first facts in the genesis of language, that roots are not words at all; that they are abstractions invented by scholars; titles or headings, used for assorting the contents of the vocabulary; contrivances for classifying and describing the relations of words, as words are contrivances for classifying and describing the relations of things' (1899: 102–103).

Payne took as the mark of primitiveness in language a linguistic form which he called the 'holophrase' or 'portmanteau word'. Holophrastic languages did not analyse and structure experience in the way that the European languages could; instead, they merely gave general, undifferentiated impressions. They were more specific than the animal cry, which 'may be described as a holophrase not yet personalised' (1899: 170), and stood half-way between that and analytic languages:

> 'Circumstance, time, the mental disposition of the persons concerned, are all in due time embodied in the holophrase. This rudimentary form of speech, then, possesses a syntax, though not a syntax of words, or even of particles; it is a syntax of conceptions, which by the dissolution of the holophrase becomes a syntax of particles and words, of the new constituents of speech to which that dissolution gives birth' (Payne, 1899: 117).

The idea of the holophrase was partly prompted by the tendency for incorporation of many of the American Indian languages, since this gives rise to complex, indivisible linguistic forms. But in 1911, Franz Boas, the great American linguist and anthropologist, pointed out that it was above all the lack of overlap between the semantic systems of two very different languages, that of the observer and that of the observed, that gave rise to the idea of the holophrase.[6]

E. B. Tylor made a different attempt to find the origin of language. Tylor was keenly interested in language for its own sake, as we can tell from his writings,[7] but his particular theoretical concern was to find in the origins of language a rational explanation for the present arbitrary relation between word and idea:

> 'That the selection of words to express ideas was ever purely arbitrary, that is to say, such that it would have been consistent with its principles to exchange any two words as we may exchange algebraic symbols, or to shake up a number of words in a bag and redistribute them at random among the ideas they represented, is a supposition opposed to such knowledge as we have of the formation of language' (1865: 57).

Tylor thus touched on a problem later to be much discussed in Saussurean linguistics (Saussure, 1916; trans. 1959). Whether or not the relation between the *signifiant* and the *signifié* is arbitrary, a linguistic sign gains meaning from its place in a system of signs. Tylor had in fact realized that this was the case in the languages he spoke, because he wrote that words had 'become like counters or algebraic symbols, good to represent just what they are set down to mean' (1865: 59). What he wished to prove was that there was a time in the past when the selection of linguistic signs had been based on reason.

The primitive form of language to which Tylor directed his attention was the language of gestures used by the deaf and dumb. He himself recorded the language used in the Berlin Deaf and Dumb Institute, and compared it with the similar system used in England. He read of the French system in the work of the Abbé Sicard (1808), whose ideas on language influenced Tylor considerably. Tylor claimed that the signs used were the creation of the deaf and dumb themselves, and that the reason for their choice of signs was always obvious: 'The relation between idea and sign not only always exists, but is scarcely lost sight of for a moment' (1865: 16). Moreover, a comparison of the language of the deaf mutes with the sign language used as a lingua franca among the American Indians showed remarkable resemblances between them. Tylor therefore felt that he was close to discovering the original sign-making faculty in man which had once produced the spoken language.[8]

Tylor never claimed that gesture language had either preceded speech or given rise to it, although he thought it possible. He investigated several reports that primitive languages were more dependent on gesture than was his own, but none of them was convincing. For example, Mme Pfeiffer visited the Puris of Brazil and claimed that they had no words for 'yesterday' and 'tomorrow'. To express these ideas they were forced to use the word for 'day', at the same time pointing behind them for 'yesterday' and in front of them for 'tomorrow'. But other evidence showed that the neighbouring tribes did not lack the words in question, and Tylor very sensibly remarked:

> 'It is extremely likely that Mme Pfeiffer's savages suffered the penalty of being set down as wanting in language for no worse fault than using a combination of words and signs in order to make what they meant as clear as possible to her comprehension' (1865: 80).[9]

The importance of Tylor's theories on gesture language and its relation to speech lies in his realization that both are dependent on man's powers of symbolization and abstraction:

> 'It seems more likely than not that there may be a similarity between the process by which the human mind first uttered itself in speech, and that by which the same mind still utters itself in gestures' (1865: 76).

It was rare indeed for anyone from this period to argue that the structure of language could be paralleled anywhere else in culture. But the language of gesture most resembles speech in that it is a closed system of mutually agreed, and therefore artificial, signs.[10] By looking for a 'natural' relation between *signifiant* and *signifié*, that is, a relation subject to a rational explanation, Tylor moved away from the abstract nature of language.

Of British anthropologists who showed any interest in language, many ventured no further than the attempt to find how language was first created. In this, it cannot be claimed that they introduced any radically new approaches; they only re-argued suggestions that had been current for years. Tylor, for example, as well as investigating gesture language, discussed at length the old theory that the sounds of speech might have originated in imitations of the sounds of nature, although his conclusion was that, in the unlikely case that all language did so originate, words had deviated so far that 'to all intents and purposes they might at first have been arbitrarily chosen' (1871: 229). The theories put forward were, however, misguided in their assumptions.[11]

COGNITIVE STRUCTURES AND LANGUAGE

Myth

Almost without exception, British anthropologists of the period agreed with Müller that language was nothing more than 'the outward form and manifestation of thought' (Müller, 1871: 590). The idea, for example, that race is reflected in language depends on an initial assumption that language is no more than the passive agent by means of which thought is transmitted, the thought being physically conditioned, and thus affected by race. When languages were called 'primitive' and 'holophrastic', there was sometimes the idea that the language itself could have a limiting effect on thought. This seems to be the case in Marett's suggestion that all primitive peoples should be taught a language like the one that he himself spoke:

> 'Since thinking is little more or less than, as Plato put it, a silent conversation with oneself, to possess an analytic language is to be more than half-way on the road to the analytic mode of intelligence, the mode of thinking by direct concepts' (1912: 151).

But the idea that language could have any effect on cognitive structures was explored by only one major early writer, Max Müller:

> 'Though we maintain that thought cannot exist without language, nor language without thought, we do distinguish

between thought and language, between the inward and the outward *logos*, between the substance and the form. Nay, we go a step beyond. We admit that language necessarily reacts on thought, and we see in this reaction, in this refraction of the rays of language, the real solution of the old riddle of mythology' (1871: 593).

According to Müller, language was incapable of representing thought without distorting it, and this was a consequence of the way in which it had developed. His version of this development depended entirely upon the languages of the Indo-European group, since he was a great Sanskrit scholar, and appears to have had very little knowledge of any languages outside this group. In the period of language formation, called by Müller the 'mythopoeic period', language was still alive. Objects were named according to their characteristic attributes, with the result that one object might be named by more than one attribute, giving rise to synonyms, and more than one object might share an attribute, giving rise to homonyms. Because at this stage the relationship between name and object was still comprehensible, words carried a much greater load of meaning than at present:

> 'Every word, whether noun or verb, had still its full original power during the mythopoeic ages. Words were heavy and unwieldy. They said more than they ought to say, and hence much of the strangeness of the mythological language' (1856: 369).

All the natural phenomena were once called by the names that man used for his own actions. The sun was the 'shiner', the moon the 'measurer', and the river the 'runner' or the 'plougher'. That this had been the case could be 'proved' from Sanskrit etymology. Since all these phenomena were seen as instituting action, they were inevitably personalized. They were originally undifferentiated, but later a division was created by the introduction of new forms to make the feminine category. Neuter could not have been introduced until after language had died, since 'our problem is not, how language came to personify, but how it succeeded in dispersonifying' (1878: 189).

When this early stage was passed, language died and lost its 'etymological conscience' (1856: 357). The old weight of meaning was submerged, and became open to misinterpretation, for 'It is the essential character of a true myth that it should no longer be intelligible by a reference to the spoken language' (1856: 376).

Müller believed that, as languages decayed, the debris of their earlier stages set obstacles in the way of pure thought. Societies explained these obstacles by turning them into myths. Müller argued that the process that created these myths was essentially the same as that to be seen in the workings of folk etymology. When the reason why all the natural phenomena were named as male and female actors was no longer understood, men were forced to transform them into living beings, acting out various dramas in a world of mythology. This explained why, whenever Müller investigated a myth, he always found that the protagonists could be traced back to nature.

Müller considered that language would never be a perfect vehicle for the transmission of thought because it would never be able to lose its poetic, myth-making aspect. Mythology 'can never disappear till language becomes altogether commensurate with thought, which it never will' (1871: 590). It was no longer necessary for anthropologists to imagine 'a period of temporary insanity through which the human mind had to pass' (1856: 309) in order to explain the myths of the world; since mythology was nothing more than 'the dark shadow that language throws on thought' (1871: 590), the whole problem could be solved by appeal to the science of language.

Müller's theory is the less convincing in that it is based solely on evidence from the Indo-European languages, and the myths of Europe and Asia. For example, linguistic gender, which plays an essential part in his theory, is not, of course, characteristic of all language families. But the interest of his theory lies less in the accuracy of his hypothesis than in his realization of the way in which language works as a symbolic system. He recognized how widespread a process popular etymology is, continually reorganizing and rationalizing symbolic structures. His theory that words can say 'more than they ought to say' (1856: 369) seems to be based on a realization of the way in which an old metaphor, opaque in normal use, springs back to life when placed in a context also related to its literal sense. This resembles

Turner's theories on the polysemy of ritual symbols (1967, 1968). Müller would also have approved of Lévi-Strauss's concept of *bricolage* (1962: 26–47; trans. 1966: 16–36), which is used to demonstrate how every symbolic structure is affected by the fact that its components have been used before and will be used again. Like Lévi-Strauss, and unlike anyone of his own generation, Müller used language as the key to other symbolic structures of great importance to anthropology.

Kinship systems

The study of kinship has always been of central importance to anthropology. Two influential books on the subject were written by British anthropologists at an early date (Maine, 1861; Mclennan, 1865). But both Maine and Mclennan were interested only in the legal and political implications of their evolutionary schema of kinship systems, and it was the American L. H. Morgan (1870, 1877) who first insisted on the importance of studying the terminologies used in kinship systems. The British at this early date never seemed to grasp the importance of kinship terminology, or to consider its relevance to ideas of kinship behaviour.

The standard approach towards kinship studies, which was used in the later years of the period, was Rivers's method for the collecting of genealogies, which he developed for the Torres Straits expedition (1904). The complete unimportance of linguistic systems to Rivers, and those who used his method, is evident from his own rather breathtaking recommendation of the method:

> 'By means of the genealogical method it is possible, *with no knowledge of the language, and with very inferior interpreters*, to work out with the utmost accuracy systems of kinship so complicated that Europeans who have spent their whole lives among the people have never been able to grasp them' (1910: 10; my italics).

The government anthropologists of the early twentieth century applied Rivers's method for much the same reason (e.g. N. W. Thomas, 1910: 141).

The British were aware of some of the work being done on

kinship in America, but they assumed that terminologies were merely different ways of naming actual physical relationships. An example of the extent of their awareness can be found in Thomas:

> 'There are two systems of indicating kinship, by which we mean relationships traceable by genealogy. One of these, the descriptive, is mainly used among the white races, the other, the classificatory, is confined to the coloured races of mankind' (1910: 112).

Evidence of how far apart the British and the Americans were in this field can be found by comparing this passage with the brilliant article by A. L. Kroeber in the British anthropologists' own journal:

> 'Since, then, it is not only primitive people that classify or fail to distinguish relationships, the suspicion is justified that the current distinction between the two classes or systems of indicating relationships is subjective, and has its origin in the point of view of investigators, who, on approaching foreign languages, have been impressed with their failure to discriminate certain relationships between which languages of civilised Europe distinguish, and who, in the enthusiasm of formulating general theories from such facts, have forgotten that their own languages are filled with entirely analogous groupings or classifications which custom has made so familiar and natural that they are not felt as such' (1909: 77).

Kroeber then proceeded to a subtle analysis of the differences between physical relationships as such, the basic constituent categories of any kinship system, and the particular linguistic patterning of any one such system. It is to papers such as this that modern social anthropologists are more likely to look.

THE USE OF 'NATIVE' CATEGORIES: MANA, TOTEM, AND TABOO

That early British anthropologists were unaware of the systematic nature of linguistic structures, and of the dependence of the elements of a cognitive system one upon the other, is once again evident in their use of certain linguistic categories taken from particular primitive societies to serve as technical terms of general application. It was in the field of comparative religion that the most famous of these terms, *mana*, *totem*, and *taboo*, were used. In this field, anthropologists attempted to identify patterns of religious evolution which could be demonstrated in all societies past and present, but their material was vast and disparate. Therefore, they sought categories which would enable them to organize the evidence.

Mana, a term from the Melanesian languages, makes one of its first appearances in the literature in a letter, dated 7 July 1877, from the missionary and linguist R. H. Codrington, which was quoted by Müller as an example of 'how the idea of the infinite, of the unseen, or as we call it afterwards, the Divine, may exist among the lowest tribes in a vague and hazy form' (1878: 53). Further descriptions of *mana* in its Melanesian context can be found in Codrington's own book (e.g. 1891: 191).

In a paper published in 1909, R. R. Marett suggested that *mana* should be taken into the technical language of comparative anthropology as a term of wider application than its actual linguistic distribution:

> 'It is no part of my present design to determine, by an exhaustive analysis of the existing evidence, how the conception of *mana* is understood and applied within its special area of distribution, namely, the Pacific region. Such a task pertains to Descriptive Ethnology, and it is rather to a problem of Comparative Ethnology that I would venture to call attention. I propose to discuss the value – that is to say, the appropriateness and the fruitfulness – of either this conception of *mana* or some nearly equivalent notion, such as the Huron *orenda*, when selected by the science of Comparative Religion to serve as one of its categories, or classificatory terms of the widest extension' (1909: 101).

Marett considered that Tylor's term 'animism' could profitably be replaced by *mana*. 'Animism' was at once too specific and too general, whereas *mana*, as befitting 'the incoherent state of rudimentary reflection' (1909: 119), had an undifferentiated quality which made it suitable for describing this early state of religion:

> 'Such terms I would denominate "sympathetic"; and would, further, hazard the judgement that, in the case of all science

of the kind, its use of sympathetic terms is the measure of its sympathetic insight' (1909: 104).

Marett admitted the difficulty of using a culturally bound word as a general technical term, since there would always be some contamination in both directions between the localized and the general idea, but he still considered that the disadvantage was outweighed by the value of using a term which was itself expressive of primitive religion.

Marett's use of the term *mana* showed, on the positive side, an awareness that ethnographic data were not easily reducible to his own cultural categories. On the negative side, it assumed that all non-European cultures differed from those of Europe in much the same ways, so that they could all be classified together.[12] By taking 'opaque' terms from the same kinds of society as those from which they took their ethnographic evidence, anthropologists gave an ontological status to these particular categories that was never quite matched by ideas like 'animism', or the distinction between 'magic' and 'religion'. As Marett realized, 'animism' could itself be analysed; the linguistic term was not inviolable, and its specific reference and general value could be questioned. But a term taken from another different culture was respected as a 'true' category, however much it had been distorted from its original usage in order to fit all the heterogeneous customs subsumed under its name.

The other best-known categories of this type were *totem*, from Odjikewa, or a comparable Algonquin language, and *taboo*, *tabu*, *tapu* from the Polynesian languages. They were earlier imports, and not so obviously the responsibility of one man. Moreover, both words were adopted into general English usage surprisingly early, whereas *mana* never really spread beyond anthropology.[13] *Taboo* was first reported as a custom of the Polynesians by Captain Cook in 1777, and by the beginning of the nineteenth century it had already been fully adopted into the English language.[14]

The seventh edition of the *Encyclopaedia Britannica* (1842) carried a brief note on *taboo*, referring only to its use in the Polynesian context. The eighth edition omitted it altogether; but the ninth, of 1888, contained a long article by J. G. Frazer, in which he did not hesitate to use *taboo* as a general term for a worldwide phenomenon. He claimed in his *Golden Bough* volume on *taboo* (1911) that it was not until he came to write the article for the *Encyclopaedia Britannica* that he realized how widespread the custom of *taboo* was, thus implying that he was the anthropologist mainly responsible for its adoption as a technical term,[15] but other comparable uses of a similar date can be found, notably in Lang (e.g. 1883: 417; 1884: 73, 75), and it is more likely that Frazer merely made explicit in his article a linguistic practice which had been current among his contemporaries for several years.

It is even more difficult to discover who was the first to use *totem* as a technical term. It was first mentioned in a purely American Indian context in the early seventeenth century, and recurred frequently in the literature from that time on. By 1871 it was being used by Tylor as the name for a hypothetical universal stage of development, when he assumed an 'early totem stage of society'. It was again Frazer who used the borrowed word in a highly generalized sense in the *Encyclopaedia Britannica* (ninth edition):

> 'A totem is a class of material objects which a savage regards with superstitious respect, believing that there exists between him and every member of the class an intimate and altogether special relation' (1888b: 467).

By 1905, Andrew Lang was writing: 'Meanwhile we are concerned rather with the way into totemism out of a prior non-totemic social condition, and with the development of the various stages of totemic society in Australia' (1905: 6).

The early British anthropologists, who extracted these terms from the languages of certain societies, thought that they were thereby easing the task of anthropology. The legacy of these terms has presented anthropology in this century with problems that it has been able to overcome only by recognizing the unreality of the terms.

CONCLUSION

One reason why early British anthropology regarded the study of language as lying beyond its own bounds was that the science of language was already a well-established and autonomous discipline at a time when anthropology was still looking for its own rules of procedure. Therefore, instead of developing their own distinctive approach towards language, anthropologists assumed that the subject was already adequately developed, and, in most cases where linguistics did enter anthropological discussion, its use was based on the theories and categories already established by the Indo-European linguists. Paradoxically, Müller was the only writer of the period who made use of a specifically anthropological theory of language, yet he was himself primarily a specialist in the field of Indo-European linguistics. His theories on the relationship between language and anthropology still have a direct relevance to anthropology today, unlike the linguistic theories of his contemporaries.

It must be admitted, however, that there were a few British anthropologists who began to doubt the adequacy of some of the linguistic reports that were used to substantiate anthropological theories, and even to doubt some of the theories themselves. For example, the Rev. S. S. Dorman reported that his ecclesiastical predecessor, who had lived among the Masarwas of South Africa for more than twenty years, thought that their vocabulary possessed no more than three hundred words. From his own researches, Dorman reported: 'I have been able to collect about two thousand words . . . I am quite sure that I have not nearly exhausted their vocabulary' (1917: 61).

Hale argued that it was the faultiness in the methods of recording languages that had given rise to the idea that the languages of primitive peoples were limited and concrete (1891: 418), and he believed on the contrary that there was no such thing as a barbarous language. He came some way towards establishing a theory of the phoneme, in order to explain why 'in many languages, as is well known, there are elementary sounds of an indeterminate nature, which seem to float between two, and sometimes even three or four, diverse articulations' (1884: 233). On the other hand, Hale was prepared to argue that language should be the only definition of race, and he thought that some languages were more advanced and complex than others. His conclusion to his article (1884) on 'intermediate articulations' shows that he did not realize the importance of some of his own arguments.

As early as 1883, R. N. Cust attacked the idea that a language lacking written or scholarly traditions would also be lacking in grammar:

> 'As to the assertion that Grammarians formed a Language, it is sheer nonsense. The Grammatical features of a Language developed themselves according to the genius of the people, and it is impossible to say, why or how this took place. No rules of Grammarians could stop the process, or accelerate it' (1883: 66–67).

In 1903 Codrington produced convincing evidence to counteract arguments such as those of Payne on the rapidity of change in unwritten languages. The Spanish who discovered the Solomon Islands in 1567 recorded about forty words of the local language. A large number of these can still be identified, since 'with all the difficulties of correct hearing, remembering and writing down strange words, the Spaniards have recorded what is in great part easily recognised' (1903: 25). What is more, it appeared from the same evidence that there had been no significant change in the geographical distribution of the various dialects.

Towards the end of this period, A. M. Hocart twice published articles attacking philosophers and psychologists for their theories about the mental inadequacies of primitives, since these were based solely on misleading and limited linguistic evidence that bore no relation to the various languages as they were in use. He brought evidence against the theory that primitives are 'poor in general concepts and rich in minute subdivisions of the species', pointing out that:

> 'This view may seem quite impregnable to the thinker at home, and, as it once seemed so to me, I cannot well blame those whose faith has never been exposed to that powerful dissolvent, experience of savage life' (1912: 267).

Hocart thus heralded the dawn of a new anthropological age. It is to be regretted, however, that his expectations that the new anthropology would be capable of producing new and valid linguistic theories to challenge the old preconceptions should have been proved false once his 'powerful dissolvent' had become the orthodox, and indeed the only possible, practice in the discipline.

Mainstream anthropology largely ignored the problem of language altogether. In later years, Frazer merely remarked on the pragmatic level that he preferred the ethnographic evidence of missionaries to that of travellers, since the former were likely to know the language better (1921: 244), and he approved of Malinowski's use of the native language in ethnographic research (1922: vii–viii). His only other involvement in this area was in his championing of the use of *totem* and *taboo* as descriptive categories. It is true that Robertson Smith analysed linguistic terms as a necessary part of his anthropology, but in this he was merely following the specialized tradition of biblical exegesis.

In the early twentieth century there was a certain increase in the technical and pragmatic uses of linguistics as a tool for collecting ethnographic information and establishing 'tribal' classifications. C. G. Seligman collected his material on New Guinea by means of interpreters, pidgin English, and the filling in of questionnaires (1910). The new breed of government anthropologists and administrators such as Rattray (e.g. 1916), Thomas (e.g. 1910), and Amaury Talbot (e.g. 1912, 1923) considered that the recording of languages and texts was part of their work, and for it they tended to use standardized vocabularies and grammatical questionnaires. This became a regular practice, as can be seen from Meek (1931).

I have referred earlier to the difference in the American anthropologists' approach to language. This is no place for a detailed analysis of this approach, or of the reasons why it was so different from that of the British anthropologists, and I shall merely attempt to summarize it.

Many of the main trends in American anthropological linguistics can be found in Boas's classical Introduction to the *Handbook of American Indian Languages* (1911). Boas was aware of the relativity of linguistic categories, since he perceived that they were the artificial products of culture and in no way natural in origin. He realized that neither semantic nor grammatical categories would necessarily coincide in different languages, and developed a rudimentary phoneme theory.[16] In this way he applied 'his cardinal principle of viewing each language in terms of its own pattern instead of a preconceived or theoretical one' (Kroeber, 1943: 15). Boas was convinced that there were no such things as 'primitive' languages and that any language was capable of adapting to any situation. One of his most suggestive theories was that language was only one of many similar cultural systems, and that its value to anthropology was that, unlike any other cultural system, its categories were never consciously recognized, and thus it was not subject to the same misleading rationalizations.

Ideas similar to those of Boas were proposed by other American anthropologists such as Sapir and Kroeber, and the following generations developed them further. The reason why the American approach was so very different from the British partly derives from the personalities and interests of the founders of the subject. It was also a result of the isolation of the Americans, not only from European anthropology, but also from European comparative linguistics. Further important factors were the nature of the American Indian languages, the circumstances in which these were recorded, and the general situation of the Indian in white America. A useful summary of the causes can be found in Malmberg (1964: 159–160).

Early British anthropology, having no contacts with American ideas on language, and lacking both trustworthy linguistic evidence and the techniques for assessing it, never produced anything that remotely resembled a sociological theory of language. No one realized that language was comparable to other cultural phenomena, or that its structure was anything but an isolated system. Therefore, no traditional categories or procedures were developed which could later serve as a framework for the study of symbolic systems. Post-1920 anthropology, similarly, did not produce any linguistic theory of relevance to symbolism, as can be seen in the failure of Malinowskian anthropology to explain myth beyond a frequently naïve analysis of its integrative function. As a result, British anthropology's more recent approaches to symbolism have depended for their inspiration on work from the French tradition, and notably on that of Lévi-Strauss, who has significantly followed leads given by, among others, Boas. It might be argued that the responsibility for this state of affairs lies in the different interests of the functionalist period of systematic fieldwork.

But this alone would not have been sufficient; there was also a general ignorance of all the deeper implications of language for a study of culture in the period of British anthropology discussed in this paper.

NOTES

1. Although the approach was distinctive, the precise delimitation, both of what was British and of what was anthropological in the field, must be somewhat arbitrary. At a time when the gentleman amateur was not debarred by intense specialization from any discipline, it is difficult to distinguish the contributions of the anthropologist from those of the linguist, the missionary, or the colonial administrator. In collecting evidence, I consulted the major writings of anthropologists of the period (1850–1920), and concentrated particularly on the articles and discussions in the early volumes of the *Journal of the Royal Anthropological Institute* and the *Journal of the Ethnological Society*, since these give a clearer impression than the works of any single author of the general preoccupations of the time. Even if some of these articles were written by others than anthropologists, it can be argued that their inclusion indicates their interest to the anthropology of the day.

2. In the discussion that followed, Dr Leitner showed a strange contempt for the more cautious theories of the Indo-European linguists:

> 'Dr Hyde Clarke's researches . . . deserved every encouragement for the sake of the causes of truth, and as a protest against the literary terrorism exercised by a set of Sanscritists, who now monopolised attention in certain leading societies and journals, erroneously supposed to be devoted to impartial investigations. The collection of material, historical, ethnological and other, was far more important than the preservation of this or that philological theory. We were on the mere threshold of the science of language' (Leitner, 1874: 212).

3. A. A. Hill (1952) has traced the literary history of one such myth, that Cherokee has fourteen different words for 'wash' and no general term. He analysed the fourteen words, first quoted in 1823, and discovered that they all derived from two distinct morphs. For a general discussion of this point, and of the following, see Lévi-Strauss (1962, trans. 1966, particularly the first chapter). Payne's reports on the primitiveness of certain languages are referred to as recently as 1961 by Sir Russell Brain in an introductory chapter on the origin and nature of language (p. 6), although he does admit to doubting whether such languages can helpfully be compared with early language.

4. Hale's own interest, as evidenced in an article of 1886, was rather how to explain the origin of the various language families, which no amount of philological research could demonstrate to be all ultimately descended from the same source. He based his theory on an assumed 'strong language-making instinct' in children, this being dependent on the stories of young children, often twins, who developed a private language apparently unrelated to any spoken in their vicinity. When large groups of early, but language-commanding, men migrated across the countryside, they retained in some form their original speech. But frequently a group no larger than a single family would wander off on its own. In such cases, if the parents then died, the young children left to fend for themselves would create a new language. Hale ingeniously used this

argument to explain two further philological problems, the first being that some language families, such as the Aryan, have a wide geographical distribution, whereas within the bounds of the state of California alone, for example, a large number of different stocks can be identified. He suggested that in the inclement conditions of Europe and Northern America, no band of orphans could have survived, whereas in California, and to a lesser extent in Oregon, where a similar linguistic situation exists, conditions are such that the survival of such groups must have been frequent. The second problem, that languages of apparently different stocks can share certain grammatical features with their geographical neighbours, he explained by assuming the survival of one adult only, who would have adopted the new language of the children, but would have applied to it the grammatical system of the old language, since such infant languages apparently lack any 'grammar'.

5. It is interesting, however, that Müller tried to use the linguistic evidence of Indo-European against Darwin's evolutionary theory of the development of man from the ape. While admitting that he considered this linguistic model to be an evolutionary one ('In the Science of Language, I was a Darwinian before Darwin' – 1873: 661), he held that language itself, even in its most primitive form, was an insuperable barrier between man and beast, a barrier that no theory of gradual differentiation could overcome. The passage in which he expresses his dislike of such theories is highly significant in its unwitting testimony to the importance of all cultural systems of meaning:

> 'The admission of this insensible graduation would eliminate not only the difference between ape and man, but likewise between black and white, hot and cold, a high and a low note in music; in fact, it would do away with the possibility of all exact and definite knowledge, by removing those wonderful lines and laws of nature, which change the Chaos into a Kosmos, the Infinite into the Finite, and which enable us to count, to tell, and to know' (Müller, 1873: 668).

Is this perhaps an example of *la pensée civilisée*? As W. D. Whitney asked in a review of Müller's arguments, where is the line in nature that separates a high note from a low note? The only lines are in our musical scales, 'and they are products of art rather than of nature' (1874; 65).

6. 'The tendency of a language to express a complex idea by a single term has been styled "holophrasis", and it appears therefore that every language may be holophrastic from the point of view of another language. Holophrasis can hardly be taken as a fundamental characteristic of primitive languages' (Boas, 1911: 26).

7. From Tylor's published works, and from his notebooks now in the Pitt Rivers Museum, Oxford, we discover that he had an excellent command of French, German, and Spanish. One notebook records that in the winter of 1860–61 alone, he learnt the elements of Sanskrit, gathered some material for a book on general philology, read a grammar of Greenlandish and 'got some knowledge of the language', read Bopp and Porschmann on Malayo-Polynesian, and gained an 'elementary knowledge' of Russian. In the next summer, he began Welsh.

8. Marett in his biography of Tylor praised his approach to speech by means of the language of gesture, because gesture is 'an artifice so akin to nature that our ethnic diversity scarcely affects it' (1936: 52). Ideas similar to those of Tylor can be found in Sibree (1883) and Clarke (1894).

9. An interesting confirmation of this explanation can be found in a similar situation described in Hale's account of the Chinook Jargon: 'The Indians in

general – contrary to what seems to be a common opinion – are very sparing of their gesticulations. No language, probably, requires less assistance from this source than theirs' (1890: 18). When, however, the Indians needed to use the Jargon to communicate with someone not understanding their own tongue, they could be seen to resort to animated gestures, in order to supplement the language.

10. As Kroeber pointed out, in a discussion of the evidence on the Plains Indians' gesture language:

> 'But what is characteristic of the sign language as an effective system of communication is precisely that it did *not* remain on a level of naturalness, spontaneity, and full transparency, but made artificial commitments, arbitrary choices, between potential expressions and meaning' (1958: 16).

11. To reach the history of language, the anthropologists used two models neither of which has any historical reality: the languages of contemporary non-literate societies have no historical priority over European languages, and the Indo-European model is incapable of generating history which is not already built into it (see Ardener, p. 217 below).

12. Franz Steiner makes the same point when discussing the similar significance of 'totemism' as a general category:

> 'This significance was twofold: it bore the import of an assumed stage in human evolution; it also demarcated totemism as a solid block of "otherness", which it remained even after thinking in terms of stages had been abandoned by the earnest' (1956, 1967 edn: 18).

13. It is perhaps significant that *taboo* and *totem* both have well-documented entries in their respective volumes of the *OED* (1919 and 1926), whereas *mana* has to wait to be mentioned until the Supplement in 1933, though it must be admitted that the M volume of the Dictionary was published considerably earlier (1908).

14. Evidence for the rapidness of this adoption can be found in the use of *taboo* in the following passage from a collection of essays by Mary Russell Mitford in 1826:

> 'The mention of her neighbours is evidently *taboo*, since it is at least twenty to one but she is in a state of affront with nine-tenths of them; her own family are also *taboo* for the same reason' (1826: 63; italics in the original).

Another good example is in Charlotte Brontë's *Shirley*, where a governess is describing her experiences with earlier employers: 'The gentlemen, I found, regarded me as a "tabooed woman", to whom they were interdicted from granting the usual privileges of the sex' (1849, 1924 edn, vol. 2: 84). Such usages suggest that Frazer was not particularly original in his extension of the use of 'taboo'.

15. 'When about the year 1886 my ever-lamented friend William Robertson Smith asked me to write an article on Taboo for the Ninth Edition of the *Encyclopaedia Britannica,* I shared what I believe to have been at the time the current view of anthropologists, that the institution in question was confined to the brown and black races of the Pacific. But an attentive study of the accounts given of Taboo by observers who wrote while it still flourished in Polynesia soon led me to modify that view. The analogies which the system presents to the superstitions, not only of savages elsewhere, but of the civilised races of antiqity, were too numerous and too striking to be overlooked; and I came to the conclusion that Taboo is only one of a number of similar systems

of superstition which among many, perhaps among all races of men, have contributed in large measure, under many different names, and with many variations of detail, to build up the complex fabric of society in all the various sides or elements of it which we describe as religious, social, political, moral and economic. This conclusion I briefly indicated in my article. My general views on the subject were accepted by my friend Robertson Smith and applied by him in his celebrated *Lectures* to the elucidation of some aspects of Semitic religion. Since then the importance of Taboo and of systems like it in the evolution of religion and morality, of government and property, has been generally recognised and has indeed become a commonplace of anthropology' (1911: v–vi).

Steiner also quotes this important passage in full (1956, 1967 edn: 97).

16. Boas's excellent article 'On Alternating Sounds', 1889, where he proved:

> 'that there is no such phenomenon as synthetic or alternating sounds, and that their occurrence is in no way a sign of primitiveness of the speech in which they are said to occur; that alternating sounds are in reality alternating apperceptions of one and the same sound' (1889: 52),

should be contrasted with Hale's confused theories on this topic, written five years earlier.

REFERENCES

BARLOW, H. 1872. Vocabulary of Aboriginal Dialects of Queensland. *Journal of the Royal Anthropological Institute* **2:** 166–175.

BOAS, FRANZ. 1889. On Alternating Sounds. *American Anthropologist* (o.s.) **2:** 47–53.

—— 1911. Introduction to the *Handbook of American Indian Languages*. *Bureau of American Ethnology Bull. 40*, part 1: 5–89. Washington, DC: Smithsonian Institution.

BRAIN, SIR RUSSELL. 1961. *Speech Disorders*. London: Butterworth.

BRONTË, CHARLOTTE. 1849. *Shirley*. Edinburgh: John Grant, 1924.

CLARKE, HYDE. 1874. Researches in Prehistoric and Protohistoric Comparative Philology, Mythology and Archaeology, in connection with the origin of culture in America, and its propagation by the Sumerian or Akkad families. *Journal of the Royal Anthropological Institute* **4:** 148–212.

—— 1894. Note on Mr W. G. Aston's 'Japanese Onomatopes, and the Origin of Language', *JRAI* **23:** 332. *Journal of the Royal Anthropological Institute* **24:** 60–62.

CODRINGTON, R. H. 1891. *The Melanesians, their Anthropology and Folklore*. London: Oxford University Press.

—— 1903. On the Stability of Unwritten Languages. *Man* **11:** 25–26.

CRAWFURD, J. 1861. On the Aryan or Indo-Germanic Theory. *Journal of the Ethnological Society* (n.s.) **1:** 268–286.

CUST, R. N. 1883. *A Sketch of the Modern Languages of Africa.* 2 vols. London: Trubner.

DORMAN, S. S. 1917. The Tati Bushmen (Masarwas) and their Language. *Journal of the Royal Anthropological Institute* **47**: 37–112.

FRAZER, J. G. 1888a. Taboo. *Encyclopaedia Britannica*, 9th edition, vol. 23, pp. 15–18. Also in *Garnered Sheaves*, pp. 80–92. London: Macmillan, 1931.

— 1888b. Totemism. *Encyclopaedia Britannica*, 9th edition, vol. 23, pp. 467–476.

— 1911. *Taboo and the Perils of the Soul. The Golden Bough*, part 2, 3rd edition. London: Macmillan.

— 1921. The Scope and Method of Mental Anthropology. In *Garnered Sheaves*, pp. 234–251. Also in *Science Progress* **64**, April 1922.

— 1922. Preface to B. Malinowski, *Argonauts of the Western Pacific*. London: Routledge. Also in *Garnered Sheaves*, pp. 391–398. London: Macmillan, 1931.

GOLDIE, H. 1868. *Principles of Efik Grammar*. Edinburgh: Muir & Paterson.

HALE, HORATIO. 1884. On some Doubtful or Intermediate Articulations: An Experiment in Phonetics. *Journal of the Royal Anthropological Institute* **14**: 233–243.

— 1886. The Origin of Languages and the Antiquity of Speaking Man. *Proceedings of the American Association for the Advancement of Science and Art* **35**: 279–323.

— 1890. *The Oregon Trade Language or 'Chinook Jargon'*. London: Whittaker.

— 1891. Language as a Test of Mental Capacity. *Journal of the Royal Anthropological Institute* **21**: 413–455.

HILL, ARCHIBALD A. 1952. A Note on Primitive Languages. *International Journal of American Linguistics* **18**: 172–177. Also in D. Hymes (ed.), *Language in Culture and Society*, pp. 86–88. New York: Harper & Row, 1964.

HOCART, A. M. 1912. The Psychological Interpretation of Language. *British Journal of Psychology* **5** (3): 267–279.

— 1918. A Point of Grammar and a Study in Method. *American Anthropologist* **20**: 265–279.

KENNEDY, JOHN. 1856. On the Probable Origin of the American Indians, with particular reference to that of the Caribs. *Journal of the Ethnological Society* (o.s.) **4**: 226–267.

KROEBER, A. L. 1909. Classificatory Systems of Relationship. *Journal of the Royal Anthropological Institute* **39**: 77–84.

KROEBER, A. L. 1943. Franz Boas, the Man. *American Anthropologist, Memoir Series* 61, 45 (3), part 2: 5–26.

—— 1958. Sign Language Inquiry. *International Journal of American Linguistics* **24**: 1–19.

LANG, A. 1883. The Early History of the Family. *Contemporary Review* Sept.: 406–422. Also in *Custom and Myth,* pp. 245–275. London: Longmans, 1884.

—— 1884. Cupid, Psyche and the 'Sun-Frog'. In *Custom and Myth.* London: Longmans.

—— 1905. *The Secret of the Totem.* London: Longmans.

LEITNER, G. W. 1874. In discussion on Clarke, 1874. *Journal of the Royal Anthropological Institute* **4**: 212–214.

LÉVI-STRAUSS, C. 1962. *La Pensée sauvage.* Paris: Plon. Translated as *The Savage Mind.* London: Weidenfeld & Nicolson; Chicago: University of Chicago Press, 1966.

MACKENZIE, A. 1873. Specimens of Native Australian Languages. *Journal of the Royal Anthropological Institute* **3**: 247–264.

MACKINLAY, WILLIAM E. W. 1901. Memorandum on the Languages of the Philippines. *Journal of the Royal Anthropological Institute* **31**: 214–218.

MAINE, SIR H. 1861. *Ancient Law.* London: John Murray.

MALINOWSKI, B. 1920. Classificatory Particles in the Language of Kiriwina. *Bulletin of the School of Oriental Studies* **1** (4): 33–78.

MALMBERG, BERTIL. 1964. *New Trends in Linguistics.* Trans. E. Carney. Published under the auspices of the Nature Methods Institutes. Stockholm: Lund.

MARETT, R. R. 1909. The Conception of Mana. In *The Threshold of Religion,* pp. 101–121. London: Methuen.

—— 1912. *Anthropology.* London: Thornton Butterworth.

—— 1936. *Tylor.* London: Chapman & Hall.

MCLENNAN, J. F. 1865. *Primitive Marriage.* London: Black.

MEEK, C. K. 1931. *Tribal Studies in Northern Nigeria.* London: Kegan Paul, Trench, Trubner.

MITFORD, M. R. 1826. *Our Village: Sketches.* Vol. 2, *The Touchy Lady.*

MORGAN, L. H. 1870. *Ancient Society.* New York: Holt.

—— 1877. *Systems of Consanguinity and Affinity of the Human Family.* Washington, DC: Smithsonian Institution.

MÜLLER, F. MAX. 1856. Comparative Mythology. In *Selected Essays,* vol. 1, pp. 299–424. London: Longmans, 1881.

—— 1871. On the Philosophy of Mythology. In *Selected Essays,* vol. 1, pp. 577–623.

—— 1872. Results of the Science of Language. In *Selected Essays,* vol. 1, pp. 174–251.

—— 1873. Lectures on Mr Darwin's Philosophy of Language. *Fraser's Magazine* **7**: 525–541 and 659–678; **8**: 1–24.

—— 1878. *Hibbert Lectures.* London: Longmans.

OPPERT, GUSTAV. 1883. On the Classification of Languages in Conformity with Ethnology. *Journal of the Royal Anthropological Institute* **13**: 32–50.

PAYNE, E. J. 1899. *History of the New World called America*, vol. 2. London: Oxford University Press.

RATTRAY, R. S. 1916. *Ashanti Proverbs.* London: Oxford University Press.

RIVERS, W. H. R. 1904. *Sociology, Magic and Religion of the Western Islanders.* Reports of the Cambridge Anthropological Expedition to Torres Straits, vol. 5. Cambridge: Cambridge University Press.

—— 1910. The Genealogical Method of Anthropological Enquiry. *The Sociological Review* **3** (1): 1–12.

SAUSSURE, FERDINAND DE. 1916. *Cours de linguistique générale.* Paris: Payot. Trans. Wade Baskin. New York: Philosophical Library, 1959; London: Peter Owen, 1960.

SAYCE, A. H. 1875. Language and Race. *Journal of the Royal Anthropological Institute* **5**: 212–216.

SELIGMAN, C. G. 1910. *The Melanesians of British New Guinea.* Cambridge: Cambridge University Press.

SIBREE, JAMES. 1883. Notes on the Relics of the Sign and Gesture Language among the Malagasy. *Journal of the Royal Anthropological Institute* **13**: 174–182.

SICARD, ROCH AMBROISE C. 1808. *Théorie des signes pour l'instruction des sourds muets.* 2 vols. Paris: Imprimerie de l'Institution des Sourds Muets.

SMITH, W. ROBERTSON. 1889. *The Religion of the Semites.* London: Black.

STEINER, FRANZ. 1956. *Taboo.* London: Cohen & West; Harmondsworth: Penguin Books, 1967.

TALBOT, P. AMAURY. 1912. *In the Shadow of the Bush.* London: Heinemann.

—— 1923. *Life in Southern Nigeria.* London: Macmillan.

TAPLIN, L. 1871. Notes on a Comparative Table of Australian Languages. *Journal of the Royal Anthropological Institute* **1**: 84–88.

THOMAS, NORTHCOTE W. 1910. *Anthropological Report on the Edo-Speaking Peoples of Nigeria*, part 1. London: Harrison.

—— 1913. *Anthropological Report on the Ibo-Speaking Peoples of Nigeria.* London: Harrison.

TURNER, VICTOR. 1967. *The Forest of Symbols: Aspects of Ndembu Ritual.* Ithaca, NY: Cornell University Press.

—— 1968. *The Drums of Affliction: A Study of Religious Processes among the Ndembu of Zambia.* London: Oxford University Press.

TYLOR, E. B. 1865. *Researches into the Early History of Mankind and the Development of Civilisation.* London: Murray.

—— 1871. *Primitive Culture: Researches into the Development of Mythology, Philosophy, Religion, Language, Art and Custom.* London: Murray.

—— 1881. *Anthropology: An Introduction to the Study of Man and Civilisation.* London: Macmillan.

—— Unpublished Notebooks. Pitt Rivers Museum, Oxford.

WHITNEY, WILLIAM DWIGHT. 1874. Darwinism and Language. *North American Review* **119**: 61–88.

—— 1875. In discussion on Sayce, 1875. *Journal of the Royal Anthropological Institute* **5**: 216–217.

R. H. Robins

Malinowski, Firth, and the 'Context of Situation'

Context of situation became the basis of a theory of meaning and a significant part of a theory of language during a period of the development of general linguistics in Great Britain. Among linguists here it was most discussed during the late 1930s and during the first decade or so after the war, when linguistics was expanding from its most active centre at the time, the University of London, under the leadership and inspiration of J. R. Firth, the first holder anywhere in this country of a chair in the subject.

After Firth's retirement, too soon followed by his death in 1960, context of situation lost some of its interest among linguists. Phonological and grammatical theory, focused on the formal side of language, was all-absorbing, and in 1957 the description and analysis of languages was thrown into exciting turmoil by the publication of Noam Chomsky's *Syntactic Structures*. This heralded a great outpouring of publication and discussion on the theory of grammatical description and on the proper objectives and methods of grammatical and phonological analysis, and 1957 is considered by many to have been one of the major turning-points in modern linguistic studies.

At first Chomsky and the transformationalists (as they are called from a particular component in their theory of grammatical relations) concentrated on the formal aspect of language; but in recent years, under the influence of such linguists as Fodor, Katz, and Postal, they have turned their attention to the semantic interpretation of sentences and to semantic theory in general. This has not led them to return to the support of Malinowski's and Firth's context of situation theory – far from it – but it has reawakened interest in the problems of meaning and of semantic analysis, and in so doing it has revived the study of Malinowski's and Firth's approaches to these questions.

In trying to assess the relevance and importance of context of situation we must look at the theory in its historical context, in relation to the successive changes in the dominant outlooks that have characterized linguistic work during this century.

The nature of meaning, or, put in another way, the relations between linguistic utterances and the outside world, became a subject of discussion from the beginnings of European thought. Nineteenth-century linguistics, or philology as it was often known then in this country, inherited a body of doctrine stemming from Aristotle and the Stoics, ancient lexicographers and rhetoricians, and their successors during the Middle Ages and the Renaissance. There is no need or occasion here to rehearse this tradition in detail, but two things stand out: theories of meaning and of semantic analysis were based on the assumed identification and linguistic priority of the word as a self-evident recognizable unit in languages, and the languages within and around which study was concentrated were by and large the well-known literate languages, ancient and modern, of European and Mediterranean civilization.

A great deal of important work had been done in this tradition, and many permanently valuable insights had been gained, but none of it really answered to the needs of Malinowski in preparing his field observations for European publication. He was faced with the task of translating ethnographically vital texts into English so that they should be meaningful and informative in an English monograph for English readers.

In *Man and Culture* (R. W. Firth, 1957) anthropologists have pointed out Malinowski's place in the history of anthropology: his emphasis on descriptivism and on functionalism or structuralism (in its older anthropological sense), as against former predominantly historicist orientations in the study of cultures (significantly parallel to the contemporaneous teaching in linguistics by the Genevan Ferdinand de Saussure), and his pioneering insistence on the study of a culture in the field by living among the people and by working as far as possible through the medium of the indigenous languages. Just because Malinowski was such a gifted polyglot, as he himself felt bound to admit, he was faced with the problems of semantic statement and analysis when he tried to translate his texts.

It is scarcely necessary here to go into detail on Malinowski's context of situation theory. I will merely turn attention to the essential points as I see them. At first drawing his conclusions from the study of preliterate languages of so-called primitive peoples, in his later years he insisted that these conclusions applied equally to our own literate European languages.

1. The time-honoured conception of language as the vocal communication of thought was, as a definition, quite valueless, and as a statement of language use it was applicable only to a limited sphere of activity, e.g. the lecture-room or learned debate.

2. Language was a 'mode of activity', like other socially co-operative activities, and not a 'countersign of thought'.

3. Utterances were produced and understood not as self-contained events, but strictly within a shared context of situation, all that was relevant in the personal, cultural, historical, and physical setting in which the utterances were spoken and heard.

4. The meanings and uses of linguistic forms, words, and sentences, were acquired and understood from their occurrences in such contexts, and must be so explained by the linguist. The meaning relation should not be thought of as a dyadic one between a word and its referent, but as a multidimensional and functional set of relations between the word in its sentence and the context of its occurrence.

5. In consequence of what has just been said, the meanings of words and sentences are not universals that happen to be differently labelled in different languages, but they are in large measure dependent on and a part of the culture of the speech community. Translation is possible only in the unification of the cultural context, and the deceptively simple problems of translation between most European languages are due to the historically shared Graeco-Roman-Christian cultural inheritance of Europe. The more diverse the cultures the harder becomes translation, and, significantly, the more deeply embedded in the culture a word or a phrase is, that is to say the more revealing it is of that culture, the greater the difficulty of rendering it in a language from outside the culture area.

6. The word was not the primary meaningful unit. This was the sentence. Sentences were what was uttered and understood, and word meanings were distillations or abstractions from the meanings, the contextual functions, of sentences, and dictionary entries do their best to summarize these abstractions.

Malinowski's challenge to the semantic priority of the word ran counter to the theories of the West from Aristotle to our own day. But in ancient India (though to my knowledge Malinowski was not himself interested in this field) the question of priority was keenly debated: does word meaning arise from sentence meaning or are sentence meanings built up from word meanings? Bhartrhari (*c*. seventh century AD) argued that a sentence conveyed its meaning undivided at first, like a picture, and that analysis into individual word meanings is a subsequent critical, metalinguistic operation. He instances the sentence 'Fetch a cuckoo from the woods' (in Sanskrit, of course); unless and until the meaning of the word 'cuckoo' is known as well, the meaning of 'fetch' remains vague and undefined, since fetching a log and fetching a bird are very different operations.

It is well known that Firth took up Malinowski's concept of the context of situation and built it into the centre of his theoretical approach to language. Firth's main interest was different from Malinowski's; it has been observed that Malinowski was an ethnographer forced into linguistics by the needs of his own subject (witness the genesis of his 'Ethnographic Theory of Language' chapter from originally scattered footnotes in other parts of *Coral Gardens and their Magic*), whereas Firth was a linguist, deeply concerned with linguistic theory, who was forced into ethnography in order to achieve an adequate understanding of meaning.

Firth was convinced that since language was essentially meaningful activity the whole of linguistic description and analysis could in a sense be regarded as the description and analysis of meaning. Hence sprang his at first sight paradoxical collocations, 'phonological meaning' and 'grammatical meaning'. But we are now concerned with his semantic theory, and this was based on the context of situation. Firth's context of situation was a more abstract affair than Malinowski's 'environmental reality'. Firth envisaged it as a set of abstract categories by means of which he hoped that all the relevant factors involved in the use and understanding of an utterance and its components could be identified in situations and classified in descriptions.

At least three purposes were to be achieved in this way:

1. The identification and classification of different styles of utterance by reference to the relevant features of the appropriate situations (in addition to the formal features themselves), e.g. formalized, literary, colloquial, slangy, rhetorical, etc.

2. The description of the actual use of a given utterance in its situation as a unique occurrent.

3. The identification and description of the semantic functions ascribable to general grammatical structures and intonation sequences (question, imperative, subject and object relations, etc.) and the lexical meanings of individual words as the recurrent components of utterance.

It is notorious that Firth provided totally inadequate exemplification of a semantic analysis in terms of the theory he so ardently believed in and so assiduously preached. Beyond suggesting what he called a 'typical context of situation', he did little to fill in the details. In such a context the following categories were, he said, relevant:

features of participants: persons, personalities
verbal action, non-verbal action
relevant objects
effects of verbal action.

This schematization has been repeated several times by different writers. By far the most penetrating and revealing application is a study by T. F. Mitchell (1957) of 'The Language of Buying and Selling in Cyrenaica', in which specific locutions involved in successive stages of a grain or other produce auction, or ordinary sale, are set out and analysed in relation to the developing situation.

Mitchell's application of context of situation has been generally acclaimed. But it deals, deliberately, with a small part only of language use and language function. In fact it fulfils the first two aims of Firth's context of situation theory: the identification of a situationally determined style or mode of discourse, and the explanation and interpretation of an actual sequence of utterances in a given situation. It scarcely constitutes even an outline of a general theory of word and sentence meaning. To such a criticism Firth would probably have replied that the whole of language use, including the selection of the appropriate vocabulary items, is a vastly complex amalgam of specific language uses, and that a general explication of meaning can come about only as the end-product of indeterminately numerous detailed studies such as Mitchell's.

As was said at the outset, during the period immediately following Firth's retirement the interest of linguists was on formal analysis rather than on semantics, and the other of Firth's two main foci of attention, prosodic analysis in phonology, received far more exemplification, exposition, and criticism. What is sometimes called 'neo-Firthian' linguistics, associated with Professor M. A. K. Halliday at University College, London, and his colleagues and pupils, derives more directly than other theories from the teachings of Firth, and incorporates a good many of the fundamental tenets of Firthian theory. Halliday regards context of situation as a central and essential part of his theory of languages, making it the bridge between grammar and lexis (vocabulary) and the external world on one side, with phonology and phonetics the link between grammar and lexis and actual phonation and audition on the other. But once again, Halliday and his associates have devoted more time and print to the exposition of other aspects of language and other parts of their theory than they have to context of situation, being content for the most part to reproduce, almost unchanged and without elaboration, the typical scheme of a context of situation that Firth had originally proposed in 1950.

In the middle 1960s a revival of interest in semantic topics began to characterize linguistics on both sides of the Atlantic. In 1963 John Lyons, now at Edinburgh, published an important study of the semantics of certain key terms in the philosophical dialogues of Plato, and in the widely read and lengthy introduction to this study, for the general reader its most valuable part, he makes mention of Firth's context of situation and exploits the notion of a context progressively built up as a dialogue proceeds, conditioning and helping to determine the meaning of what is subsequently said in it.

In 1966 Longmans published a volume of studies dedicated to the memory of J. R. Firth, and in it Lyons returns to a more central line of criticism of the context of situation theory of meaning. In his study Lyons accepts Firth's claim that the occurrence or acceptability of an utterance in a situation is the only guarantee of its being significant. He furthermore applauds Firth's recognition of the multiplicity of utterance types in socially different situations, the sort of thing illustrated in one typical instance by Mitchell's Cyrenaican article. But he denies Firth's claim, or the claim made by others on Firth's behalf, to have evolved a genuine theory of meaning, one capable of dealing with the lexical meanings of the words of a language, such as are internalized by native speakers largely in childhood and are as far as possible encapsulated by the lexicographer in dictionary entries. In particular, Lyons can find no place in Firth's system for the relation of reference or denotation, whereby a large number of words, especially noun words, but by no means all such words, can be associated more or less directly with some part or parts of the observed external world. In fact, I believe that the referential function of many words can be included as part of Firth's 'relevant objects' and 'non-verbal action' categories, but it was certainly a weakness on Firth's part that he neglected to make clear his thinking on this question.

Of greater import in the revival of semantic studies among linguists has been the extension of transformational linguistics to include lexical and structural meanings. At first, in his 1957 *Syntactic Structures* and the writings immediately following this, Chomsky and his colleagues left lexical meaning and indeed meaning as a whole outside their central concern. In 1964, however, Katz and Postal published their *Integrated Theory of Linguistic Descriptions*, in which they set out the scope of description in the following introductory words: 'A linguistic description of a natural language is an attempt to reveal the nature of a fluent speaker's mastery of that language.'

In their book Katz and Postal incorporate a theory of semantic analysis outlined in an earlier article by Katz and

Fodor into a comprehensive account of transformational linguistics. Clearly they were right to attempt something on these lines, since part of a fluent speaker's mastery of his language is his knowledge of what words to use in given circumstances. It may be said that 1964 marked the re-entry of semantics into the central field of attention of American linguists and those most influenced by American work.

Katz and Postal frame their theory of semantics from a traditional word-based starting-point, with little immediate contact with Malinowski's or Firth's context of situation. It is probably significant that Malinowski's linguistic work sprang from the ethnographic analysis of remote cultures where meanings had to be discovered before they could be analysed and stated, whereas the transformational linguists (notably unlike their immediate predecessors in America) have largely worked on English and on other familiar languages, whose grammar and word meanings are, at least in an unsystematized way, already known before analysis starts.

Katz and Postal regard word meanings as combinations of 'atomic conceptual elements', and many words can have several different such combinations: 'bachelor' may consist of human + male + adult + unmarried, or of human + possessing a first degree. Normally, sentence structures and the possible coexistence of the meanings of the words they contain necessarily select only one combination in each case (e.g. as in 'Jillian is a bachelor of Oxford, having spent three years at Lady Margaret Hall'). If this does not happen then the sentence is in this respect inherently ambiguous (e.g. 'He wears a light suit in summer' – light in weight or light in colour?).

This approach bears strong resemblances to earlier 'componential' analyses of certain areas of vocabulary, notably kinship terminologies, such as Lounsbury's 'Pawnee Kinship Usage' (1956). A number of studies of this sort were brought together in a special publication of the *American Anthropologist* in 1965 (cf. Hammel). They owe much original inspiration to componential or feature analysis in phonology; but the applicability of such a system of analysis to the whole lexicon of any language must remain seriously in doubt, at least for the present.

One does not want to go too deeply here into the Katz–Postal–Fodor theory of semantic analysis, but a sketch such as has just been given is necessary, since their theory, with but slight modifications, has become the more or less officially approved approach to semantics on the part of transformational linguists; and because of their numbers and their insights into linguistic structure, the renown and vigour of most of their published work, not to mention the vociferous applause of their followers, transformational theory has become probably the strongest influence in linguistics at the present time in America and in several universities in Europe. Chomsky leads a group of the most able associates and graduate research students at Massachusetts Institute of Technology, who constitute a main diffusion centre of developments in transformational theory.

One of the ablest and most interesting members of this group is D. T. Langendoen, who has undertaken a review and evaluation of the work of what he calls the 'London school' of linguistics, first as a Ph.D. dissertation under Chomsky's supervision, subsequently published in 1968 by the MIT Press.

Much of this book does not concern us here. It comprises a critical account of work undertaken in phonological analysis in terms of Firth's prosodic theory. But the book does contain what I believe is the first fairly detailed examination, from the outside, of the context of situation concept as expounded and used by Malinowski and Firth. The theoretical starting-point for Langendoen's criticisms is the semantic theory of Katz and Postal, now accepted by linguists of Chomsky's persuasion.

Langendoen criticizes the use made of context of situation in framing a theory of semantics both by Malinowski in his later formulation of it and by Firth. It is not hard to see some of the obvious inadequacies of Malinowski's exposition, more particularly in his presentation in the 'Problem of Meaning in Primitive Languages', with its carelessness of expression and its gratuitous and unjustified assumption of a basic difference between the languages of primitives and the literate languages of civilization. This latter weakness Malinowski himself recognized and in his later 'Ethnographic Theory of Language' he specifically applied the theory of meaning he was outlining to all uses of language in all societies, primitive and advanced.

Langendoen, like J. B. Carroll before him, objects to the apparent 'particularism' of Malinowski's context of situation, in that the meaning of each utterance seems to reside, on this view, in the unique actual environment at the time and place in which it occurred. This objection Firth had intended to remedy by his interpretation of the context of situation as an abstract set of semantically relevant categories, abstracted from multitudes of actual situations, to which unique particulars could be referred.

But the main weight of Langendoen's attack falls at the same point in both Malinowski's and Firth's work, namely that they failed to distinguish a number of different things:

1. The possible use of context of situation in deciding between the different meanings of inherently ambiguous sentences ('disambiguation' is the current jargon for this). Firth, in fact, illustrated this aspect of context of situation analysis, in his 'Technique of Semantics' (1935), in referring to physical objects on the one hand and to printed agenda and the like on the other in interpreting the sentence 'It's not on the board'.

2. The relevance of context of situation in accounting for the irrelevance of the usual lexical meanings of words when used in greetings formulae and the like in the socially conditioned chatter that Malinowski quaintly christened 'phatic communion'.

3. The delimiting of different styles of speech by reference to their habitual contexts.

In all these fields Langendoen allows a place for context of situation analysis, though not necessarily in Malinowski–Firth terms; but they all relate to what he calls 'language use'. This, he says, should be strictly separated from his fourth item: language meaning; and his main charge against context of situation theorists is that by failing to make the distinction between language use and language meaning they placed more weight on context of situation than it can properly bear.

Certainly Malinowski was careless in this treatment of these very relevant distinctions, and Firth left annoyingly little exemplification of what he hoped to achieve through contextual analysis. But they were both attempting to face the problem of lexical meaning and its basis in the acquisition and the intuitive knowledge of a language on the part of native speakers, and the problem of explaining the relations between language and the rest of human experience. Western linguists, from Aristotle on, have tended to start with word meanings as in some way given; and this is the position of Langendoen, following the theory favoured by transformational linguists.

It would seem at present doubtful whether the native speaker's knowledge of word meanings can be adequately displayed in models of the type so far employed in application to words like 'bachelor' and some kinship terms that carry rather obvious and clear-cut distinctions between their different meanings. It is a besetting sin on the part of semantic theorists that they choose their illustrations from that part of the lexicon that obviously fits their theory the best and then assume that the rest will follow. A semantic theory must account also for a speaker's competence in using and interpreting words whose meanings are associated in scales and in fields, like English 'apprehensive', 'anxious', 'worried', 'afraid', 'alarmed', 'terrified', and so on, with multiple relationships and indeterminate cut-off points.

The role played by innate ideas in our knowledge of certain basic categories of cognition and perception has been a bone of contention for some centuries. It is quite possible that Malinowski, at least in some of his writings, and Firth both underestimated the *a priori* content of our linguistic competence (certainly this is the view of Chomsky and his colleagues, who align themselves on the side of the rationalists against the empiricists in a revival of the seventeenth-century philosophical controversy). But in any event, a great deal of our knowledge of the meanings of words is clearly not *a priori* and is in no sense a language universal. Somehow we acquire, intensively in childhood but continuing all our lives, by means of some sort of abstraction process from utterances heard in specific situations, the ability to use and to understand the vocabulary of our language, together with its sentence patterns and grammatical constructions.

It was precisely the nature of this acquisition and a possible theoretical frame in which to envisage and perhaps display it that Malinowski and Firth were working at in their context of situation. Language meaning is abstracted out of language use, and represents a more or less agreed semantic range of meaning associated with each word in a language, further specified on each occasion of use. And no doubt the process of feedback from use to agreed meaning goes on all the time (this is how the phenomenon of semantic change must be considered). But the point here is that, even if the model currently favoured by Langendoen and the transformationalists can be made adequate to explicate all word meanings, it will still take the acquisition and the experimental base of this semantic competence for granted, and this is just what Malinowski and Firth were trying to come to grips with, stimulated in Malinowski's case by difficulties encountered in translation and interpretation when operating between languages spoken across wide cultural divergences.

Context of situation was an attempt to suggest what lies behind our knowledge of word meanings, taken by Langendoen as a starting-point, even though it may so far have proved in practice impossible to state more than a small part of word meanings in such terms. Langendoen chides Firth and those following up his ideas with making context of situation 'a convenient dumping ground for people's knowledge about the world, their own culture, etc.' (1968: 50), and he assigns Mitchell's study of the language of buying and selling 'to the realm of ethnography and not of semantics' (ibid.: 65). But this is verbal play. It is just such areas of experience and knowledge, call them what you will, that are somehow involved in the individual's acquisition and retention of his knowledge of his vocabulary. The linguist must somehow try to explicate this.

In a recent unpublished but circulated 'working paper', Langendoen has declared himself more sympathetic towards Firthian and Malinowskian semantic notions; but he still fails to come to grips with the question of what shall and shall not properly be held to fall within that term 'meaning' in an adequate explanation of our lexical knowledge of our native language.

It may be felt that the last part of this paper has concentrated rather excessively on context of situation in relation to lexical meanings. But this is the aspect that critics, and especially Langendoen, have focused on; the more general application of the concept to styles and varieties of language use has been more readily accepted and has, in consequence, been subjected to less criticism.

In summary, I would say that the theory of context of situation, as developed successively by Malinowski and by Firth, made linguists aware of the need for a careful study of the relationships involved in meaning (hitherto this topic had been rather left to the philosophers). Very probably both these scholars thought that the application of the contextual theory was simpler and more straightforward than is in fact the case. But however undeveloped its application may still be, this theory of linguistic semantics does attempt to come to grips with the very basis of meaning relations, which others have been content to take for granted. For this reason I would conclude that, at least until it is replaced by something more effective in this area, Malinowski's and Firth's context of situation theory has something of indispensable value for both linguists and ethnographers.

REFERENCES

BAZELL, C. E., *et al.* (eds.). 1966. *In Memory of J. R. Firth.* London: Longmans.

CARROLL, J. B. 1953. *The Study of Language.* Cambridge, Mass.: Harvard University Press.

CHOMSKY, N. 1957. *Syntactic Structures.* The Hague: Mouton.

FIRTH, J. R. 1935. The Technique of Semantics. *Transactions of the Philological Society*: 36–72. Also in *Papers in Linguistics*, 1957.

—— 1950. Personality and Language in Society. *Sociological Review* **42**: 37–52. Also in *Papers in Linguistics*, 1957.

—— 1957. *Papers in Linguistics 1934–1951.* London: Oxford University Press.

FIRTH, R. W. (ed.). 1957. *Man and Culture: An Evaluation of the Work of Bronislaw Malinowski.* London: Routledge & Kegan Paul.

HAMMEL, E. A. (ed.). 1965. Formal Semantic Analysis. *American Anthropologist* **67** (5), part 2: 1–316.

KATZ, J., and FODOR, J. 1963. The Structure of a Semantic Theory. *Language* **39**: 170–210.

—— and POSTAL, P. M. 1964. *An Integrated Theory of Linguistic Descriptions.* Cambridge, Mass.: MIT Press.

LANGENDOEN, D. T. 1967. On Selection, Projection, Meaning, and Semantic Content. *Working Papers in Linguistics*, Ohio State University Research Foundation, Columbus, pp. 100–109.

—— 1968. *The London School of Linguistics: A Study of the Linguistic*

Theories of B. Malinowski and J. R. Firth. Cambridge, Mass.: MIT Press.

LOUNSBURY, F. G. 1956. A Semantic Analysis of the Pawnee Kinship Usage. *Language* **32**: 158–194.

LYONS, J. 1963. *Structural Semantics: An Analysis of Part of the Vocabulary of Plato*. Oxford: Blackwell for the Philological Society.

MALINOWSKI, B. 1923. The Problem of Meaning in Primitive Languages. Supplement I in C. K. Ogden and I. A. Richards, *The Meaning of Meaning*. London: Kegan Paul.

—— 1935. An Ethnographic Theory of Language. Chapter 1 in *Coral Gardens and their Magic*, vol. II. London: Allen & Unwin.

MITCHELL, T. F. 1957. The Language of Buying and Selling in Cyrenaica: A Situational Statement. *Hespéris* **44**: 31–71.

Dell Hymes

Sociolinguistics and the Ethnography of Speaking[1]

'Sociolinguistics' is the most recent and most common term for an area of research that links linguistics with anthropology and sociology. 'Ethnography of speaking' designates a particular approach. I shall sketch the context in which the two terms have emerged, then try to indicate the importance of the ethnography of speaking, not only to the area of research, but also to linguistics and anthropology as disciplines.

To argue the study of speech is likely to seem only a plea for linguistics. To avoid that impression, I shall treat linguistics first, and at greater length, arguing the need for ethnography there, before broaching the complementary need for linguistics in social anthropology. Behind both arguments stands a common conception of the study of speech.

I

Mixed terms linking linguistics with the social sciences, especially anthropology, are an old story. One can trace the use of 'ethnographic philology', 'philological ethnology', 'linguistic anthropology', and the like from at least the middle of the nineteenth century. Until the second world war such terms were usually phrases – coordinate ('linguistics and ethnology'), genitive ('sociology of language'), adjectival ('sociological linguistics'). Only since the second world war have one-word terms come to prominence. Their form, their relative chronology, and their prevalence, are revealing.

The form of these terms – ethnolinguistics, psycholinguistics, sociolinguistics – shows that it is linguistics, its concepts, methods, and prestige, that has become central. (Hence 'ethnolinguistics', not 'anthropology of language', for a field of research; and 'anthropological linguistics', not 'linguistic anthropology', as the prevalent term, even among anthropologists, for a sub-discipline.) To be sure, Malinowski had, much earlier, spoken (1920: 69) of urgent need for an 'ethnolinguistic theory' to help to elucidate native meanings and texts, but neither the term nor the theory received sustained attention. 'Ethnolinguistics' first emerged into prominence in the late 1940s, followed shortly by 'psycholinguistics' in the early 1950s, and by 'sociolinguistics' in the early 1960s.[2] The sequence reflects the successive impact of recent linguistics, first on anthropologists, who had helped to nurture it, then on psychologists, and, most recently, on sociologists.

The currency of the term reflects, I think, a growing sense of the importance, not only of linguistics, but also of problems of language, and a hope for a combination of rigour and relevance in their study. Interest in sociolinguistics, indeed, is far from being a matter internal to academic disciplines. There are two main sources of practical interest and support: the language problems of developing nations (cf. Fishman, Ferguson, and Das Gupta, 1968), and problems of education and social relations in highly urbanized societies such as England and the United States. With respect to both one is pretty much in the position of wanting to apply a basic science that does not yet exist.[3] The creation of this basic science (whatever its ultimate label and affiliations) I take to be the defining task of sociolinguistics, and the chief warrant for the term.[4]

A more general sort of social relevance is that of seeking to transcend a long-standing 'alienation' of language, and knowledge about language. On this view, language and linguistics often stand to human life in a relation parallel to that of goods and economics, as analysed in the first book of *Das Kapital*. Marx's comments on 'fetishism of commodities', analysis of a human power and creation made to stand over against man, and understood in categories divorcing it from its roots in social life, could be applied, *mutatis mutandi*, to language. From this standpoint, the historical origin of standard languages and linguistic study as instruments of cultural hegemony (Hellenistic study of Greek, Indian of the Sanskritic Vedas, Chinese of the Confucian classics) is unwittingly reinforced by the contemporary methodological canon of defining linguistic theory as concerned only with an ideal speaker-hearer in a perfectly homogeneous community, free from all limitations of actual use. The effect is the same, closing off study of the social realities of language by those most able to analyse their linguistic dimension. From this standpoint, sociolinguistics has a contribution to make to what Wright Mills called the task of sociological imagination, that of enabling men to understand their lives adequately in terms of the true determinants of them; here the perspective provided by ethnographic and comparative studies, although of little engineering pertinence, may be of great intellectual importance. We have yet to gain the cross-cultural perspective on speech that we have on child-rearing, sex, religion. Both in linguistics and in social science, the roles of language in human life usually are assumed or asserted. Research that seeks the actual ranges and kinds of meaning that speaking and languages have, and the conditions that support or frustrate each, has hardly begun.[5]

Whatever one's conception of the relevance of sociolinguistics, two things should be made clear about it and the terms on which it is modelled. First, these terms do not designate three disciplines, but rather problem areas that draw members of different disciplines together. The problems and the participants overlap. Not only may scholars from different disciplines contribute under the same one label, but also one and the same scholar may in different contexts contribute under each of the three. The same topic may appear under all three. (The issues raised by Whorf have been discussed as 'ethnolinguistics', 'psycholinguistics', and 'sociolinguistics' in turn.) In effect, the three terms mediate between particular social sciences and linguistics, and, increasingly, between linguistics and the social sciences as a whole. 'Sociolinguistics', the last to emerge, and the one more suggestive of social science as a whole, benefits from this trend, and tends to displace the others, where their putative content is shared. It remains true that there is more willingness to identify one's work as 'sociolinguistic' than to define oneself as a 'sociolinguist'.

Second, the domain of such terms is subject to shifting definition of the disciplines between which they mediate. For something like a generation (say, from *Coral Gardens* (1935) to Katz and Fodor (1963)), a technical study of a folk taxonomy might readily have been labelled 'ethnolinguistic'. Today, given the renewed legitimacy of semantics among linguists, such a study can be taken as part of linguistics (cf. the excellent textbook by Lyons, 1968). Given the renewed attention to cognitive structures among anthropologists, such a study can equally well be taken as part of social anthropology. A similar fate may await 'sociolinguistics'. Having arisen to fill a gap, it may find itself absorbed from both sides. A generation from now, one still may speak only of linguistics and anthropology (and of sociology and psychology) when disciplines are in question. 'Sociolinguistic', 'ethnolinguistic', and 'psycholinguistic' will remain useful adjectives for kinds of research but their corresponding plural nouns will be seen as having marked a transition.[6]

If this should happen, it will be in the context of a linguistics and a social anthropology in some respects radically recast, such that adjacent sectors merge.[7] I shall return to this prospect in the conclusion. Let me emphasize what I mean by saying here that the prediction would not be verified by increased cooperation between linguists and anthropologists, in the field and after, although there is of course much need for that. It would not be made true by some ethnographers coming to do what some linguists now do, and conversely, although that is essential; or by investigations that are jointly linguistic and ethnographic on just those occasions when the special importance of a feature (linguistic or social) dictates intensive study, although of course one wants such work. These things are needed, most obviously with regard to semantics.[8] No amount of combination of disciplines as presently constituted, however, asking just the questions each now normally asks, will serve. The essence of the prediction is in the hope for disciplines radically recast. It will become true only if linguistics and social anthropology revise their conventional scope and methodology, so that matters now let fall between them are seen as indispensable to each.

The multiplicity of terms, over the past century and more, for the common interests of linguists and anthropologists suggests a recurrent need, and a recurrent tension – a need met often by *ad hoc* coinage, a tension persisting owing to failure to resolve the relationship of the two fields in a form capable of sustained growth. Just as practical problems require an as yet inchoate scientific field, so do some of the tasks of linguists and anthropologists. Such a resolution requires changes in present ways of thinking about and working with language in the two disciplines. By 'ethnography of speaking' is meant work to bring about the change.

II

The issues are implicit in the term 'ethnography of speaking' itself. 'Ethnography' has sometimes been considered 'mere' description, not itself a theoretical task, but only fodder for one. Often it has been taken as a part of the scientific division of labour concerned with societies other than one's own. 'Speaking' has been regarded as merely implementation and variation, outside the domain of language and linguistics proper. Linguistic theory has mostly developed in abstraction from contexts of use and sources of diversity. But by an ethnography of speaking I shall understand a description that is a theory – a theory of speech as a system of cultural behaviour; a system not necessarily exotic, but necessarily concerned with the organization of diversity.

Let me now sketch what is entailed with regard to linguistics, considering first the scope and goals of linguistic theory, then issues of methodology.

THE SCOPE OF LINGUISTIC DESCRIPTION

As a term for the activity of linguists that corresponds to ethnography, I shall use simply 'linguistic description'. What portion of language linguists describe, or attend to most carefully, depends of course upon their theoretical outlook. The development of linguistic description in this century must be seen in relation to the introduction of, and changes of foci for, the notion of structure. The concern first was to secure recognition of the synchronic state of a language as a legitimate object of scientific study, as one indeed of theoretical importance and of precedence, independently of practical, historical, cultural, or other considerations. This goal is the culminating theme of Saussure's *Cours de linguistique générale* (1916), the posthumous book regarded as the starting-point of modern linguistics; it is assumed by Boas (1911) (except that cultural considerations are important), and it is the theme of Sapir's first theoretical essay (1912), developing into the leitmotiv of his book *Language* (1921).

To a great extent it was the conquest of speech sounds as an area of pattern belonging to linguistics that gave structural linguistics its impetus. (Sound had been the domain of phonetics as a *Naturwissenschaft*, only grammar the domain of linguistics, a *Geisteswissenschaft*.) The area of concentration, where battles of method and theory were first fought, thus was phonology. Boas, Sapir, and Kroeber had already criticized traditional conceptions of word structure; Bloomfield (1933) generalized the notion of morpheme, and morphology came to be intensively cultivated in the late 1930s and the 1940s. Syntax came more to attention in the 1950s, and Chomsky (1957), building on work of Harris, made it *the* centre in a way that radically challenged earlier work in phonology and morphology as well. Semantics has become a major concern in the 1960s, and in some hands in a way that would radically recast previous work in syntax (including that of Chomsky). Very recently the notion of sociolinguistic description has been advanced (Hymes, 1967b) (essentially as a synonym for 'ethnography of speaking'). Here in one sense is the theme of this paper – that the next change of focus for linguistic descriptions entails social description (ethnography), and that with this change the process that began with phonology and morphology will have come full circle – linguistic description will find its own development to require (on a new plane) considerations from which at first it sought to be free.[9]

Structure and freedom

A principal issue is the relation seen between structure and freedom, or, from another point of view, between structure and human nature. To put it in grossly simplified form: in seeking structure, Saussure is concerned with the word, Chomsky with the sentence, the ethnography of speaking with the act of speech. That is, for Saussure, the object of linguistic theory was language as a structured social fact, and its sphere was the word. Combinations of words in sentences (conventional phrases apart) were aspects of speech, a matter of individual free creation in particular acts outside the sphere of structure. Later linguists extended structural analysis to the sentence, but structure was conceived as segmentation and classification of occurrent forms. With Chomsky, both (a) the scope of syntactic structure and (b) its relation to human nature were reformulated.

As to (a): beyond occurrent forms and distributional patterns was a network of relationships, distinct from, yet basic to, them. In part, Chomsky revitalized traditional conceptions, making them explicit in a formal theory. In so doing Chomsky was carrying further a logic in the recognition of linguistic levels that can be traced from Sapir's 'Sound Patterns in Language' (1925). Briefly, the logic is this: a level (or component) of linguistic structure is to be recognized when there appear systematically two one–many relations. Thus a sentence such as 'Visiting anthropologists can be amusing' may be ambiguous. A single structure, so far as occurrent forms and relations are concerned, it may yet express two different sets of underlying relationships. In one 'anthropologist' is subject, in one object, of the verb from which the gerund 'visiting' derives. (Loosely, it is as if the sentence derived in the one case from 'Someone visits anthropologists', and 'It is amusing'.) This is the relationship Sydney Lamb calls 'neutralization'. Conversely, the same set of relationships may underlie a number of different sentences, e.g. 'Visiting anthropologists can be amusing', 'To visit anthropologists can be amusing', 'It is amusing to visit anthropologists'; or 'It is amusing to be visited by anthropologists', 'Anthropologists who visit can be amusing', etc. This is the relationship Lamb calls 'diversification'. Notice that in the last pair 'anthropologists' is object of a preposition ('by') in one case, subject of 'be' in the other, yet, fundamentally, subject of 'visit' in both. The level of underlying relationships in syntax is 'deep structure'. It is actually more abstract, more remote from the manifest forms (surface structure), than these examples show.[10]

As to (b): Chomsky also reinterpreted the relation of structure to individual freedom and human nature. The deeper structures discovered are not opposed to freedom, but its condition. The child is conceived, not as passively learning linguistic patterns, but as actively constructing a theory to make intelligible the scattered and limited sample of speech that comes his way.

Within a remarkably short period, from remarkably limited data, the child is seen to acquire essential mastery of a finite device capable of producing an infinity of sentences. These conditions of acquisition are argued by Chomsky to necessitate postulation of a quite specific innate basis (*faculté de langage*). Herein lies the 'creative aspect of language', the 'rule-governed creativity', acquired and used largely free of stimulus control, which permits a speaker to respond appropriately to novel situations. For Chomsky, the ultimate purpose of linguistic theory is to characterize this underlying ability.

The goal of the ethnography of speaking can be said to be to complete the discovery of the sphere of 'rule-governed creativity' with respect to language, and to characterize the abilities of persons in this regard (without prejudice to the specific biological basis of the abilities). In extending the scope of linguistic rules beyond sentences to speech acts, and in seeking to relate language meaningfully to situations, this approach, although compatible with Chomsky's goals, does critically recast certain of his concepts. To see how this is so, let me consider two concepts that Chomsky has made central to discussion, then discuss particular lines of linguistic research.

Competence and performance

Chomsky's work is a decisive step, not only in extending the scope of linguistic theory, but also in redefining the nature of its object. For 'language' Chomsky substitutes 'competence' defined as a fluent native speaker's knowledge (largely tacit) of grammaticality – of whether or not putative sentences are part of his language, and according to what structural relationships. The goal of linguistic description is thus changed, from an object independent of men, to a human capacity. Both changes (deep structure, human capacity) are felt to be so great as to lead transformational grammarians to reject 'structural linguistics' as a name for their work, and to use it solely to describe other schools as predecessors. From a social standpoint, transformational grammar might equally well be seen as the culmination of the leading theme of structural linguistics. To centre analysis in a deep structure, one grounded in human nature, is to fulfil an impulse of structural linguistics to treat language as a sphere of wholly autonomous form. Such a theory perfects and gives the ultimate justification to a study of language at once of human significance and abstracted from actual human beings.

Chomsky's redefinition of linguistic goals appears, then, a half-way house. The term 'competence' promises more than it in fact contains. Restricted to the purely grammatical, it leaves other aspects of speakers' tacit knowledge and ability in confusion, thrown together under a largely unexamined concept of 'performance'. In effect, 'performance' confuses two separate aims. The first is to stress that 'competence' is something underlying behaviour ('mere performance', 'actual performance'). The second is to allow for aspects of linguistic ability which are not grammatical: psychological constraints on memory, choice of alternative rules, stylistic choices and devices in word order, etc. The intended negative connotation of the first sense of 'performance' tends to attach to the second sense; factors of performance – and all social factors must be placed here – are generally seen as things that limit the realization of grammatical possibilities, rather than as constitutive or enabling. In fact, of course, choice among the alternatives that can be generated from a single base structure depends as much upon a tacit knowledge as does grammar, and can be studied as much in terms of underlying rules as can grammar. Such things equally underlie actual behaviour, and would be aspects of 'competence' in the normal sense of the term. On its own terms, transformational theory must extend the notion of 'competence' to include more than the grammatical.

The need of some such revision is being recognized within transformational theory.[11] What may not be accepted at present is a need to complement the particular thrust, and to revise the particular idealization, of transformational theory. Chomsky's interest is in moving from what is said to what is constant in grammar, and from what is social to what is innate in human nature. That, so to speak, is but half a dialectic. A thoroughgoing linguistics must move in the other direction as well, from what is potential in human nature, and in a grammar, to what is realizable and realized; and conceive of the social factors entering into realization as constitutive and rule-governed too. The present tendency is to ignore any content specific to factors external to grammar; as input to the acquisition of its use, they are depreciated, and as aspects of output, actual use, seen as no problem, or, if a problem, only as negative.

An ethnography of speaking approach shares Chomsky's concern for creativity and freedom, but it recognizes that a child, or person, master only of grammar, is not yet free. Chomsky's attempt to discuss the 'creative' aspect of language use (Chomsky, 1966) suffers from the same difficulty as his treatment of 'competence'. The main thrust is independence of situation. Chomsky specifies freedom from stimulus control, infinity of possible sentences, yet appropriateness of novel sentences to novel situations; but the first two properties, and the grammatical mechanisms he considers, can never account for appropriateness. A novel sentence might be wildly inappropriate. Appropriateness involves a *positive* relation to situations, not a negative one, and, indeed, a knowledge of a kind of competence regarding situations and relations of sentences to them. As with 'competence', so with 'creativity': I share Chomsky's goals for linguistics, and admire him for setting them, but they cannot be reached on his terms or by linguistics alone. Rules of appropriateness beyond grammar govern speech, and are acquired as part of conceptions of self, and of meanings associated both with particular forms of speech and with the act of speaking itself.

The issue is especially clear with regard to education and schooling. Chomsky's insistence on the universal capacity for linguistic fluency is essential against the pervasive tendency to blame the failures of a social system on its victims, but in itself provides only a partial remedy.

To say that children could be fluent and are not is poignant, perhaps to invite drastic intervention techniques (some American 'authorities' advise taking black children from their mothers at the age of six months). What is needed as well is a realization that the standard of the schools is not the only standard, that more than one system of speaking, each with rules, values, and satisfactions and accomplishments of its own, is involved. Lower-class black children in the United States, for example, are probably much more sensitive to the aesthetic and interactional uses of language than are many middle-class white children.

In such respects the transformational conception of linguistic theory, concerned exclusively with an ideally fluent speaker-listener in a perfectly homogeneous community, may unwittingly play into the hands of those whose views the theory's exponents would wish to reject. Not only are motivations and rules and values for use neglected, but also the 'competence' of which they speak is unlocated, merely glossed with a conventional language name, e.g. English. The theoretical potential of the formal system is imputed to individual speakers. (One leading researcher in children's language, recognizing that Chomsky's 'competence' means the formal system, and not wishing to challenge his theory, went so far as to call the actual knowledge of grammar held by an individual a sub-type of performance!) The difficulty is analogous to the circularity with which Whorf moved between an imputed world-view and the linguistic data (from one informant in New York City) from which the world-view had been inferred. In fact, of course, similar bodies of data are compatible with different underlying organization and degrees of knowledge in individual speakers. (One serious difficulty for some children is that their speech is referred by teachers to the same grammatical system as standard English, when, in the case of West Indian and many American negro children, it may have a distinct history involving past creolization; consequently, a grammar superficially similar may be in important respects distinct (cf. Dillard, 1968).)

An adequate approach must distinguish and investigate four aspects of competence: (a) *systematic potential* – whether and to what extent something is not yet realized, and, in a sense, not yet known; it is to this that Chomsky in effect reduces competence; (b) *appropriateness* – whether and to what extent something is in some context suitable, effective, or the like; (c) *occurrence* – whether and to what extent something is done; (d) *feasibility* – whether and to what extent something is possible, given the means of implementation available.

The last three dimensions would have to be 'performance' in the system of Chomsky's *Aspects* (1965), but knowledge with regard to each is part of the competence of a speaker-hearer in any full sense of the term, and 'performance' should be reserved for a more normal, consistent meaning (see below). There is no notice of occurrence in *Aspects*, or in most current linguistic theory, but it is an essential dimension. Most linguists today scorn quantitative data, for example, but Labov (1966, 1969) has shown that systematic study of quantitative variation discloses new kinds of structure and makes possible explanation of change. In general, this theoretical dimension provides for the fact that members of a speech community are aware of the commonness, rarity, previous occurrence or novelty, of many features of speech, and that this knowledge enters into their definitions and evaluations of ways of speaking.[12]

In terms of these dimensions, one can say of speech that it is, for example, grammatical, awkward, overly formal, and rare (as in the conversation of the American ambassador to the Court of St James in the TV film, 'The Royal Family'); ungrammatical, difficult, expressively appropriate, and individual (as in the speech of Leontes in Act II of *The Winter's Tale* (Thorne, 1969)); ungrammatical, awkward, appropriate, and common (as in the bumbling speech required of Burundi peasants before aristocrats (Albert, 1972)); grammatical, easy, correct, and avoided (as indicated in these remarks under 'Dukes and Duchesses . . . Style of Addressing in Speech': '. . . though the necessity for using the full title would generally be avoided . . . in conversation it is best to make as sparing a use as possible of titles' (*Titles and Forms of Address*, 1967: 46)).

One must recognize not only knowledge, but also ability to implement it, with respect to each of these dimensions, as a component of competence in speaking. Especially, one must provide for motivation and value.[13] And, as indicated, the competence to be attributed to particular persons and communities is in each case an empirical matter. Transformational theory recognizes that what seems the same sentence may enter into two quite different sets of relations, syntactically; it must recognize the same thing to be true, socially.

Finally, the negative connotation of *performance*, as the realization of knowledge and ability, must be replaced with recognition of its positive aspect as well. There are properties of performance, essential to the social role of speaking, that go beyond the knowledge and ability referable to particular persons. In part these properties are functions of the social organization of speech (complementarity of roles, etc.), in part they emerge in the actual events of speech themselves (as when one speaks to a responsive or a 'cold' audience).[14]

Such a perspective calls for a descriptive method, a methodological approach, different from that common in linguistics. To indicate what it would be like let me consider the ways in which linguistics itself is moving in the required direction.

DIRECTIONS OF LINGUISTIC DESCRIPTION

In the immediate situation in linguistics the main frontiers of relevant work have to do with the extension of analysis beyond the sentence to sequences in discourse; beyond the single language to *choices* among forms of speech; and beyond the referential function to functions that may be loosely grouped together as stylistic. Each of these can be seen as involving kinds of knowledge and ability (i.e. competence) on the part of members of a community.

Discourse: texts

Chomsky has recently alluded to coherence (1968: 11), perhaps in response to the attention given to it by Halliday, Gleason, and others (coherence was not discussed in Chomsky, 1965, despite the attribution of it here to a Cartesian view). Just as one has the ability to recognize a sentence as grammatical or ungrammatical, so one has the ability to recognize a series of sentences as discourse, rather than an arbitrary list (Hasan, 1968: 1). The ability depends in important part on properly linguistic features and is increasingly recognized as a necessary facet of investigation (cf. Daneš, 1964; Halliday, 1967). Three brief examples must suffice.

Kiparsky (1968), for example, in a brilliant article explaining diverse Indo-European phenomena in terms of a single type of rule, conjunct reduction (by virtue of which the second occurrence of a feature may be omitted or expressed by an unmarked form), notes that the scope of such rules applies across sentences (p. 34n.4) and even across change of speakers in dialogue (p. 43). Gunter (1966) explicitly attacks the restriction of *la langue* to the sentence, and notes that the placement of accent cannot be explained without the assumption that a given variety of a sentence signals its own particular kind of relevance to its context. (By variety of sentence is meant that a given sentence is in effect chosen from among what another linguist, Henry Hiz, has called a battery. There are paradigms not only of morphemes, but of sentences as well.) The format of the usual transformational grammar is criticized for obscuring the relation among the members of a paradigm of sentence varieties. With particular reference to accent, Gunter goes on to show that some placements in dialogue make nonsense of it, others provide intelligibility; that in general one has a knowledge of 'context grammar' that enables one to tell whether a sentence is relevant to what has just been said, or whether relevance to an implicit (non-verbal) context must be sought; if the former, what the connection is, and if the latter, what limits the form and content of the non-overt must satisfy. (See Gunter's article for detailed interpretation of English examples.) As a third example, let me cite Wheeler (1967), who found that his Siona informants would allow variation in the enclitic chosen to mark subject and object relations, where single sentences were involved, but would stubbornly refuse to vary the presence or choice of enclitic in texts. There was decidedly a fixed order for use or non-use of the markers, if a narration or dialogue was to be acceptable, yet no clue within the sentence as to the rationale. Wheeler discovered (partly with the aid of kinesic behaviour on the part of informants) that not one but two dimensions underlay the grammatical markers in question. The markers signalled both subject, object, or goal within the sentence, and degree of focus – emphatic, normal, or none – within the discourse. This last, purely discourse, function is indeed their primary function.

The study of texts is of course familiar to linguists and ethnographers both; and transformational grammar itself began in work of Zellig Harris in the early 1950s on certain recurrent properties of texts. The work cited above makes clear the development of text analysis in terms of an extended understanding of the competence of speakers. There is much to be learnt just from such study of syntactic relations. At the same time, analysis must go beyond purely linguistic markers. Much of the coherence of texts depends upon abstract rules independent of specific linguistic form, indeed, of speech. Such are the kinds of knowledge that the sociologist Harvey Sacks analyses as hearers' and viewers' maxims. One such maxim in brief form is: if the first of two sentences can be heard (interpreted) as the cause of the second, hear it that way. Sacks (1972) uses the start of a children's story as illustration: 'The baby cried. The mommy picked it up.' He notes that we spontaneously take the mommy to be *its* mommy, and to have picked the baby up *because* it cried, although neither relationship is stated (or implied by the underlying syntax).[15]

A familiar example of structural analysis of texts is of course the work of Lévi-Strauss, Greimas, and others. From the standpoint of an ethnography of speaking, such work has a complementary limitation: it has little or nothing to do with specific linguistic form at all. This is not to deny the existence of narrative structures independent of linguistic form, but to question that their function can be validly inferred apart from a knowledge of such form. In a Chinookan myth, for example, any translation, even an abstract, would make clear the presence of a structure, 'Interdiction: Interdiction violated', and imply that the outcome (a murder) follows from the violation, as so often is found to be the case. Analysis of the myth in terms of its specific development, in Clackamas Chinook, discloses structures that place almost an opposite significance on the myth. The myth is to be understood in terms of a specifically Chinookan theory of myth (one requiring constant moving back and forth between linguistic form and cultural meaning for its discovery, as in the classic structural linguistic principle of form–meaning covariation) such that it is here not the violator, but the one who issues the interdiction, who, in Clackamas terms, is culpable. Only through control of the original linguistic form, moreover, is one able to discover that an inherited plot has been shaped to express through imagery and style a personal meaning, as well as to see that the terse myth has a unity (see Hymes, 1968b).

The particular contribution of linguistics presumably will be to explore to its limits the formally linguistic coherence of texts, and, as in the work of Gunter, Labov, and some others, to explore conversational interaction as well. The contribution of social anthropology may be to explore the structure of conversational interaction more directly and thoroughly, as part of ethnography, and to insist on understanding discourse structures as *situated*, that is, as pertaining to cultural and personal occasions in which part of their meaning and structure lies.[16] There is as yet relatively little work that integrates both aspects. These points bring us to a central concept, that of speech act.

Discourse: speech acts

To consider discourse as situated is not to refer it to an infinity of possible contextual factors. (The failure to develop a method beyond the handling of discrete instances vitiated the influence of Malinowski's work.) Linguists and perhaps others do tend to imagine that when a door is opened on a level beyond the familiar, everything in the universe outside will rush in. From the standpoint of ethnography of speaking, there is in a community a system of speech acts, a structured knowledge of kinds and occasions of speech. The level of speech acts is indeed implied by the very logic that has led, since Sapir's 'Sound Patterns in Language' (1925), to the recognition of other implicit levels in linguistics. As discussed earlier with regard to syntax, the question is one of a one–many, many–one relationship.

Just so with the status of sentences as acts of speech. A sentence in interrogative form may serve as a question, a reflective statement, a command; a question may be expressed in interrogative or declarative form ('Is this clock slow?': 'I say, this clock seems to be a bit slow'). In general, the function of an interrogative, declarative, or imperative form of sentence is not uniquely given in virtue of that form; the same functions may be served by different forms.

Some linguists, recognizing the significance of speech acts, now wish to incorporate them into syntax, so that a sentence carries with it in deep structure something like 'I ask you', 'I tell you', and the like (normally deleted in overt form). There is indeed evidence to support this approach in some cases (McCawley, 1968: 157), but as a general solution to the problem it appears a last-ditch effort to keep within the conventional boundaries of linguistics. An approach that insists on the complex, abstract knowledge of speakers with regard to other relationships quite distinct from manifest form need not cling to a literal verbal embodiment of acts of speech. Some assertions, requests, commands, threats, and the like are known to be such on the basis of a knowledge, *jointly*, of the message-form and the relationship in which it occurs. Commonly the same message-form serves as a serious insult in some relationships and as a badge of intimacy in others. (This point will be taken up with regard to code-switching.) An approach that is limited to occurrences of actual illocutionary verbs (overt or covert) cannot handle the status in some circumstances of 'Oh dear, I seem to be out of matches' as a request.

A related point – obvious, yet needing to be repeatedly mentioned – is that the rules that govern speech acts govern more than single speakers and more than speech. The Sanskrit rule for conjunct reduction across interlocutors has been mentioned. An especially nice example of both points is found among the Haya of northern Tanzania (Sheila Seitel, personal communication). When mentioning a quantity, the speaker will say something such as 'We saw this many of them', holding up a certain number of fingers. It is the listener who then says the number. When rules for summoning in English are developed (Schegloff, 1972), they are found to subsume both verbal and non-verbal acts: 'George!', a telephone ring, a knock on a door. By the same logic that rejects compartments in syntax and phonology when they prevent unitary treatment of unitary phenomena (cf. McCawley, 1968: 166 ff.), the boundary between verbal and non-verbal messages must be erased in a good many cases when sentences are studied as addressed acts of speech.

Codes and code-switching

'Code-switching' is a common term for alternate use of two or more languages, or varieties of a language. Studies of code-switching are among the most important developments in sociolinguistics, first, because bilingualism and bidialectism are significant social matters, and, second, because the work necessarily breaks with the implicit image of 'one language – one community'. Such studies show that the very notions of speech community, fluency of speakers, what counts as a 'language' as an object of description, are dependent on ethnographic and comparative study.

The linguistic and communicative boundaries between communities cannot be defined by linguistic features alone (cf. Hymes, 1968c). Forms of speech of the same degree of linguistic difference may be counted as dialects in one area, as distinct languages in another, depending on the political, not the linguistic, history of the area in question. This is so in Africa (Jan Voohoeve, personal communication) and lies beneath the appearance of linguistic uniformity in Europe. Were the standard languages removed, Europe would look linguistically much more like native America.

Three separate dimensions seem to have been confused in the usual notion of a 'language': *provenance of content, mutual intelligibility*, and *functional role*. Sometimes different forms of speech are called by the same language name because their historical provenance is seen to be substantially the same (e.g. 'English' for a variety of 'dialects' throughout the world). Sometimes two communities are said to have the same, or different, languages on grounds of mutual intelligibility, or the lack thereof. Sometimes a form of speech is said to be the language of a community because it is the primary mode of interaction (the 'vernacular'). Yet each of these criteria leads to different results. Not all forms of speech derived from a common English source (more or less common – the earlier dialect diversity of English must not be overlooked) are mutually intelligible. Some mutually unintelligible forms of speech are not distinct languages: 'pig Latin', for example, derives from English by one or two operations. Groups sometimes have a primary form of speech that conflates material of different provenance, e.g. the French-suffused speech of pre-revolutionary Russian aristocracy, or the mixed Latin–German of Luther's tabletalk. The functional variety, 'language of the demons', among Sinhalese conflates (a) Sanskrit, (b) Pali, (c) Classical Sinhalese, and (d) a polyglot mixture, according to whether (a) Hindu or (b) Buddhist deities are invoked or mentioned, or (c) origin myths are narrated, or (d) demons are directly addressed and commanded (Tambiah, 1968: 177).

An adequate approach might be developed along the following lines. *Speech community* would be defined in terms of the sharing both of some one primary form of speech, and of rules for its use. (Peoples may share a language but have different rules for its use, or may share rules of use but apply them to different languages.) *Form of speech* could be adopted as a neutral, basic term.[17] The number and kinds of forms of speech in a community would, of course, be an empirical matter. Where connection among varieties in terms of common provenance of their stock of lexical and grammatical materials is in question, one would speak, as now, of *languages* and *dialects*. Where mutual intelligibility is in question, one would speak of *codes*. This usage would allow for inclusion of such forms of speech as Mazateco whistle-talk, Jabo drum-signalling and horn-calling, Tagalog speech disguise, and the like. There are thus two dimensions to differences of code: some require the learning of new linguistic content, some require the learning of operations on linguistic content already known. Where functional role is in question, one would speak of *varieties* (cf. Ferguson and Gumperz, 1960), and, more specifically for situations, of *registers*.

Just to locate the referent of its description, then, linguistics must place the particular body of judgements of acceptability, kinds of grammatical knowledge, etc., which it wishes to analyse, among the plurality of forms of speech found in every community. For pure linguistics, the task may be only a way of excluding some phenomena and of ensuring the validity of those selected for description. For social anthropology and ethnography of speaking, such an account of the repertoire of a community is an essential framework. An interesting account of a trilingual community in this regard has been provided by Denison (1968).[18] Denison delineates thirteen factors involved in the selection of one or the other of the three languages in Sauris (German, Italian, Friulian). These factors can be seen to be aspects of four general aspects of speaking: Situation (here, formality of the scene, home setting); Genre (here, sayings, written genres – Denison reports that the basic distinction for genre depends on a relationship to what I would term Key – the attitude or spirit in which the act occurs; here, spontaneity versus non-spontaneity); participants (here, capacities and preference of sender, receiver, auditor for a variety, plus age and sex); and the Act-Sequence itself (here, shifts in topic, and the variety of the preceding discourse).

Code-selection and code-switching (more precisely variety-selection and -switching) point beyond themselves in two important ways. First, their description requires, and helps to create, an adequate general framework for the discovery and statement of rules of speaking. Varieties of form of speech may depend upon a single factor, such as setting in time and place, or culturally defined scene (*Situation*); on characteristics of *participants*; on *ends in view* (e.g. Kaska Indians switch to English to curse); the form and topics of the discourse as it unfolds (*Act-Sequence*); the tone or mood (e.g. mock:serious, warm:reserved, etc.) (*Key*); the *instrumentalities* available in terms of *channels* (oral, written, and perhaps here, use of the voice in singing, etc.); *norms of interaction* holding between or for participants and situations (e.g. whether to select the variety best known to a given interlocutor is obligatory, ingratiating, or insulting (as implying that he does not know some more prestigious variety)); *norms of interpretation* (beliefs and values, and common-sense reasoning, e.g. treating infant vocalization as a separate code, knowledge of which is shared by some men with certain guardian spirits (Wishram Chinook)); and, finally, *Genre*. More commonly, rules for use of a form of speech will involve relations among two or more factors. Just these two steps – identifying what can count as an instance of such a factor relevant to communication, and discovering the relations obtaining between such factors – are the fundamental steps of ethnography of speaking (and communication) generally.

Second, the dimensions and meanings found to underlie and explain the selection and switching of varieties are general. Intimacy versus distance, for example, is a dimension underlying choice of Spanish or of Guarani in Paraguay (Rubin, 1968); it is also a dimension underlying choice of pronouns *ty* or *vy* in Russian. If pursued in a thoroughgoing way, the problem of forms of speech brings one to the starting-point of ethnography of speaking as a whole. Very simply and very generally, that starting-point is to recognize that in any community a number of *ways of speaking* will be distinguished. Shifts in the entire provenance of the linguistic material (e.g. German to Italian) are perhaps the most salient evidence, but shifts in any other aspect of speaking provide evidence as well: from normal voice to whispering; from direct to indirect address; from rapid to deliberate tempo; from one topic to another; from one selection of grammatical and/or lexical and/or phonological features within a variety to another; and so on. Here is the kind of form–meaning covariation that is basic to ethnography of speaking and sociolinguistics, the sociolinguistic commutation test, as it were, analogous to the principle of structural contrast basic to the relevance of features in linguistics proper. In some cases it is clear how to extend the form of a grammar to comprise ways of speaking, as when it is a question of automatically selected features, when one participant is of a certain status (cf. Sherzer, 1967), or there is a discretely defined genre (DeCamp, 1968). For many aspects of ways of speaking, adequate modes of statement remain to be worked out.

Many ways of speaking, of course, require intimate command of a community's linguistic resources for their study. Choice of language varieties has the advantage for social anthropologists of being both salient and representative. It must be clear that study of varieties, and of ways of speaking, is more than a matter of merely correlating linguistic forms with situations, however; this raises the question of functional perspective.

FUNCTIONS OF SPEECH

What must be stressed here is the priority of a functional perspective, and the plurality and problematic status of functions. Discovery of structure in linguistics has proceeded mostly as if the function of language is reference alone. The common account of language as mediating merely between (vocal) sound and meaning manifests this assumption. It pictures language as structure between the two continua of possible meanings and possible sounds. The image of man implied is of an abstract, isolated individual, related only to a world of objects to be named and described. Ethnography of speaking proceeds on the hypothesis that an equally primary function of speech is *address*. Speech, including linguistic structure as a major, but not a sole, resource, mediates between persons and their situations. Ordinary linguistic structure, a constituent of the organization of speaking, cannot suffice as a starting-point from which to discover that organization. One must begin from speaking as a mode of action, not from language as an unmotivated mechanism.

This perspective has direct consequences for the handling of phenomena commonly grouped loosely together as 'style' (on 'style' as a residual category, cf. Gunter, 1966). There is a tendency to regard style as deviation from a norm set by ordinary linguistic analysis, rather than as the accomplishment of communicative purposes through more complex means; and to deal with such matters only when they intrude inescapably into ordinary linguistic analysis. Chomsky has noted the existence of rules of style with regard to word order and the case-form of pronouns in surface structure, for example, but essentially to make clear that they do not bear on the theory of grammatical structure which is his proper concern (1965: 125, 227–228n.5; 221–222n.36). There has indeed been some valuable work on these matters in various schools of linguistics in Europe, and in various centres in England and the United States. (Two selections of important work are Chatman and Levin (1966) and Steinmann (1967).) The focus of most work called stylistic is on literary or other texts. Stylistics is invaluable to the ethnography of speaking, and indeed almost indistinguishable from it (cf. Guiraud, 1961, 'Conclusion'), but the ethnographic approach must be concerned with ways of speaking generally.

From such a perspective, phenomena of style do not merely supervene, but they reconstitute elements of linguistic theory in the narrower sense. Let me give brief examples, from phonology, grammar, and from ways of speaking.

From an ordinary linguistic standpoint, aspiration and word order are relevant when subject to phonemic contrast and transformational rules, respectively, and are otherwise peripheral or irrelevant. From a more general functional perspective, these and a number of other features are empirical universals of languages, differing among languages not in the fact but in the kind of relevance. Every language has conventional elements that are 'stylistic' as well as 'referential' in function, and the two are interdependent; what is stylistic in a given context cannot at the same time be referential. If aspiration distinguishes words as lexical items, it cannot at the same time distinguish an expressive from a neutral use of a word, and conversely. In a linguistic description on ethnographic principles, then, one begins by asking not what elements are phonemic, transformationally governed, etc., but simply what elements are conventionally recognized means of verbal expression. It is a second step to treat these elements as some stylistic, some referential, in function. The same point can be made with regard to word order, only some of whose regularities are accountable in syntactic terms (cf. Chomsky, 1965: 126; Halliday, 1967, and Czech work cited there). The logic here is that of Saussure, when he argued that lexicon as well as grammar had to be part of linguistic study, since a given feature was found now in one, now in the other, in different languages.

The organizing power (and necessity) of a functional starting-point is particularly clear with regard to particles, which have no internal structure of their own, and often only limited syntactic roles, but which may display distributional structure and significance when analysed in relation to intonation and the form of social interaction. Only their substitutability as responses would lead one to group together 'You're welcome', 'Don't mention it', and 'My pleasure'; or, as leave-takings, 'Good-bye', 'Au revoir', 'See you'. Visitors to a country often make the mistake of seizing on surface equivalence in meaning, and inferring an equivalence in social distribution, for forms such as United States 'Thank you', British 'Thank you', and French 'Merci', just as they make the same mistake with regard to syntactic distribution for other words. The parallel between syntactic sets and interactional sets goes further, in that both tend to detach the forms they press into formal service from their original lexical meanings. In 'Keep going', 'keep' marks continuative aspect, not 'retain'; British 'Thank you' seems on its way to marking formally the segments of certain interactions, with only residual attachment to 'thanking' in some cases.

If one were to examine the literature on 'men's and women's speech', one would conclude that it was a rare phenomenon, found mostly among extinct American Indian tribes. It has been reported mostly by linguists who were also anthropologists, for cases in which the grammar or phonology of the language could be stated only by taking it into account. Working out from ordinary linguistics, then, one would have to conclude that in most societies men and women talk alike. That is a strange conclusion to arrive at, if language is a social instrument, given the importance of role differentiation along sexual lines in most times and places; and it is a false conclusion of course. One must begin with the functional question: do members of this community distinguish ways of speaking appropriate to men and appropriate to women? – and then seek the particular verbal means by which the distinction is implemented.

The identification of ways of speaking, and of the elements available to them, is a descriptive task at the frontiers of current linguistics. Obviously it does not exhaust functional understanding. If the goal of ethnography of speaking is to complete discovery of the sphere of rule-governed creativity with regard to language, then it must not only identify structure in discourse, in selection of language-varieties, in 'stylistic' functions, but also relate such structure to its actual use. Ultimately it would entail understanding of those complex uses of rules that underlie individual acts that are creative in the usual sense of involving unique meanings and mediations, and innovation with regard to the rules themselves (on unique mediation, cf. Tillich, 1964: 56–57; on such innovation as a general human experience, cf. Williams, 1961, Part 1, Ch. 1). By disclosing the conventional means available and organized it would make possible clearer understanding of the personal and transcendent (cf. Sapir, 1927; Tillich, 1964: 53–67). In the immediate situation it is important to stress the steps that lie at the edge of normal practice and theory, implicated by it or implicating change in it.

METHODOLOGICAL SUMMING-UP

Clearly, much of what has been discussed from the starting-point of linguistics could be approached from an ethnographic starting-point as well. That is in keeping with the prediction that an ethnography of speaking would represent a merging of the two disciplines at certain points; and it is inescapable. The logic of the discussion of linguistics has been to provide linguistic description with a necessary ethnographic base: to extend the scope of linguistic description from an isolated sentence-generating single norm to the structure of speaking as a whole, and to see description of speaking as situated and purposive. In short, to see larger structure, and to see structure as dependent on explicit broader conceptions of function. But to have presented these matters from an ethnographic starting-point would have involved a critique of social anthropology, just as much as the presentation above has been a critique of linguistics. If linguistics needs to look to the foundations of its work, social anthropology needs to look to the linguistic content. It perhaps has a special responsibility and opportunity to do so, and to this I now turn.

III

There are neglected kinds of knowledge to be made explicit as goals of analysis, in social anthropology as well. I shall be able to mention only two examples, one having to do with members of other cultures, one with those who study them.

A few years ago Max Gluckman wrote on the importance of gossip and scandal (1963). Among the groups taken as illustrations (Elizabeth Colson's Makah, English fox-hunting aristocracy), knowing how to gossip was found to be essential. This case may be taken to represent many ethnographic accounts, wherein some such ability is noted.

Consider what is entailed. Presumably it is not the case that gossiping and speaking are the same, that all speech is gossip. There must then be criteria for recognizing some speech as gossip, as being better or worse at it, as making mistakes, and as learning how. In short, members of the group presumably share a knowledge, and have ways of acquiring it, that an ethnographer might be expected to describe. Typically, ethnographers do not do so. Ethnographic accounts are rife with terms that in fact denote ways of speaking, though they are not always recognized to be such. (For reconstruction of a contrast drawn by Lowie in this respect between Crow and Hidatsa, see Hymes, 1964b.) One may be told that it is important, for men, say, to be good at a certain way of speaking. Commonly it is impossible to tell what would consist of an instance of the activity in question, or what being good at it would be like. Members of the world's cultures pray, curse, reproach, taunt, invoke, gossip, answer, instruct, report, joke, insult, greet, take leave, announce, interpret, advise, preach, command, inquire, duel verbally, etc., etc. At least they do so in the language of ethnography. What they would be found to be doing in terms of their own languages and cultures – or in terms of a general theory and terminology of speech, one that was systematic, not an *ad hoc* adaptation from the ethnographer's culture – it is seldom possible to tell. Sometimes who may or should speak, how, when, and where, to whom, can be glimpsed, but seldom in sufficient detail to permit explicit formulation.

(Here is a respect in which linguistics has a lesson for ethnography. If it does not direct its attention sufficiently to ethnographic matters, in its own domain it is explicit and vulnerable. Linguists write rules, or formalize relationships in data in other ways, and study the conditions in which one or another formalization is to be preferred, not to ape mathematics, but in order to do a decent job of work. Rule-writing commits one in explicit terms, as to what is being claimed and comprised. A good deal of the extension of ethnography into knowledge of speech is probably best handled by amplification of linguistic rules to comprise the ethnographic factors. The attitude to take toward the formalisms involved is to regard them simply as necessary book-keeping.)

Straight lexicography would sometimes serve, as when there is a specific verb stem for an act such as 'to tell *A* in the presence of *B* of the bad thing *B* has said of *A*' (Wasco Chinook). Translation itself, of course, would not suffice: 'to pronounce' is the best English gloss for Chinookan *-pghna*, but the specific constitutive force of the latter comes out only in its use in ceremonies and myths (cf. Hymes, 1966b). To define the act congealed in the Chinookan stem that can be politely rendered 'to sing of someone with whom one has slept' requires some knowledge of its place among possible types of song. Investigation of the stem 'to curse' would lead one into intonation and social relationships; with a minor exception (*qalaq baya*, something like 'darn you') there are no words in the language that are curse-words or obscene in themselves: cursing and obscenity depend on what is said, in what way, to whom. Lexicography might stop with recording the only Chinookan expression analogous to a European greeting (*dan miúxhulal*, 'what are you doing'); it would not itself lead one to explore the absence (as in many Amerindian societies) of the complex greeting patterns found in Africa, or to notice that common Wasco practice is *not* to greet someone who joins a group: courtesy requires that one does not call attention to the newcomer until he or she no longer is such – a practice in keeping with another, that one can pay a visit simply by coming and need not speak, if there is nothing more to convey. To pursue the analysis of speech acts, then, involves one in ethnography with speaking as its focus.

It would be easy to respond that such ethnography might be interesting but a luxury. In fact, I think it will prove both valuable and in some respects indispensable. First of all, inquiry into speaking – just into occasions in which speech is required, optional, or prescribed – discloses patterns of importance in a culture. Among Chinookans, for example, investigation of patterns of expected speech and required silence discloses that certain scenes are defined as formal by the fact that an audience is addressed by one whose words are repeated from another source, and that both grammar and conduct reflect a belief that matters dependent on the future, especially where relations with nature are concerned, should not be spoken while still uncertain. The pattern unites a number of practices, including the major ceremony in individual life (conferring of a name), the central public ideological activity (myth narration), and the major personal one (the guardian-spirit quest). For each there is a period in which something said (pronouncement of name, myth, guardian spirit's instructions) can be quoted but not disclosed in full, and a point at which, having been validated, the words are repeated in full. In terms of the pattern, a number of isolated and puzzling items fall into place (see Hymes, 1966b). Again, attention to the interpretation put upon infant speech may reveal much of the adult culture. Both Chinookans and Ashanti believe that infants share a first language not the adult one (on native theory, the 'native language' is always a second language). For Chinookans, the baby's talk is shared with certain spirits, and shamans having those spirits interpret it lest by 'dying' it return to the spirit world from which it came; the attempt is to incorporate the infant communicatively within the community. Ashanti traditionally exclude infants from a room in which a woman is giving birth, on the ground that an infant would talk to the baby in the womb in the special language they share, and, by warning it of the hardness of life, make it reluctant to emerge and so cause a hard delivery. The evaluation of spontaneous speech as intrinsically dangerous (and a pairing of men:women: culture:nature, in this regard) is brought out in this. Interpretations of the intent of first utterances – e.g. as an attempt to name kin (Wogeo), to ask for food (Alorese), to manipulate (Chaga) – may indeed be something of a projective test for a culture, as regards adult practices and the valuation placed on speech itself.

At the very least, then, analysis of speaking would enhance ethnographies. Beliefs and practices with regard to children may be an especially revealing area – one important for general theory, since the usual commonplaces concerning the role of language in the transmission of culture are patently inadequate to the great empirical diversity as to what is and what is not, and how much is, transmitted verbally. Some attention to speaking is in fact essential to ethnography itself, if seldom consciously thought of as part of one's analysis. In learning to get along with informants and other members of a community, to obtain information and the like, an ethnographer willy-nilly acquires some working sense of the very things with which we are here concerned. He or she does not normally make that working sense an object of conscious attention or reflection. (A number of times such patterns seem to have come first to awareness in conversation about fieldwork.) With respect, then, to what may be called the domain of *interrogative behaviour*, investigation of the sort proposed here would entail no more than making one's own process of investigation part of the object of study.

In just this respect social anthropologists can make a vital contribution to sociolinguistics and the ethnography of speaking, while perhaps contributing to their own work, whatever its main concern. A social anthropologist once posed the following problem: in a Mayan-speaking community in Mexico her questions were typically responded to by a Mayan expression translatable as 'Nothing'. She also noted that children's questions to parents would receive the same answer. I am not sure how the ethnography got done, or what solution was supposed to be drawn out of a sociolinguistic hat, but clearly, it cannot be the case that members of that Mayan community have no way of obtaining information from one another. Presumably there are appropriate ways of ascertaining things one does not already know from others who know them, and circumstances in which those who know things think it appropriate to tell them. I would suspect that a direct question was interpreted as rudeness. (Speakers seem generally to have and evaluate alternative ways of asking information and giving commands.) In any case, facts such as these – that among Araucanians it is an insult to be asked to repeat an answer, that a prompt answer from a Toba means he has no time to answer questions, that a Wasco prefers not to answer a question on the day of its asking, that Aritama prefer intermediaries for request – point to a sector of behaviour that successful ethnographers presumably master, just as they master some command of the local language. To make such matters the object of explicit attention would serve the interests of social anthropology and sociolinguistics both.

There is a second area in which these two interests appear to coincide, the study of kinship terms. Formal analysis of kinship ('componential analysis') has sometimes forgotten in practice what it honours in theory, the need of an ethnographic approach that treats verbal behaviour as situated, as answers to explicit or implicit questions, whose local status must be determined. Schneider (1969) has brought this point forcibly home. He shows that analyses of American English kinship terms have conflated two separate questions: when asked as to relatives, American informants may understand either biological relationship (relationship at all) or social relationship (relationship that counts). And he shows that the priority of terms of reference over terms of address is a dogma at best, and empirically wrong in known cases. In these respects Schneider's critique of componential analysis is at one with the critique of linguistics made earlier in this paper. To his points may be added the question of the setting of questions: Tulisano and Cole (1965) observe that informants may use different terms in introducing kin from those they use in responding to ethnographers, and Murphy (1967) reports that the Tuareg use a Sudanese system for explaining kin relations to non-kin, but an Iroquois system in address and reference among kin themselves. Conant (1961) has shown that systems of address may be more revealing than systems of reference, and at the same time contain other than kinship terms in the narrow sense, and Fischer (1964) has taken a specific setting, the family, to show the significance of patterns of address drawing upon several different domains (kinship, pronouns, personal names).

Social anthropologists are thus familiar in the area of kinship with exactly the problems that the ethnography of speaking raises about verbal form in general. The starting-point must be the purposes and strategies of persons in situations: what terms, what language indeed, what type of system even, are found in the data, will depend on that. At the same time there is, perhaps, an extension of focus. The fundamental problem may be seen to be, how do persons address each other? How are formally and comparatively distinct domains (personal names, kin terms, pronouns, titles, nicknames) integrated in the service of address?

One value of terms, or modes, of address as a focus is that it makes so clear that the relation of linguistic form to social setting is not merely a matter of correlation. Persons choose among alternative modes of address, and have a knowledge of what the meaning of doing so may be that can be formally explicated. An approach that has seemed successful with choice of speech level in Korean address would be, briefly, as follows: a mode of address (term, style, speech variety, whatever) has associated with it a usual, or 'unmarked', value – say, formality. Social relationships and settings have associated with them usual, or 'unmarked', values. When the values of the mode of address and the social context match – when both, say, are formal – then that meaning is of course accomplished, together with the meeting of expectations. When the values do not match – when, say, an informal mode of address is used in a formal relationship, or conversely – then a special, or 'marked', meaning is conveyed. The unmarked and marked meanings are each defined by a particular rule or relation, mapping the set of linguistic alternatives onto the set of social relationships and settings. What the particular marked meaning – deference, courtesy, insult, change of status – will be is of course an empirical question, as are the options available to the recipient (to overlook, acknowledge, take as irrevocable). Some generalizations seem likely to emerge, e.g. that mappings of terms onto categories higher and lower than normal matching have positive and negative import, respectively.

I stress this point because there is a strong tendency to consider the relation of linguistic form to setting only in terms of one-to-one matching. The 'rule-governed creativity' of speakers is not so restricted. 'Registers', for example, are not chosen only because a situation demands them; they may be chosen to define a situation, or to discover its definition by others (as when the choice can be taken in two different ways, depending on the relationship).

In the study of interrogative behaviour and modes of address, then, social anthropologists would serve their own interests while dealing with problems essential to an ethnography of speaking. There are other respects in which the contribution of social anthropology is essential, if it can be secured. I shall indicate four of these.

First, as noted above, analysis of the meaning of modes of address requires knowledge of the 'semantics' of social relationships as well as of the semantics of verbal forms. Attempts to deal with these problems from the standpoint of linguistic meanings alone cannot succeed; nor can treatments in terms of contexts alone. Each has structure of its own that is essential, but not sufficient. There are ten features of use of second-person pronouns in Russian, for example, according to Friedrich (1966), not two, because ten are needed to account for switching and other aspects of use. Yet this goes against the obvious fact (stressed by Einar Haugen in discussion in the same volume) that the Russian pronouns do essentially contrast on just the dimensions of authority and intimacy. If the additional features are packed into the pronouns, one obscures their semantic structure and leaves unexplained their varied efficacy in different situations. Nor would it serve to displace the meaning onto the contexts alone (as Malinowski's approach seemed in danger of doing); that way would lie sheer confusion. The pronouns, like features of address and style generally, have 'an identificational-contrastive' value (to use the term of Kenneth Pike, 1967), essentially that of authority and distance versus absence of authority and closeness. The personal relationships in which the terms are used have also their values on these dimensions. The additional features seen as needed by Friedrich contribute to defining the values of these situations. The actual implications of pronoun use so nicely explicated by Friedrich arise from the interaction of the two sets of values, or meanings (taking into account preceding discourse as part of situation).[19] In short, semantics and ethnography of speaking simply are not possible without social anthropology.

Second, it is essential for sociolinguistics, and ethnography of speaking as its part, to explain the absence as well as the presence of phenomena, and their differential elaboration. To take up again the example of men's and women's ways of speaking: one needs accounts of cases where there is little differentiation as well as of cases where there is much; of cases where grammar is affected and where it is not, in order to explain, if possible, why the cases where sex is marked in grammar occur. It is not, then, that intrusion of a social feature into grammar is unimportant; rather, it represents a particular linguistic means of implementing a universal function of speaking. An adequate sociolinguistic theory must have something to say about such relationships (cf. Tyler, 1965, for a suggestion with regard to one such relationship). In consequence, one cannot ask for the study of such phenomena only when they are salient and central to a language or society – one needs the full range of cases. (And it would be just the other side of the same error to do as some have suggested, to study such phenomena under the heading of 'marginal linguistics' in just the cases where they are *not* central.)

The point applies to linguistic marking of social status, of knowledge and responsibility, and any other feature of anthropological interest.[20] Anthropologists have tended to point to obligatory grammatical categories and terminological elaboration as direct expressions of a society. Here, as elsewhere, there are always two possibilities, and no general rule to decide between them in advance: the particular trait may be directly expressive, or it may be compensatory. Thus, Trukese personal names emphasize individuality, Nakanai names social relationships – both are compensatory, on Truk to secure some measure of individuality amidst pressing social obligation, on Nakani to remind ambitious individuals of social obligations (Goodenough, 1965). (One might refer to this as the 'Chinese music principle', agitated music accompanying quiet action, quiet music agitated action, in classical Chinese drama (I owe the example to Kenneth Burke's account of an experience with the musician Henry Cowell).) Moreover, a language is never a direct inventory of a culture, but always a selective metalanguage. The circumstances, and a theory, of linguistic explicitness ought to be a major problem uniting linguistics and social anthropology.

Third, a matter related to the preceding two, it is essential to sociolinguistics and the ethnography of speaking to develop an adequate theory of the kinds of speech acts and the dimensions of speech forms, both as a basis for analyses and as a result of them. The familiar task of anthropology – of providing comparative perspective – is especially needed here. In a sense this task could be described as that of providing a truly comparative rhetoric, drawing on, but transcending and establishing on a different basis, the insights of rhetoric and poetics in our own civilization.[21] In this respect the problem parallels that which confronted linguistics in reconstructing the basis of grammatical and phonological concepts in the light of the languages of mankind as a whole, and that which confronted social anthropology in reconstructing adequate dimensions for the understanding of kinship, the family, marriage, and the like. To cite two examples of kinds of problem:

1. Among the Bella Coola, private possession of a myth validates status privileges, and, during investiture, a special genre of 'outlining' serves simultaneously to manifest possession and conceal full knowledge of the myth; a similar practice is reported from the Iatmul, where a speaker cites a myth in terms of exoteric clichés, fragmenting its plot, in manifesting the correct knowledge that proves a kin claim to land while keeping outsiders in the dark. In contrast, among the Cashinaua of Brazil (Ken Kensinger, personal communication) the citation of a myth in dispute calls for verbal exactitude (whereas the ordinary narration may be interrupted, adapted to circumstances, etc.). What are the varieties of speech acts found with regard to the social function of myths? Where are they found? And how can their occurrence be explained?

2. Basil Bernstein has pioneered in the recognition of diverse varieties of speech within a single community, and with regard to England he has distinguished elaborated and restricted 'codes'. Ethnographic data indicate that the three dimensions linked to these types sort separately: 'now-coding' versus 'then-coding', personal versus positional social control, elaboration

versus limitation of verbal form. Thus two Quakers, both remarkable men, are described as follows:

> 'G's style has some sparkle at particular points, but, for the most part, it is unexciting. B, on the other hand, rose to great heights which enabled him to produce memorable and quotable prose. If G was asked why individual worship was insufficient, and therefore social worship required, his natural tendency was to quote the Bible, leaving the matter there, but B could invent an appropriate figure of speech. . . . G, to our ears, sounds pious, using largely predictable phrases, but B's expressions often have a startling freshness' (Trueblood, 1960: 146–147).

G was in fact a preacher of great influence through the eastern and southern United States. Trueblood ascribes the difference in part to B's being more nearly original in his thought. Neither social control nor limited verbal form seems involved. Again, among the Chaga, a proverb, an instance of then-coding *par excellence*, is used just because the personal feelings and motives of a child are taken into account: rather than speak directly to the child, a proverb is used to call attention indirectly to the matter for which he is at fault. Again, in a Newfoundland village, the genre of 'cuffing' is precisely an elaboration of verbal form, where, in the absence of actual news and controversy, argument over a past occurrence is carried on, but with the rule that personal involvement and feeling disqualify a participant. Faris (1966: 247) reports that there was marked reaction to his own attempts to gossip or attempt the technique of the 'cuffer', and anxiety that, as a 'stranger', 'my information was personal and not the formalised and routinised communication of local people'. (Faris notes that he did not persist in 'cuffering' attempts, but more from lack of sufficient skill than from community reaction.) Further, whole communities may seem to contrast on the personal:positional control dimension (Arapesh and Manus, according to Mead, 1937) in the handling of speech and communication, but a third independent type may also occur (Bali, according to Mead). The occurrence and interrelations of these features and dimensions, and possible related others, badly need cross-cultural investigation.

Fourth, social anthropologists have been concerned to explain the role and meaning of religion, kinship, myth, etc. As have linguists, they have tended to take the role and meaning of speech for granted, to note only that it is everywhere important. But it is not everywhere important in the same way, to the same extent or purpose. Communities vary grossly in the sheer amount of talk, in the place assigned to talk in relation to touch or sight, in trust or distrust of talk, in the proportion and kinds of roles dependent on verbal skills. While any one instance of these phenomena is likely to seem familiar, when two or more are seen to contrast – e.g. that the Bella Coola chatter incessantly whereas Paliyan men after the age of forty talk almost not at all (Gardner, 1966) – one begins to see a problem for comparative analysis. The place of speaking in human lives has hardly begun to be understood in the ways in which anthropologists would seek to understand the place of other aspects of life. With religion, kinship, and the like, one at least can argue in the light of data from many ethnographic accounts. For speaking, the ethnographic accounts are still to come.

IV

Ethnography of speaking, as sketched above, would be a linguistics that had discovered ethnographic foundations, and an ethnography that had discovered linguistic content, in relation to the knowledge and abilities for use of knowledge (competence) of the persons whose communities were studied. 'Sociolinguistics', it was said, is a term of a type that mediates between disciplines. Its currency reflects general recognition that inherited disciplinary boundaries do not suffice, their unity being as much social as intellectual. In the study of man, as in Christian churches and radical movements, once-vital distinctions seem about as pertinent to present needs as disputes between medieval baronies. We can no longer believe wholeheartedly in disciplines with exclusive claims on levels of reality or regions of the world. The institutionalizations that confront us appear as obstacles as often as they do as aids. Pursuing a problem, or a student's training, one continually finds the unity of both fragmented among disciplines and faculties.

Still, I do not think that the answer is to create new disciplines, even though 'sociolinguistics' may have in it the makings of one. What is needed is opportunity to combine the kinds of training and knowledge required to pursue sociolinguistic problems, in short, flexibility in institutional structures. Whether the centre be a faculty of linguistics or anthropology or sociology, a School of English, or some of these jointly, is secondary, and depends on local conditions and initiatives. What is primary, given recognition of the field, is the means to pursue it.

Anthropology has here a special opportunity and, one might say, even responsibility. Of the sciences concerned with men, it has the closest and fullest ties with linguistics. In principle it already recognizes linguistic research as part of its concern, and already includes some acquaintance with language and linguistics in its training. The required combination of training in linguistics and in social analysis can perhaps be effected under the aegis of anthropology more readily than under any other. (Important here also is the humanistic aspect of anthropology, its ties with attention to texts and verbal art.) There being a social need for such training, anthropology would enhance its recognized relevance in sponsoring it. And in so far as the internal unity and direction of anthropology are in question, it may be fair to say that problems of the sort described in this paper could be one centre of unity, a new one that would be yet in some respects but a renewal of some of anthropology's oldest concerns at the centre of contemporary social and scientific problems.

NOTES

1. I should like to thank Clare Hall for the fellowship that has made possible a year of acquaintance with linguistics and social anthropology in Great Britain; the National Institute of Mental Health (US) and the Guggenheim Foundation for support of work on which it is based; and colleagues at Cambridge for their interest in it. I have benefited from opportunities to discuss some of the matters raised here at the Universities of Birmingham, Edinburgh, Leeds, London, Oxford, and York.

2. This term also occurred at least a decade before it came into common use (Currie, 1952); cf. Wallis (1956).

3. The need for such a scientific basis has provoked critical comment (e.g. the inaugural address of Alisjahbana, 1965).

4. The practical relevance of sociolinguistics is a mixed blessing. It adds the justification of social relevance to a development that has a logic and importance within science itself; and work that is practically motivated can bring to light and help to solve issues of theory (cf. Hymes, 1971a, with regard to 'disadvantaged' children). Research funds being scarce, and their sources sometimes short-sighted, however, energies are too often diverted into providing materials for which there has not been the chance to develop a scientifically adequate basis.

Practical concerns are sometimes associated with 'macro-', as distinct from 'micro-', sociolinguistics. The distinction sometimes reflects different priorities, and differences in professional origin. Some are attracted to work on large populations, and national institutions and policies, as being of more social relevance and theoretical importance. Others are attracted to work with small communities and social interaction, as offering a greater prospect of developing secure methodology and theory. Again, sociolinguistics is for some a new application of known social science; for others, an extension (and revision) of linguistics. The former may devise new questions and scales, the latter expand the scope of linguistic rules. Each may wonder about the validity and rigour of the other.

Obviously none of these differences need be one of principle. There are advances in method and theory to be made in the comparative study of larger social systems; rules of verbal interaction in a small community may be of immediate relevance for its teachers and schools. Policies and nation-wide generalizations should be based on close knowledge of actual situations, just as local situations cannot be adequately understood in isolation. Use of quantitative and interview techniques presupposes close-grained qualitative analysis, and formal analysis of the sort congenial to linguists must come to terms with quantitative variables and social features. It remains that few have been able to balance practical relevance and scientific advance, and that perspectives that articulate the relations between 'micro-' and 'macro-' sociolinguistics are rare. (Several approaches are represented in papers by Albert, Bernstein, Fischer, Fishman, Garfinkel, Labov, and Roberts, in Gumperz and Hymes, 1972.)

5. See, now, the development of this theme by Lefebvre, 1966 (Ch. 8, 'La Forme marchandise et le discours', esp. pp. 348 ff.). Thoughts of my own are found in papers of 1961, 1966c, and 1967a: 646. The analogy with Marx's critique of economics was part of a prepared discussion of 'Marxism and Sociology' by I. M. Zeitlin, at a symposium of the Socialist Scholars Conference, New York, September 1967. Cf. Barthes's notion of *l'écriture* (1953), Bernstein (1964), Darnell and Sherzer (1972), and Hymes (1961, 1966b).

6. It will, of course, remain possible to speak of 'ethnolinguistics' as a field in which progress can be gauged (Whiteley, 1966: 154n.9), in so far as one is speaking of a relation between linguistics and anthropology, exclusive of other disciplines. This relation is most likely to remain specific for historical problems. Among social scientists, only anthropologists are likely to be found proposing genetic relationships, reconstructing vocabularies, tracing population movements and diffusion through loan-words, etc. It remains to be seen to what extent the extension of other social sciences to work in areas conventionally anthropological (Africa, Asia) will lead to a sharing of synchronic interests in language. When one wants to designate a branch of anthropology parallel to 'physical' and 'social', 'linguistic anthropology' will continue to recommend itself.

This discussion of terminology draws on Hymes (1966a), which goes into greater detail from the standpoint of anthropology. Such reflexive use of our means for understanding other cultures – here, analysis of terminology – seems to me essential. It tests our methods and our self-knowledge against each other.

7. This is not to define linguistics as part of anthropology (though some linguists have done so), parallel to, but opposing, Chomsky's definition of linguistics as a branch of cognitive psychology. Comparative Indo-European and Romance linguistics are hardly confined to being parts of either anthropology or psychology. Such statements are possible only if one ignores or denies part of linguistics itself, or moves to a level of abstraction remote from actual practice. For a view of the place of linguistics within a more general field, see Hymes (1968a).

8. As long realized, of course, and pointed out by Mair (1935) in criticizing 'linguistics without sociology', and by J. R. Firth (1935), advocating 'sociological linguistics', in the same year as *Coral Gardens* also. A decade later Nida (1945: 208 (in Hymes, 1964b: 97)) advocated a 'combination of analytical social anthropology and descriptive linguistics [as] . . . the key to the study of semantics'. Two decades later, Whiteley has advocated the combination afresh in a valuable paper (1966). The reiteration suggests that a common-sense principle has yet to become a commonplace of practice. This interpretation would seem to be borne out by a sentence in a recent Malinowski memorial lecture: 'Would not then an analysis of the words used directly in the ritual advance this kind of interpretation further?' (Tambiah, 1968: 200n.2.) That a social anthropologist should find it necessary to propose this to his colleagues in the year 33 CG (after *Coral Gardens*)! Especially since the very point is consciously important within the established church of their own society. The Scottish church insists on an order in the service the opposite of the English because a fundamental point of doctrine is involved (Buchanan, 1968: 143–144). The precise choice of words, or even use of words at all, poses unresolved problems (Buchanan, 1968: 13, 21). Regarding a desire for a 'definite association of the people' with the preparation of the Table for the eucharist, one finds:

> 'The fact that the laymen bring the elements to the Table . . . whether during a hymn or during silence, does not of itself convey any representative symbolism or include the congregation as a whole. The introduction of a formula can change that, but immediately words are introduced they seem to say too much. . . . Texts appropriate to gifts of money cannot of themselves say anything very helpful about the elements. Recourse is then had to symbolism; but . . . This is not to say that the Lambeth statement has had no effect on texts. The big effect, already noted, is in the "Accept us in him" terminology. This clearly has many years to run, as it comes not only in the LFA [Liturgy for Africans], but also in its derivatives EAUL [East African United Liturgy] and NZ [New Zealand Episcopal Liturgy]. It is a far less controversial form than open self-oblation, for it emphasizes both God's grace, and the mediation of it by Jesus Christ. But another decade may well show that this phraseology is a liturgical by-product of a late doctrinal formulation, and it may thus go back into the melting-pot, as Christians strive to find exactly what they do want to say at this point of the eucharistic prayer.'

9. There were always some linguists who insisted on the social character of linguistics, but without much effect on the character of linguistic description or the foci of attention.

10. If 'deep structure' and 'surface structure' are to be used as terms in

anthropology, any analogue to linguistic structure should be explicitly disavowed, if some such formal, transformative relationship between levels is not intended. In particular, it would wholly miss the point of Chomsky's linguistic theory to regard deep structure as simply a more abstract set of patterns of the same sort as the patterns of surface structure. The point is that the levels of structure are related in a finite system of generative principles. I should add that it is not necessary that the relation be expressed in terms of a concept of 'rule'. (Some linguists, notably Lamb, maintain that 'rule' is inappropriate.) The points made here, as to linguistics and ethnography, would still hold, whatever the manner of formulating the systematic relations underlying sentences and acts of speech.

11. In a conversation (July 1968), Chomsky remarked that the original competence/performance dichotomy was inadequate, in reference to my critique of it (Hymes, 1971a). This essay develops in more detail the points being made here.

12. Conversation interaction may proceed in terms of awareness of frequencies of features, as when Prague speakers are reported to move from the phonology of standard Czech to that of conversational Czech by degrees. Japanese are said to be able to identify foreigners who have learnt the language formally because their speech is too correct. Here belongs 'the distinction between the merely and marginally possible and the actually normal: between what one will accept as a hearer and what one will produce as a speaker' (Quirk, 1968: 195). The category also allows the feature of social life summed up in the medieval rubric, *factum valet* (Harold Garfinkel, personal communication): something contrary to rule may be accepted, in fact done, e.g.:

> 'The prefix "The" is now by general custom used in addressing the daughters of dukes, marquesses and earls, e.g., "The Lady Jean Smith". Although it should therefore be used, the practice exists only by courtesy, and is not recognized as correct by, for example, the College of Arms' (*Titles and Forms of Address*, 1967 edn: 45).

13. The simplistic view of transformational generative grammar is that competence is essentially a maturational unfolding. Many hold the equally simplistic view that quantity of exposure should shape children's speech (a view once put forward to explain linguistic change by Bloomfield, 1933). In fact, of course, maturation and exposure both play some role, but identification and motivation are equally fundamental. Many black boys use substandard speech, not through interference with unfolding or lack of exposure, but as a sign of masculinity. Is it surprising that black lower-class boys do not take white middle-class women teachers as models? Non-standard-speaking children hear as much TV and radio as other children, and their teachers all day. At Columbia Point School (Boston) last summer, in a discussion in which teachers had raised just these points, the one black mother present observed: 'I've noticed that when the children play "school" outside, they talk like they're supposed to in school; and when they stop playing school, they don't.'

14. E.g. in a review of records by Joan Chissell (*The Times Saturday Review*, 5 April 1969):

> 'Stephen Bishop . . . in Beethoven's Diabelli Variations, a work which did much to make his name on the concert platform. Here, the daemonic, visionary Beethoven takes a bit longer to break out than when aided and abetted by audience reaction, but progressively Bishop's superb strength and discipline take fire. . . .'

15. An entry from *Pears Cyclopaedia* (Barker, 1968–69) illustrates this point, and a further one of some importance:

> '1901. Queen Victoria dies, Jan. 22. Trans-Siberian railway opened for single-track traffic.'

For many people, as for myself, this entry is momentarily humorous. One can read it in terms of Sacks's maxim: *post hoc, ergo propter hoc*. The railway opened for single-track traffic *once* (because) Queen Victoria had died. This response reflects the fact that discourse, like syntax, has ambiguities, entailing relation of a surface structure to more than one underlying structure. Were only Sacks's maxim applicable, there would be only a puzzling causal relationship. Were only conventions of chronicle applicable, no relationship except occurrene in thce same year would be considered. The humour is in entertaining the causal connection of narrative where one knows it is not intended (conjuring up perhaps an image of Queen Victoria bodily blocking the single track). Notice that the discourse rules are seen to be context-sensitive to genre (narrative, chronicle). An important part of humour, and creative use of language generally, is to be understood in terms of such *conjunction* (simultaneous derivation, not selection of a single derivation, as in disambiguation). Use of this resource of language seems to vary a great deal cross-culturally, and competence for it probably depends very much upon cultural context.

16. My understanding of these issues owes much to Kenneth Burke, who has long insisted on analysis of language as the enacting of strategies to encompass situations (see the title essay in his *Philosophy of Literary Form*, 1941). Burke has also pointed out the value of theology, as well as of poetics and rhetoric, for the understanding of verbal action. In general, anthropology has much to gain from the disciplines of rhetoric, literary criticism, and textual interpretation. Both points are nicely exemplified in the parables of Jesus. The early Church interpreted the parables allegorically; critical scholarship freed them from that in the late nineteenth century, but form-criticism, despite some insights, failed when it tried to treat them in terms of formal distinctions not present in the original Aramaic folk-category (*mashal*). Recent work has established the primacy of two considerations: reconstruction of the original linguistic form (Aramaic), wherever possible, by triangulation from the variant Greek, Syriac, and Hebrew renderings, and reconstruction of the place of a parable in Jesus' career, as 'uttered in an actual situation . . . at a particular and often unforeseen point . . . they were preponderantly concerned with a situation of conflict' (Jeremias, 1963: 21). A major cause of misinterpretation was the tendency of Gospel writers and the Church to take the parables as addressed to their own subsequent situation rather than as addressed (as was the case) to an immediate situation, often to an opponent or doubting outsider. The parables are *par excellence* instances of what Chomsky (1966) terms the 'creative' aspect of language use, an essential criterion of which he gives as appropriateness of new sentences to novel situations; and they bring to the fore what Chomsky omits, the dialectic relation. Chomsky analyses the grammatical conditions for sentences to be independent of control by a situation; the ethnography of speaking investigates the conditions for sentences to define and change situations.

On the crux in Mark 4: 10–13, as to Jesus' own intention, Moule (1966: 149–151) defends the authenticity of the saying, but fails to deal with the linguistic and contextual evidence for its being an interpolation here (Jeremias, 1963: 13–18). Hunter (1964: 110–122) reviews the problem, adopting Jeremias's solution. (All authors agree that the apparent meaning that the parables are intended to prevent outsiders from understanding is wrong.) The issue hinges on two conjunctions, the original Aramaic *de*, which can mean 'who', whereas the NT Greek *hina* can mean only 'that', and the original Aramaic *dilema*, to be taken (as rabbinical exegesis shows) as 'unless', not as 'lest'. The necessity of original text – *pace* Lévi-Strauss, and some of his followers – for accurate understanding of fundamental relationships, the inadequacy of translations, could not be more clearly demonstrated.

17. Cf. Greenberg (1968: 36) for use of 'speech forms' in this sense.

18. I share Denison's approach, differing in terminology. As he implies, functional variety is fundamental. The difficulty with some recent writing on speech functions is that elaboration of categories, names, and definitions may obscure the empirical, problematic nature of the problem. What one can hope to establish as universal is relevant questions and dimensions or features of contrast, not a limited number of categorical types.

19. Cf. Gluckman (1959), where two or three Barotse terms for property concepts serve complex judicial proceedings, through interaction with a complex vocabulary for relationships among persons.

20. Missionary linguists may be specially interested in the conditions in which a language gives grammatical status to a major theological category, such as *kerygma*. The development of an approach to language as situated action, as against a purely semantic and formal approach, parallels, if much less successfully, the development of a view of theological interpretation as directed to *kerygma*, the proclamation of the Church as an act (and of Christ, indeed, in some writing, as a word-event) for which one takes responsibility, as against mere acceptance of institutional authority and credal propositions. The distinction is grammatical in Siona (Wheeler, 1967). One mode-aspect indicates awareness of the circumstances of the action of a verb, as opposed to non-awareness (definite:indefinite), and association with them, as opposed to no responsibility for them (involvement:non-involvement). Wheeler (1967: 71–73) translated Bible narrative in the 'definite involvement' mode; informants then, and most Siona still, retold it as they would a myth, or another person's experience, in the 'indefinite non-involvement' mode, 'but a few have accepted the Scripture as God's personal communication to them and narrate it to others in the definite involvement mode' (p. 73). Cf. Ebeling (1966, Ch. I, III (2), VI (3)); Kasper (1969: 29–32, 42n.1., 47–51); Richardson (1961, Ch. 5, Ch. 6: 126 ff.), from Lutheran, Catholic, and Episcopalian standpoints, respectively.

21. Cf. Burke (1950: 43): 'We are not so much proposing to import anthropology into rhetoric, as proposing that anthropologists recognize the factor of rhetoric in their own field.'

REFERENCES

ALBERT, ETHEL. 1972. Culture Patterning of Speech Behaviour in Burundi (with special attention to 'rhetoric', 'logic', and 'poetics'). In Gumperz and Hymes (eds.), 1972.

ALISJAHBANA, S. T. 1965. *The Failure of Modern Linguistics in the face of Linguistic Problems of the Twentieth Century*. Kuala Lumpur: University of Malaya.

BARKER, L. M. (ed.). 1968–69. *Pears Cyclopaedia*. 77th edn. London: Pelham Books.

BARTHES, R. 1953. *Le Degré zéro de l'écriture*. Paris: Le Seuil.

BERNSTEIN, B. 1964. Elaborated and Restricted Codes: Their Social Origins and some Consequences. In J. J. Gumperz and D. Hymes (eds.), *The Ethnography of Communication*, pp. 55–69. Menasha, Wis.: American Anthropological Association.

BLOOMFIELD, L. 1933. *Language*. New York: Holt.

BOAS, F. 1911. *Handbook of American Indian Languages*. Washington, DC: Smithsonian Institution.

BUCHANAN, C. O. (ed.). 1968. *Modern Anglican Liturgies 1958–1968*. London: Oxford University Press.

BURKE, KENNETH, 1941. *Philosophy of Literary Form*. Baton Rouge: Louisiana State University Press. (Variously reprinted.)

—— 1950. *A Rhetoric of Motives*. Englewood Cliffs, N.J.: Prentice Hall.

CHATMAN, S., and LEVIN, S. E. (eds.). 1966. *Essays on the Language of Literature*. Boston, Mass.: Houghton Mifflin.

CHOMSKY, NOAM. 1957. *Syntactic Structures*. The Hague: Mouton.

—— 1965. *Aspects of the Theory of Syntax*. Cambridge, Mass.: MIT Press.

—— 1966. *Cartesian Linguistics*. New York: Harper & Row.

—— 1968. *Language and Mind*. New York: Harcourt, Brace & World.

CONANT, F. P. 1961. Jarawa Kin Systems of Reference and Address. *Anthropological Linguistics* **3** (2): 19–33.

CURRIE, H. C. 1952. A Projection of Socio-linguistics: The Relationships of Speech to Social Status. *Southern Speech Journal* **18**: 28–37.

DANEŠ, F. 1964. A Three-level Approach to Syntax. *Travaux linguistiques de Prague* **1**: 225–240.

DARNELL, R., and SHERZER, J. 1972. A Field Guide to the Study of Speech Use. (Outline.) In Gumperz and Hymes (eds.), 1972.

DECAMP, D. 1968. Toward a Generative Analysis of a Post-creole Speech Continuum. In Hymes (ed.), 1971b.

DENISON, NORMAN. 1968. Sauris: A Trilingual Community in Diatypic Perspective. *Man* (n.s.) **3** (4): 578–592.

DILLARD, J. 1968. The Creolist and the Study of Negro Non-standard Dialects in the United States. In Hymes (ed.), 1971b.

EBELING, G. 1966. *Theology and Proclamation: A Discussion with Rudolf Bultmann*. London: Collins.

FARIS, J. C. 1966. The Dynamics of Verbal Exchange: A Newfoundland Example. *Anthropologica* **8** (2): 235–248.

FERGUSON, C. A., and GUMPERZ, J. J. (eds.). 1960. *Linguistic Diversity in South Asia: Studies in Regional, Social and Functional Variation*. (*International Journal of American Linguistics* **26** (3), Part III.) Bloomington: Indiana University Research

Center in Anthropology, Folklore and Linguistics, Publication 13.

FIRTH, J. R. 1935. The Technique of Semantics. *Transactions of the Philological Society* (London): 36–72.

FISCHER, J. L. 1964. Linguistic and Social Interaction in Two Communities. In J. J. Gumperz and D. Hymes (eds.), *The Ethnography of Communication*, pp. 115–126. Menasha, Wis.: American Anthropological Association.

FISHMAN, J., FERGUSON, C. A., and DAS GUPTA, J. (eds.). 1968. *Language Problems of Developing Nations*. New York: Wiley.

FRIEDRICH, PAUL. 1966. Structural Implications of Russian Pronominal Usage. In W. Bright (ed.), *Sociolinguistics*, pp. 214–253. The Hague: Mouton.

GARDNER, P. M. 1966. Symmetric Respect and Memorate Knowledge: The Structure and Ecology of Individualistic Culture. *Southwestern Journal of Anthropology* **22**: 389–415.

GLUCKMAN, MAX. 1959. The Technical Vocabulary of Barotse Jurisprudence. *American Anthropologist* **61**: 743–759.

— 1963. Gossip and Scandal. *Current Anthropology* **4**: 307–315.

GOODENOUGH, W. H. 1965. Personal Names and Modes of Address in Two Oceanic Societies. In M. E. Spiro (ed.), *Context and Meaning in Cultural Anthropology*, pp. 265–276. New York: Free Press.

GREENBERG, J. 1968. *Anthropological Linguistics*. New York: Random House.

GUIRAUD, P. 1961. *La Stylistique*. Third edition. Paris: Presses Universitaires de France.

GUMPERZ, J. J., and HYMES, D. (eds.). 1972. *Directions in Sociolinguistics*. New York: Holt, Rinehart & Winston.

GUNTER, R. 1966. On the Placement of Accent in Dialogue: A Feature of Context Grammar. *Journal of Linguistics* **2**: 159–179.

HALLIDAY, M. A. K. 1967. Notes on Transitivity and Theme in English, Part II. *Journal of Linguistics* **3** (2).

HASAN, RUQAIYA. 1968. *Grammatical Cohesion in Spoken and Written English*, Part one. (Programme in Linguistics and English teaching, Paper 7.) London: Longmans.

HUNTER, A. M. 1964. *Interpreting the Parables*. Second edition. London: SCM Press.

HYMES, D. 1961. Functions of Speech: An Evolutionary Approach. In F. Gruber (ed.), *Anthropology and Education*, pp. 55–83. Philadelphia: University of Pennsylvania Press. (Bobbs-Merrill Reprints.)

— 1962. The Ethnography of Speaking. In T. Gladwin and W. C.

Sturtevant (eds.), *Anthropology and Human Behavior*. Washington, DC: Anthropological Society of Washington. Reprinted in J. Fishman (ed.), *Readings in the Sociology of Language*. The Hague: Mouton, 1968.

HYMES, D. 1964a. Directions in (Ethno-)linguistic Theory. In A. K. Romney and R. G. D'Andrade (eds.), *Transcultural Studies in Cognition*, pp. 6–56. Washington: American Anthropological Association.

— (ed.). 1964b. *Language in Culture and Society*. New York: Harper & Row.

— 1966a. On 'Anthropological Linguistics' and Congeners. *American Anthropologist* **68**: 143–153.

— 1966b. Two Types of Linguistic Relativity. In W. Bright (ed.), *Sociolinguistics*, pp. 114–157. The Hague: Mouton.

— 1966c. Sociolinguistic Determination of Knowledge. Paper prepared for Research Committee on sociology of knowledge. Inter. Soc. Assn.

— 1967a. Why Linguistics Needs the Sociologist. *Social Research* **34**: 632–647.

— 1967b. Models of the Interaction of Language and Social Setting. *Journal of Social Issues* **23** (2): 8–28.

— 1968a. Linguistics – the Field. In D. L. Sills (ed.), *International Encyclopedia of the Social Sciences*. New York and London: Collier/Macmillan.

— 1968b. The 'Wife' who 'Goes Out' like a Man. *Social Science Information* **7** (3): 173–199.

— 1968c. Linguistic Problems in Defining the Concept of 'Tribe'. In J. Helm (ed.), *Essays on the Problem of Tribe*, pp. 23–48. Seattle: University of Washington Press.

— 1971a. *On Communicative Competence*. Philadelphia: University of Pennsylvania Press.

— (ed.). 1971b. *Pidginization and Creolization of Languages*. Cambridge: Cambridge University Press.

JEREMIAS, J. 1963. *The Parables of Jesus*. Revised edition. London: SCM Press. Translated from the German, *Die Gleichnisse Jesu*, by S. H. Hooke.

KASPER, WALTER. 1969. *The Methods of Dogmatic Theology*. Shannon: Ecclesia Press. Translated from the German, *Die Methoden der Dogmatik – Einheit und Vielheit*, by John Drury.

KATZ, J. J., and FODOR, J. 1963. The Structure of a Semantic Theory. *Language* **39**: 170–210.

KIPARSKY, P. 1968. Tense and Mood in Indo-European Syntax. *Foundations of Language* **4**: 30–57.

LABOV, W. A. 1966. *The Social Stratification of English in New York City*. Washington, DC: Center for Applied Linguistics.

—— 1969. Contraction, Deletion, and Inherent Variability of the English Copula. (Paper circulated to Conference on Pidginization and Creolization of Languages, Mona, Jamaica, 1968.) *Language* **45**: 715–752.

LEACH, E. R. (ed.). 1967. *The Structural Study of Myth and Totemism*. ASA Monograph 5. London: Tavistock.

LEFEBVRE, H. 1966. *Le Langage et la société*. Paris: Gallimard.

LYONS, J. 1968. *Introduction to Theoretical Linguistics*. Cambridge: Cambridge University Press.

MAIR, L. 1935. Linguistics without Sociology: Some Notes on the Standard Luganda Dictionary. *Bulletin of the School of Oriental Studies* **7**: 913–921.

MALINOWSKI, B. 1920. Classificatory Particles in the Language of Kiriwina. *Bulletin of the School of Oriental Studies* **1** (4): **33–78.**

—— 1935. *Coral Gardens and their Magic*. London: Allen & Unwin.

MANDELBAUM, D. G. (ed.). 1949. *Selected Writings of Edward Sapir*. Berkeley and Los Angeles: University of California Press; Cambridge: Cambridge University Press, 1950.

MCCAWLEY, J. 1968. The Role of Semantics in a Grammar. In E. Bach and R. T. Harms (eds.), *Universals in Linguistic Theory*, pp. 125–170. New York: Holt, Rinehart & Winston.

MEAD, M. 1937. Public Opinion Mechanisms among Primitive Peoples. *Public Opinion Quarterly* **1**: 5–16.

MILLS, C. W. 1959. *The Sociological Imagination*. New York: Oxford University Press.

MOULE, C. F. D. 1966. *The Birth of the New Testament*. Second edition. London: Adam & Charles Black.

MURPHY, R. F. 1967. Tuareg Kinship. *American Anthropologist* **69**: 163–170.

NIDA, E. A. 1945. Linguistics and Ethnology in Translation Problems. *Word* **1**: 194–208. Also in Hymes (ed.), 1964b.

PIKE, K. L. 1967. *Language in relation to a Unified Theory of the Structure of Human Behavior*. The Hague: Mouton.

QUIRK, R. 1968. *Essays on the English Language, Medieval and Modern*. London: Longmans.

REICHEL-DOLMATOFF, G. and A. 1961. *The People of Aritama*. Chicago: University of Chicago Press.

RICHARDSON, ALAN. 1961. *The Bible in the Age of Science*. London: SCM Press.

RUBIN, J. 1968. *National Bilingualism in Paraguay*. The Hague: Mouton.

SACKS, H. 1972. Two Lectures on the Analysis of Children's Stories. In Gumperz and Hymes (eds.), 1972.

SAPIR, E. 1912. Language and Environment. In Mandelbaum (ed.), 1949, pp. 89–103.

— 1921. *Language*. New York: Harcourt, Brace.

— 1925. Sound Patterns in Language. In Mandelbaum (ed.), 1949, pp. 33–45.

— 1927. Speech as a Personality Trait. In Mandelbaum (ed.), 1949, pp. 533–543.

— 1934. The Emergence of the Concept of Personality in a Study of Cultures. In Mandelbaum (ed.), 1949, pp. 590–597.

— 1938. Why Cultural Anthropology Needs the Psychiatrist. In Mandelbaum (ed.), 1949, pp. 569–577.

SAUSSURE, F. DE. 1916. *Cours de linguistique générale*. Paris: Payot.

SCHEGLOFF, E. 1972. Sequencing in Conversational Openings. In Gumperz and Hymes (eds.), 1972.

SCHNEIDER, D. G. 1969. Componential Analysis – a State-of-the-Art Review. Prepared for Wenner-Gren Symposium on 'Cognitive Studies and Artificial Intelligence Research', Chicago.

SHERZER, J. 1967. An Exploration into the Ethnography of Speaking of the Abipones. M.A. dissertation, Dept. of Linguistics, University of Pennsylvania,

STEINMANN, M., JR (ed.). 1967. *New Rhetorics*. New York: Scribners.

TAMBIAH, S. J. 1968. The Magical Power of Words. *Man* **3**: 175–208.

THORNE, J. P. 1969. *The Grammar of Jealousy*. Edinburgh Studies in English and Scots. London: Longmans.

TILLICH, P. 1964. *Theology of Culture*. New York: Oxford University Press.

Titles and Forms of Address: A Guide to their Correct Use. 1967. 13th edition. London: Adam & Charles Black.

TRUEBLOOD, D. E. 1960. Robert Barclay and Joseph John Gurney. In A. Brinton (ed.), *Then and Now: Quaker Essays . . .*, pp. 131–150. Philadelphia: University of Pennsylvania Press.

TULISANO, R., and COLE, J. T. 1965. Is Terminology Enough? *American Anthropologist* **67**: 747–748.

TYLER, S. A. 1965. Koya Language Morphology and Patterns of Kinship Behavior. *American Anthropologist* **67**: 428–441.

— 1966. Context and Variation in Koya Kinship Terminology. *American Anthropologist* **68**: 693–708. Revised in Gumperz and Hymes (eds.), 1972.

WALLIS, E. E. 1956. Sociolinguistics in relation to Mezquital

Transition Education. In *Estudios antropológicos publicado en homenaje al doctor Manuel Gamio*, pp. 523–535. Mexico, DF: Sociedad Mexicana de Antropológica.

WHEELER, A. 1967. Grammatical Structure in Siona Discourse. *Lingua* **19**: 60–77.

WHITELEY, W. H. 1966. Social Anthropology, Meaning and Linguistics. *Man* (n.s.) **1**: 139–157.

WILLIAMS, R. 1961. *The Long Revolution*. London: Chatto & Windus.

J. B. Pride

Customs and Cases of Verbal Behaviour[1]

'. . . once one admits that what we empirically observe is not "customs", but "cases" of human behaviour, it seems . . . that we cannot escape the concept of choice in our analysis: our central problem becomes what are the constraints and incentives that canalize choices'.

F. BARTH, *Models of Social Organization*

A TRANSACTIONAL APPROACH TO SOCIOLINGUISTICS

In these three thought-provoking essays Barth (1966) puts forward a transactional theory of human behaviour which seeks to describe and explain the processes that 'generate' patterns of regularity in the social structure. In place of the view that sees human behaviour as very largely predictable, in terms of 'rights and duties' associated with conventionally given status positions, there is the alternative that recognizes the crucial function of transactions between people, mediating between considerations of 'value' on the one hand and institutionalized society on the other. Participants in any interaction enter reciprocally into 'transactional bargains', in which they seek to match (by selectively expressing and playing down – E. Goffman calls this process 'impression management') their respective statuses, such that for each participant 'the value gained . . . is greater or equal to the value lost' (Barth, 1966: 4). Social institutions and social roles alike, stereotyped though they may seem to be, are the changing offshoots of individual actions and the motivations that lie behind these. In particular, the role of the entrepreneur is seen as crucial.[2]

Such forms of reasoning (here, of course, extremely curtailed) have considerable bearing on the nature of linguistic behaviour. First, a much-needed theoretical perspective is lent to the problem of reconciling the descriptive study of regularities in the social structure (including their linguistic components) with understanding of the nature of the 'autonomy of the organism' (Chomsky, 1959) – that is to say, of the individual human being himself; the study of institutions at the sociocultural level is joined with that of individual behaviours at the face-to-face level. Second, and related, one rather persistent objection to the feasibility of studying language in its 'contexts of situation', namely that contexts are 'infinite' and hence 'below the level of a general abstract theory' (Berry, 1966: xv), is countered: finiteness is provided for in the assumption of 'a much simpler set and distribution of basic values' which, as the currency of transactions, distinguish for participants which of their statuses should form the basis for their interaction; and, equally important, it is assumed that there are distinct limits on the possible number of perceived statuses for any given society. Third, the continuity of social process is asserted over the *status quo* of social system. Fourth, special attention is directed to those perhaps crucial cases in which participants face the problem of conflicting values and statuses, crucial because these may be the growing-points of new customs and institutions. And fifth – not least – one is invited to identify more closely the substantive nature of cultural values relevant to choice of language.

Present-day sociolinguistics (a common label for the study of 'language in culture and society') appears to be moving rather gradually away from the very widespread assumption of the separability (hence correlatability) of 'language' and its 'situations' of use (with or without deterministic relationships pointing one way or the other).[3] The implications of the conviction that each will, on the contrary, often be part and parcel of the other are considerable. If, for example, one takes just one aspect of 'situation', norms of social behaviour, these are taken to be (a) always communicative,[4] and (b) often inextricably linguistic; while if one throws main emphasis not on normative but on transactional social behaviour, the same holds good.

A very recent example of the approach that gives priority to the separability and correlatability (hence mutual predictability) of 'language' and 'situation', moreover that regards the latter as in all important respects observable, is Fishman's team study of bilingualism among a section of the Puerto Rican population of New York City (Fishman, 1968).[5] At one point Fishman states:

> 'The variety most likely to be employed by a *cleric* preaching to *parishioners* on a specific *religious topic* in the *place of worship* can be predicted more confidently than can more "all purpose" predictions flowing from identification with community intimacy values, or from participation in the religious domain, or from cleric–parishioner role relationships more generally' (p. 981).

The emphasis throughout this investigation on data that can be empirically observed and accurately predicted[6] underlies several far-reaching theoretical and descriptive decisions. These include decisions to relate 'value clusters' to far more concrete 'domains' of language use; to resolve domains in turn into constituent 'role relations', without attempting to reduce the huge variety of such relations to the more manageable proportions of statuses, their concomitant rights and duties, or to sets of cultural values which enter into the mechanics of impression management; and to pay relatively little attention to those cases of 'code-switching' which reflect or signal shifts in interpersonal relations rather than relate to alterations in more observable features of the environment. Each will be discussed in turn.

The value clusters that attract Fishman's attention are precisely two, namely the 'high culture' that emphasizes distance and power relationships, formality and ritual, and the 'low culture' of ethnicity, spontaneity, comradeship, intimacy, etc. Stable bilingualism (which is here called 'diglossia') is the linguistic realization of complementarity between the two sets of values, the languages being referred to accordingly as 'high' (H) and 'low' (L) respectively. H and L are said to be predictable in terms of an individual's acceptance of each value cluster, and such acceptance – it is argued – can be inferred 'from manifest behaviour by trained observers'; or by reviewing with a subject 'his daily activities, his interest and beliefs, his friends and associates, his duties and responsibilities, his likes and dislikes, etc.'; or alternatively it can be self-reported by the more sophisticated members of the community (p. 971). But Fishman goes on to point out that relationships between values and choice of language will also vary with educational, occupational, and other networks within the community. 'Value clusters are much grosser and looser abstractions than speech varieties' (p. 974). Accordingly, main emphasis is shifted to the category of 'domain', the best definition of which may be this from an earlier paper:

> 'A sociocultural construct abstracted from topics of communication, relationships and interactions between communicators and locales of communication in accord with the institutions of a society and the spheres of activity of a culture in such a way that individual behaviour and social patterns can be distinguished from each other and yet related to each other' (Fishman, 1966: 430).

Domains are 'the most common institutional arenas in which cultural identifications are enacted' (p. 974). Correspondingly, one will expect to find 'two complementary sets of domains, in each one of which one variety or another is clearly dominant' (p. 975).

It is important to note that the scope of Ferguson's earlier use of the term 'diglossia' (Ferguson, 1959) has been very considerably broadened (see also Fishman, 1967). Ferguson had used the term to designate certain very special (but not uncommon) situations in which two varieties of one language stand in markedly complementary positions in respect of rather specific prestige patterns, relative order of learning, appropriate domains, directions and modes of borrowing, structural (especially grammatical) features, etc. 'High' and 'low' are for Fishman very much more general notions, applied, moreover, to distinct languages as well as to varieties of single languages.[7] On the cultural side they seem to dichotomize a universal phenomenon which Fishman has elsewhere argued to be most fruitfully regarded as a continuous scale, that of ethnicity (Fishman, 1965). On the social-psychological side they appear to stand at opposite ends of each of two scales of interpersonal relationship, those of power (authority, dominance, etc.), on the one hand, and solidarity (intimacy, affiliation, etc.), on the other. Terms such as formality, intimacy, familiarity, distance, spontaneity, and the like recur frequently in connection with these two 'major value clusters'. This is not least the case in that part of the Report that aims to describe the major ethnographic characteristics of the New York Puerto Rican community (Hoffman, 1968), even though three value clusters, not two, are here put forward. These are, namely: sex role differentiation ('Spanish is the language of the sex roles that are more traditional, more basic and more idealized', p. 34); family unity (including kinship) and ethnic ties (Spanish is the language of the home); and 'fatalism' (the more formal the human organizations that seek to cope with forces beyond man's control the more likely they are to conduct their business in English).

The careful lack of involvement in this Report with the finer detail of cultural values[8] extends downwards from the concept of domain to the more concrete concept of their constituent role relations. It is stated:

> '. . . the role relationships themselves may be more parsimoniously (though abstractly) groupable or clusterable into a very few types, such as predominantly open and closed relationships (networks), relationships between weaker and stronger interlocutors . . . younger and older interlocutors, etc.' (p. 978).

Further comment is restricted to the question of network type. Open networks are specified as those that allow relatively greater freedom of choice as between 'high' and 'low' language; it is further pointed out that, unlike values *vis-à-vis* domains, and domains *vis-à-vis* role relations, network types do not stand in a branching relationship with role relations. Thus characteristics of open networks like 'shared experience of great danger, great intimacy, etc.' may certainly affect choice of H or L, but will bear no necessarily predictable relationship with such role relations as may happen to apply at the time. Networks 'characterize *kinds* of role relationships along the dimension of permissible role-fluidity' (p. 979). It would seem to be the case, therefore, that considerations which apply in open networks are tantamount to considerations of value which enter into transactional behaviour. But no such correspondence is developed: '. . . network types are abstractions because social relations are specifiable in terms of much more precise and naturalistically real role relationships' (p. 977).

The prevailing bias of Fishman's work is towards the concrete, away from the abstract. Cultural values are concretized in domains, domains in role relations. At each step possibilities of finiteness recede. It is therefore necessary not only to recognize the unpredictability of relationships between values and roles (moreover, the frequent priority of the former), but also to recast the latter into more abstract or finite terms. In this connection the treatment by Goodenough (1965) of the terms 'status' and 'role' is apposite. The two concepts are regarded as quite distinct. Statuses are in effect points on status dimensions (examples of which are: 'cordiality', 'reverence', 'display of affection', 'sexual distance', 'emotional independence', 'setting oneself up above another') at which particular combinations of rights and duties apply. 'Rights and their duty counterparts serve to define boundaries within which the parties to social relationships are expected to confine their behaviour' (p. 3) – and may well be, of course, at least in part, linguistic. Role relationships (Goodenough: 'identity relationships') disport themselves in all their variety along the various status dimensions, groupable in each case according to status, that is to say according to shared rights and duties.

Goodenough takes up the question of whether the numbers of status dimensions and statuses (as contrasted with identity or role relationships and rights and duties) are or are not strictly limited for any given society. It is suggested first of all that in very general terms what people learn in the normal course of their lives is not likely to be 'so complicated as to defy analysis'. But more particularly, the well-known findings of Miller (1956) in the field of cognitive psychology, to the effect that the human brain is limited to approximately seven discriminations on any one scale, are invoked to apply to discriminations on status-dimension scales. Hence one might very reasonably think in terms of five- or seven-point scales of 'deference' etc. (but, one might add, not necessarily dichotomies of 'high' and 'low', 'formal' and 'informal', etc.). Status dimensions themselves may be similarly limited in number; reference is made to some remarks of Wallace (1961) concerning a possible maximum limit of 2^6 to the size of folk taxonomies. The overall picture, then, seems to add up to one of a *few* cultural values involved in the transactional selection of a *few* status dimensions each responded to in terms of a *few* discriminations, and these together accounting for a vast number of role relationships and (in part linguistic) rights and duties.[9]

Individuals play many parts, or, one might say, enact many statuses, often simultaneously. Statuses may not always be easily compatible; nor therefore will their associated rights and duties be so. Drawing upon a phonetic analogy, Goodenough suggests three modes of response in such cases: either one of the duties is dropped, or one or both are modified, or both are replaced by a 'distinctive third'. Now this is unmistakably the point at which Barth's discussion begins to take over. He asks: what are the processes involved in such adjustments, and how do individual decisions accumulate into and modify, as well as become modified or even prescribed by, institutionalized convention and habit? The crucial cases, he believes, may well be those which face participants with 'dilemmas of choice', involving incompatibilities among values, statuses, and rights and duties alike.

Linguistic responses in such cases range over a wide variety of options. Where there is choice of two languages, one may be dropped, or retained and modified, or may borrow features or elements from the other; borrowing or learning may go so far as to give rise to a pidgin language, or, without pidginization, the two languages might 'seem to merge' into styles which at the very least mask the retention of structural identity essentially with the one rather than with the other (Gumperz, 1967a, 1967b); both may be replaced by a third (or by no language at all); or, finally, choice may alternate between the two, in what is commonly known as code-switching; and various combinations of these responses can be illustrated and observed. Where choice is between two or more dialects, varieties, styles, variants, etc. (these terms, like the term language itself, are to be taken as problematical), an equally wide range of possibilities presents itself (wider if one does not hold with the notion of language-merging) – and of course the sheer number of available dialects (etc.) will almost always be far greater.

Very special interest attaches to cases of code-switching between unambiguously distinct languages. For one thing it is normally much easier than in the case of dialects, varieties, and so forth, to specify precisely what is being switched with what;

this being so, one is in the best position to study those revealing cases of language choice in which alterations in domain, physical setting, role relationship, etc. are not observable, or do not apply.[10] The most revealing cases of all are likely to be those in which participants switch codes rather rapidly, and/or insert words or phrases from one language into the other, in either case perhaps modifying the form of each or either language in the process:[11] deterministic relationships between language and situation (as stimulus and response) seem to be particularly irrelevant. One might, of course, choose to regard all such behaviour as some kind of deviation from institutionalized norms, motivated by more or less obscure forms of 'interpersonal purpose and understanding', the 'situation' proper remaining undisturbed (see Fishman, 1968: 982, 983, 1,042) – the disciplinary corollary being that these are matters that concern the anthropologist and the social psychologist rather than the sociolinguist. It could more properly be argued, however, that Fishman's opposition to what he calls 'a basic reliance on purported interpersonal meanings' (p. 1,034) and the probing of 'momentary interpersonal subtlety' (p. 1,035) is very much akin to Skinner's renunciation of 'an outdated doctrine of the expression of ideas', and shares much the same weaknesses (see Skinner, 1957; Chomsky, 1959). Fishman's only examples of linguistic subtleties are those of humour, contrast, and emphasis, all 'marked' forms of expression, that is to say, acquiring most of their meaning from contrast with 'unmarked' forms.[12]

For the investigation of code-switching behaviour Fishman relies exclusively on self-report and interview techniques, rather than on observation or on participant-analysis of observed data. The former are common techniques which reverse those advocated by Barth for ethnographic analysis generally. Barth stresses the need to make empirical observations of particular interactions in order to infer rules of status combinability and the 'games of strategy' that lie behind these, and asserts the feasibility of doing this. Fishman, on the other hand, seeks to infer observables (domains, choice of language, etc.) from opinions of participants or their representatives. Put rather crudely, the alternatives are those of (a) the sociolinguist's (ethnographer's, etc.) inferences on the spot, and (b) informant opinion about observables more or less as it were *in vacuo*. The only advantage of the latter seems to be that of width of coverage; the investigator cannot be everywhere at once.

Nevertheless the Report does contain suggestive evidence for what one might call unstable code-switching. Hoffman goes so far as to state:

> 'Language choice in some situations is predictable by reference to the domain in which the interaction takes place. However, a description of those situations in which language choice is not so readily predictable would be of much greater interest and value for the purposes of this study' (p. 63).

He presents little more, however, than brief anecdotal pictures of 'language-switching or unexpected language choice'. One spots some suggestive factors: public versus private setting (cf. Stewart, 1963), the effect of third parties, reprimanding a child versus discussing educational goals and aspirations with him, expression of anger versus warning of impending anger, argument versus discussion, group therapy situations versus situations that do not threaten personal dignity,[13] kidding and joking and impressing the opposite sex at parties, addressing one's girl-friend's parents versus addressing the girl herself, work situations requiring the expression of authority versus lunch-hour breaks with the same people. Hoffman observes in passing that in respect of home situations 'Respondents were not able to explain why they switched, but remembered that it was always done without conscious effort' (p. 66).

Later on there is an informal account of the views of a group of Puerto Rican intellectuals on bilingualism among themselves and their compatriots. Between close friends Spanish is the preferred language but English is often used 'on particular occasions or for particular purposes' (p. 101); 'English words or phrases . . . creep into informal conversations – whether they be relaxed or heated – but they serve to signal informality itself, or humor, or contrast, or emphasis . . .' (p. 102); 'topics that are not essentially Puerto Rican or Spanish' are relevant (p. 103). The contrast formality:informality dominates these interviews, alongside ethnic feeling ('Hell! Such a beautiful treasure as that which Spain gave us – to lose it? – no! Never!' – p. 119).

There follows the complete transcript of a long and lively discussion with a group of Puerto Rican high-school students. Several informants speak of (themselves or someone else) being 'in the mood' or 'getting an urge' to speak one of the languages; there may be 'no reason' for this (p. 226), or 'maybe when I'm angry or something like that' (p. 237). The factor of courtesy or 'respect or something' (p. 237) crops up several times; this may be coupled with that of ethnic identification (p. 239). Spanish, it seems, can be strategic for asking for a favour: 'I'll just speak in Spanish a little more. You know, a little more affectionately. You know the Spanish' (p. 241). But it has to be done properly: 'They feel nice. It's just the way you say it sometime. You say it with a certain little ting to it that they like' (p. 242). Spanish slang is useful for 'kidding around' (p. 243), and might be used for getting to know someone better (p. 246). One cannot help noticing in the students' remarks a roughly even balance between considerations of domains, role relationships, settings, proficiencies, etc., on the one hand, and status relations, values, and what for the moment might be called pragmatic purposes such as asking for a favour, etc., on the other. Not unnaturally, perhaps, it is the latter that tend to develop into keen debate. One cannot then, on this evidence, easily accept the truth of such assertions as the following: 'Domain . . . is an abstraction that many bilinguals handle easily and consistently. It corresponds closely to the way many bilinguals think of their language-choice regularities' (p. 1,042).[14]

Three sorts of evidence are provided in the Report for the validity and supposedly crucial role of domain analysis in the study of language choice. Very briefly, these involve: (a) self-report instruments used with high-school students, the results from which indicate that choice of language is related to five given domains rather than to five given interlocutors (parent, friend, priest, teacher, employer), five given places, or five given topics; (b) factor analysis of the replies to questions included in a language census conducted in a Puerto Rican neighbourhood in Jersey City, which clearly points to the four domains of education, family, work, and religion; and (c) word-naming tasks in which Puerto Rican children (aged six to twelve) were asked to name as many objects as could be found in each of four settings (kitchen, school, church, and neighbourhood), which indicate a clear connection between choice of language and domain.[15] These results are, however, subject in each case to the limitations imposed by what had gone into the various questions and tasks in the first place. The technique of presenting subjects in the first type of test with two incongruent (as well as two congruent) situational components, and asking them to provide a third component to complete the situation, could perhaps have been extended to take in components having to do with status dimensions as supplementary to the rather unremarkable sets of persons, places, and topics which were in fact used. The census questions are all unambiguously domain-oriented; and the third test loses some validity not only in being restricted to the four given settings or domains but also by requiring single words in response, as opposed to other stretches of language (one cannot, for example, ask a favour very easily in one word).

Domains, unlike role relationships and settings, *may* conceivably be limited in number for any given social group (though the question of how many recognizable social groups there may be in a complex modern society immediately suggests itself), and *may* be observably related to certain regularities of linguistic behaviour. But these characteristics are not theoretically all-important. A more basic question is surely to ask *why* certain domains are marked by the use of one particular language rather than another. Part of the answer will of course invite consideration of factors which seem to be accidental, or temporary, or just as much effect as cause: locales that may be institutionally tied to that language, its relatively greater yield of technical terms, current educational policy, etc. More significantly generalizable considerations, however, will have to do with the relevance of particular statuses and status relationships to that domain, and hence to the use of one language rather than another. Back of this still are the processes of transactional adjustment among statuses (hence languages) which over a period of time have yielded observable regularities of behaviour, and which potentially stand to modify that behaviour. Transactions in turn imply considerations of values, or constraints and incentives, on the part of individual human beings.

A transactional theory of sociolinguistics does not separate, or seek to separate, 'mind' and 'event', *langue* and *parole*. The use of the term 'generative' in the following statement bears essential likeness to its use in generative linguistic theory, yet the qualification is equally important: '. . . the logical operations whereby forms are generated should mirror actual, empirical processes which can be identified in the reality which is being analysed' (Barth, 1966: v). This would seem to mean that one must reject a purely mentalistic conception of linguistic behaviour (requiring either no reference at all to social environment (Katz and Fodor, 1963) or an equally questionable assumption of 'restricted' or in effect neutral contexts (Lyons, 1968: 98, 419, etc.)). It also means that transactional processes are themselves to be taken as generative in character. The second of these consequences could be particularly interesting, although as yet (as Barth points out) the analytical status of transactions (or 'reciprocity') is far from clear. Strictly behaviouristic treatments such as Homans's 'Social Behavior as Exchange' (1958), which would interpret values as 'reinforcers' rather as corn for the pigeon (p. 598), would seem to be ruled out.

SPEECH FUNCTIONS

Some relatively neglected yet fundamental aspects of the social use of language are well focused by certain problems encountered in the use of techniques of correlation. Since one cannot correlate linguistic with non-linguistic variables if some of the defining criteria are common to both sides, correlation is possible only in the following circumstances: (1) between wholly linguistic and wholly non-linguistic variables; (2) between linguistic variables wholly or partly defined by the use of non-linguistic criteria and quite distinct non-linguistic variables; (3) as for (2), interchanging the places of linguistic and non-linguistic; and (4) between linguistic variables implicating non-linguistic criteria and distinct non-linguistic variables implicating again distinct linguistic criteria. Three problems in the use of correlation in sociolinguistics will be attended to in turn: first, its frequent *difficulty*, even when feasible; second, its equally frequent *impossibility*; and third, its fundamental *irrelevance* to much of what is important in language behaviour.

Of the second, third, and fourth cases above, one notes that the use of mixed criteria will not easily exclude variables standing on the other side of the correlation. For example (second case), if one seeks to show that the use of a 'restricted code' of English (which is not theoretically defined as a function of socio-economic class: see in particular the recent writings of Bernstein) does in fact relate to class, there must always be the possibility that judgements of class have been at least partly criterial for the analyst's identification of instances of the use of this type of English. Similarly (third case), Labov's correlations of phonological variables on the one side with socio-economic class and stylistic level (in terms of 'formality') on the other may be well justified but are not entirely straightforward: stylistic level is said to have been defined partly with the aid of linguistic or para-linguistic 'channel cues' such as rhythm, tempo, etc. (Labov, 1964: 168), but one might still wonder whether in the analytical event itself (the interview situation) distinctions between 'careful' and 'casual' speech might not have been identified to some extent from the evidence of those same phonological variables. It is just possible, indeed, that the latter, which had been chosen in the first place partly for their 'immunity from conscious suppression' and high frequency (p. 166), were both unconscious and significant indices of stylistic level for the investigator himself.

These are difficulties experienced in correlation. More suggestive for one's understanding of language are those cases in which correlation is not possible at all, since the various criteria are quite clearly mixed. Attempts to correlate, for example, equidistant points on a phonetic scale with evaluations (of correctness, prestige, etc.) on the part of different groups of people must fail if – as is surely the case – perception of phonetic distance is itself a function of such evaluations. Blom and Gumperz (1972) throw light on the significance of non-correlatability between 'linguistic' and 'non-linguistic' components of the speech behaviour of a group of Norwegian university students whose studies take them between their local home and non-local university town environments. Code-switching between, and mixtures of, standard and dialectal forms of speech mirror the two sets of experiences but do not necessarily match observable changes in the immediate situation of utterance.

Code-switching behaviour of this sort (called 'metaphorical') is therefore criterial for the identification of relevant non-observable 'non-linguistic' shifts in the situation. Latent shifts of this latter kind are very likely to have a great deal to do with social relationships holding between participants. More importantly, however, the analyst's inability to dissociate 'linguistic' from 'non-linguistic' in such cases might very reasonably be regarded as a simple consequence of the at least partial equivalence in meaning of the two terms themselves – hence the quotation marks. This type of code-switching has innumerable analogies at all levels: in shifts between language and language (thus between Spanish and English in Paraguay as described by Rubin, 1963), between variety and variety (thus between 'high' and 'low' Javanese as described by Geertz, 1960), and between variant and variant (forms of address, for example).

But there are still more far-reaching limitations on the usefulness of correlational techniques in sociolinguistics. Correlation implies a view of behaviour as conformity to and deviation from norms. Certainly, linguistic like any other behaviour *is* conditioned in many respects. Blom and Gumperz point out, for example, that their university subjects do not seem to be aware of their own metaphorical code-switching behaviour, at any rate in its more 'mixed' language guises: one assumes, therefore, that even in this case linguistic behaviour is largely conditioned by histories of exposure to different aspects of the Norwegian social-linguistic structure, and their associated values, and perhaps immediately triggered off by shifts in 'topic'. A transactional perspective, however, while recognizing that social structure determines much in individual human behaviour, allows too for the perhaps ultimately more important reverse process, in which participants estimate and weigh up the values of statuses, and in acting accordingly bring some degree of pressure to bear on the regularities of social structure.[16]

Varieties of code-switching are relevant to these considerations, but perhaps the most interesting linguistic phenomena of all are those best described as processes of language-merging: variant with variant, style with style, variety with variety, dialect with dialect, conceivably language with language. Processes of this sort seem particularly to embody at least analogous processes of cultural value or social status manipulation. One is concerned here not so much with losses in the attributed significances of maintained structural boundaries as with structural blurring itself (the two cases are not of course wholly distinct in historical perspective). But although a few examples can be cited of scholarly studies of the development of 'mixed' forms of speech, studies that are at one and the same time descriptions of (i.e. describing the only or best evidence for) the mixed sociocultural identities of emerging groups (see, for example, Gumperz, 1967a, 1967b; Richardson, 1962; Samarin, 1966), such processes are probably very much more widespread than the current literature would seem to suggest.

Most widespread of all are surely those processes of stylistic convergence (hence simultaneous divergence) *within* languages, dialects, and varieties. The opportunity here for greater understanding of the transactional nature of linguistic behaviour is at once its difficulty. Code-switching between languages and even dialects is reasonably describable in terms of what is being switched with what; merging between languages and dialects is rather more difficult to measure (as Gumperz, 1967a, points out, for many speakers in 'stable bilingual communities' there may be no 'pure' unadulterated standard forms of language which can be properly conceived of as standing in relationships of mutual interference: synchronically speaking, the 'mixed' form *is* here the standard); the description of stylistic shifts or mergers (at various levels: intonation, slang, whatever) is more problematical still, being fraught at all times with the difficulty of recognizing clear antecedents. If one is concerned to describe processes of stylistic convergence and divergence, then one has to justify one's choice of criteria for 'a' style. Various approaches suggest themselves. The least relevant of these is that which rigorously seeks to exclude all factors regarded as non-linguistic, instead asserting some kind of logical or methodological priority of 'form' over 'context'.[17] Those which involve only observables such as domains, role relations, settings, and the like are subject to the same kinds of criticism as can be levelled at similarly restricted approaches to code-switching (see the first part of this paper); that is to say, just as in the latter case one is liable to be drawn into descriptions of endless environmental determinants, so one flinches at the prospect of describing environmentally related style after style, variant after variant, one's only justification being that they are there. It is time, therefore, that the problem (essentially that of 'meaning') were approached (in its sociolinguistic aspects; there are others: see for example Whiteley, 1966) in the more finite yet more general terms of processual transactions of values and statuses.

The transactional implications of Bernstein's current work are considerable, but latent. Bernstein (1972) distinguishes three 'modes of social control' ('imperative', 'positional', 'personal'), two 'family types' ('positional' and 'personal'), and two 'codes' ('restricted' and 'elaborated'), their systematic interrelations arising from the structure of society. The two codes are conceived in terms both of mode of social control and of structural features. Family type is a function of mode of social control only, and by no means necessarily restricted by social class. The three modes of social control themselves would seem in effect to amount to the expression of the status dimensions of power, position, and personal identity, respectively. A transactional extension of this general picture would bring into consideration: (a) status points on each dimension, (b) other dimensions besides these three ('solidarity', for example, is distinguishable), (c) (rule-governed?) co-occurrences among particular statuses on particular dimensions, (d) recognition of a measure of autonomy or creativity on the part of individual speakers, and (e) partly as a consequence of this the possibility of (non-rule-governed?) incongruencies among statuses as expressed in particular utterances. In each case one reckons with linguistic realization at all levels (grammatical, lexical, phonological, paralinguistic, for example).

The putting into effect and/or reflection of status co-occurrences are the mechanics of transactional linguistic behaviour, and as such deserve a habitation and a name in sociolinguistics. It might be suggested that the notion of 'speech functions' (see Firth, 1935) provides a reasonable fit. For instance, the putting into effect of particular statuses on the power and position dimensions is likely to be referred to by native users of the language in roughly similar terms: as 'deference' increases, for example, one steps from such speech functions as ' ommands' to 'requests' to 'tentative suggestions' to 'asking for a favour' to 'pleading', to accept (for the sake of argument) just five statuses. Other dimensions (if made prominent in the communication) will have the effect of converting the above into 'advice' or 'persuasion' or 'appeal' (thus Bernstein speaks of 'positional' and 'personal' appeals as modes of social control), and so forth. The speech function 'greeting' highlights the status dimension 'acquaintanceship' (its length, lapse, renewal, etc.), plus – but of course less criterial to the definition of 'greeting' itself (although quite possibly of far greater significance to the recipient) – those of solidarity, position, emotional independence, sexual distance, intimacy, etc. Any schematization along these lines is likely, of course, to be more than somewhat arbitrary in the present circumstances, but the general principle seems clear enough: speech functions could be regarded as, at least in part, the expression of perhaps rule-governed co-occurrences of status dimensions and statuses.

More exactly, however, speech functions would seem to be expressions of statuses *and* (developmentally prior) considerations of value entering into the selective presentation of statuses ('impression management'). Barth's down-to-earth example of the transactional development over time of North Sea fishermen's institutionalized roles illustrates (1) values ('cooperation', 'responsibility', 'skill', 'qualities of leadership', 'reliability', etc.), (2) statuses (rights and duties on board), and (3) the (partly verbal) means of over- and under-communicating values associated with statuses ('argument', 'joking', 'bragging', 'never elicits comments', 'spontaneous', 'emphasis on careful rationality and finality of decision', etc.). The latter relate very closely to the notion of speech functions, and (in Barth's view: pp. 8, 9) reflect values very much more directly than statuses. With this, one might compare some remarks of Douglas (1968), writing on some factors in joke perception, who notes the often close relationship between joking behaviour and 'community', over against 'social structure':

> 'In "community" the personal relations of men and women appear in a special light. They form part of the ongoing process which is only partly organized in the wider social "structure". . . . "Community" in this sense has positive values associated with it: good fellowship, spontaneity, warm contact . . . the experience of the non-structure in contrast

to the structure . . . laughter and jokes, since they attack classification and hierarchy, are obviously apt symbols for expressing community in this sense of unhierarchised, undifferentiated social relations' (p. 370).[18]

One must, of course, be prepared to recognize *several* (overlapping) types of speech function, including: (a) those which most directly seem to realize status relationships, (b) those which more clearly answer to underlying values, and (c) others which particularly concern cognitive relationships of one sort or another, such as, for example, 'causality'. Common labels, like 'agreement', may, even on one particular occasion, amount to pegs attached to several such dimensions of meaning: the whole point of agreeing at all may very often be to reinforce or establish conventional or unusual status relationships with or without the solidarity that comes from shared values, rather than or as well as to assent to some intellectual argument or other.

An as yet largely unrealized function of descriptive linguistics is that of showing how speech functions of all sorts are realized linguistically. Any and all levels of language are liable to be implicated. The various linguistic renderings of a word like 'yes' or a phrase like 'I see' may be very subtle in phonetic or phonological terms, yet their associated meanings may very well have considerable generality–reflections in miniature of basic social and personal relationships. The language user himself is probably engaged in the more or less continuous exercise, whatever else he or the other participant happens to be interpreting or conveying, of handling status relationships and values of one sort or another, the linguistic markers of which may be quite minimal. *How* to agree, the significance of a certain kind of hesitation, precisely why the other person suddenly speaks faster (or slower) when the argument starts to get more complicated, what various people *mean* on various occasions and in various deliveries by the comment 'interesting', and so forth, matter a great deal, for all their fleeting appearance in the stream of speech.

NOTES

1. The paper owes much, but none of its faults, to Professor W. H. Whiteley for general prior orientation and to Mrs Janet Holmes for discussion and comment during composition.

2. Processes involving language and processes involving values are likely to be closely related. Probably all that Barth has to say about the latter in transactional behaviour can be liberally and directly illustrated in terms of the former. Thus, with the formation of 'overarching values' compare the formation of 'standard languages', such as Bahasa Indonesia, over against the various vernaculars, dialects, etc. Then again, differing evaluations of a single situation helped to account for the survival of Chinese pidgin English in its early days (each side giving it a very different but equally potent value). 'Faulty information' about values certainly seems to apply to the odd case of Sango, the 'prestige' lingua franca in the Central African Republic, the very existence of which as a language may be questionable (Samarin, 1966). The process of seeking value information, particularly at the early stages of interpersonal acquaintanceship, is often achieved by the judicious use of a few words in one particular language (or style, etc.) interspersed in the mainstream of another, related values being thereby brought into prominence and tested for reactions (see Tanner, 1967; see, too, the reference (below) to comments by Fishman's Puerto Rican high-school informants). Most important of all, perhaps, is the operation of 'feedback' from actions to values (the one having the effect of modifying the other), well reflected in the inevitable role of the bilingual who is in any degree 'bicultural'; he is *par excellence* the strategically placed entrepreneur.

3. McIntosh (1965) reminds us that the linguistic dog very often wags the situational tail. . . .

4. See Sapir (1933) especially.

5. This Report runs to 1,209 pages, contains thirty-six distinct sections, and lists seventeen contributors to the text itself. There are eight main parts: Introduction, Background Studies, Sociologically-Oriented Studies, Psychologically-Oriented Studies, Linguistically-Oriented Studies, Summary and Conclusions, Theoretical Addendum (by Fishman: four essays), and Appendices. This is a major achievement of its kind in sociolinguistic description, not least because its theoretical perspectives are made unusually explicit.

6. Fishman goes on to speak of a progression in analysis 'from descriptive adequacy alone to predictive power with respect to the what and the how of variety use' (p. 981). One misses in this Report an interest in what one might wish to call the study of sociolinguistic aspects of *explanatory* adequacy.

7. Ferguson recognizes this as 'the analogous situation' (1959: 429).

8. It is interesting to note that Fishman's concern to avoid 'uncontaminated' psychological, linguistic, and sociological descriptions of bilingualism (pp. 952 ff.) does not extend to the admission of a substantial anthropological dimension.

9. The *kind* of picture one might arrive at is therefore of around say twelve status dimensions combinable into some sixty-four combinations of six each (plus many more than sixty-four when less than six are combined at once), each dimension containing up to around seven discriminable statuses. Total numbers of theoretically possible status combinations would thus seem to be very large indeed. At any one moment, however, presumably no more than one or two

statuses on each of up to six or so dimensions will be expressed or perceived, and in the system as a whole there will be many non-occurring status combinations (these, moreover, relative to social group, etc). Hence the possible relevance of an approach that recognizes, at least in principle, 'context-sensitive' rules governing the selection of statuses (and associated language). At the same time, of course, rules *are* only rules, 'more honoured in the breach than the observance . . .'

10. Ma and Herasimchuk state:

> '. . . no attempts should be made at gathering data on inter-language switching since this is the more difficult kind of variation to collect and requires techniques more based on observation and participant-observation than on elicitation alone' (Fishman, 1968: 665).

The opposite might just as well be argued, namely that intra-language switching requires participant-observation in order to guide and validate choice of formal linguistic criteria for the demarcation of boundaries between varieties of the language (or indeed to demonstrate that such boundaries are often very difficult, or impossible, to identify). The minute phonological variables chosen by Labov (which serve as a model for Ma and Herasimchuk) are not necessarily the only or the best criteria. Against Labov's own justifications for their choice (they are said to be high in frequency, immune from conscious suppression, integral units of larger structures, and easily quantified on a linear scale: Labov, 1964: 166), one would wish to plead for the consideration of grammatical, lexical, semantic, or other phonological variables, or combinations of these. Moreover, given distances on a phonetic scale do not necessarily match (a) perceptions of distance or (b) their social valuation. (This is, of course, one illustration of the point, made earlier, that 'language' and 'situation' are often in certain respects part and parcel of each other, hence in such cases cannot properly be correlated: see the second part of this paper.)

11. See, for example, Whiteley (1967) on the sociolinguistic contexts of various degrees of assimilation of English loan-words in Swahili in Dar-es-Salaam.

12. It need hardly be pointed out that 'humour' (as 'joking' also) is certainly not so easily to be referred exclusively to behaviour norms: see below, on 'Speech functions'.

13. Code-switching among Pakistani immigrants in Bradford may in part be a function of attitudes being expressed at the time towards aspects of their own cultural background (Jones, 1968).

14. There are two sides to this question, namely what bilinguals think of, and how accurately. Accuracy is likely of course to depend in part on the observability of 'non-linguistic' factors under consideration: see Blom and Gumperz (1972) on this aspect of monolingual code-switching in rural northern Norway.

15. Or rather setting, but with domain implications.

16. It is worth while to note that the generative linguist takes up the position that 'language' *is* a totally distinct entity from 'situation' (or social environment, etc.), but that predictions of the one from the other will always be either uninteresting or unique or both: 'It is only under exceptional and quite uninteresting circumstances that one can seriously consider how "situational context" determines what is said, even in probabilistic terms' (Chomsky, 1966).

17. 'Neo-Firthian' approaches to the 'inter-level' of 'context' are of just this sort (see Pride, 1971).

18. Compare the treatment of 'role-fluidity' by Fishman (see p. 99 above). More positively, there is surely much of interest and relevance in Paine's

discussion of the play of individual and group 'interest' in gossip (Paine, 1967), as opposed to the more conventionally unifying pressure of feelings of group solidarity: the speech functions of gossip in this view are very much more directly tied to values than to statuses, although there will rarely, of course, be total contrast between the two.

REFERENCES

BARTH, F. 1966. *Models of Social Organization*. Occasional Paper No. 23. London: Royal Anthropological Institute.

BERNSTEIN, B. 1972. Article in J. J. Gumperz and D. Hymes (eds.), *Directions in Sociolinguistics*. New York: Holt, Rinehart & Winston.

BERRY, J. 1966. Introduction to B. Malinowski, *The Language of Magic and Gardening*. London: Allen & Unwin.

BLOM, J. P., and GUMPERZ, J. J. 1972. Some Social Determinants of Verbal Behaviour. In J. J. Gumperz and D. Hymes (eds.), *Directions in Sociolinguistics*. New York: Holt, Rinehart & Winston.

BRIGHT, W. (ed.). 1966. *Sociolinguistics*. The Hague: Mouton.

CHOMSKY, N. 1959. Review of B. F. Skinner, *Verbal Behaviour* (1957). *Language* **35**.

—— 1966. Linguistic Theory. In W. F. Bottiglia (ed.), *Northeast Conference on the Teaching of Foreign Languages*, pp. 43–49. Reports of the Working Committees.

DOUGLAS, M. 1968. The Social Control of Cognition: Some Factors in Joke Perception. *Man* **3** (3): 361–376.

FERGUSON, C. A. 1959. Diglossia. *Word* **15:** 325–340. Also in Hymes (ed.), 1964.

FIRTH, J. R. 1935. The Technique of Semantics. *Transactions of the Philological Society*: 36–72. Also in Firth, *Papers in Linguistics 1934–1951*. London: Oxford University Press, 1957.

FISHMAN, J. A. 1965. Varieties of Ethnicity and Varieties of Language Consciousness. In *Monograph Series on Languages and Linguistics No. 18*. Georgetown University.

—— 1966. Language Maintenance and Language Shift. In J. A. Fishman *et al.*, *Language Loyalty in the United States*. The Hague: Mouton.

—— 1967. Bilingualism with and without Diglossia; Diglossia with and without Bilingualism. *Journal of Social Issues* **23** (2): 29–38.

—— (ed.). 1968. *Bilingualism in the Barrio*. Final Report, Contract No. OEC-1-7-062817 – 0297. US Dept. of Health, Education and Welfare.

GEERTZ, C. 1960. *The Religion of Java*. Glencoe, Ill.: Free Press.

GOODENOUGH, W. H. 1965. Rethinking 'Status' and 'Role'. In M. Banton (ed.), *The Relevance of Models for Social Anthropology*, pp. 1–24. ASA Monograph 1. London: Tavistock.

GUMPERZ, J. J. 1967a. On the Linguistic Markers of Bilingual Communication. *Journal of Social Issues* **23** (2).

—— 1967b. How can we Describe and Measure the Behaviour of Bilingual Groups? In report of Conference on Bilingualism, Moncton, Toronto.

HOENIGSWALD, H. M. 1966. A Proposal for the Study of Folk-Linguistics. In Bright (ed.), 1966.

HOFFMAN, G. 1968. Puerto Ricans in New York: A Language-related Ethnographic Summary. In Fishman (ed.), 1968.

HOMANS, G. C. 1958. Social Behavior as Exchange. *American Journal of Sociology* **63** (6): 597–606.

HYMES, D. H. (ed.). 1964. *Language in Culture and Society: A Reader in Linguistics and Anthropology*. New York: Harper & Row.

JONES, J. H. G. 1968. Code-switching among Pakistani Immigrants in Bradford. University of Leeds dissertation.

KATZ, J. J., and FODOR, J. A. 1963. The Structure of a Semantic Theory. *Language* **39**: 170–210. Also in Fodor and Katz (eds.), *The Structure of Language*, Englewood Cliffs, NJ: Prentice-Hall, 1964.

LABOV, W. 1964. Phonological Correlates of Social Stratification. *American Anthropologist* **66** (2).

LYONS, J. 1968. *Introduction to Theoretical Linguistics*. Cambridge: Cambridge University Press.

MA, R., and HERASIMCHUK, E. 1968. Linguistic Dimensions of a Bilingual Neighborhood. In Fishman (ed.), 1968.

MCINTOSH, A. 1965. Saying. *Review of English Literature* **6** (2).

MILLER, G. A. 1956. The Magical Number Seven, Plus or Minus Two: Some Limit on our Capacity for Processing Information. *Psychological Review* **63**.

PAINE, R. 1967. What is Gossip about? An Alternative Hypothesis. *Man* (n.s.) **2**: 278–285.

PRIDE, J. B. 1971. *The Social Meaning of Language*. London: Oxford University Press.

RICHARDSON, I. 1962. Linguistic Change in Africa with special reference to the Bemba-speaking Area of Northern Rhodesia. In *Symposium on Multilingualism*. CSA/CCTA Publication 87. Brazzaville.

RUBIN, J. **1963.** Bilingual Usage in Paraguay. In J. A. Fishman (ed.), *Readings in the Sociology of Language*. The Hague: Mouton, 1968.

SAMARIN, W. J. 1966. Self-annulling Prestige Factors among Speakers of a Creole Language. In Bright (ed.), 1966.

SAPIR, E. 1933. Language. In D. G. Mandelbaum (ed.), *Selected Writings of Edward Sapir*. Berkeley: University of California Press, 1949; Cambridge: Cambridge University Press, 1950.

SKINNER, B. F. 1957. *Verbal Behavior*. New York: Appleton-Century-Crofts.

STEWART, W. A. 1963. The Functional Distribution of Creole and French in Haiti. In *Monograph Series on Languages and Linguistics No. 13*. Georgetown University.

TANNER, N. 1967. Speech and Society among the Indonesian Elite: A Case Study of a Multilingual Society. *Anthropological Linguistics* **9** (3).

WALLACE, A. F. C. 1961. On Being Just Complicated Enough. In *Proceedings of the National Academy of Sciences* **47.**

WHITELEY, W. H. 1966. Social Anthropology, Meaning and Linguistics. *Man* (n.s.) **1** (2): 139–157.

—— 1967. Loanwords in Linguistic Description: A Case Study from Tanzania, East Africa. In I. Rauch and C. T. Scott (eds), *Approaches in Linguistic Methodology*. Madison, Wis.: University of Wisconsin Press.

PART II

Multilingualism and Social Categories

W. H. Whiteley

A Note on Multilingualism

Interest in multilingualism among linguists and social anthropologists is a comparatively recent phenomenon, and represents part of a more general movement away from the views of their subject which had stressed unity and uniformity. In social anthropology such views owed something to Malinowskian institutionalism, with its emphasis on the function of an institution in maintaining the fabric and continuity of the whole society; they also stemmed partly from the consequent development of techniques for the intensive study of small communities over long periods. If such study were to form a viable basis from which to make statements about the whole society, then there must be some presumption of uniformity. In linguistics, following the Saussurean dichotomy of *langue* and *parole*, emphasis was placed on synchronic description, using a body of text collected from one or more speakers as the basis for extrapolation. Bloch and Trager's definition of the work of the linguist is well known:

> 'When he has described the facts of speech in such a way as to account for all the utterances used by the members of a social group, his description is what we call the system or the grammar of the language' (Bloch and Trager, 1942: 8).

Happy were those who could speak of *the* system! Yet variations from the system cannot be dismissed as irrelevant, and the conception of a 'common core' and 'overall pattern', discussed by Hockett (1958), represented an attempt to comprehend the awkwardness of linguistic facts, though Hockett could still find it possible to say that 'Generally speaking, the totality of speech habits of a single person at a given time constitute an idiolect' (p. 321). It was admitted that some people, e.g. Swiss-Germans, had two idiolects, and that it was even possible to find cases where idiolect boundaries were ill-defined, but such cases were rare and could be discounted.

Later writers found it less easy to account for the facts in this way, and it was shortly being quite widely recognized[1] that even in a so-called unilingual community, such as an English town, for example, there were recognizably distinct varieties of English which, so far from occurring in free variation, served as markers of social class, social roles, particular occupations, and so on. By implication, and even allowing for a certain measure of flexibility in the definition of idiolect, one could now argue that a native speaker of English controlled not one or two idiolects, but perhaps a dozen or so.[2] Creolists, especially, stressed the importance of diversity:

> 'Nearly all speakers of English in Jamaica could be arranged in a sort of linguistic continuum . . . Even the concept of a linguistic continuum is an over-simplification, for it assumes that all Jamaica is one linguistic community' (DeCamp, 1961: 82–84).

Patterns of bilingualism and trilingualism such as these were of central concern to educators and social psychologists, as a glance at recent bibliographies will testify,[3] but the social anthropologist in Britain was still too preoccupied with abstracting away from individual behaviour for such diversity to be considered important.

The label 'multilingual' as applied to countries or societies, however, is deceptively comprehensive: Kenya may be described as such, in the sense that it comprises a number of sub-societies each speaking a different first language, yet in many of these sub-societies there are a majority of people who are unilingual, and many bilinguals may spend much of their lives speaking a single language. Again, a country may be designated multilingual where several languages are used officially for different purposes, even though specific sectors of government may remain unilingual. Situations where different languages compete for recognition arouse the interest of political scientists and historians, who may account for aspects of nationalism in linguistic terms while recognizing that the extent to which language is a critical factor varies very widely. At this level some very ambitious statements have been made: the writer of one recent study feels that he can state as a proposition that 'Multilingualism is not an issue . . . in agrarian societies that are predominantly illiterate under elites that share a lingua franca' (Anderson, 1969: 24). By contrast, Fishman has made an impressive contribution to the study of language policy, with particular reference to the stages of formulation and implementation, and has recently proposed a typology of language policies and decisions relating to them.[4] That area of social life in which members of a community manipulate their language skills in accordance with social norms and aspirations has been illuminated by Gumperz.[5] Particularly revealing has been his study of code-switching, that characteristic of face-to-face interaction in multilingual situations, which is, however, equally prevalent in unilingual communities: the child at school talking to teacher and to other children; the teenager with parents and coevals; the guest at a cocktail party.

Any linguist or social anthropologist who has studied a multilingual community recognizes that it is a good starting-point from which to move to the study of a unilingual one: as Denison (1968) has pointed out, it is much easier to spot when someone shifts to a different language than it is to recognize a shift in 'register', though when he further comments '. . . for language switch can be (relatively) unequivocally determined, since it is observable independently of variation in the associated situation' (p. 582), it is less clear what is meant, since it may turn out that the switch is the only observable diagnostic feature of such a situational change. Here, the help of the sociologist is invoked: perhaps the switch is diagnostic in some situations but not in others. One must recognize, in any case, that observation of a shift from one language to another is itself only a recognition of gross features: if one argues that people who speak only one language still have control over several varieties of that language, there is no reason to suppose that speakers of several languages are denied this facility. Certainly, in a city like Nairobi, conversations can be heard daily in which at least three varieties of Swahili are being operated by speakers who also operate some English and another African language. While linguists begin to explore the implications of diversity, British social anthropologists have showed a new interest in social situations and in the dramatis personae, though a concomitant concern for language as a constituent of the total situation every bit as important as non-linguistic behaviour seems rather slow to arise. It is surprising to notice, in a recently published study of urban networks (Mitchell, 1969), the absence of linguistic observation, where as acute an observer as Epstein finds it possible to talk about a 'gossip' network without reference to the languages in which the gossip was transmitted. Parkin's work in Kampala (Parkin, 1971), and, more recently, in Nairobi, has demonstrated the importance of language choice in the shifting pattern of urban relationships, where one may wish sometimes to suppress, sometimes to underline, one's ethnic affiliation.

For the social anthropologist, recognition of the social significance of language is an important aid to descriptive adequacy, especially if he is working within a transactional, situational, or network framework. For the linguist, however, the implications of multilingualism may be more far-reaching. In a recent paper Le Page (1968) has drawn attention to the implications for linguistic description of the concept of 'interference', when, as so often happens with bilingual speakers, it is difficult to demarcate the systems between which interference occurs. To take a concrete example: a substantial number of Kenyans are quadrilingual, English and Swahili being added formally through the educational system to their first languages, one of which may be a Nilotic and the other a Bantu language. Those who live in the towns, especially, will certainly have acquired skills informally in at least one other variety of Swahili. Without considering here how the functional load on these languages is distributed, two initial problems need to be solved by the linguist:

(a) How can one relate a speaker's competence (in Chomsky's sense), acquired either formally or informally, in what for him is a second or third language to the competence shown in that language by someone for whom it is the first language?

(b) How can one account for a speaker's competence in a range of varieties of his own first language?

DeCamp has suggested that generative theory could be extended to handle the problems posed by (b), that:

> 'linguistic diversity within any speech community may be factored into a small set of sociolinguistic "structures" each of which may be represented by a simple mathematical

> function . . . and by a corresponding schema of binary features, which, if they are incorporated into a generative grammar, can result in the grammar's generating those aspects of the linguistic diversity which are attributable to that structure' (1970: 165–166).

Presumably factoring of a similar sort could account for those areas of competence manifested by a speaker for whom the language in question had been acquired as a second or third language – for example, in the Kenya situation, by a Nilotic speaker who habitually used a Bantu language in the restricted situation of buying and selling. But it is evident that where competence is bound to performance in socially restricted situations, which may themselves be rather numerous, then the specification of sociolinguistic 'structures' may turn out to be rather complex. Aside from the objections to this proposal raised by Labov (1970), it seems to me that to incorporate the principle of variety into a theory is less problematical than to account, not for the frequency of use, which DeCamp sloughs off to performance, but for the propensity to use a particular variety or combination of varieties. Here one might hope that social anthropologists would come forward with an index of probability with which DeCamp's factors might be weighted, and so bring to the study of linguistic diversity a genuine sociolinguistic contribution.

NOTES

1. Prior to this there were, of course, exceptions, like J. R. Firth, but his contributions to linguistic diversity were, I feel, of the order of flashes of insight rather than systematic demonstrations from a body of text.
2. A most readable introduction to the study of varieties of English is Crystal and Davy (1969). Labov's study (1966) of certain phonological features in New York English, which had previously been thought to be in free variation, is indispensable to students of this topic.
3. See the general statement by Lewis (1962) and that of Lambert (1971).
4. See, for example, Fishman 1968a and 1968b, and his more recent contribution to typology (Fishman, 1971).
5. From his many contributions one might cite his 1964 paper as characteristic.

REFERENCES

ANDERSON, N. 1969. The Uses and Worth of Language. In N. Anderson (ed.), *Studies in Multilingualism*. Leiden: Brill.

BLOCH, B., and TRAGER, G. L. 1942. *Outline of Linguistic Analysis*. Baltimore, Md: Linguistic Society of America.

CRYSTAL, D., and DAVY, D. 1969. *Investigating English Style*. London: Longmans.

DECAMP, D. 1961. Social and Geographical Factors in Jamaican Dialects. In R. B. Le Page (ed.), *Creole Language Studies*, II. London: Macmillan.

— 1970. Is a Sociolinguistic Theory Possible? Pp. 157–168 in *Monograph Series on Languages and Linguistics No. 22*. Georgetown University.

DENISON, N. 1968. Sauris: A Trilingual Community in Diatypic Perspective. *Man* (n.s.) **3** (4): 578–592.

EPSTEIN, A. L. 1969. Gossip, Norms and Social Network. In Mitchell (ed.), 1969.

FISHMAN, J. A. 1968a. Sociolinguistics and the Language Problems of Developing Nations. In J. A. Fishman, C. A. Ferguson, and J. Das Gupta (eds.), *Language Problems of Developing Nations*. New York: Wiley.

— 1968b. Nationality-Nationalism and Nation-Nationism. In J. A. Fishman, C. A. Ferguson, and J. Das Gupta (eds.), *Language Problems of Developing Nations*. New York: Wiley.

— 1971. National Languages and Languages of Wider Communication in the Developing Nations. In Whiteley (ed.), 1971.

GUMPERZ, J. J. 1964. Linguistic and Social Interaction in Two Communities. In J. J. Gumperz and D. H. Hymes (eds.), *The Ethnography of Communication*. Menasha, Wis.: American Anthropological Association.

HOCKETT, C. F. 1958. *A Course in Modern Linguistics*. London: Macmillan.

LABOV, W. 1966. *The Social Stratification of English in New York City*. Washington, DC: Center for Applied Linguistics.

— 1970. In discussion following DeCamp (1970) above, pp. 171–172.

LAMBERT, W. E. 1971. A Social Psychology of Bilingualism. In Whiteley (ed.), 1971.

LE PAGE, R. B. 1968. Problems of Description in Multilingual Communities. *Transactions of the Philological Society*: 189–212.

LEWIS, E. G. 1962. Conditions Affecting the 'Reception' of an Official (Second/Foreign) Language. In *Symposium on Multilingualism*. CSA/CCTA Publication 87. Brazzaville.

MITCHELL, J. C. (ed.). 1969. *Social Networks in Urban Situations.* Manchester: Manchester University Press.

PARKIN, D. 1971. Language Choice on Two Kampala Housing Estates. In Whiteley (ed.), 1971.

WHITELEY, W. H. (ed.). 1971. *Language Use and Social Change.* London: Oxford University Press.

Elizabeth Tonkin

Some Coastal Pidgins of West Africa

This is a discussion of the way in which first 'pidgin Portuguese' and then 'pidgin English' developed in West Africa, with later examples drawn particularly from Nigeria. Any history of these languages is bound to be speculative: they had no literature and their documentation is haphazard. I have found, however, that the disparate pieces of evidence become more coherent when one tries to understand the social relations that underlie them. In the course of European contact with the peoples of the West African coast, members of very different cultures created and maintained a common language. What had they in common that enabled them to do this, and how far did they understand each other? What does the structure of the language itself tell us of their relationship? My account raises as many questions as it answers, but they are questions of interest to social anthropologists, referring as they do to the nature of communication, and to the creation and choice of social identity. The place of language in culture has often been discussed, but less attention has been given to the uses of language in society.[1] The history of any pidgin is a fruitful topic for such inquiry.[2]

PIDGIN LANGUAGES AND PIDGIN SITUATIONS

What then are 'pidgins'?[3] They are languages[4] which have commonly been defined in terms of their supposed history, a 'reduced' versions of a 'source' or 'base' language. In this view of a pidgin, its vocabulary (which is small and limited in scope) is normally considered to derive mainly from such a base language, but the latter's distinctions of person, gender, tense, and the like, might have been reduced or lost altogether. One must, however, call the result a 'language' and not merely some partial or 'corrupt' form of the original, because its syntax and grammar have been restructured to form a new system. The new language may even be spoken by people who have no direct knowledge of the base language. The other important feature of a pidgin is that it appears to have developed as a means of contact between people with very different first languages, so that the base language is not the only contributor. The puzzle for linguists is to decide in what ways the other language (or languages) has influenced the restructuring I have mentioned. Obviously any solutions will be of interest to social anthropologists as well, but all explanations are tentative as yet.

It will be seen that the definition of pidgin I have sketched out is a sociolinguistic, not simply a linguistic, one, and pidgins have, in fact, usually been sociologically defined before analysis began, by the choice of languages already known popularly as 'pidgins' or 'creoles' for investigation. This has led to *ad hoc* types of classification by reference to specific social situations, usually involving Europeans in positions of power. Possible pidgins with a non-European base language have been much less fully examined.

The *linguistic* phenomena that have been attributed to pidgins do not, therefore, define them, and they do not in fact appear to be unique phenomena; rather, certain common tendencies to simplification are manifested in an extreme way. From this point of view, 'pidgin' and 'creole' are not explanatory terms. But it is clear that the process of reduction can be observed only by comparison with a base language: hence the necessity of a historical approach. Yet, since the 'mixture' of other languages is such that the changes cannot be accounted for by orthodox 'Neogrammarian' methods, they present a challenge to linguists.[5]

If the concept of mixture is limited to the notion of a base language larded with borrowings, it is too crude to account for the complex process of semantic transformation and syntactic fusion that is likely to occur if one thinks of language primarily in terms of its users – here the distinctive groups who created the new language. But such a concept is necessary if one wishes to consider the pidgin's later history. If it develops alongside the continuing presence of the base, or if that language becomes at some point important, the influence on the pidgin can be great. Not only is the base available as a source of loan-words when expansion is necessary, it may be considered the standard variety to which the pidgin is a substandard supplement or alternative. Such 'diglossic' situations are a complex problem for sociological description, and for linguistic description too.[6]

It will be noticed that I have referred to 'creoles' as a 'popular' term, but have confined my own use to 'pidgin'. This deliberately does not conform with the practice of many linguists working in this field, who have contended that a 'pidgin' is a language 'native to none of those that use it' (Hall, 1966: xii), whereas a 'creole' is a pidgin that has become 'the native language of a speech community' (ibid.: xii). These stages are made to correspond to the processes of reduction and expansion already mentioned. However, while it is in a sense true that a 'creole' must first have been a 'pidgin', they are not necessarily distinctive linguistically. The same variety can in fact be used either as a 'first language' or as a 'lingua franca'. The processes of reduction and expansion will not neatly fit these uses if the pattern of development is not a simple linear one. This point is, I think, proved by examination of the West African material. Hence I shall not make the distinction between 'pidgin' and 'creole', especially as in a multilingual situation creoles in *sensu stricto* do not exist; that is to say, creoles in the sense defined by Le Page:

> 'The second stage of development occurs when the "pidgin" becomes so widely used that it is a more valuable instrument than the mother-tongues; parents then use it to their children, the children grow up speaking "pidgin" as their first language' (1964: 40).

In the all-important initial phase of West African Pidgin Portuguese, mulattos who had learnt a form of Portuguese in the home were clearly important, but they were important partly because they knew an African language as well, and could interpret between black and white. A simple dichotomy between 'pidgin' and 'creole' is thus inadequate to account for the transmission and development that must have occurred.

If the pidgin/creole distinction is not operable either linguistically or sociologically, might not the common conceptions of pidgin and creole *situations* be equally impossible to pin down? Systematic comparison has not been applied from this angle either, but one can find references to languages with 'pidgin' characteristics which are developing in, for instance, a non-European situation. Town Bemba (a language described by Richardson (1961, 1962) as a *cikopabeeluti* or 'language of the Copperbelt') is said to be spoken among equals. Based on CiBemba, it is the language of *savoir-vivre* – a symbol of a person's identity as a modern townsman. Sango, a language of the Central African Republic, is said by Samarin (1966) to be the language of the man who has left the bush but has not enough education to speak French. The speakers of both these languages are therefore attempting, by linguistic means, to join a group. These examples of one of the commonest uses of language might in turn lead us to look critically at the accepted views of European domination in Africa. Was an accessible form of the Europeans' language sometimes a desirable social marker?

I do not, however, wish to study 'correlatability', as against the inextricable combination of language and situation described by Pride elsewhere in this volume. Rather, one can approach the two together, considering language as one element in a complex bundle which makes up a situation, defining this last as broadly as possible. As these two examples I have given show, the evidence for any one element may in turn lead us to a better appreciation of the rest. One can then look for significant relations between elements, rather than attempt to compare preconceived wholes.

PIDGIN PORTUGUESE, *c.* 1440–1750

Portuguese was the first European language used on the West African coast, and, as in the rest of the Portuguese empire, not only was it the language of communication between European and native but it remained, as a pidgin lingua franca, the accepted language which succeeding Europeans had to learn. What was the nature of the initial Portuguese contact in West Africa?

Although the chroniclers record one brutal attack after another, the Portuguese from the beginning aimed at trade in goods, as well as forcible slave-raiding. Even their attacks had a longer aim: some of the captives were treated well in Portugal and then taken back to Africa as interpreters. The fifteenth-century explorer Cadamosto describes this process (e.g. 1937:

55). When one remembers, too, that there had been African slaves in Europe since the Middle Ages, and that the Moors were not finally expelled from the Iberian peninsula until 1492, it is possible that the Portuguese were not wholly ignorant of the land they set out to explore. Cadamosto turned back when his interpreters could no longer converse with the natives; the Portuguese built up their information as they progressed down the coast (see Hair, 1966). One wonders if they had not pilots and guides up that particular river which led to the court of Benin.

We do not know how a Portuguese pidgin began.[7] Besides this indication that African languages were initially used, we can guess from the entries in vocabularies collected in the sixteenth and seventeenth centuries by European visitors to the coast that certain Portuguese words and even words from other African languages soon became 'accepted' for trading. Comparison reveals this 'common pool' of names for items such as 'chicken', 'basins', 'knife', 'kola' (see e.g. Hair, 1967). The ubiquitous *dash* was first recorded in 1556 – a word of Romance origin (Christophersen, 1953, 1959). The visitors thought that these were native words; that they were offered as appropriate to the trading situation shows the significance of the Portuguese 'model' of contact and one way in which a pidgin spread.

The vocabularies, and loan-words still in African coastal languages, offer clues to the early lexis of pidgin but not to its syntax. This must have developed in a translation situation, and it is interesting to consider also that the Portuguese may have attempted to talk in a language already 'pidginized': the Sabir or Lingua Franca of the Mediterranean. Despite many references, actual examples of the Lingua Franca are few,[8] although the name has been applied to Mediterranean contact languages since the time of the Crusades. Mr Midshipman Easy's friend Gascoigne used it to make love to a beautiful Mooress in Tetuan – but Marryat unfortunately translates their conversation! The 'Sabir' which is the language of 'le Grand Turc' in *Le Bourgeois Gentilhomme* (1670) has recognizably pidgin forms.[9]

By the end of the seventeenth century Barbot thus reported the language situation at the coast. At Sierra Leone:

'Most of the Blacks about the bay speak either *Portuguese* or

Lingua Franca, which is a great convenience to the Europeans who come hither, and some also understand a little *English* or *Dutch*' (1732: 103).

At 'the River Junk' (near Sestos) the trade was in the hands of the English, but the language was broken Dutch and Portuguese, and on the Gold Coast:

> 'Many of the Coast Blacks speak a little *English* or *Dutch* and for the most part speak to us in a sort of *Lingua Franca* or broken *Portuguese* and *French*' (p. 249).

The same pattern occurs at Fida (Whydah), although here 'some few are very perfect in French' – and the French can more easily understand 'that *Lingua Franca* or broken *Portuguese*' (p. 339). In Benin, where the Portuguese influence is waning, but still significant, the brokers (*Mercadors* and *Veadors*) 'speak a sort of broken *Lingua Franca*' (p 360). Barbot may well mean that a European attempting to speak in Lingua Franca would be understood and answered in Pidgin Portuguese, but it is interesting that the resemblance is noted; it certainly appears, too, that a pidgin has emerged.

Actually it always seems that pidgins are swiftly developed and institutionalized,[10] so that it may be assumed that Pidgin Portuguese existed from the early days of Portuguese contact. In Surinam, for instance, it is known that Negro-English was stabilized in thirty years from the beginnings of the colony (Rens, 1953: 54). By then it had already been taken over by the Dutch, who remained there, and maintained it as a slave language.

In West Africa the spread of Pidgin Portuguese was encouraged by the Portuguese policy of settlement, whereby families of mixed blood grew up speaking a sort of Portuguese as their 'father tongue'.

> 'It was the early development and constant recruitment of a cadre of fluent speakers which gave such extensive and lasting currency to the Portuguese tongue' (Bradshaw, 1965: 7).

By the middle of the eighteenth century these speakers were 'black Portuguese': communities up and down the coast who were still nominally Christian and followed some European ways. In a manner reminiscent of the Anglo-Indians, they were sharply anxious to be called Portuguese.[11] By this time the only Portuguese settlements on the mainland north of Cape Lopez were in what is still Portuguese Guinea, yet when Francis Moore knew the black Portuguese on the Gambia, 1730–35, their 'bastard sort of Portuguese scarce understood in Lisbon' (1738: 39) was still the medium of trade; but English was known to the slaves at the fort there (Smith, 1744) and it soon replaced Portuguese as a lingua franca on the coast. The black Portuguese communities for whom language had been both a sign of identity and a means of maintaining it (by interpreting between black and white traders) are little mentioned after this period (although there are references to them up to the end of the eighteenth century). That they survived so long suggests that, however brutal and contemptuous the Portuguese appear as colonizers, their language and their culture were valued, particularly by those whose stranger fathers perhaps excluded them from full membership of local society.

The history of the 'Portuguese' bears out my earlier suggestion that pidgins may offer a means of identity; it also shows that language spread is helped by 'linguistic reservoirs' – self-perpetuating sources of the language from which it can continue to be picked up as a lingua franca. But although this fact demonstrates the importance of childhood acquisition, it also shows that the language cannot have developed in a simple (1) 'pidgin', (2) 'creole' fashion. Moreover, the 'Portuguese' were a socially significant group largely because they maintained their links – including language – with their mothers' kin. They were in an ambiguous position, vulnerable to suspicion by black and by white, but equally they derived patronage from both sides.

My suggestions for the beginnings of Pidgin Portuguese do not necessarily depend on there being a model language: the Lingua Franca features might have come independently from the simplifying efforts by speaker and hearer which are likely whenever communication is urgent but difficult. Simplification, as I have said, is a common linguistic tendency; again, one may cite Town Bemba where the complex CiBemba verbal system is indeterminately used (Richardson, 1962: 192). But obviously, any available precedent is likely to be used on initial contact –

any available schema of behaviour will be applied to try to cope with a new situation.

The many similarities between the pidgins or creoles of West Africa and the Caribbean have led to assumptions of a 'proto pidgin' of Portuguese base common to them all.[12] R. W. Thompson put forward a suggestion (1961) that Lingua Franca or Sabir was (i) used by the Portuguese in West Africa, (ii) 'creolized' in their factories and settlements on the coast, and (iii) used in the succeeding centuries as a 'pidgin' in the Far East. Period (ii) seems unnecessary, especially if one rejects the 'pidgin and creole' hypothesis. It is, of course, probable that Portuguese Pidgin developed with cross-fertilization from all quarters of the empire; we know the 'world-wide nature of the "onomastic reserve" of the Portuguese language' (E. Ardener, 1968: 117n.32).

In the Caribbean as in West Africa the problem is how these pidgins were acquired – or made; but a rigid either-or stance is not, I think, necessary. One must take into account both the operation of the 'law of least effort' and the key importance specific historical events may have. (The difficulty is to know what proportion of the result is due to either cause.) Here the situation included 'language-and-behaviour' which could be swiftly diffused – either as the participants moved away to repeat the situation (e.g. to the Caribbean or to another part of the coast) or as they were joined by newcomers, such as plantation slaves.

It is possible that the Portuguese themselves used West African pidgin when they were active in the West Indies between 1580 (union of the crowns of Spain and Portugal) and their supersession by the Dutch. In the crucial early period slave numbers were small and language contact easier between black and white. Sometimes this was due to the presence of white indentured servants (as in Jamaica and Surinam); the first slaves in the Antilles were brought over from Spain and Portugal (Rens, 1953: 6).[13]

Such a hypothesis does not invalidate the more common one that a pidgin was carried from Africa by the slaves themselves, but it offers an alternative or supplementary explanation, which is useful because there is no proof of such transmission. It is true that Dutch slavers used a language described as *portugués costeño* in Africa in the middle of the eighteenth century, that slaves often spent a long time in 'barracoons' awaiting shipment, that voyages were long and some of the crew had slave mistresses (writers usually cite van Wijk (1958) for this information; it is corroborated elsewhere). But all this amounts only to a possibility of an African genesis, and, by the eighteenth century, 'creole' languages of the Caribbean seem to have been well established. It is, of course, equally possible that slaves learnt pidgin in Africa in the earlier days of the trade.

'STRANGERS' AND 'GUESTS': RELATIONSHIPS OF CONTACT

Although it is not certain that Pidgin Portuguese preceded the English- and French-based creoles still spoken in the Caribbean, such a changeover certainly did occur in West Africa. Before discussing this, however, I try to consider in more detail the types of relationship that grew up between the blacks and whites who spoke and developed the West African pidgins.

As I have already suggested, the process of development of a pidgin is complex, and demonstrates with what limited means it is possible for people of very different background to succeed in communicating, especially as one expects to find 'the European affixing the same ideas to the words spoken by the African, as if they were pronounced by one of his own nation' (Matthews, 1788: 165) – and also vice versa. But, important as these aspects of language are to social anthropologists, they require detailed linguistic attention, so I confine myself here to some of their social implications. The fact is that a European language was chosen for communication, even though the outcome was a restructuring of syntax and lexis often representing African usage, and phonologically owing more to African languages.[14] Why were the people who seemed to be 'alternately fighting, trading and fornicating' (Boxer, 1961: 35) with the Africans the main source of the language spoken between them? After all, though powerful in arms they were heavily outnumbered. I do not know the complete answer to this question but there are several possible elements involved.

Commercial exigency must have been important: it was, as

Barbot said, 'a great convenience' not to have to learn a host of remote African languages. European travellers emphasized African inferiority and grudging wonder at European wealth. This sense of inequality is important too, but the pattern of relationship becomes more complex when examined. One way of dealing with strangers is to treat them, temporarily, *as if* they are not so: 'The stranger is still regarded as an enemy, but is treated as a friend for a limited time, and for a specific purpose' (Hamilton Grierson, 1903: 84). Brought into a group's own world order, the stranger became less dangerous. But whereas a pattern of periodically suspended hostility seems often to be institutionalized among groups roughly equivalent in strength and culture, the European, conscious of his superior wealth and technology, was likely to make an unbalanced and not a reciprocal relationship. This perhaps suggests a reason for choosing the European's language as the basis for communication.

A curious form of relationship, which is described at different places and periods all along the coast, is the adoption of the names of particular ships' officers by Africans. This practice is different from the bestowal of names and titles by Europeans as a gesture of contemptuous flattery (also sometimes an attempt to translate local honorifics and terms of hierarchy). An early example of a requested entitling is described by Jobson on his ascent of the Gambia in 1620:

> '*Buckor Sano* would needs be stiled the white mans *Alcaid*; I took it kindly, and put about his necke a string of Christall and a double string of Currall . . . a solemn cry *Alcaide, Alcaide* was proclaimed' (Purchas, 1625: 924).

Atkins gives an interesting account of name-taking at Cape Lopez, which suggests that Africans might, by identifying the 'strangers' with themselves, make them into 'guests':

> 'Many of them have borrowed names from the Europeans that have put in here, and are pleased when you will adopt them to wear such a Cognizance of your Remembrance, they do not solicit this favour till after several views, that they see something to be admired, or that the person asked, has a

fancied sympathy of Temper, or likeness with themselves' (1737: 198).

Such behaviour does not entirely account for the choice of language. But it does show that the relationship was not necessarily a simple one of mutual suspicion and strictly commercial contact. Traders who lived long on the coast and founded families there might become deeply involved in the affairs of their 'affines'. The practical surgeon Atkins was disgusted to find that this was so of the governor of Cape Coast Castle, who 'doted' upon his mulatto 'wife' and preferred the fetishes on his wrists to European medicine. Many became impressed by African beliefs. Their view was candidly put by the Irishman Nicholas Owen in his journal: 'There's a great many whites that thinks all those things are false, but what a man sees and imploys his reason upon . . . must have some grounds of truth' (1930: 17).

Today's historians, anxious to counterbalance the traditional picture of white power, can easily show how limited it was, and how Africans hated and despised the Europeans. The details above show, however, that this too is an over-simple picture. Yet several instances of African admiration can also be seen as envy – it was the wealth and technological mastery that were, in the older sense of the word, 'admired'. Even the long-attested fondness for European finery can be interpreted as an attempt to take on the Europeans' symbols of wealth and status. Europeans seem often to have been considered outside the natural order (despite the evidence of their all-too-human failings); it is reasonable to suppose that, even more than their clothes, acquisition of their language could be a means to achieving some of this supernatural power.

PIDGIN ENGLISH, *c*. 1650–1750

The choice of language once made, Portuguese pidgin developed as part of the act of trading. When the first Englishmen visited the West African coast in 1553 (led by a renegade Portuguese)[15] they found a world already adjusted to Portuguese contact, and although they and their successors, together with the French and Dutch, struggled to break this monopoly, Pidgin

	Senegal				*Goree*				*Gambia*				*Cacheu/ Bissau*				*S. Leone/ Sherbro*			
	P	F	D	E	P	F	D	E	P	F	D	E	P	F	D	E	P	F	D	E
1450–1550	t								t				ct				ct			
1550–1650	t	ct					c		t			t	ct				t			t
1650–1750	*t	ct				ct			*t	ct		ct	ct				*t			ct

Key: P = Portuguese
F = French
D = Dutch
E = English

Notes: 1. *Incidence of Europeans:* This table is an attempt to show, in a very broa and generalized way, the distribution of European settlement during th first 300 years of contact. It does not show the incidence of *ships*, which depending on the political *status quo*, might call at any of the point named and be of nationalities other than the four nations listed.

2. *Density of settlement:* The names listed are 'ports of call' commonl recorded in the literature, but they are again simplified and selected they do not represent equal density of settlement (cf. e.g. the two isolate posts on the Grain Coast with the 30 odd forts on the Gold Coast, an their attendant lodges).

Portuguese seems to have remained the lingua franca. Pidgin English eventually succeeded it, but long after the Portuguese influence had become negligible. The choice of language, therefore, did not directly or immediately reflect the balance of power.

Some light is thrown on this process of shift to English by an analysis of the agents of transmission, the loci of contact (in which pidgin would be used), and their distribution among the different European powers (see table above). For one needs to know also why English succeeded, rather than French or Dutch. On the Gold Coast a Danish pidgin also developed (Christophersen, 1953 *passim*), but it appears to have been confined to the Danish settlements.

The ownership of the fortified posts did not necessarily match that of the ships which plied the coast and could anchor

Guinea coast c. 1450–1750

Grain Coast				Gold Coast				Whydah				Benin/ Gatto				Bonny, Calabar, Cameroons				São Tomé & Principe			
P	F	D	E	P	F	D	E	P	F	D	E	P	F	D	E	P	F	D	E	P	F	D	E
				ct								t								ct			
	c	c		ct		ct		c	c		c	t		t	t			t		ct			
				*t		ct	ct	c	c	c	c			t	t					ct			

c: castles and larger fortified posts, broadly discriminated from
t: smaller factories, lodges; independent traders;
*t: black 'Portuguese' (dates when white Portuguese ceased settling are not exactly known).

Notes: 3. *Attestations:* Isolated Europeans may well have settled without record. In the 'Rivers' column, for instance, the Dutch entry is found in Brun (1624: 39) as a casual reference to one supercargo from the Cameroons; there might have been more. But settled traders are not referred to in the literature (there were no fortified posts, apparently), nor is the date of first settlement on 'hulks' known to me, though I think regular European settlement is post-1750. For a discussion of the earliest visits of *ships* see E. Ardener (1968).

The entries in the table are derived mostly from Fage (1965), Ryder (1959, 1965), and Lawrence (1963). Note that contrary to Lawrence's statement there is some evidence of French settlement on the Grain Coast (at Sestos: see de Marees (1602: 12–14) and Brun (1624: 39) with the notes by their editor, S. P. l'Honoré Naber, in 1912 and 1913 respectively).

far from settled areas. By 1680 the Royal African Company, for instance, consigned more goods to the Windward Coast in this 'ship trade' than to any other area (Davies, 1957: 222 f.). 'Interlopers' always outnumbered official vessels. Sloops and yachts were also sent out from the forts and from visiting ships, and were thought better value than the lodges or factories, where one or two European agents and a small staff could be easily robbed by the local people, or could do the robbing themselves.

Lawrence thinks, however, that 'there must have been dozens, probably hundreds, of lodges which have left no intelligible remains' (1963: 85), and it is equally by chance that we learn, from the casual remark of a traveller or a manuscript preserved, of individual traders who hived off on their own and settled in places like the Banana and Plantain Islands (see e.g. Smith,

1744: 54–55). Atkins reported about thirty private traders near Bence Island, 'loose privateering blades' (1737: 40). There was more informal contact with the local people in such situations than in the self-contained castles. Any social history of language must take them into account, but unfortunately documentation is not likely to appear.

How and why did Pidgin English replace Pidgin Portuguese as the lingua franca of the coast? We know that several European languages were used in the regular trading areas, and therefore several pidgins might develop, especially as there was a model – Pidgin Portuguese – available. As this original pidgin ceased to be the most useful choice, one of such secondary pidgins would be more and more used (and developed) instead. It is not likely that any French pidgin gained wide currency, since even though French ships at different periods visited the whole coast, the only land bases consistently held by the French were in Upper Guinea. (They were also active at Whydah, but here other nations were equally important.) 'Linguistic reservoirs' of French pidgin would therefore be geographically concentrated.

As for a Dutch pidgin, it might lie hidden behind an English calqued upon it; but although the Dutch were in their time more powerful than the English, their period of dominance was relatively short. It did not last into the beginning of the eighteenth century, when Portuguese and English are generally quoted as the languages of commerce on the Gold Coast. In other parts of their empire the Dutch were said to be 'more interested in spreading Dutch trade than the Dutch language or culture' (Boxer, 1961: 56), and to use the Pidgin Portuguese already established. This also happened in Surinam with Negro-English, and with Portuguese at the Cape (Kindersley, 1777: 66; and see Valkhoff's arguments, 1960, 1966). One can infer from Bosman that Portuguese was used to servants, slaves, and townspeople at Elmina (1967: 153, 199).

There were Africans who spoke Dutch well (see the story quoted by E. Ardener, 1968: 104). Similarly there are instances, throughout the years of European contact, of Africans educated in Portugal, France, and England. But such people do not appear to have been the important language models. More influential were their subordinates, the skilled slaves and the 'gromettas' (freemen) who worked at sea and ashore. Often highly mobile, they might even cross the Atlantic, especially as 'linguists' (interpreters).[16] From at least the eighteenth century, Kru from Liberia were employed (as they are still) in gangs working on ships. They must have been important diffusers and standardizers of Pidgin English, for their employers included slavers, traders, explorers, and the English Navy, and they worked for them even as far as South Africa (see, among many references, Allen, 1840; Marsh, 1944; Lloyd, 1949; Fraenkel, 1964). African pidgin-speakers such as these became the main agents of language transmission, and it is likely that the wide spread of English settlement (see table, p. 140–141) favoured the choice of their pidgin.

The Gold Coast, with its history of intensive contact, is a likely centre for the development of Pidgin English (although it could have developed as well in the Gambia and at Sierra Leone). Pidgin Portuguese was well known and could serve as a model, while Gold Coast natives travelled far along the coast. Although, as with Portuguese pidgin, independent growth is possible, it seems more likely and economically explained as essentially a secondary growth. Such an explanation would be equally possible for the Caribbean creoles, and it has been quite persuasively argued for Afrikaans by Valkhoff (1960, 1966).

PIDGIN ENGLISH IN NIGERIA FROM 1750

In this section I draw my examples from Nigeria[17] though any findings may apply more widely. In this period it is an important area because the growing demands of the transatlantic plantations drove the slavers further eastward. The coast from Dahomey to Cameroon, which had been largely ignored (partly because of its difficult sailing conditions) and sometimes hardly known, even to the Portuguese, became deeply involved with the Europeans. But until the middle of the nineteenth century, the great expansion in the slave trade did not alter the pattern of relationships between European and African middlemen or between slave and free. In the 'Rivers' however (where the slavers had been coming since the middle of the seventeenth century) an additional form of contact developed. Ships might be anchored for months in the estuary while slaves were collecting, and later (e.g. when the palm-oil trade replaced slaves) 'hulks' moored there for good were the dwelling- and trading-places of the European supercargoes. The heads of the Delta 'Houses' (described by Dike, 1956, and Jones, 1963) developed long-standing commercial relationships with the Europeans. These somewhat cynical friendships were not a new phenomenon, but the 'trading states' themselves evolved partly in response to European trading needs, and their leaders enjoyed the fruits of Western technology. Reading and writing were seen as trading skills, like book-keeping and arithmetic. This is limited literacy, which is much commoner than full literacy, as Goody and Watt point out (1968), but in Old Calabar it seems to have developed a momentum of its own, so that by the end of the eighteenth century letters and journals were being written there, in fairly fluent English.[18] It was, interestingly, at Old Calabar that the first missionaries were *invited* to settle, in 1846.

The missionary impact 1841–1891

This has been well documented by Ajayi (1966). It appears (to generalize) that the first missionaries, mostly Protestant Evangelicals, were committed consciously to the current British belief in the civilizing influences of trade, and unconsciously to the universal rightness of a Victorian middle-class morality. Heavily dependent anyway on the traders, who gave them transport and supplies, they were hardly to be differentiated from them by the Africans. The latter welcomed the missionaries usually when they realized they could teach English and arithmetic. If the Africans' image of white men remained unchanged, the missionaries' stereotype of the African was in some ways more destructive than the traders'. Traders despised Africans, but at least drank and slept with them; the missionaries' contempt was benevolent but could be infinitely patronizing. It is especially sad, too, that the rise of European philanthropy and sensibility, which made disinterested action to 'strangers' a new ideal, coincided with a great rise in coastal wealth, which, measured in slaves (and refused Western-type capital investment), could result in potlatch displays of human sacrifice which convinced European observers of African brutality.

The missionaries were under heavy pressure to work through the schools. As Protestants, they preached God's Word and 'to establish the Gospel among any people, they must have Bibles and therefore must have the art to make them or the money to buy them. They must read the Bible and this implies instruction' (Bowen, cited in Ajayi, p.126). Thus though both the missionaries and the pupils wanted English to be known, they had very different motives. The conflict deepened as the administration and commerce needed more clerks, and literacy became for Africans a means to affluence and status. There was a more subtle conflict too, between the missionaries' wish to reach the people through their own mother tongues, and their deep feeling that 'civilization' demanded an 'advanced' form of expression.[19] As we know, the idea that there are 'primitive' languages dies hard.

These divergent, incompatible aims still exist in Nigerian education. One is led to suggest a new reason for the low level of English, so often deplored: expatriates, who if not teachers are still often advisers, often unconsciously equate the learning of English with learning to participate in British culture, whereas Nigerians very often understand English as just another skill, learnt in parallel with other subjects, not as a means of command over them.[20] There is also a split between the written language and the spoken; and the speaker's expressive use may be basically Pidgin, picked up unconsciously and adequate for conversation, but not for jobs that require the marshalling of abstract information.

Nineteenth- and twentieth-century uses of Pidgin

Although the mission educators taught 'standard' English this has not displaced Pidgin in Nigeria. Here one has to see, once again, the purposes that Pidgin serves, and its deficiencies. Pidgin was well established as a means of communication for black and white; it had already served as a means of identity. Both these uses increased in the nineteenth century.

At the end of the eighteenth century the colony of Sierra Leone was set up. Among its earliest members were 'Settlers' from Nova Scotia and Jamaica (the Maroons); Krumen also were important additions from the beginning. Soon these were overwhelmed in numbers by 'Liberated Africans' – rescued off the slave ships. From these related sources a more or less homogeneous style of pidgin developed[21] and even became the only language for many members of the 'Krio' community. As a bilingual or second language it was one of the useful skills picked up by the 'emigrants' or 'Saros', those Sierra Leonians, mostly of Yoruba, but also of Hausa and Ibo origin, who started making their way back to Nigeria in the 1840s, and continued for years as important members of the administration, commerce, and the churches. They therefore helped to establish English as a major link language in Nigeria, English ranging from standard to pidgin.

When the Europeans, so long familiar at the coast, began to be seen inland, the resulting confrontations were not a simple drama of black and white. The terms of the contact, as with the early Portuguese encounters, depended on white force, but also on the vital interpreters, who might be returning emigrants or traditional middlemen or people from rival groups who had been 'pacified' earlier. They were therefore quite possibly foreign or hostile to the Africans with whom they were supposed to communicate.[22] The Europeans and the interpreters might understand little of each other either. In such circumstances any translation language has a great burden of meaning to carry. Pidgin English, which must have seemed a very convenient medium, was in fact incapable of reconciling such different world-views and made its users look foolish. For the whites, as their reminiscences and travelling accounts show, it was comic evidence of African incapacity; for many Africans, on the other hand, it was evidence of what the white man spoke.

No wonder that Pidgin became devalued – and yet more popular than ever. For with the establishment of colonial rule many new kinds of relationship needed a medium for communication, and Pidgin penetrated inland at last, finally losing some of its special coast connotations. Barracks, police posts, offices, schools (and later universities); the *sabon garis* (strangers' towns) of the north and the new urban centres of the south: these were the places where Pidgin spread – in situations analogous to those already described for Town Bemba and

Sango. It provided a neutral lingua franca for people of different tribes, and, once again, was a means to a new identity.[23] It sometimes became a first language for children of tribally 'mixed' parentage (Mafeni, 1965: 85): this occurred on a much larger scale in the plantation world of the Cameroons (Ardener, 1956, 1967). Nevertheless, though Pidgin might be adequate for such *internal* uses, additional knowledge of English was necessary to enter the world of Western ideas. The language of reading and writing in Nigeria, the language of newspapers, is necessarily near 'standard' or, better, 'international' English. Hence a 'diglossic' situation is likely to arise, with spoken varieties tending towards the 'pidgin' end of the continuum and literacy requiring a command of 'standard' forms. Such a pattern is far from unique, but in a multilingual country it does pose extra problems in education.

An anthropological approach to a topic usually dealt with by linguists may modify their conclusions – for I think that the history of West African pidgins shows that some linguistic descriptions of the way in which a 'pidgin' becomes a 'creole' are faulty. But the anthropologist also relies on linguistic data, with which he can explore social situations more subtly. In a truly sociolinguistic approach the linguist's and the anthropologist's points of view cannot be divided.

It is rewarding to attempt a social history of a language because in so doing one studies processes of social definition: how groups define themselves in opposition to other groups and also how groups bring themselves into relationship with others – what form their communication takes. Pidgin may seem a marginal subject in the ethnography of West Africa, but its long history itself needs explaining, its study throws light on the economic significance of 'outsider' groups, and an understanding of its uses is important in an examination of the period of European contact and annexation or conquest (see Ardener, 1956). It is, as I have said, through Pidgin-speaking intermediaries that black and white largely took stock of one another.

Pidgins are useful test cases for sociolinguistic inquiry, but their study, it must be emphasized, is necessarily circular – for one can never assume in advance what value is placed on the use of a language variety: one can only try to derive from the same body of evidence what such values are likely to be.

NOTES

1. For a linguist's look at the subject, see Pride (1971). Tanner (1967) argues the advantages of the social over the cultural approach for anthropologists.

2. I am particularly grateful to Edwin Ardener for his help and attentive criticism, and to Professor Dell Hymes for information and suggestions. The work on which this paper is based was made possible by the award of an SSRC Studentship.

3. The origin of the word 'pidgin' is unknown. Commonly said to be a Chinese rendering of 'business', and thus taken from Chinese pidgin English, it has also been derived from 'pidian', a local word used by Legh's colonists to describe the local people, around the present borders of Guyana and Brazil, 1605–06. See Hall (1966: 7).

4. The difficulties of delimiting varieties of language are described by Pride and Denison in this volume. The topic is a big one and there is no room to discuss it in this paper, so Pidgin is simply treated as one variety available to a speaker, without any discussion of its status. One may add that the usefulness of any language–dialect division has been criticized by several linguists (see e.g. Dalby, 1967): linguistically speaking, the two 'languages' of two different countries may differ as little as two 'dialects' elsewhere; also, *language* and *people* need not be identical.

5. See the discussion by Ardener in this volume (section IV, pp. 219–222, especially).

6. The point is discussed by Le Page (1968) with reference to some varieties of Caribbean English. Here it is hard to see a consistent use of distinctive systems, in contrast to the conscious code-switching claimed for French-based creoles (see Ferguson's well-known extension of 'diglossia' to cover the Haitian case, 1959).

7. W. Günther (at the School of Oriental and African Studies, London, 12 June 1969) suggested a history for the languages still spoken on São Tomé and Principe. He believes that they developed independently of other pidgins and that, after a period of 'chaos' and gesture, 'broken Portuguese' was redeveloped by the slaves as a language unintelligible to their masters. These seem unlikely assertions, and it is preferable to look for a model than to conjure a language *ab nihilo*. The island pidgins resemble other Portuguese pidgins closely, and it seems curious to alter Portuguese syntax (while retaining its lexis) as a means of deception – itself an unlikely act in the face of Portuguese miscegenation, and the retention of the language elsewhere by 'coloured' communities.

8. The only detailed evidence I have found is in Kahane, Kahane, and Tietze, *The Lingua Franca in the Levant* (1958). This learned study covers only 'Turkish nautical terms of Italian and Greek origin' – reconstructed from contemporary language, for which combined skill in Arabic and Romance philology was required. (None of the terms appears to be in West Coast vocabularies, but they are very specialized.)

9. A literary critic remarked (in 1873) that at

> 'Alger . . . on parle une langue qui n'est que le turc de Molière. La première fois qu'on entend les Arabes vous apostrophiser dans ce langage pittoresque:

si te sabir, ti respondir! on se tâte pour voir si l'on n'est pas sur le plancher du Théâtre Français' (cited in *Œuvres*, Tome VII, 1883).

An example of Molière's 'turc' is:

Se ti sabir,
Ti respondir;
Se non sabir
Tazir, tazir.

Mi star Mufti:
Ti qui star ci?
Non intendir:
Tazir, tazir. (Act IV Sc. V.)

10. Reinecke gives an interesting example of how a polyglot ship's crew acquires a working vocabulary of about 300 words in common after a couple of months together (1938, in Hymes, 1964: 535).

11. By the eighteenth century, English references to the Portuguese usually mean this community: see e.g. John Newton's journal entry for Bunce Island in 1750:

> 'Have had no appearance of trade today, the white men being all exhausted and I have not seen one Portuguese since I have been in the river' (Martin and Spurell, 1962: 13).

12. There is considerable dispute about the origins of Caribbean creoles – see contributions to the Mona Conference on the subject, 1968 (in Hymes, 1971).

13. When Jamaica was captured by the British in 1655, the Spaniards had had slaves there since 1515. Barbados was first settled in 1625, and open to the slaves of any country.

14. The sound system of a pidgin can vary according to the first language of the speaker. The more a pidgin was spoken among Africans the more its phonology 'Africanized', but it remained an independent system, including attempts at European phonemes; it likewise did not mirror any *single* African language. See Mafeni (1965) for a description of this in Nigeria.

15. This was Windham's visit to Benin (available in Hakluyt).

16. In the eighteenth century there was an employment register for linguists in Liverpool. 'The position was often held by "ladies of colour" ' (Williams, 1897, vol. I: 18). Women are most important transmitters and developers of pidgin. This is shown for Town Bemba by Richardson (1961); one can illustrate from Ardener (1962) and from the novels of Ekwensi their pivotal linguistic role in the unstable connections of urban and plantation life in Lagos and Cameroon.

17. By 'Nigeria' I mean the country which was consolidated as such under British rule. The Cameroons are excluded from full consideration.

18. Antera Duke's diary (ed. Forde, 1956) and the letters to Ambrose Lace quoted by Williams (1897) are examples of this.

19. Actually, the missionaries' translations were not necessarily welcomed, see S. Ardener (1968: 13). I found that Nigerian students usually preferred English – the language of the King James version is the sacred language of Christianity here too (a point amusingly illustrated by Nicol, 1960).

20. A recent Ford Foundation Survey (1967) on English language teaching never recognized that British–American and Nigerian evaluations of needs in

language-learning were not necessarily identical. It recommended psychological research but did not mention sociologists or social anthropologists.

21. This minimal summary is based on the analysis of the earliest population (see Hargreaves, 1962) and agrees with Berry's conclusions as to sources (1959), except that I think Kru English must have been a significant contributor. The close similarities between this, other varieties of coastal Pidgin heard in the colony, and the 'Jamaica Talk' of the Maroons explains why the Nova Scotians (the largest single group of Settlers) did not form the main language models.

22. In *Things Fall Apart* (1958) Chinua Achebe makes the over-zealous converts precipitate clashes in Iboland, while corrupt and hostile court messengers (who are also interpreters) become a new power element. This is borne out in other sources. A similar account is given in Oginga Odinga's autobiography, for the Kenya Luo (1967: 21).

23. See note 16. The range of Pidgin can be grasped from a reading of Nigerian novels, though it should be said that its use here is generally conventional in that it is contrasted absolutely with 'standard' English. (Cf. the common use of 'comic Cockney' to type lower-class characters, in much English light fiction.)

REFERENCES

ACHEBE, CHINUA. 1958. *Things Fall Apart*. London: Heinemann.

AJAYI, J. F. ADE. 1966. *Christian Missions in Nigeria 1841–1891*. London: Longmans.

ALEXANDRE, PIERRE. 1967. *Langues et langage en Afrique noire*. Paris: Payot.

ALLEN, CAPT. WILLIAM. 1840. *Picturesque Views on the River Niger, sketched during Lander's last visit in 1832–3*. London: Murray & Ackerman.

ARDENER, EDWIN. 1956. *Coastal Bantu of the Cameroons*. London: International African Institute.

—— 1962. *Divorce and Fertility: An African Study*. London: Oxford University Press.

—— 1967. The Nature of the Reunification of Cameroon. In A. Hazlewood (ed.), *African Integration and Disintegration*. London: Oxford University Press.

—— 1968. Documentary and Linguistic Evidence for the Rise of the Trading Polities between Rio del Rey and Cameroons, 1500–1650. In I. M. Lewis (ed.), *History and Social Anthropology*. ASA Monograph 7. London: Tavistock.

ARDENER, SHIRLEY. 1968. *Eye-witnesses to the Annexation of Cameroon 1883–1887*. West Cameroon: Government Press Buea.

ATKINS, JOHN. 1737. *A Voyage to Guinea, Brasil and the West Indies*. York and Scarborough: Printed for Ward & Chandler.

AZURARA, GOMES EANNES DE. 1896. *The Chronicle of the Discovery and Conquest of Guinea*. Trans. C. R. Beazley and E. Prestage. London: Hakluyt Society.

BARBOT, JOHN. 1732. A Description of the Coasts of North and South Guinea. In Messrs Churchill, *A Collection of Voyages*. London: Thomas Osborne.

BERRY, J. 1959. Origins of Krio Vocabulary. *Sierra Leone Studies* (n.s.) **12**: 298–307.

BOSMAN, WILLIAM. 1967. *A New and Accurate Description of the Coast of Guinea*. Edited by J. D. Fage, Introduction by J. R. Willis. London: Frank Cass.

BOXER, C. R. 1961. *Four Centuries of Portuguese Expansion 1415–1825: A Succinct Survey*. Johannesburg: Witwatersrand University Press.

BRADBURY, R. E., and LLOYD, P. C. 1957. *The Benin Kingdoms and the Edo-speaking Peoples of South-Western Nigeria ... together with a section on the Itsekiri*. London: International African Institute.

BRADSHAW, A. T. VON S. 1965. Vestiges of Portuguese in the Language of Sierra Leone. *Sierra Leone Language Review* **4**: 5–37.

BRUN, SAMUEL. 1913. Schiffarten, 1624. Edited by S. P. l'Honoré Naber in *Werken Uitgegeven door de Linschoten-Vereeniging*, Vol. VI. 's Gravenhage: Martinus Nijhoff.

CADAMOSTO. 1937. *The Voyages of Cadamosto*. Trans. by G. R. Crone. London: Hakluyt Society.

CASSIDY, FREDERIC G. 1961. *Jamaica Talk*. London: Macmillan.

—— 1962. Toward the Recovery of Early English–African Pidgin. In *Symposium on Multilingualism*. CSA/CCTA Publication 87. Brazzaville.

CHRISTOPHERSEN, PAUL. 1953. Some Special West African English Words. *English Studies* **34**: 282–291.

—— 1959. A Note on the Words 'Dash' and 'Ju-Ju' in West African English. *English Studies* **40**: 115.

CURTIN, PHILIP. 1964. *The Image of Africa*. Madison: University of Wisconsin Press.

DALBY, DAVID. 1967. Levels of Relationship in the Comparative Study of African Languages. *African Language Studies* **7**: 171–179.

DAVIES, K. G. 1957. *The Royal African Company*. London: Longmans.

DIKE, K. ONWUKA. 1956. *Trade and Politics in the Niger Delta 1830–1885*. Oxford: Clarendon Press.

EKWENSI, CYPRIAN D. O. 1954. *People of the City*. London: Andrew Dakers.

—— 1961. *Jagua Nana*. London: Hutchinson.

FAGE, J. D. 1965. *An Atlas of African History*. London: Edward Arnold.

FERGUSON, C. A. 1959. Diglossia. *Word* **15**: 325–340. Also in D. Hymes (ed.), 1964.

FORDE, C. DARYLL. 1951. *The Yoruba-speaking Peoples of South-Western Nigeria.* London: International African Institute.

— (ed.). 1956. *Efik Traders of Old Calabar.* London: International African Institute.

— and JONES, G. I. 1950. *The Ibo and Ibibio-speaking Peoples of South-Eastern Nigeria.* London: International African Institute.

FRAENKEL, MERRAN. 1964. *Tribe and Class in Monrovia.* London: Oxford University Press.

— 1966. Social Change on the Kru Coast of Liberia. *Africa* **36** (2): 154–172.

GAMBLE, DAVID. 1957. *The Wolof of Senegambia.* London: International African Institute.

GOLDIE, HUGH. 1890. *Calabar and its Mission.* Edinburgh and London: Oliphant, Anderson & Ferrier.

GOODY, JACK, and WATT, IAN. 1968. The Consequences of Literacy. In Jack Goody (ed.), *Literacy in Traditional Societies.* Cambridge: Cambridge University Press.

HAIR, P. E. H. 1966. The Use of African Languages in Afro-European Contacts in Guinea 1440–1560. *Sierra Leone Language Review* **5**: 5–26.

— 1967. An Ethnolinguistic Inventory of the Upper Guinea Coast before 1700. *African Language Review* **6**: 32–70.

HAKLUYT, RICHARD. 1904. *The Principal Navigations.* Facsimile of 2nd edn, Vol. VI, James MacLehose & Sons. Glasgow: Glasgow University Press.

HALL, ROBERT A., JR. 1966. *Pidgin and Creole Languages.* Ithaca, NY: Cornell University Press.

HAMILTON GRIERSON, P. J. 1903. *The Silent Trade.* Edinburgh: William Green.

HARGREAVES, J. D. 1962. African Colonization in Nineteenth Century Sierra Leone and Liberia. *Sierra Leone Studies* (n.s.) **16** (June): 189–203.

HYMES, DELL. 1962. The Ethnography of Speaking. In T. Gladwin and W. C. Sturtevant (eds.), *Anthropology and Human Behavior.* Washington: Anthropological Society of Washington.

— (ed.). 1964. *Language in Culture and Society.* New York: Harper & Row.

— (ed.). 1971. *Pidginization and Creolization of Languages.* Cambridge: Cambridge University Press.

JACOBS, ROBERT (ed.). 1966. *English Language Teaching in Nigeria.* (Private publication.)

JONES, G. I. 1963. *The Trading States of the Oil Rivers.* London: Oxford University Press.

KAHANE, HENRY, KAHANE, RENÉE, and TIETZE, ANDREAS. 1958. *The Lingua Franca in the Levant.* Urbana, Ill.: University of Illinois Press.

KINDERSLEY, MRS. 1777. Letters from the Islands of Teneriffe, Brazil, the Cape of Good Hope and the East Indies. London: Printed for J. Nourse.

LAWRENCE, A. W. 1963. *Trade Castles and Forts of West Africa.* London: Jonathan Cape.

LE PAGE, R. B. (ed.). 1960. *Creole Language Studies,* I. London: Macmillan.

—— 1964. *The National Language Question.* London: Oxford University Press.

—— 1968. Problems of Description in Multilingual Communities. *Transactions of the Philological Society:* 189–212.

LLOYD, CHRISTOPHER. 1949. *The Navy and the Slave Trade.* London: Longmans.

MAFENI, BERNARD O. W. 1965. *Some Aspects of the Phonetics and Phonology of Nigerian Pidgin.* Unpublished M.Litt. thesis, University of Edinburgh.

MAREES, P. DE. 1912. Beschrijving Van de Gout-Custe. . . 1602. Edited by S. P. l'Honoré Naber in *Werken Uitgegeven door de Linschoten-Vereeniging,* Vol. V. 's Gravenhage: Martinus Nijhoff.

MARRYAT, CAPT. FREDERICK. 1836. *Mr Midshipman Easy.* London: Saunders & Otley.

MARSH, JOHN H. 1944. *Skeleton Coast.* London: Hodder & Stoughton.

MARTIN, BERNARD, and SPURELL, M. (eds.). 1962. *The Journal of a Slave Trader, John Newton, 1750–1754.* London: Epworth Press.

MATTHEWS, JOHN. 1788. *A Voyage to the River Sierra-Leone. . .* London: Printed for B. White & Son.

MOLIÈRE. 1670. *Le Bourgeois Gentilhomme.* In *Œuvres de Molière,* Tome VII, edited by E. Despois and P. Mesnard. Paris: Hachette, 1883.

MOORE, FRANCIS. 1738. *Travels into the Inland Parts of Africa.* London: Printed by Edward Cave for the author.

NICOL, ABIOSEH. 1960. As the Night, the Day. In Langston Hughes (ed.), *An African Treasury.* New York: Pyramid Books.

ODINGA, A. OGINGA. 1967. *Not Yet Uhuru.* London: Heinemann Educational Books.

OWEN, NICHOLAS. 1930. *Journal of a Slave Dealer.* Edited by Eveline Martin. London: Routledge.

PHILLIPS, THOMAS. 1746. A Journal of a Voyage made in the *Hannibal* of London, 1693, 1694. In Messrs Churchill, *A Collection of Voyages,* Vol. VI. London: Henry Linton & John Osborne.

PRIDE, J. B. 1971. *The Social Meaning of Language.* London: Oxford University Press.

PURCHAS, SAMUEL. 1625. *Purchas his Pilgrimes.* London: Printed by William Stansby for Henrie Fetherstone.

REINECKE, JOHN. 1938. Trade Jargons and Creole Dialects as Marginal Languages. Reprinted in Hymes (ed.), 1964.

RENS, L. L. E. 1953. *The Historical and Social Background of Surinam's Negro English.* Amsterdam: North-Holland Publishing Co.

RICHARDSON, I. 1961. Some Observations on the Status of Town Bemba in Northern Rhodesia. *African Language Studies* **2**: 25–36.

—— 1962. Linguistic Change in Africa with special reference to the Bemba-speaking area of Northern Rhodesia. In *Symposium on Multilingualism.* CSA/CCTA Publication 87. Brazzaville.

RYDER, A. F. C. 1958. The Re-establishment of Portuguese Factories on the Costa de Mina to the Mid-eighteenth Century. *Journal of the Historical Society of Nigeria* **1** (3): 157–183.

—— 1959. An Early Portuguese Trading Voyage to the Forcados River. *Journal of the Historical Society of Nigeria* **1** (4): 294–321.

—— 1961. The Benin Missions. *Journal of the Historical Society of Nigeria* **2** (2): 231–259.

—— 1965. Dutch Trade on the Nigerian Coast during the Seventeenth Century. *Journal of the Historical Society of Nigeria* **3** (2): 195–210.

SAMARIN, WILLIAM J. 1966. Self-annulling Prestige Factors among Speakers of a Creole Language. In William Bright (ed.), *Sociolinguistics.* The Hague: Mouton.

SMITH, WILLIAM. 1744. *A New Voyage to Guinea.* London: Printed for John Nourse.

SNELGRAVE, CAPT. WILLIAM. 1754. *A New Account of Guinea and the Slave Trade.* London: J. Wren.

TANNER, NANCY. 1967. Speech and Society among the Indonesian Elite: A Case Study of a Multilingual Society. *Anthropological Linguistics* **9** (3): 15–40.

THOMPSON, R. W. 1961. A Note of Some Possible Affinities between the Creole Dialects of the Old World and those of the New. In R. B. Le Page (ed.), *Creole Language Studies,* II. London: Macmillan.

VALKHOFF, MARIUS. 1960. Contributions to the Study of Creole, I, II and III. *African Studies* **19**: 77–87, 113–115, 230–244.

—— 1966. *Studies in Portuguese and Creole with special reference to South Africa.* Johannesburg: Witwatersrand University Press.

VAN WIJK, H. L. A. 1958. Originés y Evolución del Papiamentu. *Neophilologus* **42**: 169–182.

VOORHOEVE, J. 1962. Creole Languages and Communication. In *Symposium on Multilingualism.* CSA/CCTA Publication 87. Brazzaville.

WADDELL, REV. HOPE MASTERMAN. 1863. *Twenty-nine Years in the West Indies and Central Africa.* London: Thomas Nelson.

WHINNOM, KEITH. 1956. *Spanish Contact Vernaculars in the Philippine Islands.* Hong Kong/London: Oxford University Press.

WILLIAMS, GOMER. 1897. *The Liverpool Privateers: with an account of the Liverpool Slave Trade.* 2 vols. London: William Heinemann, and Liverpool: Edward Howell.

WILSON, W. A. A. 1962. *The Crioulo of Guiné.* Johannesburg: Witwatersrand University Press.

N. Denison

Some Observations on Language Variety and Plurilingualism

Recent work[1] on the sociolinguistics of plurilingualism[2] has shown that it can be most illuminatingly and economically treated within the same conceptual framework as diglossia[3] and register[4]. These are all manifestations of language variety, and, more specifically, of what I prefer, with Gregory (1967), to call diatypic variety. 'Diatypes' are varieties of language within a community, specified according to use (purpose, function), whereas dialects are specified according to groups of users. Like so many of the lines drawn in the social sciences, such distinctions are fuzzy at the edges, but they are no less serviceable for that. It is important to remember that, in drawing them, one is distinguishing not so much between different bodies of material as between different ways of looking at the same material. People may, as Fishman (1967) has pointed out, be bilingual or bi-dialectical with or without participation in diatypic (diglossic) situations; moreover, the same utterance may best be described dialectically to meet one particular explanatory aim, diatypically to meet another.

Diatypic structuredness, like phonological or grammatical structuredness, is a characteristic of the *linguistic* part of an act of communication. Accompanying or independent gestures and other non-linguistic activities are part of the *extra-linguistic context,* as are also, for instance, the persons, age, sex, status, and roles of the sender(s) and receiver(s) of the message and of any other participants (those persons whose presence is relevant even though they may neither send nor receive messages); and those circumstances of season and clock, place and physical scene, which together form the *setting.* Paralinguistic features such as voice-timbre may be best treated as part of the *linguistic text,* and certainly, in the analysis of associated texts, as part of the *linguistic context.* Linguistic and extra-linguistic context together form the *situation* of a linguistic text. It is also convenient to treat as part of the situation the *mood* of the participants and the *purpose* and *topic* of the occasion, though these can normally be ascertained only from a complexity of linguistic and extra-linguistic indications.

A register is any one of those diatypic varieties which the members of a given speech community are accustomed to thinking of as belonging to one language. Register difference in British English is exemplified by the difference in lexical, phonological, and grammatical structure between 'Please place litter in receptacle provided' and 'Put your rubbish in this bin, would you?', in French by the selection, in addressing a single individual, of *tu* or *vous*, with concomitant grammatical, lexical, and phonological (including suprasegmental) selections.

It is both necessary and interesting to ask what in principle distinguishes diatypic selection from the mere selection of one rather than another item or sequence in the phonological system of a language, one rather than another component or sequence of components in the grammatical system, one rather than another word or sequence of words in the lexis.

The most important difference lies in the kinds of meaning carried. Apart from the specific 'meanings' which may attach to certain selections at the purely phonological level, such as onomatopoeia and suprasegmental patterns of rhythm, pitch, stress, and quantity, the main function of the phonology is to provide the differential means of constructing discrete morphological units. The essential function of grammar and lexis is to provide sufficient items and operations in the linguistic expression to distinguish between what we would normally think of as different meanings – though not, of course, on a one-for-one basis. Language simply could not perform its communicative function without these levels of organization. At first sight, however, there would appear to be no logical necessity for further organization into separate diatypes, so far as the basic communication of thoughts and intentions is concerned. Yet it appears likely that all speech communities do in fact have diatypic conventions[5] over and above the indispensable primary conventions of phonology, grammar, and lexis. There is at present no reason to believe that the former are any less arbitrary; yet the fact that diatypic distinctions seem to be universally present suggests that they reflect a universal factor in human affairs: and that factor is the presence of systems of social attitudes which imply a social analysis and categorization of situations by participants over and above the primary semantic analysis presupposed by any linguistic text in an act of communication.

One may establish a difference between diatypic and *stylistic* variation parallel to the difference between dialect and idiolect. A diatype implies a conventional connection of a language variety with a given category or categories of situation. In order to communicate without risk of misunderstanding, members of a linguistic community must submit to diatypic convention just as they must submit to the primary linguistic conventions of phonological, grammatical, and lexical rules. The margin for individual interpretations of diatypic convention in situation is, however, wider than the margin for differences in individual applications of primary phonological, grammatical, and lexical rules, and it is not difficult to see why: there is greater scope for individual assessments to differ slightly as to the degree, for instance, of formality which a given occasion calls for in a given culture, than for differences about whether to refer in English to a given animal as a horse or a cow (lexis), a cow or a sow (phonology), or whether it has been or will be slaughtered (grammar). The exploitation of this margin by individuals, even the violation of diatypic convention in a more or less regular and ultimately predictable manner, we may call stylistic variation.

If we ask what it is in the linguistic expression which distinguishes diatypic organization from the organization of the primary levels of linguistic structure, then we may note that diatypic features are not confined to a particular one of the primary levels of phonology, grammar, or lexis, but may be – and typically are – distributed throughout any or all of these levels. In other words, diatypic organization is superimposed as a set of secondary selections over and above the primary selections at the levels mentioned. Diatypes are therefore normally identifiable with confidence only over longish stretches of text, and their features include not only the presence or absence of specific items, but also, and more importantly, particular frequencies of occurrence and concurrence of items.

To return for a moment to the example quoted above of

English register difference: the two alternative forms of request belong respectively to the formal, impersonal register of relationships between authority and the public; and to the informal, friendly register of small-group relationships between people among whom equality of status is implied, if not necessarily objectively a fact. The roles of requester and requested are in the informal instance not institutionalized, whereas in the formal instance they are felt to be less interchangeable. No English person has difficulty in assigning the formulaic 'Please place litter in receptacle provided' to the visual medium, and specifically to notices in public settings; or in contextualizing 'Put your rubbish in this bin, would you?' as spoken medium or the visual reporting or simulation of it, probably private setting, probably between participants who know each other. The linguistic selections which provide the identifying clues are distributed throughout the primary levels. In the formal request, from the grammatical point of view, the absence of the possessive adjective 'your' before 'litter' and of the definite article before 'receptacle' assign the text to the visual medium, or to reading or quoting from it; the grammatical pattern of 'receptacle provided' is almost as specifically diagnostic. Lexically, the selection of 'place' versus 'put', 'litter' versus 'rubbish', 'receptacle' versus 'bin', 'box', 'basket', etc. points to a formal and public administrative context. In the informal request, the tag-question formula is a grammatical device (whereas the corresponding item in the formal request is the lexical 'please') supported in the phonology by an appropriate intonation pattern.

A register, then, involves a combination of selections, potentially at all the levels of organization of the total linguistic repertoire which a sociolinguistic community shares; hence a register has certain structural characteristics in common with whole languages. That is why it is possible to transpose from one register into another. Note that transposition is not the same as translation. In translation we endeavour – or should endeavour – to achieve matching at all levels of linguistic and extra-linguistic contextualization, including the sociosemantic contextualization implicit in register;[6] whereas in transposition from one register to another of the same language this is automatically excluded.

Generally speaking, it is normal for different registers of the same language to make use of considerable amounts of linguistic material which is indifferent as to register, or common to more than one register. In the two English utterances contrasted above, it so happens that the only shared lexical item is the preposition 'in'; but their phonological systems (assuming that the formal request receives secondary phonological realization), though by no means identical, are closely related.

In those plurilingual communities where the main diatypes can be tentatively identified as separate languages, each with its own functional specializations, it would seem theoretically possible for the linguistic systems of some or all of the diatypes to be absolutely distinct and unshared. Whether this is ever the case in practice, if we take usage within the community as the basis for our analysis, is extremely doubtful; some sharing there would always appear to be, though it may well be unidirectional rather than reciprocal (see below, p. 165). Nevertheless, it has been generally recognized that the investigation of functionally specialized plurilingualism offers more explicit and independent linguistic clues to certain types of social relationship than does any other kind of diatypic variation. As Ervin-Tripp so pertinently remarked (1964: 86): 'One of the major problems for sociolinguists will be the discovery of independent and reliable methods for defining settings.' Her use of the term 'setting' may broadly be equated with our 'categories of situation'. The relative ease with which language selection can be observed without reference to the extra-linguistic context seems to provide precisely the kind of reliable and independent criterion we are looking for.

It is of course not claimed that language is the key to *all* social attitudes and systems which are of interest to the sociologist or the social anthropologist. There are doubtless many aspects of human culture for the proper understanding of which linguistic behaviour is irrelevant or downright misleading. Nor is it the contention of the sociolinguist that these social relationships which *are* reflected in linguistic behaviour receive separate linguistic recognition on a one-to-one basis. On the other hand, it may be that certain such relationships are reflected primarily in linguistic behaviour and only minimally in non-linguistic behaviour; an example would be the didactic transactions between parents and children of a certain age-group in some cultures, including our own.

One can approach situational analysis in the sociolinguistic sphere from either end: one may tentatively set up social categories of situation on general evidence or hunch, and then examine linguistic usage to see whether it provides corroborating evidence; or else one may first examine linguistic usage and then use one's analysis to establish tentative correlations with such extra-linguistic factors as observation suggests may be crucial. One can then test one's hypotheses by seeking or contriving situations in which the only variable is the factor under investigation. Sociolinguists whose disciplinary background is sociology or anthropology will perhaps prefer the former approach. The present writer has begun applying the latter mode of investigation to a particular plurilingual situation which seems particularly to lend itself to the diatypic approach (Denison, 1968, 1969). The remainder of this paper further explores certain aspects of that situation and suggests some parallels.

Historically speaking, Sauris (German: *die Zahre*) is a German linguistic island in north-east Italy, physically isolated until recently by its remote location high in the Carnian Alps (it lies between 1,000 and 1,400 m) and, according to all the available evidence, separated for over 700 years by intervening Romance territory from its nearest German-speaking neighbour, Sappada (German: *Pladen*),[7] which lies just south of the Austrian frontier and is itself virtually a linguistic island, since the high watershed of the Alps separates it from the Lesach valley in Austria.

The German dialect of Sauris[8] has retained some archaic features of South Bavarian and has developed other specific features of its own, and these two characteristics combine to make it relatively inaccessible to other German-speakers. As part of the province of Friuli, Sauris was severed from the Austrian empire and incorporated in the Italian state in 1866. Its political history has therefore been quite different from that of South Tyrol, from the eastern limits of which it is separated by some 50 km of mountainous terrain, and its linguistic position reflects this difference. The linguistic evidence, in the absence of a documented history, makes it highly probable that

Sauris was settled from the southernmost borderland between Carinthia and East Tyrol, in the Lesachtal/Pustertal area, not much later than the year 1200.[9] The population of Sauris now stands at about 800, and seems unlikely ever to have been greatly in excess of that figure.

Of the German–Friulian–Italian trilingualism of most adults in Sauris Giovanni Lorenzoni observed:

> 'Vi si parla con la medesima facilità e scorrevolezza il dialetto tedesco e il friulano; anzi non è raro il caso che un medesimo gruppo di interlocutori salti dal tedesco al friulano e da questo a quello senza un' apparente ragione, forse anche senza che essi stessi se ne accorgano . . . Nel servizio militare hanno poi perfezionata la conoscenza della lingua nazionale, appresa nella scuola elementare' (1938: 23).
>
> ('The German dialect and Friulian are spoken there with equal facility and fluency; it is in fact not infrequently the case that the same group of speakers switches from German to Friulian and back again to German without apparent reason, perhaps even without noticing it . . . During military service they have subsequently perfected their knowledge of the national language learnt at elementary school.')

To what Lorenzoni says about the acquisition of Italian one must add that nowadays most children acquire it either as their first language, from their parents, or at kindergarten from the age of two. Lorenzoni (1938: 10) also mentions the familiarity of some adult males with some form of standard German, acquired during periods of work in Austria or Germany. This is less common nowadays, especially in the fractions of Lateis and Sauris di Sotto, but there is some familiarity with other Italian dialects, especially Veneto, Triestino, and Cadorino.

Fulgenzio Schneider (b. 1864), the late Saurian peasant-poet, writing in 1919, says of the use of Italian between Saurians:

> 'e questo anche per necessità delle cose, ma spesse volte anche per bravura, e questo si riscontra più volte, che nelle conversazioni si vuole intavolare un discorso per italiano, come per dare maggiore importanza,[10] ma poi per incapacità non potendolo seguitare viene finito nella madre lingua' (Magri, 1940/41: xviii).

('and this out of sheer necessity, for one thing, but often as a way of showing off, too; and not infrequently one encounters conversations in which there is an attempt to set up a speech in Italian, but because of inability to carry it through it finishes up in the mother tongue.')

Lest it be assumed that the use in Sauris of Friulian and Italian is of very recent date, it is interesting to note that 120 years ago Joseph Bergmann (1849) gave German no chance of surviving there:

> 'Sie [die Sauraner] sprechen eine gedehnte, verdorbene deutsche Mundart, die mit italienischen und unverständlichen Wörtern untermischt ist, so daß auch hier die deutsche Zunge bald abgestorben sein wird' –
>
> ('They [the Saurians] speak a broad, corrupt German dialect, in which Italian words and incomprehensible words are mixed, so that here too the German tongue will soon be extinct')

– and before the end of the century it was pronounced dead by Franz Kießling (1897: 13):

> 'In der Pfarre Sappada wie in Sauris bestand noch vor drei bis vier Jahrzehnten die Sprache aus mit italienischen (und in letzter Örtlichkeit auch mit slawischen) Worten verdorbener deutscher Mundart. Vom Deutschtum in dem ehemals deutschen Gebiet . . . ist heute nichts mehr zu merken.'
>
> ('In the parish of Sappada, as in Sauris, the language still consisted, up to three or four decades ago, of German dialect corrupted with Italian (and in the latter locality also Slav) words. Today there is no longer any sign of German language and culture in this formerly German area.')

The German dialect is still very much alive and spoken[11] in Sauris, but it is easy to see how Kießling was misled. It is still possible for a visitor to spend a whole day there during the summer and never hear a single word of German spoken: apparently the same was true in 1897.

Whatever the position may have been in 1919 (Schneider, quoted by Magri, 1940/41: xviii) or in 1938 (Lorenzoni, 1938: 23), close and repeated observations[12] have revealed that language selection among adults in Sauris in the 1960s shows a high degree of correlation with situational categories; so that the three languages may indeed be regarded as diatypes. Briefly, Italian correlates with the H end of the scale of situational categories and the German dialect with the L end, Friulian occupying the middle ground (M) [13] – for a more detailed account, see Denison (1968). A number of facts of especial interest emerge. First, in order to retain the concept of separate languages functioning as diatypes, the language of a text must be defined as the language of its macro-structure: this is most relevant to the German dialect, for which 'macro-' has to be particularly generously interpreted, in order to cope with Friulian and Italian intrusions of up to a sentence in length. Sharing of linguistic material in the diatypes is, ideally, unidirectional: Italian material is available to Friulian for micro-structure, both Italian and Friulian are available to the German dialect for micro-structure; but German is not available to Friulian for micro-structure and neither German nor Friulian is available to Italian. Great pains are taken to avoid infringements in the direction L → H, and when they happen they are involuntary and minor. Almost the only intrusion of German into the other diatypes which is tolerated (because the villagers are unaware of it) is in suprasegmental phonology: Friulian speakers from the surrounding area say that people from Sauris speak with a 'characteristic lilt'. Segmental intrusions from German are very rare, and are greeted with extreme ridicule. The only examples that have come to my knowledge were produced by a deaf old woman (whose performance in Friulian and Italian was judged to be poor by her fellows) and a small child. The 'mistake' produced by the child was retailed to me by an adult informant as something he once heard a playmate say when the informant was a child. He still found it very funny. The deaf woman is one of the very few adults in Sauris who is not a competent trilingual. Another is a mentally retarded adolescent female, who is said to know only the German dialect. In each of these two cases my informants clearly considered the restricted diatypic access to be natural.[14]

Interference of Friulian on Italian in Sauris is slightly more often encountered. The following excerpt from an account produced orally for me first in German, then in Friulian, and finally in Italian, shows slight Friulian influence on the Italian at the points printed in italics. It is possibly attributable to the formulation in Friulian which immediately preceded it; there was no evidence of segmental interference from the German version in either the Friulian or the Italian (B shows my prompting):

A E stato una cosa disas—disastrosa, perchè non *si ha*[15] *mai visto* una—un tempo simile. Ha provocato diversi—malanni, come nel bosco—una buona parte del bosco, anzi. E poi *scoperto*[16] diverse—diversi tetti in scandole, e anche lamiera. Poi i prati sono andati in frane, le strade rovinate, chè una cosa simile non *si ha*[15] *mai visto*.

B [Oggidì, a Sauris, si vive bene insomma, c'è lavoro?]

A Sì, si vive abbastanza bene. Basta darsi da fare, lavorare, e se uno ci ha la buona volontà si troverà a far bene, ecco!

B [Cosa fanno come lavoro?]

A Una parte si dedica a far il contadino. Sì, e una parte a *far-sù*[17] qualche villetta, ovvero-sia nel lavoro sotto certe imprese.[18]

The functions of Italian in Sauris are in the main eminently H: Italian is the language of organized religion (it has recently displaced Latin from most of the ritual part of this sphere), of school, and of kindergarten. Most of the villagers can read and write no other language. Italian is used in speaking to outsiders (unless they are known as Friulian-speakers) and, more significantly, it is used between 'Saurians' when outsiders are present. The chief apparent breach in this H pattern is the now widespread use of Italian by parents in the home to their children of pre-school and school age. Many parents use only Italian with their children, so that, as a group, children in Sauris – at least in Lateis and Sauris di Sotto – constitute a monoglot anomaly in a trilingual community. This is not quite accurate, for most children have at least some degree of passive comprehension of Friulian and German as a result of their exposure to these languages: for although most adults address their children in Italian in the home, they continue to use German among themselves. The reason given by informants for this use of Italian is in almost all cases the desire to ease the path of their children at school; a few have mentioned the general usefulness of Italian as compared with the other languages (especially the German dialect), and one family recalled that they had been asked by the schoolteacher to use Italian with their children. In other words, Italian is used in order to teach it: the home is here an extension of school. Seen in this light, this is an H function like all the others. No parents professed to feel any conflict between this function and the dimension of intimacy, which among adults leads to the selection of German in the home, the intimate connotations of which they will explicitly acknowledge.

Any conflict that may have been felt initially has apparently been overcome in the very short time since German began to be displaced in the home in dealings with children – about twelve to fifteen years, judging by the present upper age-limit of the almost monoglot Italian generation. The switch is not quite complete, even in Lateis and Sauris di Sotto; some families still speak German with their children, but the following remark made about one such child by the mayor's mother will illustrate the trend: 'Povero bambino, non parla neanche friulano.' The child was two years old!

Here we seem to have an indication of the value placed by a community (in this case, both by the macro-community of the Italian nation and by the micro-community of the village) on a particular language variety as a passport to 'better' things. Similarly, the use and teaching in English schools of a particular register for the formal imparting and acquisition of macro-community knowledge is an H activity which reflects the value that community places on the transactions associated with that particular register. Many English parents address their children in an approximation to the 'school' register when they assume a particularly pedagogical or admonitory role, perhaps with the aim, conscious or otherwise, of acquiring the authoritative nimbus of the teacher. We may note that a common assumption among parents (and even some teachers) is that the 'school' register is *the* English language, and that all other registers (and dialects) are merely corruptions of it. Hence, where we note the pedagogical use of a particular diatype (or diatypes) in a community we may, by observing other, extra-linguistic, activities with which it correlates, make objective deductions about the value placed by a society (or an influential sector of it) on those activities. Where such values are in the process of (or in need of) rapid change, there may well be a time-lag before appropriate adjustments are made in the 'school' diatype; and it would be interesting to know, in a society such as exists in present-day Britain, whether any such sociolinguistic time-lag actually acts as a brake on social change. Conversely, if a change of diatypic function in a macro-community framework runs ahead of the needs of a particular micro-community (i.e. precedes any evidence of internal forces there tending in the same direction), then we must ask whether such a process may not in itself help to bring about or hasten conformist change in the micro-community, the linguistic end of the sociolinguistic innovation acting as a 'fifth column' or 'softening-up agent' for a more general acculturation (cf. Fox, 1968). It is in this light that we must view the language policies of nation-building in developing nations (see Le Page, 1964, and Fishman, 1968c), and the resistance they often encounter.

The Carnian variety of Friulian[19] spoken in Sauris is used with acquaintances from the surrounding Friulian-speaking area, and also, in their presence, by Saurians to each other. Friulian is used, too, for shouting to attract attention. The cry for help is Friulian 'ajuuuut!'; and villagers hailing each other from a distance use Friulian – e.g. 'Giovanin, ven cà' – even though they switch to German as soon as they are within normal talking range. The habitual use of Friulian for conversation within the group is a marker of those males in their twenties and thirties who have enjoyed the benefit of a secondary school education in Ampezzo, also of the mayor and his family who lived for many years outside Sauris in a Friulian environment and now run a hotel, restaurant, and bar at La Maina, the southernmost cluster of houses in the parish. Perhaps because it is the most accessible and the nearest part of Sauris to the outside world (though still some twelve kilometres by a thought-provoking mountain road), Friulian appears to have become the predominant language at La Maina, though German is still in use between spouses in some of the families there. Friulian is commonly used for ordering drinks and for talk at the bar, not only in 'La Nuova Maina', run by the mayor's family, but elsewhere in Sauris too. However, there is apparently no automatic correlation between the language and this particular setting: as in general in Sauris, other ingredients in the situation, especially the roles of the participants, have greater priority than physical setting in diatypic selection (Denison, 1968: 583, 585). The two brief excerpts that follow, both recorded in 'La Nuova Maina', illustrate this fact, and also serve as short samples of the two Saurian diatypes not yet exemplified.

The first text is Friulian, and is part of a conversation at the bar between a male customer – A – aged about forty, from Lateis, and the mayor's sister – B – who was serving behind the bar:

B [What are you working on at present?]

A Una vileta ch'i ai vinduda a Lateis.
(A small villa I've sold at Lateis.)

B 'ndulà? (Where?)

A Là—dongja cjasa mè—chè cjasuta, si la viôt di chì, sot cjasa mè, propi lì.
(There—close to my house—that little house, you can see it from here; below my house, just there.)

C (*another male customer from Lateis, friend of* A*'s*) Tu as vindut chè cjasuta vecja, sì?
(You've sold that old cottage, have you?)

B Chè vila nova là-sù? Plui in bas di chè?
(That new villa up there? Lower down than that?)

A La scuela, sas-tu dulà ch'e jè la scuela?
(The school, d'you know where the school is?)

B Sì, la scuela sai.
(Yes, I do know the school.)

A E dongja la scuela e cjasa mè, no? Chè granda e mè, no? E chè cjasuta-lì, l'ai vinduda cumò al diretôr da . . . dal . . . la Cassa di Risparmio a Tulmieč. Sin daûr a lavorà lì.
(And by the school there's my house, are you with me? That big one's mine, all right? And that little cottage is the one I've just sold to the manager of the Savings Bank in Tolmezzo. That's the one we're working on.)

B Aha, sì. Alora, sù . . .
(Ah, yes. You mean up . . .)

A Chè che tu viodis se tu vas via chì.
(The one you can see as you leave here.)

The only Italian micro-element in this short stretch of text is the designation of the savings bank 'Cassa di Risparmio' – and that is almost certainly thought of as a proper noun. In general, there is far less *parole* recourse to specifically Italian elements in the Friulian of Sauris (though, being closely related languages, the two have quite a lot of structure in common anyway) than, say, in that of the environs of Udine, the provincial centre, where Friulian is the L diatype in a very complex three-term system with Veneto and Italian. Indeed, for Saurians, Friulian possesses the degree of integrity that goes with a modest dignity – less than they associate with Italian, but far more than they see in the German dialect. This is commensurate with the role that Friulian performs for them as a regional language, and also with its internal diatypic status midway between Italian and German. This has a curious consequence for transactions between the natives of Sauris and some of the middle-class citizens of Udine who drive up to Sauris for a weekend in the heat of August. For them, Friulian has decidedly L connotations, and they tend to reserve it, so far as any attempt at sustained discourse is concerned, for rather patronizing dealings with the rural population. The rural population is in general well aware of this, and often defends itself by replying in Italian, the H connotations of which, although they do not conceal the inequality of status of the participants, nevertheless restore distance and a certain dignity to the transaction. I have noted many instances of this kind of sociolinguistic skirmishing in Friuli. A typical occurrence, which I was able unobserved to tape, was a consultation between building workers on a site near Ampezzo and the architect, who was from Udine. Only the foreman felt secure enough to respond consistently in Friulian to the architect's Friulian, the remaining workers frequently replied in Italian, though they carried on side discussions among themselves in Friulian. Now in Sauris, when middle-class Udinesi use Friulian with patronizing intent, or on patronizing assumptions, the operation misfires completely, leaving both sides happy after an exchange in Friulian, of which both sides have understood the primary semantics whilst retaining intact their divergent interpretations – L for the Udinesi, M for the Saurians – of the sociosemantics.

The following is a short sample of the German dialect of

Sauris, extracted from a tape made, unobserved, of a highly unusual occurrence. One morning, a woman sent her husband, aged fifty–sixty, with the milk to the cooperative dairy in Sauris to make cheese. At 2 p.m. he had still not returned. The bar at 'La Nuova Maina' had just opened for the Easter season, and the cheese-maker had found his way there. Now, several glasses of schnaps later, he was conducting a quiet conversation with an old friend at one of the tables when his wife – A – burst in and began to harangue him excitedly in German. Our extract begins just as she was slowing down to get her second wind, thus giving her husband – B – a chance to insert one or two half-hearted attempts at self-defence:

A diər tsa gəla:ban ɛpas tuən man holt zinte.
(It's a waste of time to believe anything you say.)

B *ööö*! *no stà rabiàti, capîs-tu*!
(Oh, don't lose your temper, d'you understand!)

A *eee*?! *no cor rabiàsi*! gɛa ha:m! vaspe:gn tuəʃt peisar.
(No need to lose my temper, indeed! Go home! You('d) do better, that's why.)

B unt ɔxtər, dəha:me, bas tu:i?
(And then, at home, what do I do?)

A beinst k^ha:n o·rbat ɔʃt, gɛəʃtə i:bər də bi:ze auf . . .
(If you've no work to do, you can take a walk up over the meadow . . .)

A gea ha:m, ɔni gəzo:ṭ, tuəʃt peisar.
(Go home, I said, you('d) do better.)

B bein du: ʃaubəʃt mi ʃbɔrts ɔn, net . . .
(If you give me a black look, well . . .)

A *ma*! miər mɔxʃtə a:n tsourn, bein də mɔxəšt zötəna kɔmɛdias—*cjo*—i:beis-i net biə man tuən tsa gɛan in a burtshaus tsa neman-di di:. man mu:sn na·r—bis-net-bas-i: —in gaiʃt aufge:bn mu:səman.
(You make me angry when you play the fool this way. I don't know what it's coming to, to (have to) go into a pub like this to fetch you. It's enough to make a body—I don't know what—give up the ghost, it is.)

B tuəʃt na·r tsbiə s i ba:rat a diəp . . .
(You act as if I were a thief . . .)

This text illustrates once more the low diatypic selective power of setting (as narrowly defined above) in Sauris, as compared with other factors in the situation. Even where there seems at first sight to be a high degree of correlation – as for instance with Friulian in bars, German in the home, Italian at church and in school, there turns out to be a more accurately predictive correlation with some other factor or factors present. Thus, in the case of Friulian at the bar, it is probably the semi-public nature of the primary transaction (ordering drinks, counting change, the frequent presence of outsiders) which is responsible, together, at 'La Nuova Maina', with the habitual use of Friulian by the landlord's family. For German in the home, one important condition is that the participants be adults. For Italian in church and at school, it is the highly institutionalized, formal (in church, ritual) nature of the activities which is most relevant, not the actual buildings.

I have elsewhere (1968: 583–584) described how the formation of small groups (especially if for drinking) can effectively narrow and transform the total situation and lead to language-switching at 'La Nuova Maina'. The above text shows how anger can have the same effect, for the wife's voice was obviously louder than her husband felt appropriate for any language, especially German, given the other factors in the situation. This seems to have added to his embarrassment; at any rate, his own small part in the total exchange was at a very subdued decibel level. The most interesting point is the attempt made by the husband to shift the situation, bringing in the participation, and hence the support, of other males present, by the sudden switch to Friulian: 'no stà rabiàti'. This was a true switch of diatype, not one of the many established Romance micro-structural elements in the German dialect like *ma* and *kɔmɛdias* in our text, not a normal part of the code, but an act of creative *parole* improvisation. At this point the husband lifted his head, which had hitherto been bent rather despondently over his glass, and looked for approval from the other males present. In the event, the ploy failed to get him off the hook by retrieving the situation from the domain – to use Fishman's term – of conjugal dispute and putting it back in the domain of good-natured talk in Friulian at the bar, in which all present would feel free to participate. For a moment, but alas! only for a moment, his wife was thrown off balance, and was constrained to make her immediate response – an ironic echo (note that it was not mere repetition) – in Friulian also. Here, as in the retaliatory use of Italian by Friulians, described above, we have an instance of the way in which individuals, by skilful manipulation of diatypes, seek to steer situations – or better, perhaps – to *create* situations to their own advantage.

For German in Sauris, the determination of the precise status of a micro-element of Romance origin is a relevant, if in many cases an extremely difficult, task: it seems highly probable that the introduction of non-established Romance elements in German *parole* has different register and sub-register implications from the presence of the many established loan features.[20] For certain items it would be possible to make the degree of phonological or grammatical adaptation to the German basic systems decisive. With the most recent loans, however, there are often only two possible criteria: the first is the frequency of their occurrence in German macro-structure texts, and the second is the presence or absence of an alternative in the speaker's idiolect.[21] Granted that neither of these latter criteria is theoretically or practically very satisfactory, it nevertheless proves possible more often than not to make an assignment to one or more of the three main diatypes. Where a feature is common to more than one diatype, it would sometimes be possible to specify differential functions or meanings or frequencies of occurrence for it for each diatype: there remain those items where even this is hardly possible (e.g. *ma* – 'but' in all three main diatypes). Nevertheless, the description of features according to their diatypic distribution in a plurilingual community like Sauris remains a less formidable task than the description of features in register terms for a monoglot community.

Direct questioning of informants on this point in Sauris is not very helpful. With their trilingual competence in the diatypes concerned they easily recognize the 'foreign' origin of all but the very oldest Romance loan features, at least those in the lexis, including such relatively old, integrated and non-substitutable items as *də vouʃ* (pl. *de veiʃe*) – 'voice'; *d'arantse* (pl. *-n*) – 'orange'; *dər saldo:t* (pl. *-n*) – 'soldier'. There is one rare activity in which this ability has been strikingly in evidence. The sparsely documented written mode of the German diatype has ranged from poems by two parish priests towards the end of the last century and a festive oration by one of them (all reprinted by the Patronato di Udine in a Sauris commemorative volume *Sauris nelle Nozze d'Oro di Antonio Troiero* in 1932), through the moralizing and partly autobiographic verses by Fulgenzio Schneider in Giuseppe Magri's unpublished doctoral thesis (1940/41), to the anonymous verse contributions over the past few years in the church bulletin, one of them so bawdy that the present priest would blush if he could read what his bulletin has given space to. Throughout, there is a quite remarkable purist (in the linguistic sense) streak: Romance features are avoided wherever possible. This is the more striking when one bears in mind the readiness of Saurians to accept Romance features in whatever quantity the situation calls for in their spoken German. I intend to give this matter the fuller treatment it deserves on a future occasion. For the moment, suffice it to say that there may well be a parallel of a kind here with the relative scarcity of French intrusions in the very rare samples of written English produced in the decades that followed the Norman–French conquest, a period when we must assume those few who did write in English to have been bilinguals of a sort.

The almost exclusively L functions which macro-structure German performs in its spoken mode show a high degree of correlation with close participant relationships among adults, most regularly of all among female adults (regardless of topic). Non-rural technicality of topic makes for a greater incidence of Romance micro-structure (lexis, grammar of short groups); as between Italian and Friulian micro-elements, the former are more, the latter less, formally technical within an overall framework which belongs to the informal end of the scale so far as participant relationships are concerned. Rural topics, due allowance made for technological innovations, are among those which in Sauris correlate best with a high incidence of historically and synchronically 'German' micro-structure and hence with a greater degree of homogeneity in L situations. Other things being equal, the oldest speakers tend to show least, the youngest adults most, Romance micro-structure in their German, females less than males, age-for-age. Within such overall tendencies there is stylistic variation between individuals on this point, and the picture is further complicated by what among Saurians under fifty strikes one as being an almost incredibly random factor in linguistic transmission. Thus, of two males, close acquaintances aged about thirty, one knew and used the word *stiəfpruədər* – 'stepbrother', whereas the other knew only (Ital.) *fratellastro*. This second individual, however, knew and used *uməgɔŋk*^{h}, 'procession', whereas the first used only (Friul.) 'procession' and thought he had heard the German word in the form *umədɔŋk*^{h} ('folk etymology'!). Not infrequently, one hears Saurians of this generation asking each other, or a senior, for an explanation of some item of German lexis which one of them has used, and of which one or more participants are ignorant. Apart from providing the investigator with an opportunity to establish a reputation for well-nigh divine omniscience (a temptation to be resisted, as anthropologists will appreciate), this may lead him to ponder with Hymes (1967b: 634) the case of Bloomfield's White-Thunder who 'speaks less English than Menomini, and that is a strong indictment, for his Menomini is atrocious. His vocabulary is small; his inflections are often barbarous; he constructs sentences of a few threadbare models . . .' – A young man in Sauris who failed to ask linguistic questions could easily become a White-Thunder so far as his German was concerned – and there is evidence of a general impoverishment of the language, as a result, it seems, of the combined circumstances of its restricted diatypic function, its consequent low prestige (which reinforces the restriction of its diatypic function), and the random element in its diachronic transmission in these circumstances by a tiny community which never seems to have greatly exceeded 800 souls.

The survival in German among older, and some younger, Saurians of the general lexis of external church affairs such as processions, Christian feasts (Christmas, Easter, All Saints, All Souls), and verbs for 'pray', 'confirm', 'confess', is a reminder that Italian has assumed the H functions of religious observance within living memory; about fifty years ago a long line of native Saurian priests came to an end, and, with their succession by non-German-speaking priests from outside, sermons in German were discontinued. Up to about the same time German dialect explications (but Italian textbooks!) were used by the schoolteacher during the very brief exposure (one to three years) to formal schooling which children in Sauris then received. These facts, together with the recent penetration by Italian into relationships between parents and children in Sauris, show that what at first sight looks like a tolerably neat synchronic picture of diatypic distribution is none the less part of a rapidly shifting sociolinguistic scene.

At present, adults in Sauris may be said to inhabit three main diatypic spaces. It is likely that when the forefathers of the present population (better: *some* of the forefathers of *most* of the villagers) first settled their valley – which, on toponomastic evidence, had no settled population before that time (Lorenzoni, 1938 – some twelve and a half centuries ago, these three 'worlds' were spatially delimited, and could have been adequately described by drawing three concentric circles round ego, the first encompassing the village, the second the region (Friulian), and the third the great outside world (Italian – and earlier, to some extent, non-Saurian German).[22] Now that the region and the outside world are so unmistakably represented inside the village and its daily activities, the diatypic spaces which now coexist there have become psychologically rather than physically distinct. When a Saurian, using German (*inzəra ʃpro:xe*) says *bier* – 'we', he normally means himself and his fellow-villagers. A visitor from the nearest town, Ampezzo, who may be in the next room, is spoken of and identified in German as *dər be:liʃe*, as are all other Italians, Carnians, and Friulians. In German, a Saurian will today still speak of having worked *in variaul* – 'in Friuli' – almost as though it were a foreign country. When our Saurian speaks Friulian, however, *noatris* refers to himself and his fellows as Friulians, or, at least, as Carnians, though it will more often than not exclude 'talians'. When a villager speaks Italian he sees himself as part of the Italian nation: 'Se non ci siamo noi' ('If we are not here'), said the deputy mayor, lamenting the depopulation trend in the high Alpine valleys, 'chi è che difende questi confini?' ('who will defend these frontiers?').

Saurians are certainly not unique in having access to more than one social identity. However, it may be that in marking these off by such distinct diatypes adult Saurians constantly remind themselves that they cannot assume all their identities simultaneously.

'There are three ways of seeking unity in the phenomena of language ... one peculiarly open to the sociolinguistic approach is to seek a unity in the future – to see the processes of sociolinguistic change that envelop our objects of study as underlain by the emergence of a world society' (Hymes, 1967b)).

In becoming trilingual, Sauris took a major step towards membership of a world society – a step matched only in recent years by those which the world, with its modern means of communication, has taken towards Sauris. Today, in abandoning German and Friulian, the children of Sauris are being thrust even further towards a world society. In the process, they and world society are abandoning much of what was Sauris and much of what was Friuli. Let us hope that the bargain is worth its price.

SUMMARY

In this paper I have attempted to discuss, within a general sociolinguistic framework, samples of specific material from a particular trilingual case-study. The following are some of the notions of more general scope and possibly wider application which I have sought to air:

1. In Sauris, different parts of the linguistic structure appear to be sensitive to different kinds of situational factor – macro-structure specifically to participant relationships and purpose, micro-structure specifically to topic and mood. This suggests that we should not be in too much of a hurry to generalize at too high a level of abstraction in the categorization of situational factors under such labels as formality, technicality, closeness, distance, and the like. A detailed examination of the language in particular sociolinguistic situations will lead us to ask, more discriminatingly: Formality in what respect? What kind of technicality, closeness, distance? Which factors in the situation correlate with which parts of the diatypic system?

The anthropologist or sociologist must be prepared to find that a given language bundles situational factors together in diatypic correlation in what may strike him as an arbitrary, and from his point of view a highly inconvenient, manner. Arbitrary it certainly will be, from a synchronic or logical point of view, in the same way as the connection between the English sound sequence in 'mind' and the senses 'object to', 'move or behave cautiously in respect of', 'look after', and 'human thinking faculty' is arbitrary (incidentally, only the last of these senses is indifferent as regards register). The bundling may be inconvenient, but it is infinitely better than none at all: it is the best starting-point we have for the detection and scientific re-categorization of the particular factors bundled.

2. The assignment of linguistic material at the various primary levels of analysis to particular diatypes is not a simple matter. A number of different criteria may be useful here, including, for plurilingual communities, phonological evidence of assimilation of 'borrowed' lexis, frequency distribution of doubtful items according to situation category, substitutability or otherwise of loaned items by 'native' items in the sum of idiolects (with or without diatypic implications if a given substitution is made), statistically determined norm specifications as in Labov's work. We cannot shirk the *langue/parole* issue for specific occurrences of items if this is relevant for their sociosemantic effect. If it could be demonstrated for particular cases that their *langue/parole* status is sociolinguistically irrelevant, then, so far as this writer is concerned, there would be no need to pursue the matter for merely doctrinaire or theoretical linguistic reasons.

3. It is because there are sociolinguistic norms of expectation that participants are able to some extent to *create* social situations by skilful switching of diatypes. Some indication of the circumstances in which this may happen has been given above. To this extent it is legitimate to talk of the linguistic tail wagging the situational dog, and to insist on the inextricability of linguistic and non-linguistic behaviour in a sociolinguistic sense, as do Pride (note 3, p. 113) and Hymes (p. 62) in their contributions to this volume. Note, however, that a participant will be unable to impose a sociolinguistic situation if it is rejected as inappropriate by the others. To this extent the individual is no more a completely free agent sociolinguistically than he is linguistically in other respects, or in his social behaviour in general. In the words of Hymes (p. 54 above), the creativity of speakers is 'rule-governed creativity'.

4. In Sauris intra-diatypic influence and diachronic development are almost exclusively in the direction H → L. This is simply another dimension (and an illuminating one) of the well-known diachronic facts about the direction of linguistic influence between 'separate' communities of different cultural levels, or, as I would prefer to express it, of unequal prestige. Seen in this light, the synchronically arbitrary distribution of lexis according to register in English (most H words being of Latin or Romance origin, most L words being of Germanic origin) receives a diachronic 'explanation' in earlier periods (for an elite) of complete diglossia (Latin/English, later French/English) or even trilingualism (Latin/French/English) in diatypic function. Those who today possess all the relevant registers (especially at the H end of the scale) are the social heirs of those who were plurilingual, and exercised similar power by virtue of that fact. In terms of its methodological implications, this means that for communities whose history is not known, careful diatypic synchronic analysis may enable a hypothesis to be framed about a probable historical profile of social contacts and influences, for comparison with, and supplementation of, the cultural-historical inferences that can be drawn from the well-tried method of comparative and historical linguistic analysis at the primary levels of linguistic structure, especially lexis. In this sense, the arbitrariness of sociolinguistic convention may to a certain extent be dispelled.

NOTES

1. See especially Fishman (1967, 1968a, 1968b); Hymes (1967a, 1967b); Le Page (1968).

2. I prefer this term to 'multilingualism', which suggests a large number of languages; it conveniently glosses German *Mehrsprachigkeit* and French *plurilinguisme;* it includes, of course, 'bilingualism', the most frequently encountered form of plurilingualism, and more particularly its societal counterpart, 'diglossia' (see next footnote).

3. As originally put forward by Ferguson (1959) and subsequently broadened by e.g. Fishman (1967).

4. 'Register' was first used as a linguistic technical term by Reid (1956), and given wider currency by Halliday and associates in e.g. Catford (1965), Ellis (1966), Halliday, McIntosh, and Strevens (1964), Gregory (1967), Leech (1966), Ure (1967).

5. Compare, for instance, Frake's account of drinking talk in Subanun (in Gumperz and Hymes, 1964: 127–132), Dixon's description of 'mother-in-law'

language in Dyirbal (Dixon, 1968, and his correspondence on the subject in *Man* (n.s.) **3** (4), 1968), and Ferguson's survey of baby-talk in six languages (in Gumperz and Hymes, 1964: 103–114); also Mitchell (1957) on the language of buying and selling in Cyrenaica.

6. See Catford (1965).

7. Bruniera (1937/38); Hornung (1960, 1964, 1967).

8. Denison (1968); Hornung (1960, 1964); Kranzmayer (1956); Lorenzoni (1938); Lucchini (1882); Magri (1940/41).

9. See Hornung (1964: 133–143, 1960: 10); Lorenzoni (1938: 10–19).

10. A parallel here is the similar use of English by bilingual speakers of Urdu within an otherwise Urdu text, to lend weight to a point considered important. The normal procedure is first to make the point in Urdu and then to repeat it slowly and deliberately in English. In a sense, the speaker appears to be not entirely convinced by his own argument until he has heard it in the language of authority.

11. However, a generation of children is now reaching adolescence for whom Italian is the first and often the only active language; so that it really does now seem as if the years of survival of the German dialect (and, indeed, of Friulian also) are numbered.

12. I have made one or two study trips annually, for periods of up to six weeks, since 1964. Direct consultation with informants, whose accounts are cross-checked, supplements the analysis of taped material, some of it taped without the knowledge of all but one participant and without the author's presence, some of it taped without the knowledge of any participant.

13. 'High' and 'Low', as first put forward by Ferguson (1959) and developed in e.g. Fishman (1968a). See also Pride's comments in his paper in this volume (pp. 97 ff.). The values do, of course, form a continuous scale, but the attachment of identifiably distinct linguistic macro-structures to different parts of the scale does force a choice upon the speaker for each situation. In *di*glossic situations the two terms of the dichotomy correlate with H and L reaches of the scale. For the *tri*lingual system in Sauris we require an extra term: German is then L(ow), Italian is H(igh), and Friulian is M(id).

14. The choice of diatype for deaf people and imbeciles (often grouped together as one category) is interesting. In a German/Romansch bilingual community in Oberhalbstein, Grisons, Switzerland, the only adult who knew no German was an imbecile. In Pöckau, in the Slovene/German bilingual strip of Austrian Carinthia, there is a mentally backward old man whose German is poor in the extreme, but whose house-to-house mimicry of the parson's Slovene sermon on feast-days assures him of a few days' splendid eating annually. On the other hand, a deaf middle-aged male in the same area knows no Slovene but only German. There has been a change here over recent decades from Slovene to German as the language spoken by most parents to their children. Hence, in all these cases, the language learnt by imbeciles and the deaf is the language of the home, as one would expect. Yet in each instance the facts were explained to me by bilingual relatives or acquaintances of the individuals concerned, in terms of the alleged greater inherent simplicity of the language selected.

15. Standard Italian requires construction with auxil. *essere* – 'be'. Friulian permits either *jessi* – 'be' or *(a)vê* – 'have'.

16. Standard Italian requires *scoperchiato* – 'stripped, uncovered'. Friulian has *scuviart*, which is normally translatable by Italian *scoperto* – 'discovered'.

17. Standard Italian would normally have simply *fare* or *costruire*. Friulian is *fà-sù*.

18. A translation of the excerpt quoted is given below:

A It was a disastrous thing, because we have never seen such weather. It caused various kinds of damage, like in the woods, indeed, in a considerable part of the woods. And then – stripped a number of shingled roofs, and metal roofs, too. Then, the meadows were broken up by landslides, the roads ruined, so we've never seen such a thing.

B [But do you live well in Sauris nowadays, is there work?]

A Yes, we live pretty well. It's enough to be enterprising, work hard, and if a person shows willing he'll get on well, that's how it is.

B [What kind of work do people do?]

A Some devote themselves to farming. Yes, and some to putting up the odd house, or else working for certain firms.

19. See Bender *et al.* (1952); Francescato (1967); Iliescu (1964, 1969); Marchetti (1952); Pirona *et al.* (1935).

20. Le Page (1968) provides a critical survey of attempts to carry out the assignment of 'interference phenomena' to *langue* or *parole* according to various criteria.

21. Labov (1966) approaches the specification of 'norms' for individual speakers in New York City on a comparative frequency basis.

22. Of course this is rather an over-simplification. The oldest Latin and Romance loan-words in Saurian German show that long before the Saurian migration the 'worlds' they inhabited were already beginning to merge. We are really concerned with a difference of degree here, but it is such a large degree of difference that it is easy to think of it as a difference of kind.

REFERENCES

BENDER, B., FRANCESCATO, G., and SALZMAN, Z. 1952. Friulian Phonology. *Word* **8**: 216–223.

BERGMANN, J. 1849. Die deutsche Gemeinde Sappada nebst Sauris. *Archiv für Kunde österr. Geschichtsquellen* **III** (1/2). Vienna: Akademie der Wissenschaften.

BRUNIERA, MARIA. 1937/38. Il Dialetto Tedesco dell'Isola Alloglotta di Sappada. Dissertation, University of Padua.

CATFORD, J. C. 1965. *A Linguistic Theory of Translation*. London: Oxford University Press.

DENISON, N. 1968. Sauris: A Trilingual Community in Diatypic Perspective. *Man* (n.s.) **3** (4): 578–592.

—— 1969. Sociolinguistics and Plurilingualism. *Acts of the Xth International Congress of Linguists* **10**: 551–559.

DIXON, R. M. W. 1968. The Dyirbal Language of North Queensland. Dissertation, University of London.

ELLIS, J. O. 1966. On Contextual Meaning. In C. E. Bazell *et al.* (eds), *In Memory of J. R. Firth*. London: Longmans.

ERVIN-TRIPP, SUSAN. 1964. Interaction of Language, Topic and Listener. In Gumperz and Hymes (eds.), 1964.

FERGUSON, C. A. 1959. Diglossia. *Word* **15:** 325–340. Also in D. Hymes (ed.), *Language in Culture and Society.* New York: Harper & Row, 1964.

—— 1964. Baby-talk in Six Languages. In Gumperz and Hymes (eds.), 1964.

FISHMAN, J. A. 1965. Who Speaks What Language to Whom and When? *Linguistique* **2:** 67–88.

—— 1967. Bilingualism with and without Diglossia; Diglossia with and without Bilingualism. *Journal of Social Issues* **23** (2): 29–38.

—— 1968a. Sociolinguistic Perspective on the Study of Bilingualism. *Linguistics* **39:** 21–49.

—— (ed.). 1968b. Bilingualism in the Barrio. Final Report, Contract No. OEC-1-7-062817-0297. US Dept of Health, Education and Welfare.

—— 1968c. Sociolinguistics and the Language Problems of the Developing Countries. In J. A. Fishman, C. A. Ferguson, and J. Das Gupta (eds.), *Language Problems of Developing Nations.* pp. 3–16. New York: Wiley.

FOX, ROBIN. 1968. Multilingualism in Two Communities. *Man* (n.s.) **3:** 456–464.

FRAKE, C. O. 1964. How to Ask for a Drink in Subanun. In Gumperz and Hymes (eds.), 1964.

FRANCESCATO, G. 1967. *Dialettologia Friulana.* Udine: Società Filologica Friulana.

GREGORY, M. 1967. Aspects of Varieties Differentiation. *Journal of Linguistics* **3:** 177–197.

GUMPERZ, J. J., and HYMES, D. (eds.). 1964. *The Ethnography of Communication.* Menasha, Wis.: American Anthropological Association.

HALLIDAY, M. A. K., MCINTOSH, A., and STREVENS, P. 1964. *The Linguistic Sciences and Language Teaching.* London: Longmans.

HORNUNG, MARIA. 1960. Die Osttiroler Bauernsprachinseln Pladen und Zahre in Oberkarnien. *Osttiroler Heimatblätter* **98:** 1–14.

—— 1964. *Mundartkunde Osttirols.* Vienna: Akademie der Wissenschaften.

—— 1967. Romanische Entlehnungen in der deutschen Sprachinselmundart von Pladen. In *Mundart und Geschichte* (Kranzmayer Festschrift), pp. 41–69. Vienna: Akademie der Wissenschaften.

HYMES, D. 1967a. Models of the Interaction of Language and Social Setting. *Journal of Social Issues* **23** (2): 8–28.

— 1967b. Why Linguistics Needs the Sociologist. *Social Research* **34**: 632–647.

ILIESCU, MARIA. 1964. Zu den in Rumänien gesprochenen friaulischen Dialekten. *Revue Roumaine de Linguistique* **9**: 68–78.

— 1969. Observations sur le bi- et multilinguisme des frioulans de Roumanie. *Acts of the Xth International Congress of Linguists* **10**: 777–781.

KIESSLING, F. 1897. *Verwelschtes und verlorenes deutsches Blut.* Vienna.

KRANZMAYER, E. 1956. *Historische Lautgeographie des gesamtbairischen Dialektraumes.* Vienna: Akademie der Wissenschaften.

LABOV, W. 1966. *The Social Stratification of English in New York City.* Washington, DC: Center for Applied Linguistics.

LEECH, G. N. 1966. *English in Advertising.* London: Longmans.

LE PAGE, R. B. 1964. *The National Language Question.* London: Oxford University Press.

— 1968. Problems of Description in Multilingual Communities. *Transactions of the Philological Society:* 189–212.

LORENZONI, G. 1938. *La Toponomastica di Sauris.* Udine: Istituto delle Edizioni Accademiche.

LUCCHINI, L. 1882. *Saggio di Dialettologia Sauriana.* Udine: Patronato di Udine.

MAGRI, G. 1940/41. Il Dialetto di Sauris. Dissertation, University of Padua.

MARCHETTI, G. 1952. *Lineamenti di Grammatica Friulana.* Udine: Società Filologica Friulana.

MITCHELL, T. F. 1957. The Language of Buying and Selling in Cyrenaica: A Situational Statement. *Hespéris* **44**: 31–71.

PIRONA, G. A., CARLETTI, E., and CORGNALI, G. B. 1935. *Il Nuovo Pirona: Vocabulario Friulano.* Udine: Società Filologica Friulana.

REID, T. B. W. 1956. Linguistics, Structuralism and Philology. *Archivum Linguisticum* **8**: 28–37.

URE, JEAN N. 1967. *The Theory of Register and Register in Language Teaching.* Colchester: University of Essex.

D. Crystal

Prosodic and Paralinguistic Correlates of Social Categories

Research into the linguistic correlates of social categories has been almost exclusively based on the study of lexical, grammatical, and segmental phonetic and phonological characteristics. What are generally referred to as 'speech styles', i.e. modes of speaking restricted to or primarily associated with a particular social group, are illustrated solely with reference to restricted usage of items of vocabulary and of grammatical inflections or structures, and to differences in the articulations of vowels, consonants, and vowel–consonant sequences. There is remarkably little attention paid to one other aspect of speech, which I would hold is of major importance for the linguistic definition of social categories, namely, the *non-segmental* phonetic and phonological characteristics of utterance. These features I shall describe in more detail below; meanwhile, it will suffice to say that they refer to vocal effects due to contrasts in pitch, loudness, and speed of utterance, or to the use of qualities of voice such as nasalization or breathiness in order to communicate specific meanings. 'Intonation', or 'speech melody', clearly comes under this heading, therefore, as does 'rhythm', and what is regularly, albeit vaguely, called 'tone of voice'. Certain aspects of tone of voice are sometimes studied separately under the heading of 'paralanguage'. More precisely, non-segmental effect would include any sound effect which cannot be described by reference to a single segment (or phoneme) in the sound system of a language, but which either continues over a stretch of utterance (minimally one syllable), or requires reference to a number of segments in different parts of an utterance that are all affected by a single 'set' or configuration of the vocal organs – as when velarization of certain sounds produces a cumulative impression and a semantic interpretation that affect the whole of the utterance. Goffman (1964: 133) looks at this area from a different viewpoint, referring to the expressive aspects of discourse which cannot be clearly transferred through writing to paper – he refers to them as the 'greasy' parts of speech! 'It's not *what* you say, but the way that you say it' summarizes the scope of this field, from the formal point of view. Functionally, it is generally agreed that non-segmental phonology provides the main method of communicating emphasis and personal attitudes (sarcasm, surprise, etc.) in language; and that it may also be used with a grammatical role, as when intonation distinguishes between restrictive and non-restrictive relative clauses in English (cf. the use of commas in writing, as between 'My brother, who's abroad, wrote me a letter' – one brother – and 'My brother who's abroad wrote me a letter' – more than one brother). I would add that non-segmental phonology is also one of the main ways of establishing the identity of social groups in speech.

Reasons for the general absence of reference to the function of non-segmental phonology in this area of interdisciplinary overlap are not difficult to find. These features of language are among the most difficult to subject to analysis, being relatively difficult to perceive, transcribe, and measure. Most of us are unused to listening to differences in pitch and loudness, for example, and few people know what kind of phenomenon to look for. Also, the differences between these contrasts are typically less discrete than those between segmental contrasts: the distinction between a |p| and a |b|, or even between two vowel sounds adjacent in articulation, is relatively clear-cut; whereas the distinction between a falling tone and a rising–falling tone, or between one and two degrees of stress, is sometimes extremely difficult to hear. Labov (1964: 166, and 176n.7), while allowing the importance of non-segmental phenomena in language, considers them to be essentially unquantifiable at the present stage of study, and therefore omits them from his own work on the ground that 'we lack the large body of theory and practice in codifying intonation which we have for segmental phones'. There is also less of a tradition of study for these features than for other aspects of language organization. Features such as intonation ('prosodic features', as they are usually called) are referred to only sporadically, either as part of an attempt to explain the function of punctuation marks, or to define the phonetic correlates of metre. The simplified patterns used in textbooks for teaching English to foreigners, which have been around since the beginning of this century, are quite inadequate for research purposes, even as a basis for description; and in any case very little work has been done on languages other than English.

More recently, linguists have begun to examine non-segmental vocal effect in detail, but so far there has been little attempt to describe systematically the range of non-segmental features which are in principle operative in a language, or to work out a theory that will define and interrelate them satisfactorily. Work by Pike (1944) and Trager (1958, 1961), particularly the latter's research into paralanguage, the definition of the subject of *semiotics*, viz. the study of patterned, human communicative behaviour in all modalities (see Sebeok *et al.*, 1964), and recent work on voice quality (see Laver, 1968) have all done a great deal to stimulate interest in non-segmental vocal effect, but little of this has so far been used in social anthropology. The very important collection of papers on the ethnography of communication edited by Gumperz and Hymes (1964) provides another move in the right direction. Hymes in his introduction to the volume (and also in his contribution to the present monograph) demonstrates very clearly the need to develop an 'ethnography of speaking' – informally defined as a specification of what kinds of things one may appropriately say in what message forms to what kinds of people in what kinds of situation, and, given a set of alternatives, what consequences stem from selecting one rather than another – and refers to the need for semiotic and other studies. Most of the contributors to the volume underline this point at various places. Albert, for example, refers to the training in tone of voice and its modulation, *inter alia*, for men in Burundi, and shows its relevance to age, sex, kinship, and other relationships, referring to certain highly conventionalized speech patterns such as those used in visiting formulae, petitioning situations, rules of precedence, and respect patterns. Distinctions are made, many of them non-segmental, according to the social role of those present, the degree of formality (especially relating to whether the situation is public or private), and the objectives of the speech situation. 'Together, social role and situational prescriptions determine the order of precedence of speakers, relevant conventions of politeness, appropriate formulas and styles of speech, and topics of discussion' (1964: 43). But despite this much-needed emphasis on theoretical principles, neither Albert nor any of the other contributors to the volume present any detailed account of the non-segmental phonology involved: the references stay at a maximally general level.

It should be emphasized that this collection of papers is quite exceptional in its orientation in this area. On the whole, most fieldworkers, even in linguistics, are still unaware, in principle, of the *kind* of linguistic phenomenon they are liable to come into contact with in this part of language, how they should label phenomena that they hear, or how they should integrate these with other aspects of any linguistic description they may happen to be making. The present paper is therefore an attempt to outline this area of study, so that the functional range of non-segmental features in a social anthropological context may be more readily recognized. But first I ought to indicate the extent to which non-segmental features *have* been noted in the description of social categories, either by linguists or by anthropologists, as this may help to clarify the nature of these features and underline the need for research in this area. A partial survey of the literature in this respect is not all that meaningful, in fact, because, in the absence of any generally agreed theory, there is no guarantee that different scholars are using such terms as 'melody', 'tone', and 'stress' in the same way (it is frequently obvious that they are not); and there have been few attempts to transcribe utterances in order to indicate the frequency of occurrence and distribution of specific effects. But at least some of the references used here may help to provide a context of situation for those not too familiar with the subject.

I have divided the main references into five generally recognized categories (though there is, of course, some overlapping): institutionalized non-segmental correlates (or indications, depending on the point of view) of *sex*, *age*, *status*, *occupation*, and *functions* (*genres*). I shall add some references to English in order to indicate further the kind of information involved.

1. *Sex*

It is probable that there are important non-segmental differences between the speech habits of men and women in most languages, though very little data have been analysed from this point of view. Cf. such informal remarks as 'Stop clucking like an old woman', or references to 'sexy' voice and the like (see Laver, 1968: 49). Intuitive impressions of effeminacy in English, for example, partly correlate with segmental effects such as lisping, but are mainly non-segmental: a 'simpering' voice, for instance, largely reduces to the use of a wider pitch-range than normal (for men), with *glissando* effects between stressed syllables, a more frequent use of complex tones (e.g. the fall–rise and the rise–fall), the use of breathiness and huskiness in the voice, and switching to a higher (falsetto) register from time to time. (This provides an interesting contrast with Mohave, for instance, where a man imitating a woman (or transvestite) does not change to falsetto, but uses his normal voice, and rather imitates verbal and segmental effects (see Devereux, 1949: 269).) According to Ferguson (in Sebeok *et al.*, 1964: 274), velarization in Arabic indicates, among other things, masculinity, whereas avoidance of velarization indicates the opposite. In Darkhat Mongol, women front all back and mid vowels (see Capell, 1966: 101). In Yana, men talking to men 'speak fully and deliberately', whereas when women are involved (as either speakers or hearers) 'a clipped style of utterance' is used (see Sapir, in Mandelbaum, 1949: 212). Also in Yana, to express interrogation, women lengthen final vowels, whereas men add a segmental suffix, *-n* (Sapir, op. cit.: 179–180, cf. also p. 211), though it is a descriptive problem whether the length should be interpreted non-segmentally or not. In Chichimeca, where male and female names in the same family may be identical, it is reported that 'tone' may be used to differentiate the sexes being addressed (see Driver and Driver, 1963: 108). Syllabic tone differences may distinguish between sexes in Koasati (Haas, 1944). Sex differences, moreover, sometimes correlate with age. According to Garbell (1965), many female speakers over seventy of Urmi, a dialect spoken by Jews in north Persian Azerbaijan, replace practically all 'plain' words by 'flat' words, i.e. words consisting of 'flat' phones, which in Garbell's metalanguage means such features as the strong velarization of all oral consonants, the articulation of all labials with marked lip protrusion and rounding, and pharyngealization. Again, *responses* to non-segmental vocal effects can be a valuable part of a description, e.g. in Mohave, the breaking of the male voice in adolescence is not considered an important, or even a relevant, indication of puberty (Devereux, 1949: 268), whereas, of course, in English it is a feature that is regularly remarked upon. And, as a last example, one could note the training in voice modulation that Burundi men receive, but women do not (Albert, 1964: 37).

2. *Age*

References to the non-segmental correlates of age are very sporadic indeed in the sociolinguistic literature, though this was one of the most readily demonstrable correlations in the early work in social psychology (see Kramer, 1963; Allport and Cantril, 1934), and one has a perfectly clear intuitive impression of 'old', 'young' voices, and the like. In fact, the only regular references are to baby-talk (i.e. the speech characteristics of adults addressing babies). Kelkar (1964), under the heading of *paraphonology*, refers to the extended pitch and loudness characteristics, and the relatively slow and regular speed of baby-talk in Marathi, and mentions certain general vocal effects, such as pouting and palatalization. Ferguson (1964), with reference to English, also cites the higher overall pitch of baby-talk, the preference for certain pitch contours, and labialization, but does not discuss it further. Ervin-Tripp (1964) refers to some general characteristics of children's play-intonations, and Burling (1966) shows that broad rhythmic similarities exist between samples of children's verse from a number of languages. It is highly likely that older groups are also discriminated by non-segmental features (and not just by grammar and vocabulary, which are the only areas generally cited), but there is no published evidence on the point, apart from a few general remarks, as in Albert (1964) and Garbell (1965).

3. *Status*

Non-segmental phonology is frequently used to indicate the social identity of the speaker on a scale of some kind (his 'class dialect', as many would say), or the identity of the receiver in these terms. Certain tones of 'respect' might be conventionalized indications of a particular kinship or caste relation, for instance, or may indicate different social roles. John Boman Adams mentions the importance of stereotyped pitch patterns and tones of voice in order to establish status between participants in one dialect of Egyptian:

> 'The villager is ordinarily conditioned to give and receive communications whose content is so stereotyped that he pays little attention to it other than to note that it conforms to the norms of traditional utterances and that the speaker is socially acceptable. . . . These statuses are often established in the exchange of stereotyped expressions of esteem and concern that are obligatory whenever two or more persons meet. Since the same expressions are always uttered, interpretations of "friendliness" or "enmity" depend upon meanings conveyed by subtle qualities of tone, pitch, and melody. These qualities, in their different modes, are interpretable to one who is acquainted with their culturally defined meanings' (1957: 226).

In Cayuvava, a rapidly disappearing language in Bolivia, there is a set of nasal phonemes, but nasalization also occurs with 'honorific' stylistic function (according to Key, 1967: 19): an individual of lower social or economic status addresses one of higher rank with a prominence of nasalization for all vowels of the utterance; and similarly with a woman being polite to her husband, or a man asking a favour. Albert (1964) refers to a number of similar examples, also instancing a typical sociolinguistic use of silence in this respect: in Burundi conclave, the silence of the highest-ranking person negates the proceedings, indicating total disapproval (whereas silence of lower-ranking people would have no comparable effect) (p. 41). Gumperz (1964: 144) distinguishes between two forms of the vernacular in Khalapur, moṭī bolī and saf bolī, the former being used primarily within the family group, the latter being used in external relationships, and refers to particular distributions of pitch glides occurring in the former but not in the latter. Longacre (1957) notes a very restricted formal third person enclitic in Mixtecan, which adds length and nasal quality to the syllable. What Shapiro (1968) calls 'explicit' and 'elliptical' codes in Russian are generally distinguished, *inter alia*, by tempo, the latter being faster. Bernstein (1964) makes some reference to intonation in his distinction between restricted and elaborated codes in English.

Many of these oppositions imply a distinction between formal and informal (non-casual and casual, etc.) kinds of speech, which has been frequently referred to in English (e.g. by Joos, 1962). Speed of utterance is presumably one of the features that would distinguish formal from informal speech; and there is, as usual, a fair amount of informal evidence for the existence of status styles in English, e.g. 'How dare you talk to me like that! I'm not one of your employees/students/secretaries . . .', and reference to 'la-di-da' voices, 'talking down', and so on. Hoenigswald (1966: 19) makes the point that in this field it is important to study the *ideals* of speech behaviour cherished by a group as well as the actual speech behaviour used, and an interesting area of research will be the systematic examination of elocution handbooks – not to condemn them, as linguists generally do, but to view them descriptively, as data concerning the desired (real or imagined) correlates of genteel, educated speech and the reverse. Non-segmental effect is regularly referred to here: see, for example, the influential work of the American elocutionist Rush (1827) in this respect. One should also note the vocal effects used, sometimes as mocking forms, when addressing a member of a stigmatized group, e.g. Sapir refers to the 'thickish' sounds of s and ʃ 'pronounced with the lower jaw held in front of the upper' when talking to hunchbacks in Nootka (see Mandelbaum, p. 183), and to the way of satirizing cowards in this language, when either addressing them or referring to them, by 'making one's voice small' (i.e. using a 'thin, piping voice') (p. 184). Cf. children's sing-song cat-calls in English, using the tune

Gumperz, finally, mentions the importance of sentence speed and pause (as hesitation) in the analysis of status, and suggests that it is about time that scholars broadened the range of their linguistic investigations to take account of these matters (in Bright, 1966: 46). The points mentioned in this section are certainly only some of the possibilities. There are hardly any data to illuminate the question of the covariance of change in social status with change in tone of voice (e.g. after marriage, or after some initiation rite), though the existence of such phenomena can hardly be doubted.

4. *Occupation*

In English we are all familiar with the 'tone of voice' that is generally attributed to people acting in their professional capacities, such as the clergyman, lawyer, and undertaker. Phrases such as 'you sound like a clergyman' are conventionally meaningful, and would be interpreted (e.g. in an attempted imitation) as referring to a vocal effect in which pitch-range movements were narrowed, there was frequent use of monotone, rhythm was regular, tempo fairly slow, and overall pitch-height and resonance of the voice were increased. There are many occupations that would be recognized primarily on the basis of the non-segmental features involved, e.g. the disc jockey, barrister, preacher, street vendor, parade-ground commander, sports commentator, and many other kinds of radio and television announcer. Certain of these roles naturally overlap with status to some extent. Miller (1956: 181) talks about *authority roles*, by which he means 'a conceptualized position within a system of interpersonal relations whose incumbent is authorized to perform designated regulative functions for a designated action group during designated activity episodes', and many of those he cites (perhaps all?), e.g. drill sergeant, coxswain, foreman, cheer leader, involve the use of non-segmental features. The notion of a 'professional voice' is commonplace, if ill defined. Lecturers are generally aware of the kind of feature they have to introduce into their voice in order to awaken enthusiasm or promote participation in an otherwise dead class or audience.

Many of these matters have been given some experimental support, and it is not difficult to plan tests in order to verify one's impressions. A great deal of work has already taken place in the related area of defining personality traits, usually in the form of presenting judges with various non-segmental patterns (the verbal side of the utterance having been removed, e.g. by using nonsense-words, or acoustic filtering devices, or by articulating the different patterns on a single, neutral sentence – see Kramer, 1963), and asking them to rate the function of these patterns in terms of various traits. ('Trait' is fairly broadly defined in such work, and subsumes age, sex, and certain occupational characteristics.) This research, largely reported in psychology journals between about 1935 and 1950, is methodologically unsatisfactory in many respects (e.g. insufficient attention was paid to the backgrounds (i.e. the preconceptions) of the judges, and there was a blurring of theoretical concepts which should have been kept apart – the difference between voice quality and linguistic contrasts, for instance, which I shall discuss further below), but certain correlations between non-segmental patterns and features of extra-linguistic situations did emerge – and were generally referred to as *voice stereotypes* (see Crystal, 1969, Ch. 2, for a review of this literature). An important theoretical distinction which was not made in this work, but which must be made in future research, is that between *recognition* and *production* stereotypes (cf. the distinction between passive and active in vocabulary study); for example, it is part of our competence that we can discriminate various kinds of radio and television styles of speech, but I would agree with Labov that few speakers are ever directly influenced by such patterns as far as production is concerned (see 1967: 74).

There seem to be few occupational differences involving non-segmental features mentioned in foreign language descriptions. The only area that receives a regular mention is religious and magical language, and this really overlaps my next category, speech functions.

5. *Speech functions*

Particular modalities, or genres of speaking, are generally signalled through the use of non-segmental characteristics, as elocutionists are well aware. In the context of oral literature, one would also expect frequent use of these features, as they would provide an important means of adding further variation to the very restricted, stylized scope of a poem or story. Jacobs (1956: 127) emphasizes that

> 'stylized devices such as connectives, pauses, and vocal mannerisms, to effect transitions from Scene to Scene or Act to Act in a longer story, are invariably discernible in its dictation in the native language. But publications infrequently if ever preserve evidence of these devices.'

In Mohave, when a traditional, memorized text is being uttered, it is delivered in a staccato, rapid manner, which the speakers find very difficult to slow down (sometimes impossible, when the utterance is in front of other people from the same tribe – Devereux, 1949: 269). Henry (1936: 251) refers to changes in force, pitch, vowel quality, aspiration, and pharyngealization as Kaingang story-telling devices which were commonplace rhetorical forms in the language, e.g. 'the Kaingang always raise their voices when they are describing some long drawn-out activity, and their voices even take on what might be to us a complaining tone' (which tone, incidentally, 'was the usual tone to describe the slow climbing of a hill'!). Sapir talks of *styles of recitative* in Paiute, referring to the speech of certain mythological or traditional characters designated by certain sounds and tones of voice (in Mandelbaum, p. 186, and cf. p. 465). Related to this is the tone of voice adopted by a community when imitating another: cf. Sapir's remarks about the Nootka's imitations of other tribes, e.g. adopting velar resonance (speaking 'in a rumbling fashion') for the Uchucklesit (Mandelbaum, p. 193), or speaking in a 'drawling' manner (i.e. 'a somewhat exaggerated rise in pitch towards the end of a sentence') for the northern Nootka (p. 194). The vocal stereotypes adopted by comedians, stage villains, and certain traditional pantomime characters in our own culture would be further cases in point.

Distinct genres also exist in conversation in some languages. In Shiriana, different types of conversation can be distinguished on a non-segmental basis. Migliazza and Grimes differentiate between 'one-sided' and 'balanced' types (1961: 36–37). They illustrate the former by reference to 'myths' and 'narratives', and their distinction is worth quoting at length because of its detail:

> 'Phonologically a myth is characterized by an initial period in which only lento pause groups occur, a body in which combinations of lento and andante pause groups occur, many of

which contain ideophonic feet,[1] and a termination in which one or two lento pause groups occur, with extra length on the vowel of the final stressed syllable in the contour and at times a voiced breath intake after the end of the final pause group . . . four pitch levels [adequate for normal speech, DC] do not handle the pitch patterns, which range over a wide area and move largely in long glissandos.'

As an example of 'balanced conversation', the authors cite the *bargaining dialogue*, which is

> 'delivered at night by a trading partner from one village to his partner from another in the presence of all hosts and members of a trading party, in which each partner's speech has the general characteristics of a monologue, except that the intonation is replaced by a chant form' (p. 38).

They also mention the relevance of *crescendo, decrescendo*, and laryngealization for the definition of certain speech styles.

Another well worked-out example is Conklin's study of ways of modifying normal speech patterns for purposes of entertainment or concealment (most frequently as part of voice disguise in customary courting behaviour) in Hanunóo, a language of the Philippines. There may be both segmental and non-segmental aspects of this, but the latter vary independently of the former. There are four types: *yanas* (barely audible whispering), *paliksih* (utterance involving clipped pronunciation, greater speed, greater glottal tension, expansion of the intonational contours, and shortening of the long vowels), *padiqitun* (falsetto), and *paha·gut* (any sequence of articulations during which the direction of air flow in normal speech is reversed, i.e. inhalation).

Malinowski implies the relevance of non-segmental phonological effect at many places in *The Language of Magic and Gardening*, and makes explicit reference to it in his notes about 'modes of recitation' of magical formulae. Fischer (1966: 180–181) refers to the variation in the recitation of magical formulae between Ponape and Truk: the repetitions of the former are as exact as possible, but the latter make great use of expressive variations. Genres of religious speaking are regularly prosodically distinctive. Conwell and Juilland (1963: 30) refer to the distinctive rhythmicality of prayers in Louisiana

French, which is apparently very similar to the rhythmicality of litanies and other liturgical languages in English (see Crystal and Davy, 1969: Ch. 6). West reports that in Mikasuki, the language of the Seminole Indians in Florida, stress and tone differences are minimized in sermons (1962: 90). The introduction of song and chant characteristics into Welsh preaching (*hwyl*) involves markedly different pitch, length, and speed characteristics, as well as such paralinguistic effects as resonance and tremulousness.

A typology of speech functions in language has not yet been established, though there have been numerous attempts at it. The scattered comments collected in this section clearly indicate that non-segmental effect will be a major part of the definition of the physical basis of these functions. In English, phatic communion, routine requests, avoidance ploys, routine format (sports results, weather forecasting, etc.), public-speaking, official announcements, ceremonial language, sports commentary, telephone conversation, television advertising (and other forms of persuasion): these are just some of the areas where intonational and related phonological features are markedly different from those used in spontaneous utterance. For further references to speech functions, see Stern (1956, esp. pp. 382–383) and Frake (1964).

There has, then, been considerable sporadic, impressionistic comment as to the sociolinguistic function of non-segmental effects, though the utility of this has been marred by lack of an adequate theory, inexplicitness of definition, and certain methodological weaknesses. As an example of the latter, it is sometimes difficult to know the extent to which the description of a given effect is intended as referring to a linguistic feature of an individual, a group, or the language as a whole. When data are restricted to the output of one or two speakers of a language, there is always the danger of a lack of perspective causing misinterpretation (a problem that takes an extreme form in the Cayuvava language mentioned above, where there were apparently only six living speakers at the time the description was made). Also, too little reference is made to voice-quality norms for the languages as wholes, e.g. establishing overall pitch-range, loudness, speed, and so on. But enough has been done to show clear lines of research, and the links that exist between linguistics and related, non-linguistic, semiotic fields. Here one might instance the importance of *speech surrogate* systems, such as the use of conventionalized whistling patterns, which may reflect intonational or paralinguistic patterning in the language (cf. wolf-whistles and rise–fall intonations in English), or the co-occurrence of kinesic features with speech (cf. La Barre, 1964), or the relationship between intonation and primitive music (cf. Herzog, 1934). Stankiewicz (1964) provides further comment on this point.

It is possible that an 'integrated theory' of all the observations made in this area may prove as valuable to social anthropology as Trager's framework has been in stimulating and helping to codify psychiatric research in America (see the references in Sebeok *et al.*, 1964). The descriptive framework outlined in Crystal and Quirk (1964), and developed in Crystal (1969) and elsewhere, allows for the incorporation of all the effects noted in this paper, and groups them into systems on the basis of shared formal characteristics. The following conceptual stages need to be distinguished:

1. *Non-linguistic vocal effects*

(a) *Voice quality.* Speech (or any act of communication) takes place against a personal and environmental background, which has to be identified by the analyst, in order to be discounted. Voice quality is the idiosyncratic, relatively permanent, vocal background of an individual, which allows us to recognize him, as opposed to other members of the group. It may be both segmental and non-segmental in character, but the latter is usually the dominant factor. It is a physiologically determined activity, over which most individuals have little or no measure of control. For a useful model of voice quality, see Laver (1968). In the present paper, I am concerned only with those non-segmental features which display – to however small a degree – a group-identifying function.

(b) *Physiological reflexes,* such as coughs, sneezes, or husky voice due to a sore throat, may also occur along with speech, and must also be discounted as background 'noise'.

2. *Semiotic frame*

A model of an act of communication in semiotics is generally viewed as a bundle of interacting events or non-events from different communicational sub-systems, or *modalities*, simultaneously transmitted and received. This communicative activity has been variously called a 'signal syndrome' and a 'communication configuration' or 'network'. It is distinct from the personal and physical background in that (a) it is variable with reference to the biological characteristics of the individual communicator, but is a pattern of behaviour shared by a group, and (b) the activity has always some culturally determined, relatively conventionalized value, or 'meaning'. The sub-systems are five in all, corresponding to the five senses, vocal/auditory, visual, tactile, olfactory, and gustatory; but only the first three are regularly used in normal communication (the latter have little potential structure, but are none the less of some importance as carriers of information to such people as doctor and chemist, e.g. in analysing body odours). The study of patterned, conventionalized, visual human bodily behaviour (facial expressions and bodily gestures) is known as *kinesics*. Non-vocal communicative sub-systems have not been the subject-matter of this paper: their relevance to anthropology is discussed in La Barre (1964).

3. *Vocal-auditory component*

The vocal-auditory component in communication can be broken down into the following categories:

(a) *Segmental-verbal*. This, the traditional centre of linguistic attention, would in its widest definition cover segmental phonetics and phonology, morphology, syntax, and vocabulary. A sub-set of verbal items is usually distinguished in semiotic literature: these, generally referred to as *vocalizations*, cover such items as 'mhm', 'shhh', 'tut tut', and the like, which are articulated using sounds outside the normal range of phonetic resources in the language. These overlap, formally and functionally, the next category.

(b) *Pause phenomena*. These comprise the various degrees of silence and 'voiced pause' (e.g. the 'ers' of English) that exist in a language. These features are clearly segmental, from the formal point of view, but functionally silence overlaps non-segmental features, as it enters into the physical definition of such effects as rhythmicality and intonation contour (and is partly subsumed under the notion of juncture, by some scholars).

(c) *Non-segmental features.* These are aspects of the phonic continuum which have an essentially variable relationship to the phonemes and words selected as defined by (a) above. Detailed illustration of all features is provided in Crystal (1969). They may be grouped into two general categories:

Prosodic features

These are meaningful contrasts due to variations in the attributes of pitch, loudness, and duration (which have a primary, but not an identifying, relationship to the fundamental frequency of vocal-cord vibration, amplitude of vocal-cord vibration, and speed of articulation respectively), either singly or in combination. Some values from these three variables permanently characterize speech. Prosodic features sharing a similar formal basis and displaying some mutual definition of contrastivity are grouped together into *prosodic systems*. The following systems have been distinguished:

(i) *Pitch.* There are two systems of pitch, *tone* (referring to the direction of pitch-movement in a syllable, as when it falls, rises, or stays level, or does some of these things in rapid succession) and *pitch-range*. By pitch-range, I mean the distance between adjacent syllables or stretches of utterance identified in terms of a scale running from low to high. Speakers and groups have a normal pitch-level and -range, and they may depart from this in different ways to produce extra-high or -low speech, either in a sudden step-up or -down, or gradually. The normal distance between adjacent syllables may be narrowed (perhaps reduced to monotone) or widened, and different languages display different kinds and degrees of pitch-range variation. The patterns of pitch-movement that occur in a language are referred to as the *intonation*. Connected speech is considered as analysable into a series of *units* of intonation (variously called *tone-units* or *tone-groups*), which have a definable internal structure, and which function in sequences to produce melodic contours of a more general nature.

(ii) *Loudness*. Degrees of loudness which affect single syllables are generally referred to as degrees of *stress*. (*Accent* refers to a syllable which has been made prominent owing to a combination of both loudness and pitch factors.) Speakers and groups have a norm of loudness, which they may depart from in different attitudes, styles of speech, etc. Over stretches of utterance, there may be *forte* or *piano* loudness, to various degrees. As with pitch-range, the change from one level of loudness to another may be sudden or gradual (as with *crescendo* and *diminuendo* utterance.)

(iii) *Tempo*. Single syllables may be shortened or lengthened (clipped and drawled respectively); stretches of utterance may be faster or slower than normal for a speaker or group, to various degrees (*allegro*, *lento*), and, as above, the change may take place suddenly or gradually (*accelerando*, *rallentando* speech).

(iv) *Rhythmicality*. Combinations of pitch, loudness, and duration effects produce rhythmic alternations in speaking, distinct from the rhythmic norm of the language, e.g. increasing the perceived regularity of a sequence of stressed syllables in an utterance, or decreasing it; clipping certain syllables to produce staccato speech, or slurring them, to produce *glissando* or *legato* utterance. There are numerous possible contrasts here, and of course the physical correlates of each would have to be carefully defined in any description.

Paralinguistic features

Non-segmental variations *other* than those caused primarily by pitch, loudness, and speed, i.e. where other physiological mechanisms in the oral, nasal, or pharyngeal cavities are being used to produce an effect, are referred to under this heading. Prosodic features, being permanent features of utterance, of course enter into these effects, but they are variable in respect of their definition: any of the features listed below can be uttered with variable pitch, loudness, and speed (with one or two minor restrictions). Paralinguistic features are discontinuous and relatively infrequent in speech. They do not display such clear-cut formal and functional contrasts as do prosodic features, consequently the systemicness of their function is more difficult to demonstrate. One possible system would group together the different kinds of tenseness that may occur in a language, e.g. tense, lax, slurred, and precise articulations; others would involve degrees and kinds of resonance of articulation, contrasts in register (e.g. falsetto, chest), degrees of pharyngeal construction (e.g. huskiness), types of whisper and breathy articulation, spasmodic articulations (i.e. the pulsations of air from the lungs are out-of-phase with the syllables of an utterance, as when one laughs or sobs while speaking, or says something in a tremulous tone), general retraction or advancement of the tongue (e.g. velarization), distinctive use of the lips (labialization), and various kinds of nasalization. A complete description of the possibilities here has not been written, but this cannot really be carried out in the absence of reliable data.

If one examines the data discussed in the first half of this paper in the light of the categories outlined in the second, it will be seen that all the vocal effects cited (or, at least, plausible interpretations of all these effects) can be described in terms of one or more of these categories. A great deal more work is needed before such an approach could be formalized as part of any general phonological theory; meanwhile, it may be the case that even a tentative formulation could stimulate fieldworkers to look more closely at this aspect of language, thereby providing the reliable and wide-ranging data that this corner of linguistics so badly needs.

NOTE

1. An ideophonic foot is a highly conventionalized effect, referring to a rhythm unit 'accompanied either by an anomalous pitch pattern . . . or by a voice quality that stands out in contrast with that of the rest of the utterance

(usually laryngealized or breathy in relation to the overall voice quality)' (Migliazza and Grimes, 1961, p. 35).

Lento and *andante* are differentiated partly in terms of speed and partly in terms of the number of contours involved.

REFERENCES

ADAMS, J. B. 1957. Culture and Conflict in an Egyptian Village. *American Anthropologist* **59**: 225–235.

ALBERT, E. M. 1964. 'Rhetoric', 'Logic', and 'Poetics' in Burundi: Culture Patterning of Speech Behavior. In Gumperz and Hymes (eds.), 1964.

ALLPORT, G. W., and CANTRIL, H. 1934. Judging Personality from Voice. *Journal of Social Psychology* **5**: 37–55.

BERNSTEIN, B. 1964. Elaborated and Restricted Codes: Their Social Origins and Some Consequences. In Gumperz and Hymes (eds.), 1964.

BRIGHT, W. (ed.). 1966. *Sociolinguistics*. Proceedings of the UCLA Sociolinguistics Conference, 1964. The Hague: Mouton.

BURLING, R. 1966. The Metrics of Children's Verse: A Cross-linguistic Study. *American Anthropologist* **68**: 1418–1441.

CAPELL, A. 1966. *Studies in Socio-linguistics*. The Hague: Mouton.

CONKLIN, H. C. 1959. Linguistic Play in its Cultural Context. *Language* **35**: 631–636.

CONWELL, M. J., and JUILLAND, A. 1963. *Louisiana French Grammar*. Vol. 1, *Phonology, Morphology and Syntax*. Series Practica I. The Hague: Mouton.

CRYSTAL, D. 1969. *Prosodic Systems and Intonation in English*. Cambridge: Cambridge University Press.

—— and DAVY, D. 1969. *Investigating English Style*. London: Longmans.

—— and QUIRK, R. 1964. *Systems of Prosodic and Paralinguistic Features in English*. The Hague: Mouton.

DEVEREUX, G. 1949. Mohave Voice and Speech Mannerisms. *Word* **5**: 268–272.

DRIVER, H. E., and DRIVER, W. 1963. *Ethnography and Acculturation of the Chichimeca-Jonaz of Northeast Mexico*. International Journal of American Linguistics Publication 26. The Hague: Mouton; Bloomington: Indiana University Research Center in Anthropology, Folklore and Linguistics.

ERVIN-TRIPP, S. 1964. An Analysis of the Interaction of Language, Topic and Listener. In Gumperz and Hymes (eds.), 1964.

FERGUSON, C. A. 1964. Baby-talk in Six Languages. In Gumperz and Hymes (eds.), 1964.

FISCHER, J. L. 1966. Syntax and Social Structure: Truk and Ponape. In Bright (ed.), 1966, pp. 168–183.

FRAKE, C. O. 1964. How to Ask for a Drink in Subanum. In Gumperz and Hymes (eds.), 1964.

GARBELL, I. 1965. *The Jewish Neo-Aramaic Dialect of Persian Azerbaijan*. Linguistic Analysis and Folkloristic Texts. Series Practica III. The Hague: Mouton.

GOFFMAN, E. 1964. The Neglected Situation. In Gumperz and Hymes (eds.), 1964.

GUMPERZ, J. J. 1964. Linguistic and Social Interaction in Two Communities. In Gumperz and Hymes (eds.), 1964.

— 1966. On the Ethnology of Linguistic Change. In Bright (ed.), 1966, pp. 27–38; discussion pp. 39–49.

— and HYMES, D. (eds.). 1964. *The Ethnography of Communication*. Menasha, Wis.: American Anthropological Association.

HAAS, M. R. 1944. Men's and Women's Speech in Koasati. *Language* **20**: 142–149.

HENRY, J. 1936. The Linguistic Expression of Emotion. *American Anthropologist* **38**: 250–256.

HERZOG, G. 1934. Speech Melody and Primitive Music. *Musical Quarterly* **20**: 452–466.

HOENIGSWALD, H. M. 1966. A Proposal for the Study of Folk-Linguistics. In Bright (ed.), 1966, pp. 16–20.

JACOBS, M. 1956. Thoughts on Methodology for Comprehension of an Oral Literature. In Wallace (ed.), 1956, pp. 123–130.

JOOS, M. 1962. *The Five Clocks*. International Journal of American Linguistics Publication 22. The Hague: Mouton; Bloomington: Indiana University Research Center in Anthropology, Folklore and Linguistics.

KELKAR, A. 1964. Marathi Baby-talk. *Word* **20**: 40–54.

KEY, H. 1967. *Morphology of Cayuvava*. Series Practica 53. The Hague: Mouton.

KRAMER, E. 1963. Judgment of Personal Characteristics and Emotions from Non-verbal Properties of Speech. *Psychological Bulletin* **60**: 408–420.

LA BARRE, W. 1964. Paralinguistics, Kinesics, and Cultural Anthropology. In Sebeok, Hayes, and Bateson (eds.), 1964, pp. 191–220.

LABOV, W. 1964. Phonological Correlates of Social Stratification. In Gumperz and Hymes (eds.), 1964.

— 1967. The Effect of Social Mobility on Linguistic Behavior. In Lieberson (ed.), 1967, pp. 58–75.

LAVER, J. 1968. Voice Quality and Indexical Information. *British Journal of Disorders of Communication* **3**: 43–54.

LIEBERSON, S. (ed.). 1967. *Explorations in Sociolinguistics.* International Journal of American Linguistics Publication **33**. The Hague: Mouton; Bloomington: Indiana University Research Center in Anthropology, Folklore and Linguistics, Publication 44.

LONGACRE, R. E. 1957. *Proto-Mixtecan.* Bloomington: Indiana University Research Center in Anthropology, Folklore and Linguistics, Publication 5.

MANDELBAUM, D. G. (ed.). 1949. *Selected Writings of Edward Sapir.* Berkeley, Calif.: University of California Press; Cambridge: Cambridge University Press, 1950.

MIGLIAZZA, E., and GRIMES, J. E. 1961. Shiriana Phonology. *Anthropological Linguistics* **3:** 31–41.

MILLER, W. B. 1956. A System for Describing and Analysing the Regulation of Coordinated Activity. In Wallace (ed.), 1956, pp. 175–182.

PIKE, K. L. 1944. *The Intonation of American English.* Ann Arbor, Mich.: University of Michigan Press.

RUSH, J. 1827. *The Philosophy of the Human Voice.* Philadelphia: Lippincott.

SAPIR, E. 1910. Song Recitative in Paiute Mythology. In Mandelbaum (ed.), 1949, pp. 463–467.

—— 1915. Abnormal Types of Speech in Nootka. In Mandelbaum (ed.), 1949, pp. 179–196.

—— 1929. Male and Female Forms of Speech in Yana. In Mandelbaum (ed.), 1949, pp. 206–212.

SEBEOK, T. A., HAYES, A. S., and BATESON, M. C. (eds.). 1964. *Approaches to Semiotics.* The Hague: Mouton.

SHAPIRO, M. 1968. *Russian Phonetic Variants and Phonostylistics.* University of California Publications in Linguistics 49. Berkeley: University of California Press.

STANKIEWICZ, E. 1964. Problems of Emotive Language. In Sebeok, Hayes, and Bateson (eds.), 1964, pp. 239–264.

STERN, T. 1956. Some Sources of Variability in Klamath Mythology, 3: Style and Elements of the Myth. *Journal of American Folklore* **69:** 377–386.

TRAGER, G. L. 1958. Paralanguage: A First Approximation. *Studies in Linguistics* **13:** 1–12.

—— 1961. The Typology of Paralanguage. *Anthropological Linguistics* **3:** 17–21.

WALLACE, A. F. C. (ed.). 1956. *Men and Cultures.* Selected papers of the 5th International Congress of Anthropological and Ethnological Sciences. Philadelphia: University of Pennsylvania Press.

WEST, J. D. 1962. Phonology of Mikasuki. *Studies in Linguistics* **16**: 77–91.

PART III

Social Anthropology and Language Models

Edwin Ardener

Social Anthropology and the Historicity of Historical Linguistics

This paper approaches the relations between social anthropology and linguistics from a relatively novel direction. I hope the reason for the choice will emerge. In discussing the relations between two disciplines, we run the risk of not realizing that certain specialist approaches must always remain of little mutual relevance, because of the technical requirements of their disparate subject-matters. Others when stripped of their technicalities turn out to be genuinely of dual reference. Here we consider certain implications of historical linguistics (born in the same period as social anthropology itself) for some common problems of the two modern disciplines.[1] In so doing we shall set out from a careful consideration of the historicity of the Neogrammarian model of language.

I

There was a time when 'historical linguistics' (or 'comparative philology' as it was long almost exclusively called) was all the systematic linguistics that existed, or at least that was recognized. Since at least the advent of Saussure that time has ended. More conservative practitioners of the old comparative philology have in some universities hardly recognized that this is so. The result is that many who are concerned with general linguistics still face a certain isolation from philologists, especially from those working with the European languages. Almost *a fortiori*, then, the kinds of linguists who are likely to be interested in social anthropology or 'sociolinguistics' are likely to be least involved in historical linguistics.

Now, if this is so it is a pity, because it is the question of the very 'historicity' of historical linguistics that is of especial interest to social anthropologists. Historical or 'historical' linguistics raises a problem inherent in the consideration of models based on clearly expressed operations and rules. Such models are in themselves 'timeless', or neutral in regard to time – *achronic*. Ethnographic models, almost above all others, have since Malinowski exhibited this timelessness. The 'ethnographic present' is eternal. The timelessness has been, however, perceived in conflicting ways. The rejection of 'history' by Malinowski was, in its best expression, the rejection of models falsely purporting to offer 'historicity'. (Among such were some affected, as it happens, by the 'historicity' of historical linguistics: Evans-Pritchard, 1965).

The 'timelessness' was not understood at all by many functionalists who seemed to think that their models pertained to a real 'present', to which indeed notional dates were often ascribed. This confusion was a result of a misinterpretation of the practice of fieldwork. The social anthropologist had, of course, obtained his material at certain chronological dates. Nevertheless, the structures he imposed upon the data were 'timeless', precisely through the paradox that they had implications for notional 'states' of the society other than the state at the time of the visit. The model of a segmentary lineage system of the type described by Fortes (1945, 1949) for the Tallensi thus appears to make statements about the past relationships of the ancestors of present Tallensi one to another. The historical plausibility of such past states having actually occurred in such systems is low or nil (Ardener, 1959: 116–117). Lévi-Strauss (1963: 283–289) refers to models of this kind as 'mechanical'. He had in mind those called 'Newtonian' by Wiener ('mechanical' from the system of mechanics): '. . . in any such theory the future after a fashion repeats the past. The music of the spheres is a palindrome, and the book of astronomy reads the same backward as forward' (Wiener, 1948, 1961 edn: 31; see also Postscript, p. 233 below).

Functionalist ethnographic models 'generate' states of society that may never, almost certainly will never, occur. It was, indeed, the failure of such models to 'predict' (that is to make only 'right' predictions) that precipitated some of the dissatisfaction that began to characterize post-Malinowskian social anthropology. A common expression of such dissatisfaction lay in arguments that functionalism could not express change (Pocock 1961: 103; Jarvie, 1964), which had been much aided by arguments that history was not foreign to the work of social anthropology (Evans-Pritchard, 1950; 1961). The dubbing of functionalist models as *synchronic*, in opposition to supposed *diachronic* models which would build in the dimension of time, did not however succeed in producing true diachronic models in social anthropology. Those that were attempted were merely more satisfactorily explicit about the significance of states generated by the model for 'true' states of society. They represented a higher (more explicit) stage of functionalism. Thus Leach (1954) produced an 'oscillatory' or 'cyclical' model for the states of Kachin society, which is also timeless; it is an orrery working in its own eternity. In this respect it is not inferior to that devised by Toynbee for material of broader scope. The use of the term *diachronic* thus states merely an expectation of certain models, which is usually neither clearly expressed nor truly realized. Of a truly diachronic model it is required that the workings of the model shall generate, not possible 'pasts' or 'futures', but a 'real' past and a 'real' future; the issue may be avoided somewhat by an acceptance of 'pasts' and 'futures' that shall be 'probable'.

The *kind* of model that might generate time has been talked about for many years. In social anthropology, Lévi-Strauss opposed 'statistical' models to 'mechanical' models (1963: 283–289). In this he again followed Wiener. The terminology has caused misunderstanding; it is not about models based on quantified material, but models of the type devised in 'statistical' mechanics: probabilistic, yes, but concerned with that movement towards more and more randomization known as entropy. Leach (1961) shows that this idea of time (in itself, our only sure appreciation of its passage) is usually rendered symbolically by society in quite other ways that are essentially cyclical or repetitive, and, thus, mechanical. In this respect, then, the search for true diachronic models tends to be abortive for others as well as social anthropologists.[2] Nevertheless, through the problem of historicity, social anthropologists stemming from functionalist backgrounds have come upon similar ground to that with which linguistics have become familiar through the generative grammarians after Chomsky (1957). General linguists, on the other hand, have frequently turned their backs on historicity, because it has for them been over-examined. As a result, many non-linguists believe that it has been already solved for language.

For linguistics, the terminology *synchronic* and *diachronic* was firmly developed by Saussure (1916). In thus labelling two approaches he was misled by that very historicism which he set out to reject. He was concerned with two modes of analysis which in themselves were no more concerned with time than were those of social anthropologists. That *synchronic* models are timeless (that they have nothing to do with a chronologically 'present' or momentary state) has become self-evident since Saussure. At least, most people on reflection will concede that the progress from Saussure's 'synchronic' linguistics, to 'structural' linguistics, and to 'transformational' or 'generative' linguistics, has been a real progression away from a special concern with the 'present state' of a language. The 'timelessness' of the *diachronic* linguistic model is by no means as self-evident and needs some demonstration. The diachronic linguistics of Saussure (1916) was the comparative philology of Indo-European in which he was bred, and which he helped significantly to establish. The system in its full maturity, as bequeathed by Brugmann and the Neogrammarians,[3] provides a model which in principle reduces the multiplicity of documented forms in the set of languages it is concerned with to a dictionary of 'starred' or hypothetical forms, plus a set of rules whereby the original forms ('reflexes') may be built up again from them. The form of the model is totally 'generative', and requires no historical interpretation for its operation.

For example: *u̯l̥qᵘ̯os generates Sanskrit vŕ̥kaḥ, Lithuanian vil̃kas, Gothic wulfs, and Old Bulgarian vlŭkŭ, through rules (for example phonemic ones) of the type:

*l̥ → Sanskrit r̥
Lithuanian ir, il̃
Gothic ur, ul
Old Bulgarian lŭ

The rule-books for what *u̯l̥qᵘ̯os will generate are much more complex than this simple example at a phonemic level would indicate. Any starred form in Indo-European generates intermediate phonemic sequences which themselves generate further sequences, until ultimately *u̯ḷq$^{\text{u̯}}$os generates, for example, English *wolf*, Russian *volk*.

Even linguists are sometimes puzzled by 'generative' models; social anthropologists tend to be even more bemused because of the specialist guise in which they have been discussed by linguists. All models are 'generative': the trouble is that many so-called models are not models of formal systems. The generative terminology is that of mathematics; for example:

> 'In any formal system one encounters the following constituents:
> (i) Certain constant symbols . . .
> (ii) An alphabet of variables . . .
> (iii) A set of rules, which state which strings of variables and constants constitute sensible statements: the so-called well-formed formulae . . .
> (iv) A set of well-formed formulae, known as axioms, from which others known as theorems are to be deduced . . .
> (v) A set of rules of inference which enables the deduction of theorems from other theorems or from axioms . . .' (Kilmister, 1967: 70).

For a formal system to provide a model for a corpus of given data, it must generate all and only the forms in the corpus: these are the well-formed items.

Neogrammarian linguistics provided a model of precisely that kind. The generativeness is protected by:

(a) the rule of *analogy*: e.g. Middle English wa + c [c → a non-velar consonant] → wɔ [e.g. /wɔz/ 'was', /swɔn/ 'swan']. The rule does not generate *swam*. The 'exception' is generated by the analogy rule in some such way as: 'sit': 'sat' [sæt] → 'swim': 'swam' [swæm] (Ross, 1958: 34).[4]

(b) the rule of *loan effect*: e.g. I-E *g$^{\text{u̯}}$ → Latin w. The rule does not generate Latin bōs ('cow'). It does generate Oscan bōs, which is thus defined as a 'loan-word' in Latin.

(c) an *exclusion* rule: items that the model does not generate are outside the model (usually expressed: 'phonetic laws admit no exception'). This necessary tautology is of importance to us only because of the question of historicity. The transformation of the idea of etymology by Neogrammarian linguistics made it possible to say that a word had 'no' etymology: 'Not every word has an etymology; thus MnE *girl* and much of the Hungarian vocabulary are totally without one' (Ross, 1958: 39). Such statements should be noted as clear confirmation that the model is not one of 'history'. The definition of the 'corpus' of Neogrammarian linguistics is thus that corpus that the model has generated or will generate. The excellence of the Neogrammarian model is revealed precisely because of its approximation to a total formal system.

The model as such is timeless. Its status is already that to which generative grammar merely aspires. To claim that *u̯ḷq$^{u̯}$os existed at a chronologically earlier time would be as if to claim that the elements in 'deep structure' existed in the past before the presented elements in 'surface structure'. The question may not always be irrelevant (see now King, 1969), but generative grammar is not thereby 'historical'. The starred forms 'exist' in the known corpus: Old Bulgarian, Sanskrit, . . . Modern English, Russian, or the like. *u̯ḷq$^{u̯}$os 'is' vṛ́kaḥ, wulfs, . . . *plus* certain rules.

Then wherein lies the apparent historicity of the model? (a) The corpus to be generated is already ordered *a priori* by chronologically marked elements. (b) In addition, all 'chronologically' marked sequences are required to be generated sequentially by the model. The model does not, however, generate only these chronologically marked sequential forms. Other sequences are generated as part of the calculus: they are the source of 'surplus historicity' in that they *may* perhaps have happened; they are a kind of guess, which may turn out to be well or ill substantiated according to other criteria outside the model (e.g. certain notions about universals).[5] This may seem tediously self-evident, but that it is not is demonstrated by the common belief that the model generated ('predicted') forms not previously attested. In particular, that it 'predicted' Hittite. In fact that would be an exaggeration of its achievement. A part only of the Hittite vocabulary and morphology was defined by the model as Indo-European, and the shears of the 'rule of analogy' were liberally applied. The situation was confused by the supposed confirmation by Hittite of the hypothetical laryngeals, which precisely did not belong in the true Neogrammarian model. The model for any post-Hittite 'Indo-European' is in fact a revised model, and the 'historicity' of such revisions has been seriously questioned by comparativists themselves.[6]

The preceding argument is concerned only with the most rigorous interpretation of historicity in Neogrammarian linguistics: and thus with the confusion in the model itself. The looser historical expectations based on the model have always been precarious. The discovery of Tokharian, for example, brought ideas of the dialectal distribution in Indo-European into flux (Meillet, 1950). Forms like *u̯lq$^{u̯}$os do have a double life: they are formulae expressing rules of generation in the model. They are also phonological test-words for a theory of history ('derivation'). The confusion has lasted well into our own days. Thus the well-formed model for a Neogrammarian etymology outlined by Ross (in terms of symbolic logic) is perfectly satisfactory in its aims save in this particular: he interprets the two axioms that he permits himself as statements of an existential past (1958: 28–42).[7]

II

Not only linguists must be concerned with this problem, as it is intuitively felt that the Neogrammarian model generates more 'history' than it puts in. Neogrammarian linguistics is indeed the model of all models for a diachrony of social phenomena. Other disciplines, including history, archaeology, and forms of anthropology, have even used the cart-before-the-horse term 'reconstruction' in the firm belief that at least linguistic reconstruction has taken place already. Once more we may start from Saussure. In his chess analogy he was able to illustrate *synchrony* in language by the state of the board at successive moves of the game, and *diachrony* by the rules of movement of the different pieces from one state to another. The notion of *value* was used to denote the 'synchronic' relationship of any one piece at any one state of the board to all other pieces on the board at that state. In so far as a synchronic value is an expression of a diachronic rule, how far can a study of synchronic values enable the diachronic rules to be deduced? The recovery of the rules of chess from individual states of the board is in part possible. Certain rules are not deducible until the last state of the board (e.g. the rule that mate closes the game). Past existential states of the board cannot be deduced regularly in this way. Saussure was content to point out that the rules of synchrony and those of diachrony belong in two separate fields: that one set was not reducible in practice to the other. But recently Vendler in another context has said:

> 'Suppose that while watching a game of chess I see two Pawns of the same colour standing in the same column. Then I say: "One of them must have taken an opposing piece in a previous move." Is it sufficient to say that in all chess games we ever witnessed this correlation held? No, given the rules of the game, the relation holds *a priori*; the contrary is not something unusual or unlikely: it is inconceivable. . . . Thus seen through the conceptual framework constituted by the rules of the game, two contingent historical states of affairs appear to be necessarily connected. Moreover, obviously any "game", or, in a larger context, almost any rule-governed activity, will be the source of such propositions. And this domain may range so far as to include mathematics or the rules governing the synthesis of the manifold of experience' (Vendler, 1967: 18)

Some of the 'surplus' historicity of sequences generated by the Neogrammarian model derives from rules of the two-pawns-in-a-column type. For example, the Germanic sequences:

1. p t k → f þ χ
2. b d g → p t k

Transformation (2) will have occurred after transformation (1); otherwise all p t k from b d g would fall together with 'original' p t k and generate only f þ χ.

Many traditional comparativists honestly believe that if all chronological markers were stripped from their corpus of items, and thus were not built into the model, they would still be able to order the material into sequences that would be 'chronological'. This is partly a misunderstanding. It is not sufficient to ensure that the analyst will be presented with merely *undated* material from Middle High German, Gothic, Old English, and the rest. The material is chronologically marked by more than the matter of carrying a literal date, the least of all requirements. The markers and the material are indissoluble. As will be seen in the next section, the real absence of chronological markers is no trivial empirical problem.

The case of two-pawns-in-a-column sequences is more important, for critics of the position expressed here retire to a level that implicitly states that these logical sequences will always have chronological implications. In fact, the matter is more like this: sequences that were chronologically marked reveal logical sequences on analysis, which, in so far as the marked chronology was 'correct', have other chronological implications. To take yet another analogy: in the so-called 'painting by numbers', 1 = red, 2 = blue, and the like, on a set of outlines drawn on a plain sheet. The painted configurations revealed on the canvas when the numerical rules are obeyed are, of course, autonomously open to interpretation by a 'reality codebook'. 'It is a weasel', or even 'A weasel is fighting a dog'. But a revision of the numerical markers is quite sufficient to dissolve all these other analyses, which derive their cogency or force from general rules of interpretation, which are quite separate from the rules defining the system. So it is with this 'surplus historicity' of the Neogrammarian model: it is a revelation of the full implications of chronologically marking one's material. This is exactly why it is a good model: like all such, its apparent novelties are logical implications.

The Neogrammarian model of language is always interpreted as if its rules really were those of a game that had been actually played. A sequence in the calculus is always interpreted as a *necessarily* chronological sequence in the languages of the corpus. Its achievement is tautologous, as we have seen: (1) the corpus includes prior established chronological sequences; (2) it defines as chronological all new sequences in the calculus; (3) the rules exclude from the corpus all of language to which the rules do not apply (as if there were spare pieces on a chessboard to whose operation the rules of chess did not apply). Such are the 'shears of Brugmann'.

III

The application of 'comparative philology' beyond the Indo-European 'family' brought with it the establishment of other similarly defined *corpora* of linguistic data. Certain of these contained chronologically marked material of as much variety as did the Indo-European. Some, however, had very little or no chronological marking. We may take, for example, the Bantu family. Here, starred forms generate regularly all and only forms designated Bantu (Guthrie, 1948). The model is, however, jejune compared with Neogrammarian Indo-European. There is no regular ordering of the sets generated; there are no intermediate forms equivalent to asterisked 'Celtic' or 'Germanic', or even to 'Middle English' or the like.

Possible orderings are from time to time suggested, but no rules exist compelling their acceptance. The starred Bantu forms generate at the model level (and that is the only level at which 'Bantu' exists) all the extant reflexes, without intermediate grouping. The absence of chronological markers is clearly the reason for this. The Bantu model fails historically in much the same way that the Indo-European model fails with the so-called Indo-European dialects (Italo-Celtic and the like) and the centum/satem division, where the entry of Hittite and Tokharian found the Indo-European model precisely at its weakest (Meillet, 1950). The historicity that was built into Neogrammarian models was, as has been argued, the amount that they truly yielded. The rich documentation that obscured this for Indo-European did not exist for Bantu. Thus the discovery that diachronic Bantu linguistics did not yield history was easier to make.

A firm hold on the logical bases of Neogrammarian linguistics would have helped Bantuists to avoid the historical controversies that surround their subject. Their most austere representative (Guthrie, 1948, 1953) has attempted to employ rigorously the Brugmannian shears to protect the generativeness of the Bantu model. Yet their operation has not been accepted as readily as in Indo-European studies, especially that of the *rule of exclusion*: that phonetic laws admit of no exception. The position of Guthrie is undoubtedly formally correct. Its effect is to define as non-Bantu a range of languages which others (like Greenberg) wish to call Bantu (e.g. Tiv). For the social anthropologist in the area in which these languages occur, the Bantu line (that historico-linguistic figment) swings back and forth bewilderingly over vast stretches of country, fortunately to no great danger to the inhabitants (Richardson, 1956–57; Greenberg, 1963; Crabb, 1965; Ardener, 1967: 294–295).

The Brugmannian model for Indo-European shows similar ambiguities, in the Anatolian zone. Is Hittite any closer to 'reconstructed' Indo-European than Tiv is to 'reconstructed' Bantu? Would Hittite not have been called 'semi-Indo-European' by the adherents of 'semi-Bantu'? The Indo-Hittite hypothesis (Sturtevant, 1942) echoes several hypotheses in African linguistics, but there is no firm party-line to put them finally down.

The Greenbergian hypotheses (1963) for the interrelations of the African languages are bold, but (*or*: and therefore) they are not rigorously Neogrammarian.[8] They resemble the activities of the adherents of 'internal reconstruction', or of students of relations between Basque and Caucasian, or of those attempting to establish a 'Mediterranean' family. All these interesting preoccupations are proscribed by traditional historical linguistics even today. Having declared for freedom, however, the adherents of the new formulations cannot guarantee at the same time the old Brugmannian rigour. Murdock (1957) has mistakenly used Greenberg's scheme, as if it contained even the historicity of Indo-European, in order to build a 'conjectural history' of Africa, which has gone on to influence historians.

On the other hand, Guthrie (1962) has attempted by an injection of statistics to raise the generative powers of his essentially Neogrammarian model. In so doing, he has departed from that model completely. His model is in effect a new one: based upon the geographical distribution of the percentages of known reflexes of starred Bantu reported in the known vocabularies of a fixed number of Bantu languages. The ordering of such percentages produces *prima facie* geographical possibilities. That this model of Bantu is no longer self-defining in a Brugmannian way is demonstrated by Guthrie's inclusion of a 'non-Bantu' controversial language (Tiv).

IV

The statistics of the new Bantuists have not yet received the critical execration that was heaped upon the glottochronologists. The latter were accused essentially of publicly practising vices that are the private predilections of all naïve historical linguists. It is unnecessary to refer to the detailed literature in view of Hymes's invaluable survey (1960), which covers in effect the *Blüteperiod* of the theory. In brief, Swadesh and others in various publications (e.g. Swadesh, 1950; Lees, 1953) attempted to derive a measure of the rate of change of vocabulary over time. To do this, Swadesh took a control group of languages with long-documented histories (in the order of millennia). He devised two word-lists (of 100 words and 200 words) which set out to represent the area of vocabulary that would be most resistant to change (the 'core vocabulary'). The percentage of each list retained per millennium was purported to be constant for the control group. Much refinement of assumptions and method was attempted, and for a time the glottochronological method was cited at length in American textbooks of linguistics (Gleason, 1955a, 1955b; Hockett, 1958). The chief value of the method was hoped to be the provision of chronological dates, rather like carbon dates, for the separation of languages, apparently lexically related but without documentation. The method was another reaction, in fact, to the unsatisfactory historicity of the Neogrammarian model, when applied to exotic (here originally Amerindian) languages.[9]

As is well known, historical linguists did not react with much satisfaction to this attempt to quantify the rate of linguistic change. The scholarship and skill with which the theory was demolished evoked much admiration (e.g. Bergsland and Vogt, 1962). The question whether glottochronology survives or not may be debated, but it is true to say that it does not exist as the source for a simple rule for the quick determination of chronological dates of linguistic separation, except with the most extreme qualifications. It should, however, be noted that the assumptions about comparable lexical units (lexemes of cognate form and meaning) that enabled a glottochronological statement to be made, and about a 'core' vocabulary, were merely crudely explicit versions of those that lay behind the 'genetic' view of linguistic relationship.

Thus, what is it that makes it possible for a historical linguist to say that English 'continues' Old English and not Old French? This question was solved by the Neogrammarians in characteristic manner: a second row of protective conventions lay beyond the protective rules of analogy, loan-effect, and exclusion. These were: (1) 'there are no mixed languages'; (2) 'there are no substratum effects'. On reflection it will be apparent that convention (1) preserves the generative model from generating contradictions in the 'same' language; it is merely a statement that in such a case recourse must be made to the rule of loan-effect. Convention (2) similarly excludes the possibility of a language demonstrating change, except through the principle of phonetic laws admitting of no exception. These I have termed 'conventions' because, although they are mere corollaries of existing rules, they were not readily perceived as such by many historical linguists who brought them from time to time into debate.

The Neogrammarian view is that in all cases of doubt the correct relationship will be determinable by examination. At a conference in Oxford as recently as 1967, one eminent visitor said that a 'mixed' language could occur only in the case (stated rightly to be absurd) of one language being exactly composed of 50 per cent of one language and 50 per cent of another. The naïveté of this view quite equals the naïveté of the more extreme exponents of the idea of mixed languages, against which it is directed. The problem has been recognized, however, as a real one: for example, the ambiguity of classification for a long time of Albanian and of Maltese. In the end the rules about loan and analogy do not take into account even all examples of these two phenomena. As Meillet said of Sorabian and German in Lusatia: 'le parler sorabe n'est souvent, avec de formes slaves, qu'un calque de l'allemand' (1933: 168). In the case of some modern spoken Welsh it can be said to be, at the level of phrase and sentence, a calque upon English: a one-to-one code. In the terms of generative grammar the 'deep structure' is shared in part with English. Here the findings of the modern descendant of 'synchronic linguistics' clash with those of the traditional historical linguistics. For what is more 'historical' about Modern Welsh? Its English connections? Or those with Irish, Breton, and epigraphic Gaulish?

The idea of 'core' vocabulary is also not far from the minds of historical linguists. There is in any language classified by an Indo-Europeanist what amounts to a minimum 'register' generated by the model. An essential part of any such register might be (for example) numerals, some kin terms, some bodily activities, but probably not (for example) house-building 'registers'; or those pertaining to trade. It is, in effect, assumed that all registers but one (or one small set) can be borrowed without ascribing the language to a different 'genetic' family. The intuitive basis of the term 'genetic' is that this smallest register will equal that learnt at the mother's knee.

The lesson for historical linguistics from 'exotic' languages, then, was not glottochronology, but a more serious one about the bases of the initial assumptions of any 'genetic' historical model of language. Thus the problem of Hittite is hardly solved by its triumphant attribution to Indo-European, when the very adverbial suffix used to mean 'in the language of' (*-ili*) is not generated by the model. Nor can the problem of why such an 'old' language looks so much less 'conservative' than the 'younger' Sanskrit or Greek (Meillet, 1937, 1964 edn: 56; Hauschild, 1964: 36) be solved without some consideration of processes, of which creolization is an extreme case, that 'speed up' linguistic change.[10]

V

So far we have discussed only the model of 'Neogrammarian historical linguistics' rather than the methods by which the model was built up. This has been necessary for reasons which have been partly made obvious. The system of historical linguistics is received as a system, and as one that is historical. For many of its traditional adherents the bases in method have become subsumed in the aims of the system. The method is usually referred to as one of 'reconstruction', although it is rather a method of 'construction'. It is a 'comparative' method, indeed the original method to be so-called, and one that strongly influenced social anthropology in the nineteenth century (Evans-Pritchard, 1965: 15; Henson, above). Since those days the method of comparison has become commonplace, but it has become clear that it does not in itself produce historical generalization. That it should briefly have been thought to do so results from the historical concerns of comparative philologists and Darwinian biologists.

The method of 'reconstruction' in historical linguistics is in principle not very different from the procedures used in other branches of linguistics. The same kind of approach abstracts 'phonemes' from the corpus of speech sounds, reducing the latter to series of simpler constructs which generate the original corpus by means of rules. In the heyday of their 'discovery', phonemes, when constructed, caused the same existential problem as did *u̯ḷq^{u}os and the like. If they could be constructed, where were they? Or, where had they been? A historical explanation was not seized upon, as might have occurred in another age, although it lurks behind such ideas as that of the 'archiphoneme'. It is, however, interesting that the development of laryngeal theory in Neogrammarian Indo-European was in effect a conventional internal phonemic analysis applied to the 'reconstructed' Indo-European vowel system. The historical interpretation of the proposed laryngeal phonemes produced a debate such that quite recent introductory manuals of Indo-European philology still do not deal with them.[11]

The arbiter for the 'well-formedness' of constructed phonemes in some approaches was the 'native speaker'. The question of the relationship of an analyst's model of human activity to the interpretation made by the people involved is an old one in social anthropology. That historical linguistics implies a similar 'native speaker' problem has been obscured by the circumstance that comparative philology grew up in opposition exactly to 'native speakers' in the field of etymology. The native speaker was defined out, and in much historical linguistics he still is. The very success of this operation is of some interest to social anthropology because of its undoubted dependence on him.

The transformation of etymology by Neogrammarian linguistics can be illustrated by these two sequences (Ross, 1958: 42):

1. I-E *g^{u}ōu̯s → Common Germanic *kwōz → Old English cū → Modern English 'cow'.

2. I-E *g^{u}ōu̯s → Oscan bōs → [by borrowing] Latin bōs, accusative bōvem → [by the accusative stem] Anglo-Norman bœ̄f → [by borrowing] Middle English bēf → Modern English 'beef'.

These are etymological 'sames'. Yet in English, as is well known, 'cow' and 'beef' are not the same. No folk-etymology of the two words would turn up a suggestion more apparently improbable at first sight. For Leach (1964) the two words clothe categories of great importance in the English symbolic system. These categories have, however, no place in any etymology deriving from Brugmann. Vendryes (1933), in his discussion of the tasks of 'la linguistique statique', understood the problem as one of those deriving from the 'synchronic section' of Saussure's *langue*. As he presciently put it:

> 'C'est au point de vue de l'homme qui parle que le linguiste staticien doit se placer. La seule étymologie qui compte pour lui ne peut être que l'étymologie dite populaire . . .' (p. 176).

In the absence of chronological markers, however, the clear distinction between etymology and folk-etymology cannot be so crisply maintained. The field of folk-etymology is close to the zone of dead metaphor. For example, Chinese: hwǒ ('fire'), chē ('cart'), yields hwǒ chē ('train'), but 'electric train' is dyànlì-hwǒchē (dyànlì, 'electric power'), not, for example, dyànlì-chē (Colby, 1966: 10; Hockett, 1954: 111). Similarly, 'steamroller' in English was for many speakers incorporated in 'diesel steamroller'. The possibility of recovery of a dead metaphor is recognized by native speakers. Often they will say that the 'real' meaning of a word is 'x' or 'y', referring to the process of pointing out such a dead metaphor. A serious discrepancy between Neogrammarian and folk-etymology soon became marked, however. For example, 'asphalt' is a material which among English builders is commonly pronounced 'ashfelt'. This situation produces two etymologies:

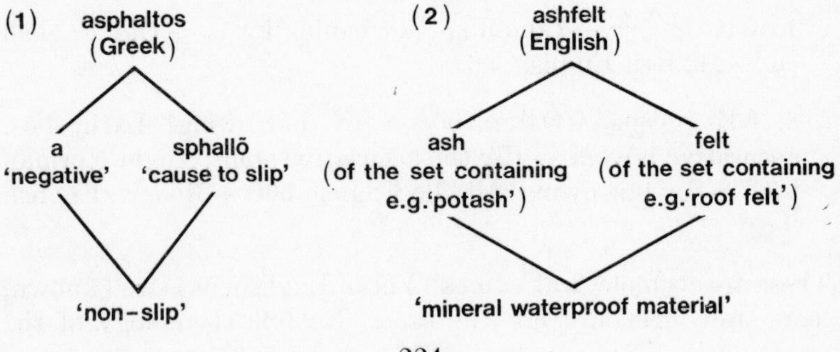

'Ashfelt' is to the untutored user a form of the same status as 'steamroller'. While the latter is a dead metaphor for the drivers of 'diesel steamrollers', 'ashfelt' is a dead metaphor that never existed. Indeed, it might better be considered a 'living' metaphor calqued on 'asphalt'! The essential neutrality of the Neogrammarian model in relation to history, in the sense of the generation of 'real' sequences, is clear when we consider that if 'ashfelt' were declared to be 'English' by some consensus of usage, a Neogrammarian etymology of the elements 'ash' and 'felt' could be supplied, and might be thought necessary. The true historicity of the sequence asphalt → ashfelt is a separate matter: it is a sequence given by a chronological record. It is the independent record, not (of course) the etymology, that validates it.[12]

The same problem occurs for the social anthropologist in the study of non-linguistic symbolism. He is offered 'folk-etymologies' by the native speaker; he attempts 'etymologies' of his own. Try as he may, however, the historical kind of etymology cannot be surely constructed without the historical records. Thus, in the Oxford degree ceremony there are striking passages in which the two proctors march up and down, and then sit down again. The folk-etymological faculty is continually exercised by spectators, who produce interpretations such as 'they are pretending to think', 'they are pretending to open the doors'.[13] We are told by the historians of the ceremony that the proctors are providing an opportunity for any member of Congregation who wishes to object to the presentation of the degree to do so by plucking a proctor's gown. The operation is linked by the historians with taking the vote in a normal assembly of Congregation (Wells, 1906). Is it possible to 'reconstruct' the etymology from the present ceremony? By hindsight no doubt certain approaches are possible. One might note that an opportunity for dissent also occurs at marriage rites. In the two rites there is, then, a symbolic space which may be filled by walking up and down, in one case, and by a formal utterance by the celebrant, in the other. The corpus of all rites in the society might be analysed and an alphabet of the possible symbolic spaces be prepared. The mode whereby such a symbolic space is realized in any given rite ('walking up and down', 'an utterance') would be a separate level of study, drawing upon further comparative material for its elucidation. Once we have got so far in trying to replicate a 'historical' etymology of a feature of a certain rite, we discover that (as the previous argument would lead us to expect) we are, in the absence of the given historical documentation, replicating post-Saussurean linguistic methods: the basic method of structural linguistics, of historical linguistics, and of social anthropology, turns out to be the same. Once more: there is no historicity in the method as such. (For similar conclusions from a different standpoint see Ellis, 1966.)

There is a further problem in the attempt at an etymology of symbolism which is inherent in the method of reconstruction. If the symbolic spaces to be compared have identical 'realizations' little more can be said. If in the wedding service the clergyman had walked up and down, made no admonitory utterance, we should be no further forward. In such a case the 'native speaker' may be our only guide in new directions. The societies that social anthropologists study frequently have formal or informal bodies of lore-guardians who characteristically operate at the level linguists would refer to as folk-etymology: collecting such 'etymologies', creating new ones. Their function may be seen as one of continually blocking up the fortuitous gaps in the symbolic sets. The remains of old systems may be seen propping up bits of the new. These *bricoleurs* (Lévi-Strauss, 1966a: 16–17) turn out indeed to be village Brugmanns with a clear grasp of the principle that a model should generate only what it has been designed to generate.[14]

It is no surprise that the narrow 'historicity' aimed at in the method of reconstruction falls into relative insignificance in front of problems of a social anthropological type. History is continually re-created in the wake of society in such a way that no one model of historicity can do more than hint at a possible aspect of a possible past. Say that 'ashfelt' and 'silverside' (a certain cut of beef) both exist in a dialect of English, and that folk interpretations 'ashfelt' = 'ash' + 'felt', and 'silverside' = 'silver' + 'side', are made. The latter is a 'real' dead metaphor; the former is created to look like a dead metaphor: the distinction has here been rescued from the very teeth of oblivion. The ability of human beings to rearrange Saussure's chessboard to look as if a game has been played so far which did not occur makes the quest for narrow 'historicity' almost meaningless. The vexed question of whether Adam had a navel led Edmund Gosse's father to make the answer, in effect, that the evidences of man's past were created with him.[15]

VI

The purpose of this paper has been to show that a consideration of Neogrammarian historical linguistics yields insights for social anthropologists which are helpful both in approaching their own problems and in appreciating the directions in which recent developments in 'non-historical' linguistics have moved. The grandeur of the Neogrammarian model for historical linguistics literally left nothing more to be said. This grandeur lay in its perfect generativeness. It did not, however, generate history. The Chomskyan generative model is in comparison incomplete, but its aims are more ambitious. Social anthropologists have had models which on their small scale were 'generative'. They are likely to waste their time in trying to find analogies with particular details of the Chomskyan system. They are likely to repeat the failure that attended Lévi-Strauss's early efforts to find social 'phonemes': a confusion of the peculiar data of linguistics with the broad 'semiological' principles (Lévi-Strauss, 1963, Chapter II).

The words of Hjelmslev (1963: 14–19), originally written in 1943, may now be translated into the terms of my argument: He speaks of two factors in his use of the word *theory*:

> '(1) A theory . . . is in itself independent of any experience. In itself, it says nothing at all about the possibility of its application and relation to empirical data. It includes no existence postulate . . .' (Thus we define *the model of a well-formed system*.)
>
> '(2) A theory introduces certain premisses concerning which the theoretician knows from preceding experience that they fulfil the conditions for application to certain empirical data. These premisses are of the greatest possible generality and may therefore be able to satisfy the conditions for application to a large number of empirical data.' (These are the '*reality conventions*' for the interpretation of the model.)

Hjelmslev goes on: 'The first of these factors we shall call the arbitrariness of a theory . . .' (this is the consistency of the model, and thus its *generativeness*), 'the second we shall call its appropriateness' (this is the *fit* of the model). Finally, for what is to be generated (the *corpus*), his wording is of striking familiarity:

> 'For example, we require of linguistic theory that it enables us to describe self-consistently and exhaustively not only a given Danish text, but also all other given Danish texts, and not only all given, but also all conceivable or possible Danish texts, including texts that will not exist until tomorrow or later, so long as they are texts of the same kind, i.e. texts of the same premissed nature as those heretofore considered' (p. 16).

The generative views of Hjelmslev, of the Neogrammarians, and of Chomsky are all expressed in a stubbornly linguistic guise, which obscures their general relevance, and in a stubbornly individual manner, which disguises from the untutored the essential similarity of their approaches. Of all these Hjelmslev has been the least understood. He had a message for synchronic and diachronic linguistics when few ears were ready to hear, even had he not published in wartime, and in Danish (he himself says somewhere in *Essais linguistiques*, 1959, 'to write in Danish is to write in water'). It is no surprise that he was regarded by Bally as the most Saussurean of Saussure's successors (Hjelmslev, 1959: 31).

The great advance of the new linguistics for non-linguists is in the making explicit of the idea of 'transformation'. In this direction, however, Lévi-Strauss has already independently made the necessary first steps for social anthropology (1962, 1964, 1966b, 1968). These more ambitious models generate sequences some of which no doubt will be of historical significance. But the problem of historicity is of course ultimately the problem of history itself. In discussion with working historians one sometimes notes in them a reluctance to concede that historiography offers a choice of pasts – even though their own theoreticians have long said no less. Each historian's model generates the data it was made to generate, with the operation of an exclusion law: the guillotine of relevance. Historians are reluctant because 'propaganda', 'legend', and 'myth' share these procedures, a fact that to social anthropologists is of especial interest (Leach, 1969: 25–30 and notes). The lesson of historical linguistics is that good models can be made, but that there can be no winning outright in the attempt to generate 'the past'.

POSTSCRIPT

Any social anthropologist setting out under the watchful walls of both historical linguists and the transformational generative grammarians will be fortunate to escape back into his own trenches from the hail of fire. It has been particularly encouraging, therefore, that although this paper has occasioned debate both at the Conference in Sussex at which it was first delivered (it was written in this form in December 1968), and before historical linguists and some transformationalists at Oxford in 1970, its main conclusions have remained standing. Consequently, I have left the text substantially as it was, save for the paragraphs on 'surplus historicity' in section II, which are essentially an expansion of the argument already summarized by my quotation from Vendler (1967). Some further remarks are required, however, in order to make clear what I am *not* saying, and also to explain my use of 'historicity'. Furthermore, we now have R. D. King's book on *Historical Linguistics and Generative Grammar* (1969) received only shortly before this volume went to press; I should like to add a few words upon it here also. Finally, not all the anthropologists were in agreement with me about the relevance of any of this to them. I shall take these three groups of points in order.

It should first of all be self-evident that this paper is not 'anti-historical' and not 'anti-historical-linguistics'. So much so, indeed, that some have justly seen it as strongly 'pro-Neogrammarian'. The paper is about the nature of formal systems, a subject that at least the writings of Lévi-Strauss, Leach, and Needham (e.g. 1962) have made well known to social anthropologists. Although the title refers to 'historical linguistics' (in part for euphony and brevity), it should be clear that the model I discuss is that of Neogrammarian historical linguistics in its most 'German' heyday (which for many is not over). This model was almost totally generative. Suggestions that one should look towards other more 'liberal' exponents of the general approach miss the point: the latter have ceased to work as if they had a totally generative model. Rather, there are many partial models but none fully articulated. Lehmann and Malkiel (1968), in an important compilation, and especially Weinreich, Labov, and Herzog (1968) therein, now present a rich programme for historical linguistics, which builds on Saussure and the Neogrammarians 'without leading to positions which disregard the achievements of past theory' (p. 20). Nevertheless, one can say that where historical linguistics is still understood to be equivalent to comparative philology, as in some quarters in my own university, the Neogrammarian model remains substantially unamended.

In stressing the generativeness of the Neogrammarian model in its most rigorous form, I have also said something about generativeness itself for non-mathematical people in the humanities tradition who, in this country at least, think there is a holy mystery in it. Furthermore, it should be clear that generativeness is not a sign of modernity. Awareness of its nature possibly is. For literary people, if a model is rigorous it is 'too rigid': they believe all models are *of* reality (which is not rigid), instead of being models *on* reality, which must be rigorous. The principle must be: 'let a hundred flowers blossom' – or 'let a hundred properly articulated formal systems contend'. When new masses of data arrive, tinkering with the old models (if they are any good) simply destroys their formal properties. A new model or set of models is required. While these are being created there is rarely any doubt of whether they work: usually they chew up facts for a generation before their implications are exhausted.

The emphasis on the neutrality of model-building principles means that each model must be used with a set of 'reality' conventions. The 'historicity' with which Neogrammarian philology is concerned derives from the 'book of conventions' for the interpretation of the model. For this reason, 'extreme' statements such as those of Ross have real integrity because of their appreciation of this. Historical linguistics, in so far as it is *not* Neogrammarian, is not a gloss on Neogrammarian history: it is based on, or hopes for, different models. Yet another comment must be made: the Neogrammarian *model* was not the only apprehension of language the Neogrammarians, as people, had. But an apprehension is less easily taught (see Osthoff and Brugmann, 1878, now easily accessible in Lehmann, 1967: 197–209).

This brings me to a final misunderstanding of my paper from the 'traditional' side. What is true of one model of history is true of all: the 'surplus historicity' it generates, over and above the chronological markers that are fed in, derives from the possibility of establishing necessary logical sequences which will be expressible by the reality conventions for the model as if they had actually happened in time. We act as if we generate reality, whereas not only is the 'truth' of the whole structure dependent on the values given to the essential minimum of chronological marked documentation, but (and this is where social anthropologists can place the problem in broader perspective) the evidence is not (as Kingsley thought of geology) 'written by God upon the rocks'. I cannot express this part of my case any more clearly than in Section V above. For people in the old humanities the lesson of modern social anthropology is that their 'science' is no worse than that of the scientists; it is merely more difficult.

To turn now to the generative grammarians. My audiences have tended to be afraid of them: for good reasons. When a group of academics acquires a powerful formal system, woe betide any naïve argument in its path. Mine here is self-evident: the terms 'generative' and 'transformational' are signals that the transformationalists care about the formal properties of models. When I say that the Neogrammarian model is generative, I do not mean *either* that I have done a detailed rewrite of it in the modern transformationalist notation (that is obvious) *or* that a modern generative model for historical linguistics would take the form of the Neogrammarian model, in whatever notation it is expressed. King (1969) provides an account of what such a modern generative model might be, while partially rewriting the Neogrammarian one. Many of the conclusions of the Neogrammarian reconstructions are not dislodged – they are described by different rules, and by a much more sophisticated notion of a rule.

As the differences between synchronic dialects are expressed by the transformationalists in terms of the presence or absence of specific rules, so between chronologically ordered dialects the differences can be expressed in terms of the acquisition or loss of rules. In simple terms the phonological and other developments of historical linguistics are, in the model, a set of statements of rule-acquisition and rule-loss. Two further principles operate also: those of rule-reordering and of simplification. For the first time, therefore, the operational elements in a synchronic and a diachronic comparison can be expressed in the same terms. The transformationalist approach to historical linguistics does not as yet produce a totally generative model as we have considered it here. It is not logically necessary, for example, in the establishment of their model, to have also a theory of the psychological or social mechanisms of rule-acquisition or rule-loss, but reference to such theories is (as usual) made. As in the 'synchronic' field, the generative grammarians are aiming at including all the phenomena that determine 'competence' in language. This aim has not been achieved, although it is a grand one, worthy of their best endeavours. The narrow 'historicity' of the Neogrammarian view has not, however, been retained:

> '[T]he proper historical phonology of a language is clearly much more than a set of rules that derive the sounds of let us say, West Germanic from proto-Indo-European. Even if these rules are made as simple as possible in terms of the distinctive features involved, there is not the slightest reason to suppose that they correspond meaningfully to historical reality. Historical reality includes restructuring, and a simple enumeration of the innovations in a language need not bear any resemblance to what happened historically if the grammar has been restructured' (King, 1969: 104).

And yet it seems that there remains a residual belief that a real 'history' is still demonstrable from a model: 'A proper historical phonology is the history of the *grammars* of a language, of the competences of successive generations of speakers' (ibid.). The strength of the transformationalist movement lay initially in its attempt at self-awareness at the model level. It should not be forgotten, then, that the grammars of the transformationalists are (as they are usually themselves aware) 'only' *models* of the competence of individuals. Indeed, the term 'competence' is a Saussurean 'signified' – itself an abstraction. While the code-book for the interpretation of the Neogrammarian model was labelled 'history', that of the transformationalists is labelled 'competence', to which their historical interests add only an appendix. The Chomskyan shears are sharper than those of Brugmann, for the aim is even more ambitious.

Mechanical and statistical models

For social anthropologists, first of all, a digression upon the derivation of Lévi-Strauss's terms, which some have questioned. Nutini (1970 edn: 85) says: 'Lévi-Strauss's most distinctive and important contribution to the theory of social structure was his dichotomizing of models into mechanical and statistical.' Nutini rightly points out the ambiguities in Lévi-Strauss's own usage, and the different interpretations of it of, for example, Nadel and Leach. He also notes: 'Models of the same scale as the phenomena are called "mechanical"; those on a different scale are called "statistical". Lévi-Strauss never explains what he means by "on the same scale as" . . .'

The sources of the terms are, however, quite clear. Lévi-Strauss's explicit and laudatory references to Wiener occur in his 1951 paper (Chapter III of Lévi-Strauss, 1963), and the remarks 'on the same scale' derive from Wiener's discussion of the Maxwell's Demon problem (this volume, pp. liv, lxxxiii). In the article on 'Social Structure' (1963, Chapter XV) the linkage with Wiener occurs as follows (p. 284):

> 'the theory of a small number of physical bodies belongs to classical mechanics, but if the number of bodies becomes greater, then one should rely on the laws of thermodynamics, that is, use a statistical model instead of a mechanical one . . .'

And further (p. 286): 'Anthropology uses "mechanical" time, reversible and non-cumulative . . . On the contrary, historical time is "statistical"; it always appears as oriented and non-reversible.'

In Wiener (1948/1961) Newtonian mechanics and Newtonian time are discussed in Chapter I, and statistical mechanics in Chapter II. Gibbsian irreversible time, and the movement towards increasing entropy, is compared with Bergsonian time. Wiener is rich in sources of the imagery of Lévi-Strauss and Leach (*entropy, topology, transformation groups* – Ardener, 1970). Wiener again:

> 'The succession of names Maxwell–Boltzmann–Gibbs represents a progressive reduction of thermodynamics to statistical mechanics: that is, a reduction of the phenomena concerning heat and temperature to phenomena in which a Newtonian mechanics is applied to a situation in which we deal not with a single dynamical system but with a statistical distribution of dynamic systems; and in which our conclusions concern not all such systems but an overwhelming majority of them' (1961 edn: 37).

Lévi-Strauss does not get the images quite right, and no doubt (as Nutini says) there was an association with Durkheim's 'mechanical' and 'organic' solidarity to confuse the issue. Lévi-Strauss also slipped over into the use of 'statistical' to refer to notionally quantifiable averages – the 'statistical norms' of Leach. Beattie in *Other Cultures* understands the matter similarly.

Wiener plays the role, in the genesis of Lévi-Strauss's view of models, that Trubetzkoy and Jakobson play in the 'phoneme' stage of his structural view (see this volume, Introduction, p. lii). Remember the pun that *anthropologie* is *entropologie* (Lévi-Strauss, 1955). Nevertheless, a careful reading of Wiener does elucidate Lévi-Strauss, despite the latter accretions. Wiener, indeed, puts it very clearly in his final chapter on Information, Language, and Society':

> 'It is in the social sciences that the coupling between the observed phenomenon and the observer is hardest to minimize. On the one hand, the observer is able to exert a considerable influence on the phenomena that come to his attention. With all respect to the intelligence, skill, and honesty of purpose of my anthropological friends, I cannot think that any community which they have investigated will ever be quite the same afterward. . . . On the other hand, the social scientist has not the advantage of looking down on his subject from the cold heights of eternity and ubiquity. . . .

> Your anthropologist reports the customs associated with the life, education, career, and death of people whose life scale is much the same as his own. . . . In other words, in the social sciences we have to deal with short statistical runs, nor can we be sure that a considerable part of what we observe is not an artifact of our own creation. . . . There is much which we must leave, whether we like it or not, to the un-"scientific", narrative method of the professional historian' (1948, 1961 edn: 163–164).

What Lévi-Strauss has enabled us to add (through his own later work) to Wiener's far from negligible insights is that the method of the anthropologist and of the professional historian (as well as that of the linguist) is also a method of models.

Finally: this paper has departed from its simple task of suggesting a few parallels in the modern trends of thought in social anthropology and linguistics, by looking back on a branch of linguistic theory which was the product of a revolution in method and conceptualization, and which has passed through many stages of growth, decay, and reordering. Even if my treatment is distorted, or in some real linguistic senses wrong, the case is clear. The newer social anthropology and the newer linguistics both have similarly wide-ranging aims. The linguists have so far been more successful in making their point, because their body of common material is relatively more copious and slightly less difficult to obtain, but we should not retire simply because 'the task may be too much for us' (Lévi-Strauss, 1963, dedication).

NOTES

1. The writings of Professor L. R. Palmer (in particular his *The Latin Language*, 1954) have long been one stimulus of my interest in this subject. I should like to acknowledge this here, although I have reason to believe that this paper does not carry his complete approval. Professor Guthrie's writings on Bantu linguistics and the problem of Cameroon linguistics provided another and more empirical stimulus. The debate on this paper at the ASA Conference was very lively and enjoyable, and I should like to thank Dr E. R. Leach and Dr G. Milner, who took up positions in support, as well as Professor Dell Hymes, who raised cogent points of disagreement.

2. For an amplification see the Postscript to this paper (pp. 233–235).

3. The basic statements were Brugmann and Delbrück (1886–1900) and Paul (1880) in various editions. See also, in declining complexity: Brugmann

(1902–04), Pedersen (1931), Meillet (1937), Krahe (1962–63), Bloomfield (1933). An early version of the Neogrammarian creed (their term) is Osthoff and Brugmann (1878: iii–xx); see also Brugmann (1885).

4. Only a simplified notation is used. See Chomsky (1957, 1965a, 1965b, 1966a, 1966b), Chomsky and Halle (1965).

5. Greenberg (1963, 1966). 'Universals' belong, if attested, in the axioms of the model. Neogrammarians often treated them as if they were generated by the model. The uncertain status of some 'universals', however, makes them best regarded as part of the conventions of interpretation.

> 'Our work as historical linguists is narrowly constrained by our judgements of what is and what is not a universal property of natural language, and we can expect the progress of historical linguistics to be closely connected with the search for linguistic universals' (King, 1969: 16).

6. Crossland (1951). Meillet (1937) expressed a certain disappointment with Hittite: 'Le nombre, encore assez petit, des textes interprétés, les obscurités d'une notation qui n'est pas faite pour une langue indo-européenne, les incertitudes qui subsistent sur bien des points, le degré avancé d'évolution de la langue à certains égards, font que le hittite ne rend pas tous les services qu'on souhaiterait' (1964 edn: 56). The discredited 'Indo-Hittite' remains in the 1964 edition of Hockett (1958). Leroy (1967) states concisely the methodological flaw:

> 'It consists in comparing the newly-deciphered languages with this Indo-European that was reconstructed on the basis of all the *other* Indo-European languages – i.e. excluding the new ones – and indeed in some respects, on the basis of two or three languages [especially Sanskrit and Greek] that are quite arbitrarily considered as being especially typical. So it is not in the least surprising that characteristically Hittite features, for example, do not appear in this reconstructed Indo-European. . . . It is obvious that if Hittite and Tokharian had been discovered fifty years earlier, Brugmann's Indo-European would have looked very different' (p. 115).

7. Thus: 'Axiom I. "Two languages are related if, and only if they were once one language" ' (p. 28). Ross's attempt is merely a sketch. The systematization by Hoenigswald (1960), in terms of American post-Bloomfield structural linguistics, is much more interesting, since he is quite explicit that the analysis can begin only after the corpus is chronologically marked. This is the burden of his remarks about the palaeographical preliminaries required (p. 3).

8. The treatment of Bantu as a greatly dispersed sub-category of a Niger–Congo family is particularly attractive.

9. Haas (1969), whose basic position is unashamedly Neogrammarian (in that non-pejorative sense that my argument implies), notes rightly that the full power of the method in its classical form has not yet been fully exploited among historical linguists of exotic languages (p. 16). She falls into the error of confusing model with reality with statements like 'Every protolanguage was . . . once a real language' (p. 32).

10. Hauschild (1964) even uses the term *Mischsprache.* See also Cowgill (1963: 105).

11. 'Die "Laryngaltheorie" kann . . . weder in ihrer Substanz noch in ihrer Methodik als gesichert gelten' (Krahe, 1962, I: 101).

12. The field of historical linguistics that most closely touches on these interests of social anthropologists is associated with the names of Trier (1931),

von Wartburg (1943, 1969), and, in this country, Ullmann (1951, 1959, 1963) This is discussed in the Introduction to the present volume. The whole question of loan, analogy, and the like is discussed by Lyons (1968: 36–38). It can be argued that 'asphalt' never existed in the speech of the users of 'ashfelt'.

13. For the older folk-etymology of the 'Proctor's Walk' see Wells (1906: 9–10):

> 'The Proctor's walk is the most curious feature of the degree ceremony; it always excites surprise and sometimes laughter. It should however be maintained with the utmost respect, for it is the clear and visible assertion of the democratic character of the University. . . . But popular imagination has invented a meaning for it, which certainly was not contemplated in its institution; it is currently believed that the Proctors walk in order to give any Oxford tradesman the opportunity of "plucking" their gown and protesting against the degree of a defaulting candidate. . . . There is a tradition that such a protest has actually been made within living memory and certainly it was threatened quite recently. . . .'

14. Linguistic folk-etymology links directly with the mythopoeic faculty The Mycenaean Greek place-name *Aptarwa* (Ventris and Chadwick, 1956), of dubious origin, is rendered in later Greek *Aptera*. Stephanus of Byzantium, like Isidore a true *bricoleur*, explained that it was there that the Sirens, after being defeated in a contest with the Muses, were so disgusted that they threw their wings from their shoulders, turned white, and jumped into the sea: hence *Aptera*, 'wingless', and the name of the nearby islands, *Leukai*, 'white'. (I am indebted to Miss G. Hart for this reference.)

15. Gosse (1907, 1949 edn: 87–88). Of P. H. Gosse's *Omphalos*, Charles Kingsley could only cry that he could not 'believe that God has written on the rocks one enormous and superfluous lie'. For those who doubt the real problem, onomastic studies are a good introduction. I have offered a detailed example (1968).

REFERENCES

ARDENER, E. W. 1959. Lineage and Locality among the Mba-Ise Ibo. *Africa* **29** (2): 113–133.

—— 1967. The Nature of the Reunification of Cameroon. In A. Hazlewood (ed.), *African Integration and Disintegration*. London: Oxford University Press.

—— 1968. Documentary and Linguistic Evidence for the Rise of the Trading Polities between Rio del Rey and Cameroons 1500–1650. In I. Lewis (ed.), *History and Social Anthropology*. ASA Monograph 7. London: Tavistock.

—— 1970. 'Galileo' and the 'Topological Space'. *Journal of the Anthropological Society of Oxford* **1** (3).

BEATTIE, J. H. M. 1964. *Other Cultures*. London: Cohen & West.

BERGSLAND, K., and VOGT, H. 1962. On the Validity of Glottochronology. *Current Anthropology* **3**: 115–158.

BLOOMFIELD, L. 1933. *Language*. New York: Holt, Rinehart & Winston; London: Allen & Unwin, 1935.

BRUGMANN, K. 1885. *Zum heutigen Stand der Sprachwissenschaft*. Strassburg: Carl J. Trübner.

— 1902–04. *Kurze vergleichende Grammatik der Indogermanischen Sprachen*. Strassburg: Carl J. Trübner.

— and DELBRÜCK, B. 1886–1900. *Grundriss der vergleichenden Grammatik der Indogermanischen Sprachen*. Strassburg: Carl J. Trübner.

CHOMSKY, N. 1957. *Syntactic Structures*. The Hague: Mouton.

— 1965a. *Current Issues in Linguistic Theory*. The Hague: Mouton.

— 1965b. *Aspects of the Theory of Syntax*. Cambridge, Mass.: MIT Press.

— 1966a. *Topics in the Theory of Generative Grammar*. The Hague: Mouton.

— 1966b. *Cartesian Linguistics*. New York and London: Harper & Row.

— and HALLE, M. 1965. Some Controversial Questions in Phonological Theory. *Journal of Linguistics*. **1**: 97–138.

COLBY, B. N. 1966. Ethnographic Semantics: A Preliminary Survey. *Current Anthropology* **7** (1): 3–32.

COWGILL, W. 1963. Universals in Indo-European Diachronic Morphology. In Greenberg (ed.), 1963.

CRABB, D. W. 1965. *Ekoid Bantu Languages of Ogoja*, Part I. Cambridge: Cambridge University Press.

CROSSLAND, R. A. 1951. A Reconsideration of the Hittite Evidence for the Existence of 'Laryngeals' in Primitive Indo-European. *Transactions of the Philological Society*: 88–130.

ELLIS, J. 1966. *Towards a General Comparative Linguistics*. The Hague: Mouton.

EVANS-PRITCHARD, E. E. 1950. Social Anthropology: Past and Present. *Man* **50**: 118–124.

— 1961. *Anthropology and History*. Manchester: Manchester University Press.

— 1965. The Comparative Method. In *The Position of Women in Primitive Societies and Other Essays in Social Anthropology*. London: Faber & Faber.

FORTES, M. 1945. *The Dynamics of Clanship among the Tallensi*. London: Oxford University Press.

— 1949. *The Web of Kinship*. London: Oxford University Press.

GLEASON, H. A. 1955a. *An Introduction to Descriptive Linguistics*. New York: Holt, Rinehart & Winston.

— 1955b. *Workbook in Descriptive Linguistics*. New York: Holt, Rinehart & Winston.

GOSSE, E. 1907. *Father and Son*. London: Heinemann. Harmondsworth: Penguin Books, 1949.

GREENBERG, J. H. (ed.). 1963. *Universals of Language*. Cambridge, Mass.: MIT Press. Paperback edition, 1966.

—— 1966. Synchronic and Diachronic Universals in Phonology. *Language* **42**: 508–517.

GUTHRIE, M. 1948. *The Classification of the Bantu Languages*. London: International African Institute.

—— 1953. *The Bantu Languages of Western Equatorial Africa*. London: International African Institute.

—— 1962. Some Developments in the Pre-history of the Bantu Languages. *Journal of African History* **3**: 273–282.

HAAS, M. R. 1969. *The Prehistory of Languages*. The Hague: Mouton.

HAUSCHILD, R. 1964. *Die Indogermanische Völker und Sprachen Kleinasiens*. Berlin: Akademie-Verlag.

HAYES, E. N. and T. (eds.). 1970. *Claude Lévi-Strauss: The Anthropologist as Hero*. Cambridge, Mass.: MIT Press.

HJELMSLEV, L. 1943. *Omkring sprogteoriens grundlaeggelse*. Copenhagen: Munksgaard.

—— (ed.). 1959. *Essais linguistiques*. Copenhagen: Nordisk Sprog- og Kulturforlag.

—— 1963. *Prolegomena to a Theory of Language*. (Translation by F. J. Whitfield of Hjelmslev, 1943.) Second edition. Madison, Wis.: University of Wisconsin Press. (First edition, 1961).

HOCKETT, C. F. 1954. Chinese versus English: An Exploration of the Whorfian Hypothesis. In H. Hoijer (ed.), *Language and Culture*. Chicago: Chicago University Press.

—— 1958. *A Course in Modern Linguistics*. New York: Macmillan.

HOENIGSWALD, H. M. 1960. *Language Change and Language Reconstruction*. Chicago: Chicago University Press.

HYMES, D. 1960. Lexicostatistics so far. *Current Anthropology* **1** (1): 3–44.

JARVIE, I. C. 1964. *The Revolution in Anthropology*. London: Routledge & Kegan Paul.

KILMISTER, C. W. 1967. *Language, Logic and Mathematics*. London: English Universities Press.

KING, R. D. 1969. *Historical Linguistics and Generative Grammar*. Englewood Cliffs, NJ: Prentice Hall.

KRAHE, H. 1962–63. *Indogermanische Sprachwissenschaft*. Vol. I, 1962, Vol. II, 1963. Berlin: De Gruyter.

LEACH, E. R. 1954. *Political Systems of Highland Burma*. London: Bell.

—— 1961. Two Essays concerning the Symbolic Representation of Time. In *Rethinking Anthropology*. London: Athlone Press, University of London.

LEACH, E. R. 1964. Anthropological Aspects of Language: Animal

Categories and Verbal Abuse. In E. H. Lenneberg (ed.), *New Directions in the Study of Language*. Cambridge, Mass.: MIT Press.

— 1969. *Genesis as Myth and Other Essays*. London: Cape.

LEES, R. B. 1953. The Basis of Glottochronology. *Language* **29**: 113–127.

LEHMANN, W. P. (ed. and trans.). 1967. *A Reader in Nineteenth Century Historical Indo-European Linguistics*. Bloomington and London: Indiana University Press.

— and MALKIEL, V. (eds.). 1968. *Directions for Historical Linguistics*. Austin: University of Texas.

LEROY, M. 1967. *The Main Trends in Modern Linguistics*. Oxford: Blackwell.

LÉVI-STRAUSS, C. 1955. *Tristes Tropiques*. Paris: Plon.

— 1958. *Anthropologie structurale*. Paris: Plon.

— 1962. *La Pensée sauvage*. Paris: Plon.

— 1963. *Structural Anthropology*. (Translation of Lévi-Strauss, 1958.) New York: Basic Books.

— 1964. *Mythologiques I: Le Cru et le cuit*. Paris: Plon.

— 1966a. *The Savage Mind*. (Translation of Lévi-Strauss, 1962.) London: Weidenfeld & Nicolson; Chicago: Chicago University Press.

— 1966b. *Mythologiques II: Du Miel aux cendres*. Paris: Plon.

— 1968. *Mythologiques III : L'Origine des manières de table*. Paris: Plon.

LYONS, J. 1968. *Introduction to Theoretical Linguistics*. Cambridge: Cambridge University Press.

MEILLET, A. 1933. Sur le bilinguisme. *Journal de Psychologie* **30**: 167–171.

— 1937. *Introduction à l'étude comparative des langues indo-européennes*. Reprinted 1964, Alabama: Alabama University Press.

— 1950. *Les Dialectes indo-européens*. Paris: Champion.

MURDOCK, G. P. 1957. *Africa: Its Peoples and Culture History*. New York: McGraw-Hill.

NEEDHAM, R. 1962. *Structure and Sentiment: A Test Case in Social Anthropology*. Chicago: Chicago University Press.

NUTINI, H. G. 1965. Some Considerations on the Nature of Social Structure and Model Building: A Critique of Claude Lévi-Strauss and Edmund Leach. *American Anthropologist* **67**: 707–731. Also in Hayes and Hayes (eds.), 1970, pp. 70–107.

OSTHOFF, H., and BRUGMANN, K. 1878. Introduction to *Morpologische Untersuchungen auf dem Gebiete der indogermanischen Sprachen* I, pp. iii–xx. Leipzig: Hirzel.

PALMER, L. R. 1954. *The Latin Language*. London: Faber.

PAUL, H. 1880. *Prinzipien der Sprachgeschichte.* Tübingen: Niemeyer. Eighth edition, 1968.

PEDERSEN, H. 1931. *Linguistic Science in the Nineteenth Century.* Trans. by J. Spargo. Cambridge, Mass.: Harvard University Press. Reissued, Bloomington: Indiana University Press, 1962.

POCOCK, D. F. 1961. *Social Anthropology.* London and New York: Sheed & Ward.

RICHARDSON, I. 1956–57. *Linguistic Survey of the N.W. Bantu Borderland.* 2 volumes. London: International African Institute.

ROSS, A. S. C. 1958. *Etymology with special reference to English.* London: Deutsch.

SAUSSURE, F. DE. 1916. *Cours de linguistique générale.* Paris: Payot.

—— 1959. *Course in General Linguistics.* (Translation by W. Baskin of Saussure, 1916.) New York: Philosophical Library; London: Peter Owen, 1960 (reprinted, 1964).

STURTEVANT, E. 1942. *The Indo-Hittite Laryngeals.* Baltimore, Md: Linguistic Society of America.

SWADESH, M. 1950. Salish Internal Relationships. *International Journal of American Linguistics* **16**: 157–167.

TRIER, J. 1931. *Der deutsche Wortschatz im Sinnbezirk des Verstandes.* Heidelberg: Carl Winter.

ULLMANN, S. 1951. *The Principles of Semantics.* Glasgow: Jackson.

—— 1959. *The Principles of Semantics.* Second edition, with additions. Oxford: Blackwell.

—— 1963. Semantic Universals. In Greenberg (ed.), 1963.

VENDLER, Z. 1967. *Linguistics in Philosophy.* Ithaca, NY: Cornell University Press.

VENDRYES, J. 1933. Sur les tâches de la linguistique statique. *Journal de Psychologie* **30**: 172–184.

VENTRIS, M., and CHADWICK, J. 1956. *Documents in Mycenaean Greek.* Cambridge: Cambridge University Press.

WARTBURG, W. VON. 1943. *Einführung in Problematik und Methodik der Sprachwissenschaft.* Tübingen: Max Niemeyer.

—— 1969. *Problems and Methods in Linguistics.* (Translation of von Wartburg, 1943.) Oxford: Blackwell.

WEINREICH, U., LABOV, W., and HERZOG, M. I. 1968. Empirical Foundations for a Theory of Language Change. In Lehmann and Malkiel (eds.), 1968, pp. 95–188.

WELLS, J. 1906. *The Oxford Degree Ceremony.* Oxford: Clarendon Press.

WIENER, N. 1948. *Cybernetics.* Cambridge, Mass.: MIT Press. Second edition, 1961.

G. B. Milner

The Quartered Shield: Outline of a Semantic Taxonomy

In an article published a few years ago in France, Dr Edmund Leach asked the following question:

> 'Comment la pensée mathématique (logique) se développe-t-elle dans l'esprit d'un homme simple? C'est cette question-me semble-t-il, qui forme le noyau du problème de Lévi, Strauss' (Leach, 1964: 1,106).

Since those words were written, three important contributions to a solution of this riddle have been published by Professor Lévi-Strauss himself. In the second of these he makes the request that we should suspend judgement on his case until all the evidence has been given in full (1966: 7). Since the latest includes the promise of at least one more volume in the same series (1968: 34), the mass of evidence will surely be very large, and when the jury is empanelled it will be fully occupied for a considerable period. In the meantime those of us who are also interested in this problem may not want to run the risk of duplicating isolated aspects of the *Mythologiques* without having a fuller understanding of its master plan.

This is not to say that we should not attack the problem from other angles. It has, after all, not yet been claimed that myth, however it is defined, subsumes all other mental activity. In addition to kinship and social structure, other sources of information, such as language, art, music, dancing, comedy, and architecture, all offer abundant material for investigations parallel, or complementary, to those currently being carried out in the field of myth.

I recently completed a detailed investigation of a corpus of traditional sayings from Samoa. This was the principal windfall of a dictionary project begun in 1955 and ended (as far as a dictionary can be said to be at an end) eleven years later. Over 1,300 separate sayings were examined from the point of view of their linguistic, and more especially their semantic, structure, and of the bearing that this might have on Samoan culture as a whole. A number of them heard in actual use were also analysed from different angles, and suggestions were made as to the particular functions served by traditional sayings in relation to other uses of language, both formal and informal.

In order to arrange this material in a manner that would allow one to see, in addition to the trees, the parts of the wood and the wood itself, I had to make a kind of *catalogue raisonné*. This took the form of a numerical card-index with cross-references, and notes under various headings: Samoan text, English literal translation, ostensible reference (i.e. what each saying appears to be concerned with), virtual reference (i.e. what it hints at or alludes to under the cloak of the ostensible reference), and indications as to the main types of function that can be served according to context, matter in hand, and situation.

This work was carried out over a period of some eighteen months. As familiarity with the material increased, I was struck by the fact that many of the traditional sayings were divided into two parts of roughly equal length which appeared to balance each other. This was made all the more obvious by the fact that many of these balanced halves rhymed.[1]

That many proverbs take the form of distichs has been pointed out fairly frequently (e.g. Raymond Firth, 1926: 263–264; Evans-Pritchard, 1964: 1). There was therefore nothing original or remarkable in finding the same feature in Samoan sayings.

A closer look showed, moreover, that there was evidence that each half of these distichs was in turn unmistakably made up of two distinct portions, which also seemed to be of roughly equal length, and to balance each other. In addition to having *matching halves*, that is to say, it was clear that many Samoan sayings also had *matching quarters*. This happened in a sufficiently large number of cases to merit closer study. Thus:

396:	'A 'ua teu, 'ia ma teu	: If you're to fix it, then fix it
	'A 'ua fai, 'ia ma fai.	: If you're to do it, then do it.
449:	Na ta alu fo'i, 'ua tai lelei	: When I departed, the coast was shallow
	'A 'ua ta sau, 'ua tai pupu	: But when I returned, the coast was bold.

748:	'O faiva o ai, malo?	:	Who is there, who wins every time?
	'A 'o faiva o ai to i lalo?	:	Who is there, who loses every time?

As regards frequency, out of a total of 1,386 sayings that were examined, 254, or 18 per cent, can be regarded as distichs. Of those 254, 75, that is to say 30 per cent, rhyme.

A closer study of the two halves of distichs and of their component quarters shows that the effect of quadripartite balance is due partly to syntactic and partly to semantic factors. Thus there is often complete syntactic symmetry in both halves as in the three examples above. For instance, a verb phrase (*vp*) followed by a noun phrase (*np*) occurs in each half:

620:	Togi	(*vp*):	le moa	(*np*):	Play your rooster
	'Ae 'u'u	(*vp*):	le 'afa	(*np*):	But keep a grip on its tether

or in both halves a noun phrase is followed by a noun phrase:

639:	'O le uo	(*np*):	i aso 'uma	(*np*):	A friend for every day
	'A 'o le uso	(*np*):	mo aso vale	(*np*):	But a sibling for evil days.

At least six other similar syntactic patterns occur, four with complete symmetry, and two with partial symmetry. There is also an unmistakable semantic counterpart to this syntactic parallelism. Thus we find:

(i) two contrasted and antithetical statements, as in examples 620 and 639 above. The two halves then often describe (or prescribe) one course of action as opposed to another, they stress contradictions, make comparisons, or point to reciprocal or complementary activities.

(ii) two paratactical statements, especially when the two halves are syntactically similar, and rhyme, but have different lexical items. Then they often stress the same point and reinforce each other:

278:	'Ua mama	i oa	:	It leaks at the gunwale.
	Mama	i taloa	:	It leaks in the keel.

662:	'Ua mativa	le fau	:	The kava strainer is ragged
	'Ua papa'u	le laulau	:	The kava bowl is running low.

(iii) two conjectural statements, with a premiss or hypothesis in the first half, and a conclusion in the second half:

142:	'A gau	le pou tu	: When the main post breaks
	E le tali pou lalo		: The side posts will not take the weight.

(iv) two consequential statements, with an event or cause in the first half, and its alleged or predicted result in the second half:

200:	'Ua mu	le lima	: (He) has burnt his hand
	Tapa	le i'ofi	: (So he) asks for a pair of tongs.

Even in cases where either one half, or both halves, consist(s) of a single verb phrase or noun phrase, it is a curious fact that the component parts of a single phrase somehow preserve the essentials, or at least the appearance and effect, of the same secondary division into quarters. For in addition to the head-word (verb or noun) and to the particles (if any) which identify the single phrase as being either nominal or verbal, at least one other 'slot' (i.e. syntactical position) is filled.

In the case of a verb phrase it may be a negative or an adverbial slot that is filled:

453:	E nana fua	(*vp*)	: le tetea	(*np*)	: In vain is an albino hidden
	'Ae le	(*negative*)	: lilo	(*v*)	: It is not concealed.

In the case of a noun phrase, it may be a pronominal or adjectival slot that is filled:

1,268:	Solo	(*vp*)	: 'i tua	(*np*)	: Be blown out of sight
	Ni ao	(*n*)	: taulia	(*adjective*)	: Any black clouds

(i.e. Let any black clouds (hovering over us) blow away.)

That is to say because, in addition to the headword of a single verb phrase or noun phrase, another important slot is filled, it is often possible to identify the nucleus of what I shall from now on call a *quadripartite structure*, even in sayings which have only one phrase either in the first half or in the second half, or in both halves.

An important question now arises. If a quadripartite syntactical structure is preferred or deliberately sought after in Samoan sayings; if, as we have just seen, the nucleus of such a structure is preserved even where the syntax is asymmetrical; if, moreover, as we saw earlier, the two *halves* of a binary structure can be identified on semantic as well as on syntactic grounds, can the *quarters* of the quadripartite structure also be identified on *semantic* grounds? If so, in what relationship does each quarter stand to its partner in the same half, and to the two quarters in the other half? Put more simply, does the tendency of Samoan sayings to be quadripartite affect their meaning?

I wish to suggest that the most important characteristic of a typical Samoan saying is the symmetrical structure not only of its syntactic form, but also of its semantic content, and, as a corollary, that its value and popularity are a direct function of the extent to which the symmetry of the semantic content matches the symmetry of the syntactic form.

In its most typical (though not necessarily its statistically most common) expression – and we shall see the implications of this later – a Samoan saying is a statement in four parts. It consists of two *halves* (major segments) each divided in two *quarters* (minor segments) standing in a balanced and structured relationship to one another, and it is the precise nature of the relationship between the separate parts that determines the cogency and meaning of the saying as a whole.

Each *quarter* includes at least one constituent with a referent that may be 'good' or 'bad' (i.e. desirable or undesirable, useful or useless, safe or dangerous, friendly or hostile, valuable or despised, attractive or unattractive, and so on). It is this main constituent that gives the quarter in which it occurs its value within the half, and indirectly within the saying as a whole, though other constituents occurring in the same quarter may modify that value.

Within each half, the two quarters have independent values which modify and affect each other, but do not modify the quarters of the other half.

For greater ease of reference we shall call the main constituent of a quarter *plus* if its referent is 'good' (i.e. safe, useful, friendly, etc.) or conversely *minus* if its referent is 'bad' (i.e. dangerous, useless, hostile, etc.). The quarters in which these constituents occur will also be called *plus* or *minus* according to the value of the main constituents (modified, or, as the case may be, unmodified, by other constituents in the same quarter).

Within each half, the two quarters may both be *plus*, or both be *minus*, or they may be opposites.

If they are both *plus*, or if they are both *minus*, then in accordance with the principle that a Friend's Friend is a Friend, and that a Foe's Foe is a Friend,[2] the semantic value of the half in which they occur will be called *positive*.

If they are opposites, then in accordance with the principle that a Foe's Friend is a Foe, and that a Friend's Foe is a Foe,[2] the half in which they occur will be called *negative*.

Accordingly, any one Samoan saying thus defined consists of a positive or negative opening half, which we can call the *head*, followed by a positive or negative closing half, which we can call the *tail*. All sayings of this type can therefore be allocated to four main classes. Each of these is subdivided into four subclasses which, as we shall see, are non-significant. A Samoan example for each of the sixteen classes is given in *Table 1* (see Appendix, p. 261 below).

If the identification of the quarters (and of their constituent parts) as *plus* or *minus* is to carry conviction, it must clearly be not only consistent, but if possible open to verification. It follows that once a constituent has been allocated a *plus* or *minus* value for a reason that is compelling (short of making nonsense of a major segment and hence of a saying as a whole), that value cannot be changed in all other sayings in which that constituent occurs. If it can be so kept without disturbing their major segments, it will give a measure of confirmation that the original allocation was correct.

If, on the other hand, it cannot be kept without disturbing the major sayings and making nonsense of them, then either the original choice must have been wrong, or what appears to be the same constituent in more than one saying is in fact not the same. We may be dealing with more than one sense of the same word, or even with different words which happen to be homonyms.

When faced with conflicting evidence, and in deciding whether to allocate *plus* or *minus* values to different words or different senses of a single word, one may have to make choices that are to some extent gratuitous and arbitrary. These choices, however, are heuristic and open to revision. What matters is that once they are made they should be applied consistently and tried out over the whole corpus of available materials, in order to see not only whether they are satisfactory, but whether they disturb the choices previously made for other words[3] as evidenced in the resulting equations.

Certain other rules must also be observed:

1. A negative particle such as *le* (not) necessarily either constitutes a minor segment in its own right or combines with a *plus* to make a *minus* (or with another *minus* to make a *plus*). Examples can be found in 610 and 844 (below) as well as in D3 and D4 of *Table 1*.

2. Unless a constituent has an obviously pejorative meaning, such, for example, as a word denoting pain, hunger, death, disease, danger, violence, etc., it is given a *plus* value, unless or until the values of other constituents in the same major segment, or the value of the major segment itself, shows that it cannot be other than *minus*. An example of this is provided by the following saying:

118:	'Ia	gase	:	manu	vao	+	Let the wild birds perish
		–		(+	–)		
				–			
	'Ae	ola	:	manu	fanua	+	But the tame birds shall live.
		+		(+	+)		
				+			

This saying has its origin in the traditional words of the leader of a pigeon-netting party at the conclusion of the hunt, i.e. 'Let the wild pigeons which have been caught be killed, but the tame (literally: 'cultivated') pigeons (i.e. the decoys) be spared.'

In the above saying *vao* (uncultivated land, bush) is given a *minus* value, while its antonym *fanua* (cultivated land) is given a *plus* value, partly on grounds of common sense (just as *gase* 'perish' and *ola* 'live', which are also antonyms, are respectively *minus* and *plus*), and partly on grounds of well-known Samoan (and generally Polynesian) values. Thus *tai* (the sea-coast, seaside) is associated with chiefs and is therefore *plus*, while *uta* (the interior of an island, the bush), is associated with commoners and is therefore *minus* (cf. *uta* in A4, *Table 1*). *Manu*, however, is assumed to be *plus* since there is no evidence to the contrary.

3. Constituents may be contrasted without necessarily being opposites. Thus in the following saying:

142:

'A gau : le pou tu − (+ +) +	−	When the main post breaks
E le tali : pou lalo (− +) (+ +) − +	−	The side posts will not take the weight

although *pou tu* (main post) and *pou lalo* (side post) are in a sense contrasted, they cannot be regarded as opposites since they perform the same function in the structure of a building. The second and fourth quarters of this saying are therefore given *plus* values, and this seems to be the only way to make both its halves negative, as common sense requires it.

4. In order to allocate a saying to its proper class and subclass, care must be taken to identify the *head* and the *tail* correctly. Normally, the statement in the second half of the saying tends to be the result, conclusion, reiteration of, or the counterweight to, the statement in the first half. Not infrequently, however, it can happen that the first half is in fact the tail, and that the head is the second half. This may be due to at least two reasons:

(a) First, in unemphatic Samoan word order, the predicate usually *precedes* the subject. For instance in:

610:

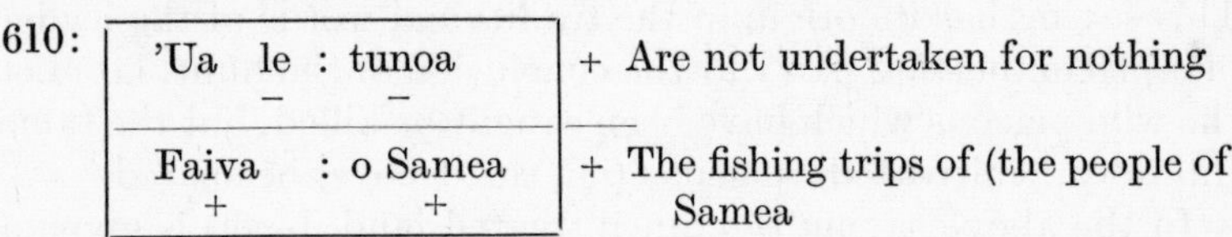

(i.e. Samea people do not go fishing for nothing), the word order is the normal one for unemphatic utterances. Since the predicate is in the first half and not in the second, in this particular case the 'conclusion' comes before the 'observation'. That is to say: 'If it's the Samea people who are fishing, you may be sure that there is a good reason for it.' To allocate this saying to its proper subclass one must therefore bear in mind that the tail comes before the head. Consequently it belongs

not to subclass A4: $\left\{\begin{smallmatrix} - & - \\ + & + \end{smallmatrix}\right\}$ but to subclass A3: $\left\{\begin{smallmatrix} + & + \\ - & - \end{smallmatrix}\right\}$.

(b) Second, there may be a stylistic reason. In order to focus attention on what is actually the tail of a saying, when it consists of two separate verb phrases, one being the 'cause' and the other the 'effect', the latter may actually come first:

704:

'Ua le aoga	: paopao	– Are no longer of any use the outrigger canoes
(– +) –	+	
'Ua tu'utaula	: manuao	– Have anchored the men-of-war
+	–	

(i.e. Now that the men-of-war have anchored, outrigger canoes are no longer of any use), so line 2, the second half, is the head, and line 1, the first half, is the tail.

All sayings of the type illustrated in 4(a) and 4(b) above may be said to have *inverted halves.*

The reader should now turn to *Table 1* in the appendix to this paper, which gives one Samoan example for each of the sixteen subclasses that are theoretically possible. It will be noted that the examples given for B1, B4, and D3 have inverted halves.

It should be added that the sixteen types of structure that are set out vary a great deal in the frequency with which they are represented in Samoan sayings. This is reassuring: if the distribution was purely random, it would throw considerable doubt on the validity of the original assumption.

As a further argument in support of the theory put forward here, I wish to draw the reader's attention to a type of quadripartite saying which can be called *expanded* or *explicit*:

There are instances of Samoan sayings which do not merely leave the value of each half to be guessed or inferred from the bare statement of the quadripartite structure itself, but actually spell it out, outside its framework, in the form of a separate comment or commentary on each half. In the following example each comment even rhymes with the half to which it is attached:

844:

'A gapa	: le toa	gau loa	If ironwood cracks, it breaks clean off
–	+	(– +) –	
'A gapapa	: le fau	'ae le gau	If hibiscus creaks, it doesn't break.
–	–	(– –) +	

Conversely, if a Samoan saying is very familiar, it may not always, or not often, be quoted in full. As a result, what is actually a quadripartite saying (though the complete structure may not be known to everyone) will generally be used in an abridged form which may be tripartite, bipartite, or even unipartite.

Thus both halves of the next example make the same point, with an ostensible reference to two different sports: (i) spear-throwing at the up-ended stem of a coconut-tree, used as a target, and (ii) pigeon-netting with long-handled nets and with decoys:

1,186:

'O le tao +	:	tafi tao (− +) −	– A spear that dislodges other spears (already well placed)
'O le manu +	:	tafi manu (− +) −	– A decoy that scares the game (instead of drawing it).

(i.e. a trouble-maker, an unpopular person). It is sufficient for a Samoan orator to use the unipartite idiom: *'Ua tafitaoina* (It has been dislodged (like) a spear (from) its target) to allude to or to imply the entire quadripartite structure from which it is derived. Such sayings can be called *contracted* or *implicit*.

Now it is a *semantic* taxonomy that the subtitle of this article promises, albeit only in outline. If, that is to say, the method that has just been sketched is suitable only for the classification of Samoan sayings, we shall not be much advanced.

In actual fact, during the early stages of this investigation, the temptation to look for parallel structures in English sayings and proverbs was very difficult to resist. Some of the results of yielding to temptation, and of refusing to be a purist outside working hours, are set out in *Table 2* of the Appendix. Its contents will of necessity be more immediately accessible to assessment and criticism[4] than are those of *Table 1*.

Before coming to any provisional conclusions, it is appropriate that we should turn our attention to a number of more general considerations.

If it is true that man succeeds in maintaining a balance

between despair and over-confidence by his ability to laugh at his environment and at himself, and that laughter usually has both a social and a linguistic component, it is extraordinary to note that, apart from honourable exceptions (Piddington, 1933; Douglas, 1968), social anthropologists as well as linguists have neglected to study the causes of laughter.[5] Linguists, for example, do not even understand fully the mechanism of a pun in the widest sense of the term. In transformational and generative grammar notably, there is much evidence of a concern to explain cases of accidental similarity and resulting ambiguity in 'surface structure' by pointing to dissimilarity in 'deep structure'. The fact, on the other hand, that, far from being objectionable, and thus deliberately avoided, ambiguity is often sought after for its exploratory and laughter-raising possibilities, has been largely overlooked.

There is a special reason why a better understanding of laughter is relevant to a discussion of traditional sayings: the processes by which a joke is triggered off seem to have much in common with the manner in which a traditional saying makes an immediate impact. One does not, that is, have to think either about a joke or about a traditional saying. Both achieve their effect instantaneously and at least partly unconsciously or intuitively.[6]

During the sixties of this century both in anthropology and in linguistics increasing attention has been given to the implications of the fact that man's intellect may be no more than the tip of an iceberg of unknown dimensions, and that new techniques must be elaborated to establish the relations between the conscious and the unconscious levels of social and linguistic activity. This awareness is as evident, say, in the abstractions of the French school of structural mythology as it is in the deep structures posited by the American school of transformational grammar.

In the light of these current preoccupations, this article also represents an attempt to peer below the surface and to discover whether a structural analysis of traditional sayings might provide a better understanding of these hidden depths and of their dimensions.

If it is true that, in addition to conscious linguistic messages, we receive and respond to other messages addressed to the subconscious or unconscious levels of our minds, it may be asked how they reach us and what form they take.

To answer these questions it is necessary to ask another, which at first flush appears to be naïve as well as irrelevant to social anthropology, but which in fact is neither. Namely, why is poetry written in short lines which are superposed and not placed end to end as in the case of lines of prose? The reason is, of course, that lines of equal length placed one above the other are better able to convey visually the regular recurrence of rhyme, rhythm, assonance, alliteration, or other messages of a similar nature, which in the traditional use of poetry are conveyed orally, and which have a paradigmatic basis.

This effect is strictly comparable to that of musical chords, with the difference that in poetry it is achieved not simultaneously and synchronically, but successively and cumulatively. If there is one characteristic of traditional sayings that has not been noticed and examined sufficiently, it is that, like poetry, sayings frequently have rhyme, rhythm, alliteration, assonance, and, perhaps even more significantly, they often incorporate a syntactic pause or some other junctural feature between their first and their second half.

The significance of this, as much for anthropologists as for linguists, has a special bearing on an axiom of all linguistic analysis: namely, that all language has both a paradigmatic and a syntagmatic axis:

syntagmatic axis
←——————→

paradigmatic axis ↕				
	John	is coming	tomorrow	by air
	Bill	arrived	this morning	by car
	Ian	will go back	on Sunday	by train

To know the context, that is to say, is a matter not only of knowing which words precede and which follow, but also, at any given point of the syntagmatic chain, of knowing which words have been (or could have been) used instead by the same (or by another) speaker in the same or in a similar situation, and with reference to the same or to a related topic. Paradigmatic chains, that is, function virtually and implicitly, as opposed to syntagmatic chains which function ostensibly and explicitly.

The two axes, moreover, define a continuum which has special properties. In an article published in the French anthropological quarterly *L'Homme* (Kristeva, 1968), this space has been called *l'espace paragrammatique*. The author points out that not infrequently a French poet will deliberately rewrite a line from one of his predecessors, in a different syntactic order but at least partly in the same words. Consequently, the meaning of many poetic statements can be understood only in relation to, and by contrast with, reminiscent statements in the history of French poetry.

This of course is restricted neither to French poetry nor to poetry in general. As we listen to a message along its syntagmatic axis, paradigmatic messages, more or less deeply embedded in our memory, which contrast or agree with what we are now hearing, are continually reaching us. Meaning therefore has a paradigmatic dimension in the sense that it is to be found *between*, i.e. *by contrast with*, antonymous or synonymous messages as well as *in* them.

A striking instance of this is found in *La Pensée sauvage* where a particularly telling point is made, not by putting it in the author's own words, but by taking a very well-known quotation from Pascal's *Pensées*:

'Le cœur a ses raisons que la raison ne connaît point',

and transposing it as follows:

'La langue est une raison humaine, qui a ses raisons et que l'homme ne connaît pas' (Lévi-Strauss, 1962: 334).

The relevance of this to traditional sayings is that their constituent parts, like the lines of poetry, should be superposed and not juxtaposed, if their paradigmatic messages are to be properly analysed and understood. Acrostics, which are intended to be read and not heard, exercise a special fascination, but patterns of rhyme and rhythm, like acrostics, also constitute paradigmatic messages which produce a cumulative impression and the effect of which may be partly subconscious or unconscious. In this sense the contrast between the first half and the second half of a traditional saying forms a semantic paradigm.

That this is so can be shown most clearly by reference to two related types of structure. The first is known in Western culture as the chiasmus, by analogy with the outline of the Greek letter χ. The second is known by different names according to languages, or in some cases, like English and German, the structure was known but until fairly recently it was not given a special name. It is called a spoonerism in English, a *Schüttelreim* in German, and a *contrepet* in French.[7] These structures also have a wide distribution outside Europe. Thus the chiasmus is known to specialists in African proverbs as cross-parallelism (Lestrade, 1937: 307; Nyembezi, 1954: 22; Westermarck, 1930: 22; 1932), and spoonerisms have been reported from Southeast Asia, notably from Burma (Hla Pe, 1962: 11).

A chiasmus can be defined as a structure in which the order of words (A B) in one clause, which I shall call the first half, is inverted in a second clause, which I shall call the second half (B A). It is thus a strikingly symmetrical form of quadripartite structure, and its appeal lies in the fact that the symmetry of the inversion, in the second half, of two concepts that occur in the first half, is reinforced by the accompanying inversion of two sequences of sounds. For this reason a chiasmus is particularly effective in framing statements that are intended to have a high mnemonic value. Here, for example, is a famous statesman giving advice to men in public life on the importance of making the right use of leisure:

> It is no use doing what you like;
> you have got to like what you do
> (Churchill, 1964: 11).

It is not surprising, therefore, to find that chiastic structures frequently occur also in traditional and proverbial sayings from many parts of the world:

Anglo-Saxon
(*c.* AD 1000): He that will not, when he may
When he would, he shall have nay.
(Whiting, 1968, W 275;
Heywood, 1963, lines 125–126)

English
(sixteenth
century) : As you shall give me as you cost me
So shall you cost me as you give me.
(Heywood, 1963, lines 1118–1119)

Moroccan
Arabic : If a wealthy man steals, they say that he forgot, and
if a poor man forgets, they say that he stole.
(Westermarck, 1930: 22)

Zulu : Umenziw' akakhohlwa: The one who is offended never forgets
Kukhohlw' umenzi : The one who forgets is the offender.
(Nyembezi, 1954: 22)

Zande : I ni rigi nduka : They feed the ridge
Nduka ki rigi ira ha: And the ridge feeds its owner.
(Evans-Pritchard, 1964: 1)

Chinese : Blame yourself as you blame others
Forgive others as you forgive yourself.[8]

Persian : Once I had strength but no wisdom;
Now I have wisdom but no strength.
(Elwell-Sutton, 1954: 93)

Samoan : Leave the lucky fish-hook and take the unlucky fish-hook
Leave the unlucky fish-hook and take the lucky fish-hook
(that is to say: do not go by appearances, the justification for this interpretation being found in a well-known Samoan myth).

It should be noted here that the spoonerism and the chiasmus are closely related in their structure. It is true that what is usually understood by a spoonerism is a transposition of two consonants or syllables. In actual fact it is logical to subsume also under that term transpositions of larger units, such as lexical items, phrases, and clauses, which can in certain circumstances generate laughter, and indeed may actually be contrived with that end in view:

My confusions are rather dicluse
The Subdegrees Higher Committee

Alterations as usual during business
Do unto yourself as others would like to be done unto.

Yet, as we have seen, it is not always for purposes of amusement, but either to make a point more clearly or to raise its mnemonic value, that a syntactical spoonerism is resorted to.[9] We can see also that since the spoonerism rests on the inversion (B A) of a well-known sequence (A B), it is related to the chiasmus in the sense that both rest on a quadripartite structure which is outlined in the former while it is fully revealed in the latter.

It is also worth noting that a chiasmus is particularly effective when it occurs in one of the explicit sayings mentioned earlier, that is to say when the two comments apposed to each half invert a part of the quadripartite structure:

Folowe	pleasure	and then will pleasure flee
Flee	pleasure	and pleasure will folowe thee

(Whiting, 1968, C 526)

Those	who	mind	don't matter
+		−	(− +)
			−
Those	who	matter	don't mind
+		+	(− −)
			+

Oignez	vilain	il vous poindra
+	−	−
Poignez	vilain	il vous oindra
−	−	+

Si elles	sont	belles	elles	ne sont	pas	fidèles
+		−	+	−		+
				−		
			−			
Si elles	sont	fidèles	elles	ne sont	pas	belles
+		+	+	−		−
				+		
			+			

Tamil:

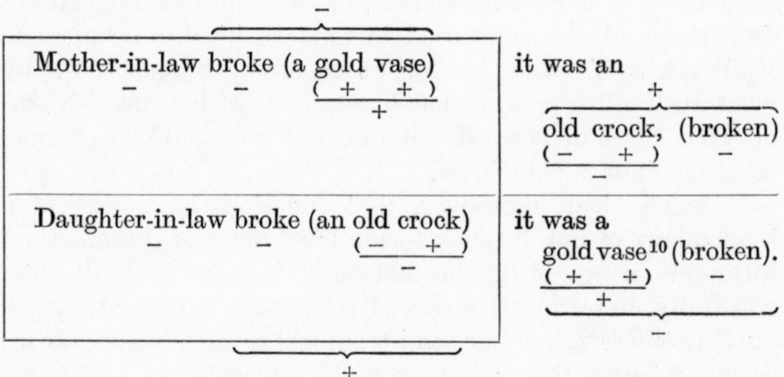

To sum up, one needs, first, to draw attention to a remarkable phenomenon and one that is so much taken for granted that its implications have seldom been elaborated in detail. In spite of the very large range of quantitative and qualitative differences between cultures, societies, and linguistic communities, in time and space, in spite of the wide variety of purposes to which languages are put and of their structural diversity, the existence of traditional and proverbial sayings has been reported so widely (if far from universally) that they not only constitute a phenomenon of great importance, but also present a challenge from a cross-cultural and taxonomic point of view.

Second, the concepts and terminological aids at present available for the analysis and description of traditional sayings are completely inadequate, and may be said to be backward, at least in comparison with what has been achieved in this century alone, in the field of, say, phonemic analysis or kinship studies. As a result, every fieldworker, every man in the street, is on a par with every paroemiographer: everyone knows or recognizes intuitively a proverb when he hears one in his own language, but no one is able to give adequate and generally acceptable criteria of recognition within a single language, let alone cross-cultural criteria.[11]

Third, it seems likely that the principal reason for this lack of progress is that analysis has in general been limited to a single language and culture, and too rigidly determined by the existence of lexical definitions which in any case are imprecise and overlap one another, as well as being valid only within a single linguistic community. Because, that is to say, definitions are arrived at arbitrarily and not in terms of a series of absolute dimensions of the type used in modern kinship or phonemic studies, it is, if not impossible, at least very difficult to discover what an English proverb has in common with a Spanish *refrán* or with German *geflügelte Worte*, not to mention a Samoan *muagagana* or a Zulu *isaga*.

It seems clear, moreover, that conscious as we are of the inadequacy of our English terms for figures of speech, we are incapable of accepting the fact that they are lexically, hence culturally, determined terms of reference. Yet faced with the great proliferation of our semi-technical terms[12] we are far from certain whether they represent valid categories, and, if they do, what exactly it is that marks one off from another. Resorting to dictionaries is not much help: these show that there are many blurred edges and much disputed territory.

The prestige of lexicography is such, however, that we not only accept what dictionaries tell us uncritically, but assume that their definitions are valid universally and cross-culturally. Thus an authority on Africa[13] (Doke, 1947: 102) comes to the conclusion that 'aphorism' is the most suitable term for certain Bantu figures of speech – this almost certainly after consulting an English dictionary, hence one likely to give definitions in terms of Western culture, and apparently without pausing to consider what there is about the concept and term of 'aphorism' that makes it absolute, and more suitable for cross-cultural analysis than any other term. This procedure is analogous to that of an early student of Australian languages who had come to the conclusion that the only part of speech he could recognize in them was the gerund, and it is open to the charge of ethnocentricity.

Fourth, one possibility that should be looked into is that, varied and discrete as the form, content, and functions of figures of speech may be, either within a single language and culture or cross-culturally, they often share a similar underlying structure. Too much attention, that is to say, has been devoted in the past to the meaning of traditional sayings, and not enough to their structure. Before we decide in our own minds what the characteristics of, say, a proverb or an aphorism are, or ought to be (these are in any case likely to clash with the next man's notions), we should perhaps concentrate on the common characteristics of all traditional sayings, and in particular on those useful and general enough to remain valid from one language to another and one culture to another.

In conclusion, what the present paper set out to show was that *quadripartite structures* were characteristic of both Samoan and English traditional sayings. If the arguments in support of this view are cogent and the thesis is accepted, then, bearing in mind the width of the cultural gap that separates Western European from Polynesian language and culture, the possibility must be examined that quadripartite structures are characteristic of traditional sayings in general.

If the present approach to traditional sayings can be used elsewhere, and if further investigations bear out that it is a valid and productive one, it is likely to provide a useful additional technique for arriving at the internal and mutually consistent (though at times ambiguous and even contradictory) values of words from little-known and exotic languages such as Samoan. In particular, it may provide a more rigorous method, available to non-native speakers, of checking the favourable and unfavourable connotations of words, without necessarily having recourse to translation into a Western language.

Appendix

Outline of a Scheme for the Cross-cultural Classification of Quadripartite Traditional Sayings

TABLE 1 SAMOAN EXAMPLES

In the first class (A), all four subclasses have a *positive* head and a *positive* tail:

A1:	'Ua logo +	: le na i ama (+ +) +	+	(A fish) is felt (biting) on the outrigger side
	Logo +	: le na i atea (+ +) +	+	(A fish) is felt (biting) on the hull side

(All is well, the undertaking has been completed successfully.)

A2:

Head	Tail		
E valavala (–)	: a tumanu (–)	+	Spindly like immature bananas
E lafulafu (–)	: a tama seugogo (– +) –	+	Dirty like boys catching sea-birds

(Do not be deceived by unfavourable appearances, unpromising beginnings often have successful endings.)

A3:

Head	Tail		
E lelei (+)	: pule (+)	+	Sharing generously is good
'Ae leaga (–)	: fa'aalualuo (–)	+	Taking the lion's share is bad

(Be generous when sharing out a feast.)

A4:

Head	Tail		
'A 'ua sala (–)	: uta (–)	+	If a mistake has been made inland
'Ia tonu (+)	: tai (+)	+	It should be put right by the shore

(If we have made a mistake, let it be put right.)

In the second class (B), all four classes have a *negative* head and a *positive* tail:

B1: (*NB: Inverted halves*)

Head	Tail		
Solo (–)	: 'i tua (–)	+	Slip to the back (i.e. out of the way)
Ni ao (+)	: taulia (–)	–	Any black clouds

(Let no untoward happenings cloud our happiness.)

B2:

Head	Tail		
'Ua taili (–)	: le matagi toga (+)	–	The wind from the south soughs
'Ae ta'alili (–)	: le si'u maui (–)	+	But the tail (of a hurricane) roars

(It is always darkest before the dawn.)

B3:

E mafuli −	: le ului +	−	The parent tree has fallen over
’Ae tupu +	: le suli +	+	But one of its saplings is growing

(Men die, but descent groups and titles continue.)

B4: (*NB: Inverted halves*)

Se’i lua’i +	: lou +	+	(One) should first fetch down
’Ulu +	: taumamao −	−	(The) breadfruit hanging on ‘remote’ branches

(The difficult part of a job should be done first.)

In the third class (C), all four subclasses have a *positive* head and a *negative* tail:

C1:

E toa +	: le loto +	+	The will is strong
’Ae pa −	: le no’o +	−	But the hips are broken

(A desire or hope that cannot be fulfilled.)

C2:

’Ia seu +	: le manu +	+	Catch the bird (if you can)
’Ae silasila +	: ’i le galu −	−	But keep your eye on the breaker

(Go ahead with your plan but look out for hidden dangers.)

C3:

’O le misa −	: e faia i Toga (+ −) −	+	The quarrel may break out in Tonga
’Ae tala −	: i Samoa +	−	But it will be reported in Samoa

(Secrets will out.)

C4:

E sola –	: le fai –	+	The sting-ray escapes
'Ae tu'u +	: le foto –	–	But it leaves its barbed sting

(The evil that men do, lives after them.)

In the fourth class (D), all four subclasses have a *negative* head and a *negative* tail:

D1:

'O le tao +	: tafi tao (– +) –	–	A spear that removes other spears (already well placed on the target)
'O le manu +	: tafi manu (– +) –	–	A decoy pigeon that drives away wild pigeons (instead of drawing them)

(A trouble-maker, a man no one wants to associate with.)

D2:

'Ua mativa –	: le fau +	–	The kava strainer is ragged
'Ua papa'u –	: le laulau +	–	The kava bowl is running low

(The party is over, the session has come to an end.)

D3: (*NB: Inverted halves*)

'Ua le aoga (– +) –	: paopao +	–	The outrigger canoes are of no use now
'Ua tu'utaula +	: manuao –	–	The men-of-war have dropped anchor

(People of low rank are of no consequence now that people of high rank are here.)

D4:

E asa –	: le faiva +	–	A fishing trip may come back empty-handed
'Ae le asa (– –) +	: le masalo –	–	But suspicion is never empty-handed

(Suspicion always finds something to feed on.)

TABLE 2 ENGLISH EXAMPLES

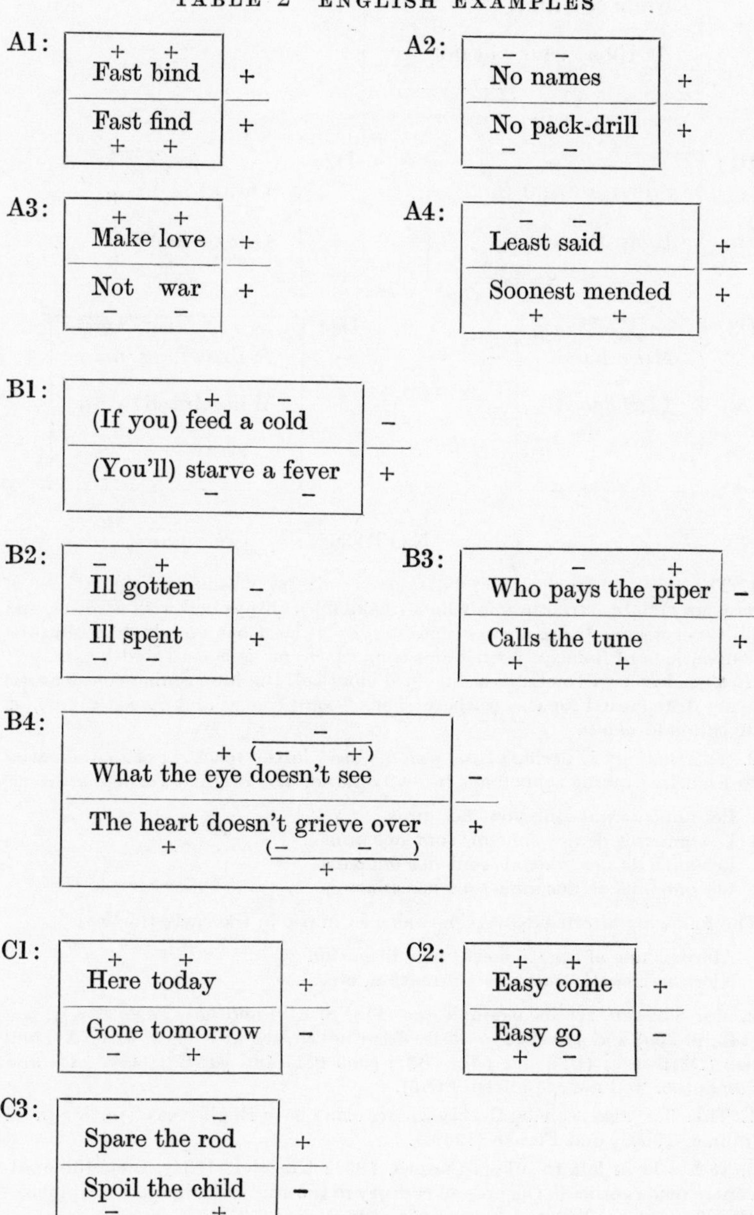
A1:
+ +
Fast bind +
Fast find +
+ +
A2:
– –
No names +
No pack-drill +
– –
A3:
+ +
Make love +
Not war +
– –
A4:
– –
Least said +
Soonest mended +
+ +
B1:
+ –
(If you) feed a cold –
(You'll) starve a fever +
– –
B2:
– +
Ill gotten –
Ill spent +
– –
B3:
– +
Who pays the piper –
Calls the tune +
+ +
B4:
–
+ (– +)
What the eye doesn't see –
The heart doesn't grieve over +
+ (– –)
+
C1:
+ +
Here today +
Gone tomorrow –
– +
C2:
+ +
Easy come +
Easy go –
+ –
C3:
– –
Spare the rod +
Spoil the child –
– +

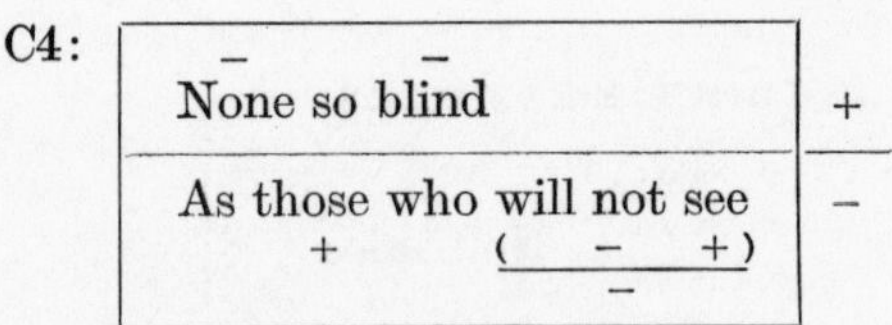

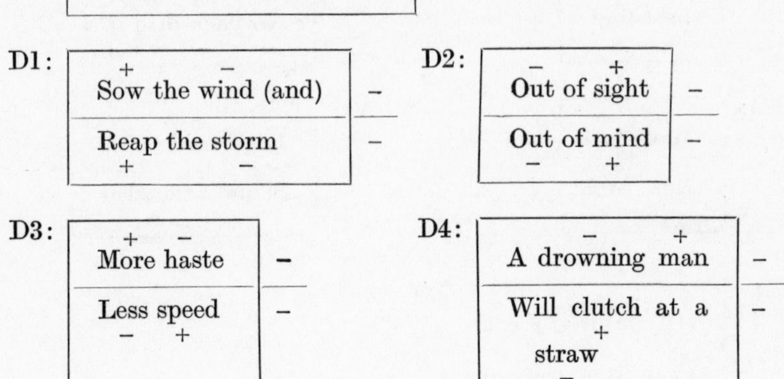

NOTES

1. The term 'rhyme' should be understood: (a) within the limitations of Samoan syllabic structure, in which (i) syllables always end with a vowel, and (ii) two consonants are always separated by at least one vowel; (b) within the conventions of Samoan poetry and song. A rhyme is constituted by the fact that the last two vowels of a 'line' are identical, the intervening consonant(s) being disregarded for this purpose. Thus *Toga* (Tonga) and *Samoa* rhyme, as do *galu* and *manu*.

2. This analogy is derived from axioms used in the teaching of mathematics to French-speaking schoolboys in Switzerland. The original version was:

Les amis de nos amis sont nos amis
Les ennemis de nos ennemis sont nos amis
Les amis de nos ennemis sont nos ennemis
Les ennemis de nos amis sont nos ennemis.

The following alternative version was also in use in the early thirties:

Affirmer une affirmation est une affirmation
Nier une négation est une affirmation, etc.

3. For Samoan, see for example *vao* (118, p. 249) and *uta* (*Table 1*, A4); *gau* (142, p. 250) and *gau* (844, p. 251). For English, see in *Table 2*, *least* (A4) and *less* (D3); *spent* (B2) and *pays* (B3); *gone* (C1) and *go* (C2); *said* (A4) and *names* (i.e. 'tell names, inform') (A2).

4. This has also been argued elsewhere, using both English as a starting-point (Milner, 1969a) and French (1969c).

5. It has been left to others (Monro, 1951; Koestler, 1964) to continue advances made earlier in the present century in the study of laughter by a philosopher (Bergson, 1900) and a psychoanalyst (Freud, 1916).

6. Some of the implications of this view have been discussed elsewhere (Milner, 1969b).

7. Recent studies of the spoonerism in English and in French also give references to other works on the same topic (Robins, 1966; François, 1966). Robins shows that the structure that is now called a spoonerism antedates the life-span (1844–1930) of the Rev. Dr W. A. Spooner, Warden of New College, Oxford, by at least two centuries. Denise François records instances of the *contrepet* in the works of Rabelais. Like 'spoonerism', the German term *Schüttelreim* is of recent origin, but *contrepet*, derived from Old French *contrepéter*, 'to take off, imitate', is on record in the form *contrepéterie* (or *contrepetterie*) as early as the sixteenth century.

8. I owe this example to my colleague Dr R. Ng.

9. The quotation given earlier from *La Pensée sauvage* is a case in point.

10. I am indebted for this suggestive example to Mr Mark Holmström of the University of East Anglia, and to my colleague Dr J. R. Marr. The original is:

> Māmiyār uṭaittāl, maṇ pāṉai
> Maṟumakaḷ uṭaittāl, poṉ pāṉai

that is to say:

> If Mother-in-law broke (it), an earthenware pot
> If Daughter-in-law broke (it), a golden pot.

An analysis of this proverb according to the principles put forward in the present article indicates that missing segments must be supplied if the equation is to be acceptable. I wish to suggest, therefore, that Mr Holmström's version is an abridged or implicit one, and that it has replaced an earlier structure of the explicit (or expanded) and chiastic type:

> If Mother-in-law broke (a gold pot): an earth pot (was broken)
> If Daughter-in-law broke (an earth pot): a gold pot (was broken).

See also Kaṇapatippiḷḷai, 1956: 90, proverb no. 1050.

11. A leading American authority on proverbs and riddles even suggests that it is futile to attempt to define a proverb:

> 'The definition of a proverb is too difficult to repay the undertaking; and should we fortunately combine in a single definition all the essential elements and give each the proper emphasis, we should not even then have a touchstone. An incommunicable quality tells us this sentence is proverbial and that one is not' (Archer Taylor, 1962, p. 3, opening paragraph).

12. Consider, for example, the following and their definitions as given in the *Shorter Oxford English Dictionary:*

> Saw; dictum; adage; saying; slogan; motto; maxim; moral; idiom; axiom; precept; proverb; by-word; sentence; epigram; aphorism; apophthegm; catch phrase; golden rule.

13. I am indebted for this reference to my colleague Mr D. K. Rycroft.

REFERENCES

BERGSON, H. 1900. *Le Rire: essai sur la signification du comique.* Paris: Alcan.

CHURCHILL, W. S. 1964. *Painting as a Pastime*. Harmondsworth: Penguin Books. (Reprinted from *Thoughts and Adventures*, 1932.)

DOKE, C. M. 1947. Bantu Wisdom-lore. *African Studies* **6**: 101–120.

DOUGLAS, MARY. 1968. The Social Control of Cognition: Some Factors in Joke Perception. *Man* (n.s.) **3**: 361–376.

ELWELL-SUTTON, L. P. 1954. *Persian Proverbs*. London: Murray.

EVANS-PRITCHARD, E. E. 1964. Zande Proverbs: Final Selection and Comments. *Man* **64**: 1.

FIRTH, RAYMOND. 1926. Proverbs in Native Life, with particular reference to those of the Maori. *Folk-lore* **37**: 134–153, 245–270.

FRANÇOIS, DENISE. 1966. Le Contrepet. *Linguistique* **2**: 31–52.

FREUD, S. 1916. *Wit and its relation to the Unconscious* (translated by A. A. Brill). London: Kegan Paul.

HEYWOOD, J. 1963. *A Dialogue of Proverbs* (edited by R. E. Habenicht from first edition, 1546). Publications in English Studies No. 25. Berkeley and Los Angeles: University of California Press.

HLA PE. 1962. *Burmese Proverbs*. London: Murray.

KAṆAPATIPPIḶḶAI, M. 1956. *Payiṛcci Ttamiḻ* (*Practical Tamil*), Part 2. Madras: Shanti Press.

KOESTLER, A. 1964. *The Act of Creation*. London: Hutchinson.

KRISTEVA, JULIA. 1968. Poésie et négativité. *L'Homme* **8**: 36–63.

LEACH, E. R. 1964. Telstar et les Aborigènes ou la pensée sauvage. *Annales* No. 6, Nov.–Déc.: 1100–1116.

LESTRADE, G. P. 1937. Traditional Literature. In I. Schapera (ed.), *The Bantu-speaking Tribes of Africa*, pp. 291–308. London: Routledge.

LÉVI-STRAUSS, C. 1962. *La Pensée sauvage*. Paris: Plon.

—— 1966. *Du Miel aux cendres*. Paris: Plon.

—— 1968. *L'Origine des manières de table*. Paris: Plon.

MILNER, G. B. 1969a. What is a Proverb? *New Society* No. 332, 6 February: 199–202.

—— 1969b. Siamese Twins, Birds and the Double Helix. *Man* (n.s.) **4**: 5–23.

—— 1969c. De l'armature des locutions proverbiales: essai de taxonomie sémantique. *L'Homme* **9** (3): 49–70.

MONRO, D. H. 1951. *Argument of Laughter*. Melbourne: Melbourne University Press.

NYEMBEZI, C. L. S. 1954. *Zulu Proverbs*. Johannesburg: Witwatersrand University Press.

PIDDINGTON, R. 1933. *The Psychology of Laughter: A Study in Social Adaptation*. London: Figurehead.

ROBINS, R. H. 1966. The Warden's Wordplay: Towards a Redefinition of the *Spoonerism. The Dalhousie Review* **46**: 457–465.

TAYLOR, ARCHER. 1962. *The Proverb.* Hatboro, Pennsylvania: Folklore Associates. Copenhagen, Denmark: Rosenkilde and Bagger. (First edition, Cambridge, Mass.: Harvard University Press,1931; London: Oxford University Press, 1932.)

WESTERMARCK, E. A. 1930. *Wit and Wisdom in Morocco: A Study of Native Proverbs.* London: Routledge.

—— 1932. The Study of Popular Sayings. In W. R. Dawson (ed.), *The Frazer Lectures 1922–1932*, pp. 190–211. London: Macmillan.

WHITING, BARTLETT J. 1968. *Proverbs, Sentences and Proverbial Phrases.* Cambridge, Mass.: Harvard University Press.

Caroline Humphrey

Some Ideas of Saussure applied to Buryat Magical Drawings[1]

This paper is the result of a preliminary attempt to apply some of the ideas of Saussure to ethnographic data. The point of the exercise is to see if the Buryat material, which consists of various combinations and series of symbolic objects, could be better understood by an anthropologist if it were seen as a semiological system. Any culture must contain many such systems because objects, patterns of behaviour, illustrations, and so on, can signify, and in so far as these miniature systems are equivalent to languages, linguistic tools and methods can be used to analyse them. It seems to me that the Buryat material is particularly suitable for this kind of analysis for three reasons: the symbolic objects in question can be isolated as a more or less autonomous system on their own, they are significant for the Buryat people as a whole, and, like a language, they convey a great many complex ideas with rather few elements, ordered by specific rules. In making the analysis I have been guided by the ideas of Saussure and Barthes, but I have not so far gone into the general Saussurean literature and must apologize for the inevitable lack of finesse in this paper as regards his concepts.

The Buryat are a people of Mongol origin who live round the shores of Lake Baikal in the Soviet Union. At the present time the magical objects I refer to, which are called *ongon*, are no longer found commonly among them, and the 'ethnographic present' of this paper refers to the period 1910–30.

I

Buryat *ongon* are a series of models or representations of spirits which are thought to have magical power in specific circumstances. The word *ongon* means both the spirit and the material representation of the spirit, and the verb *onguulakh*, 'to make into an ongon', is used, for example, of a shaman entering an ecstasy – that is, when the spirit enters his body – or of an animal that is possessed by a spirit.[2] The Buryat think of all objects and living creatures as naturally having a spirit or soul of their own, but ongon are those beings which, through the agency of man, have been made to accommodate a spirit that is not their own – in most cases the spirit of one of the distant 'ancestors' of the Buryat. The essential ongon consists of a collection of subjects, cloth, woods, feathers, beads, and so on, which is then consecrated by a shaman – that is, he makes the spirit enter it. After consecration, the ongon[3] or representation has magical power in particular circumstances depending on the nature of the spirit – one may bring luck in hunting, one eases difficult childbirth, one prevents cattle disease, and so on.

Each adult Buryat makes his own representations of the common ongon spirits. Some ongon are made almost automatically by a young couple setting up house; others are made at any time during life when circumstances indicate the need for the protection of a particular spirit. Thus a person's ongon reflect his social role, men have different ongon from women, hunters have different ongon from herders, and so on. Ongon require sacrifices and are expensive to keep, so a family may have as few as fifteen of them, or as many as a hundred. There are perhaps sixty–seventy ongon spirits known to all the Buryat, but there are many more that belong to particular lineages and regions, and some of these may be virtually unknown outside their own particular areas.

Every Buryat knows the myths about the ancestor spirits who live in ongon, and in fact there are very few legendary ancestors of whom ongon are not made. But a person will make his own model of an ongon only if he thinks that its magical power is relevant to him. Sacrifices are made regularly to all the ongon, but when the services of one are particularly required there may be an additional ceremony in which the spirit leaves the ongon representation and enters the body of a shaman and speaks through his mouth. The ongon may also manifest itself, through the shaman, in dance or music, and it becomes clear that each of these concrete representations (that is, the material or graphic ongon, the speech, and the dance or music) is separate both in structure and in meaning from the myth. Thus it would be a mistake to regard the myth as the expression in words of the (material) ongon; in fact, the ongon has its own separate representation in language, this being the speech through the mouth of the shaman.

In this paper I have chosen to analyse only the material or graphic representation of the ongon. This is because the words and music exist only for some ongon and not others and hence it is doubtful whether they can be seen as a system. There are no ongon whose only representation is in language or music.[4]

There is no single 'correct' model of a particular ongon spirit, just as, in the class of objects of clothing called 'jackets', no one jacket is more of a jacket than any other. All examples of a particular ongon are correct, provided they have been made with the recognized pattern in mind. An individual making an ongon knows this pattern and does his best to conform to it, given the materials he has to hand. Any ongon consists of a varied combination of recurring elements (for example, silk, wood, metal, buttons, animal skins, blood, paint, feathers) which must conform to one of the available patterns. The maker of an ongon need conform to the pattern only to the extent of ensuring that his model of it can be either (a) recognized on its own as a model of that ongon, or (b) distinguished from other ongon of the same maker by some part of the required pattern.

The ongon made by one individual, and the ongon of one region, may be in some ways idiosyncratic, just as a person's speech may be pervaded by a particular intonation, etc., that is, in linguistic terminology, the *idiolect*, but they are always socialized. The making of the ongon may be supervised by the lineage shaman, but even if this is the case, the ongon cannot be consecrated (that is, the spirit will not enter it) unless it is, to the Buryat mind, what it purports to be; if something is 'wrong' in the construction of the ongon, the spirits will be angry. The ongon-maker has an interest in combining his materials as nearly to the pattern as possible. Thus it is only from an abstract point of view that one can present the large range of variations in the making of a single ongon; in fact, the individual can choose only from a limited range determined by the conventions of his social circle.

If, to use Saussure's terminology, the whole range of actual models of ongon is *speech* (this term is used here as equivalent to *la parole*), the patterns or system on which they are constructed is *language* (equivalent to *la langue*).

The *language* of the system of ongon emerges from the norm of the usage of the *speech* of all the Western Buryat. There is no deciding group that determines which ongon are to be made and how they are to be made (the lineage shaman may decide locally which ongon are to be made in the case of certain misfortunes, but by definition he cannot decide for the Western Buryat in general). However, there are known cases of the invention of ongon by individuals. Here, a new combination of units, couched in the ongon *language*, becomes institutionalized and becomes a stereotype. Most of these inventions never spread very far (e.g. 'kitten, son of the cat ongon', invented at the time of collectivization as a joke but in fact taken seriously by much of the population for a few years; a parallel in the system of food of a particular society might be a dish invented during a local shortage), but at least one ongon known to have first appeared as late as the mid-nineteenth century has become almost universal in a large part of Western Buryatia (the 'two Khori girls ongon').

II

The materials used to make an ongon may be separated into units, that is, into objects with properties. Each of these units has a symbolic meaning derived from the place assigned to it in Buryat culture among other similar units. The use of Saussurean linguistic theory and terminology makes this system clearer. The basic units of the ongon can be termed *signs*, that is, a compound of *signifier* and *signified*.

In the case of ongon, the sign is the union of a concept (the signified) and the material object that may be used (the signifier). This enables us to see more clearly the nature of the units that make up ongon. It would appear that they could simply be defined as concrete entities – unlike the units of language, which, to someone who is unfamiliar with it, are a series of undistinguishable sounds. But, in fact, the units of ongon, like the units of language, must, at least at a certain level (and there will be other levels of meaning), be defined as the signifiers of certain concepts. Thus, for example, two buttons sewn on an ongon represent two units because a button signifies the soul of a person; but two beads sewn on an ongon represent one unit since they signify a single person by means of showing only his eyes.

The signified

Linguists have agreed that the signified is not a 'thing' but a mental representation of the 'thing' (Barthes, 1967a: 43). The signified of the word 'ox' is not the animal 'ox' but its mental image. The signified is the 'something' meant by the person using the sign. Linguists have further distinguished between phenomena in which the signifier and the signified cannot be

FIGURE 1 *Suns and moons*

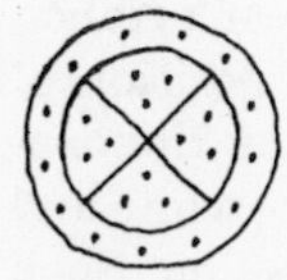
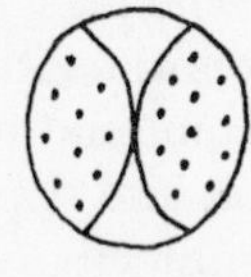

(M. N. Khangalov Archive, SME, collection no. 28, book 36, p. 1,067)

(SME, collection no. 403-62)

(SME, collection no. 365-13)

(From S. V. Ivanov, 1954: 725)

dissociated (*isologic*), and those in which the signified and its signifier can be juxtaposed (*non-isologic*).

The units of Buryat ongon are non-isologic signs, if only because they can be expressed by words as well as things. There are thus two levels among the signifieds, which may not be equivalent to one another, since words continually refer back to the semantic classification of the language itself and not to a classification having its bases in the ongon system. Thus, for example, there are drawings of many ongon of which one might simply *say*, 'This represents a sun, that represents a moon', but on another level the signifieds of these drawings are not the ideas of 'sun' and 'moon', but ill-defined concepts (which need not exist outside the ongon system) of 'south-west' and 'north-east', or 'purity' and 'impurity', which cannot be adequately expressed in words (see *Figures 1* and *3*).

Briefly, one can distinguish two types of signified in Buryat ongon. One derives from a culturally standard relation between an object and a concept. An example of this type is the coloured ribbon that is included in many ongon. Ribbons are used uniformly in almost all Buryat ceremonies to indicate direction: white ribbon is always at the (cultural) south-west, black or dark blue is always at the north-east, red is at the north-west, and yellow is at the south-east. South-west in Buryat culture is associated with seniority and purity, while north-east is the place of the inferior, impure, or female. The presence of a ribbon of one of the four colours thus indicates the ritual position of this ongon. There are rules for the combination of ribbons: white and red combined are superior to, and oppose, white and yellow; red and yellow may not be combined, and so on. Such combinations are not so much the addition of one meaning to another as stereotypes in themselves, and as such they are part of both *language* and *speech*.

The other type of signified, which may exist side by side with the first in one sign, depends on the context of the unit in the myth of the ongon. Thus the signifier 'a shaman's drum' may have many signifieds in Buryat culture as a whole, but when it is included as part of the hunting ongon and the structure of the hunt is compared with the structure of the drum, then the signifieds of the drum become more precise. It is the myth that indicates the context in which the units of ongon are to be understood. Within this context signifieds are part of oppositions – objects or actions which may be compared as similar things. For example, among trees, the myth may present the birch and the pine in such a way that they oppose one another. They can therefore be classified in relative terms as 'pure'/'neutral'/'impure' (a shorthand to indicate the inequality of opposed things and their mediator). There may be several levels of analysis of the signified, of which this, indicating 'purity' or 'impurity', is the most superficial.

If one takes the ongon as a whole to be a sign, the function of the ongon (curing syphilis, giving painless childbirth, etc.) must not be confused with its signification. Although there must surely be a relation between the functions of particular ongon and the 'messages' they convey as signs, these two are analytically separate. Barthes (1967a: 42) draws an analogy with objects of everyday use such as coats: coats protect people, but they are (unavoidably, because they are socialized) also signifying objects: 'But once the sign is constituted, society can very well refunctionalize it, and speak about it as if it were an object made for use: a fur-coat will be described as if it served only to protect from the cold.'

The signifier

In attempting to discover the nature of the relation between signifier and signified in Buryat ongon, I have made use of the linguistic distinctions between *arbitrary* and *non-arbitrary*, and *motivated* and *non-motivated*, signs. Starting from the fact that in language the choice of sounds is not imposed by the meaning (the ox does not determine the sound 'ox' since in other languages the sound is different), Saussure has spoken of an *arbitrary* relation between signifier and signified. Benvéniste (1966: 49–55) has criticized the use of this term on the grounds that Saussure has confused the animal ox, whose relation with the sound is certainly arbitrary, with the concept ox, whose association with the sound is not arbitrary but on the contrary necessary, since no one is free to change it. If we consider Buryat ongon in these terms it is clear that, even though ongon are occasionally invented (just as words may be invented), the system of ongon as a whole is non-arbitrary – whereas fashion, Barthes's example, which is created not by convention but by unilateral decision, is arbitrary.

The original problem posed by Saussure, whether or not the relations between signifier and signified are analogical, has been expressed by the terms *motivated*, for signs that are analogical, and *unmotivated*, for signs that are not analogical. In Buryat ongon, there are more and less motivated signs: the signified 'a human being' may have as signifier anything from a drawing of a stick-like human figure to a tuft of red silk representing hair and hence a person. Sometimes ongon are very lifelike, as in the 'husband and wife ongon' (see colour plate),

FIGURE 2 *Ongon of Anda-Bar*

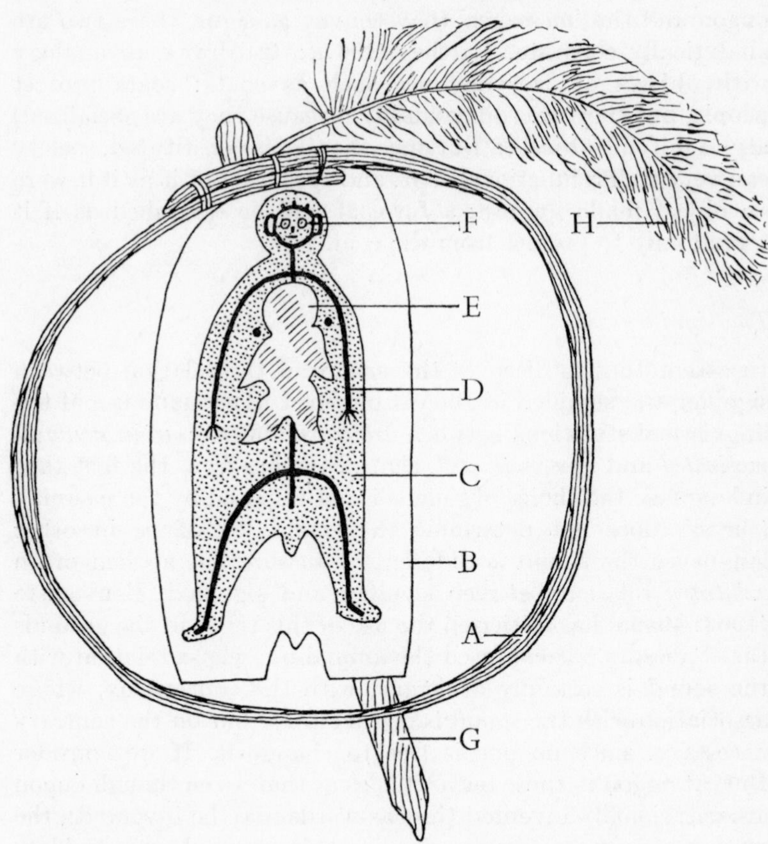

A Wooden circle representing the sides of a drum

B White cotton cloth

C Pink cotton cut in the shape of a man and sewn onto the white cloth

D The figure of a man drawn in red paint

E A man cut out of tin

F White beads sewn onto the pink cloth, representing eyes

G A wooden stick

H An eagle-owl feather

(SME, collection no. 365-2c)

but even here there are many unmotivated signs – the colour of the figures, their respective sizes, the ribbons, the chamois leather of the husband's coat, and even the whips, which signify magical power (since whips of this kind are owned only by shamans, who wave them up and down in the air, receiving magical strength from the spirits through the thongs). The majority of signs in ongon are unmotivated, for example, ribbons, which represent direction, and painted tables, which represent status. One can compare Buryat ongon in this respect with Russian icons. In icons the figures are stereotyped but they are expressive. Different aspects of one saint (signifieds) are represented by different stereotyped icons (signifiers). Thus there are several types of icon of the Virgin Mary in which various signifieds (expressed verbally by their names, 'the softening of the cruel hearts', 'the blessed silence', etc.) are represented by icons which show to a greater or lesser extent, depending on the ability of the artist, the required quality.[5] In ongon paintings it is often not possible to determine the sex of a human figure, let alone any more subtle information about it. A human about whom detailed legends have been told for centuries may be represented in his ongon by a pair of beads (his eyes).

I noted above that there may be different signifiers for one signified (that is, one object may be substituted for another but retains the same meaning); it is also true that one signifier that recurs in several ongon may be interpreted differently in each. Thus the eagle-owl feather, which signifies 'ability to fly to another world', has a different meaning in the ongon of the 'pure' hunting-spirit Anda-Bar (see *Figure 2*) from its meaning in other 'impure' ongon. So unmotivated are Buryat ongon that three physically similar ongon may refer to madness, shepherding, and fertility. In the ongon system, prior knowledge of the context is essential in order to make the link between signifier and signified.

However, the non-motivated nature of the signs in ongon does not mean that the ongon is not intelligible and even moving to the Buryat. In this respect, it may be compared with the simple cross hung on the wall by a Roman Catholic.

The sign

Another linguistic distinction is useful in the study of the semiological system of ongon. This is the introduction by Hjelmslev[6] of two strata, form and substance, within the planes of the signifiers (the plane of expression) and the signifieds (the plane of content). According to Barthes (1967a), the form is what can be described by linguistics without resort to extra-linguistic premisses; the substance is the set of aspects of linguistic phenomena that cannot be described without resort to extra-linguistic premisses. Since both form and substance exist on the plane of expression and the plane of content, we therefore have:

(i) A substance of expression: in the case of ongon this would be the material objects used in making the ongon (it would also include the words, gestures, etc. involved in the performance of an ongon).

(ii) A form of expression: the rules for the combination, exclusion, opposition, spatial allocation, etc. of the substance of expression. The same form might apply to two different 'substances', that is, to the words spoken by the ongon through the shaman, as well as to the material objects used in making a model.

(iii) A substance of content: this includes the emotional, ideological, or notional aspects of the signified; for example, the idea, signified by the eagle-owl feather, of ability to reach the upper world.

(iv) A form of content: this is the organization of the signifieds among themselves. As applied to ongon, this means the organization of elements in the context to which the ongon refers, or upon which it comments. In linguistics, this has been called (by Saussure) *value*, which comes from 'the reciprocal situation of the pieces of the language'. It is more important than signification: 'What quality of idea or phonic matter a sign contains is of less import than what there is around it in other signs.'[7] Barthes gives as an example the word 'mutton', which derives its value from its coexistence with the word 'sheep', the meaning being truly fixed only at the end of this double determination. In the analysis of the signs in ongon, the idea of value is essential.

To the Buryat, the *value* is given by the complex of beliefs and evaluations that surround the subject-matter of the ongon. This subject-matter is usually presented in the myth about the ongon spirit in which its life-story is told. We must therefore examine the relation between the ongon and the myth that is told about it.

Analysis of such a myth shows that it attempts to present a logical model in order to solve a contradiction (this contradiction will be related in some way to the practical problem that the ongon is intended to solve by its magic, but the two are not identical – for example, Anda-Bar ongon brings luck in hunting, a good catch, but the myth about the spirit Anda-Bar is concerned with ideas of purity and creativity in relation to the hunter). If the contradiction is a real one in Buryat culture the myth can reach no conclusion, and, as Lévi-Strauss says, 'se développera comme en spirale, jusqu'à ce que l'impulsion intellectuelle qui lui a donné naissance soit épuisée' (1958: 254).

The ongon (the material representation) consists of isolated objects which have also occurred in the myth, but it is not the case that the ongon merely reduplicates the myth in material or graphic form. In fact, the ongon could not simply copy the myth since it has a different structure (or, in linguistic terms, a different language); more precisely, the form of expression of the ongon is different from that of the myth, although they share in common a set of signifieds and values. While the myth sets out its contradiction in terms of signs expressed in language, the ongon answers, or comments upon, the contradiction in terms of the same signs expressed as material objects. In the case of the ongon, the starting-point is the combination of objects which then reveals its own structure. The myth works the other way around, as Lévi-Strauss pointed out: it uses a structure to produce what is an object consisting of a set of events. The ongon proceeds from the object to a discovery of its structure; the myth starts from a structure by means of which it constructs an object (Lévi-Strauss, 1966: 25–27).

How do the two structures differ? As we have said above, the myth presents, by means of a theoretically infinite number of oppositions and mediations, a logical model for the solving of contradictions. In following up the possible variations within the logical model, a cycle of myths is created which has a common structure. The actual events of a myth are seldom necessary – other events may be substituted which serve the same purpose. In the ongon, on the other hand, it is the objects (that is, units equivalent to the events in myths) that matter, or, more exactly, it is the signifieds of the objects that are important. The relations of these objects among themselves – the structure of the ongon – are secondary in the sense that many ongon can be understood simply as single objects (signs). Even where ongon consist of more than one object, the structure of the ongon serves only to make the combination of objects intelligible – it does not itself act as a source from which other ongon might be derived. An analogy may be drawn with the representation of the Christian cross: when made of gold and hung round the neck of a believer it is important as a holy object whose power comes from the value of its signified in a myth; the same is true even when the cross is represented in an icon – the aesthetic structure of the icon painting is not what gives the cross its power as a sign, and every icon of the Crucifixion, however badly painted, has equal religious status. To return to the linguistic terminology, it can be seen that the structure we have been referring to corresponds with the *form of the expression.*

The form of the expression of ongon is of two kinds: the most common is simply the addition of one object to another, the whole being tied in a bundle or put in a wooden box with a lid. Here, we find that the objects are of only one type or value. Instead of consisting of 'pure', 'impure', and 'neutral' images, as in the myth, the units of this kind of ongon are all of one type, either 'pure' or 'impure'. Since the combination of units *is* the material manifestation of a certain spirit, the consistent value of these units amounts to a declaration about the spirit.

To take an example: the myth of the hunting-spirit Anda-Bar ('Friend Snow-Leopard') says that he was banished by his mother in favour of Buryat step-sons; he was called a Tungus and forced to eat fish-heads in the forest; he became a 'white' shaman by inheritance from his mother; he was a good hunter and killed a deer belonging to his enemy Ergil-Buga ('Capricious

Stag'); he slept with an impure woman and in consequence lost his power and lost his shaman's drum. The myth of Ergil-Buga, on the other hand, goes as follows: he turned himself into hail and had himself born of a virgin, who then married, during the pregnancy, an old and distinguished Buryat of the famous Khangin lineage; he grew up and married the daughter of a famous shamaness; he became a black shaman and the enemy of Anda-Bar. Ergil-Buga is the spirit of procreation. These myths show a preoccupation with the purity of the hunter, his relationship with society (which he must leave in order to go hunting), and his relationship with women, but because of their nature as myths they come to no conclusion about hunting as such. They simply present the problem.

The ongon of these spirits, it seems to me, consist of answers to the questions presented in the myths. Anda-Bar ongon (see *Figure 2*) may have many elaborate forms but essentially it must contain the following elements: a miniature shaman's drum (or a piece of tanned wild goat skin), the representation of a male figure (drawn on cloth, or cut out of tin, or both), and red and white cloths. The minimum elements of Ergil-Buga ongon are: a complete, natural skin of the Siberian yellow polecat, the representation of a male figure, and yellow and white ribbons. If the symbolism of these elements is analysed it will be seen that Anda-Bar ongon has only 'pure' units and Ergil-Buga only 'impure' ones (and this is also the case for any additional units such as feathers, straw, bells, etc. which may be added at will and which I have not included here for reasons of space). Besides being 'pure' in value, both in everyday life and in the myth, the shaman's drum[8] is metaphorically appropriate in the hunting ongon: the drum is thought (a) to contain the wild animal helpers of the shaman, and (b) to carry him safely from this world to other worlds. The upright wooden handle of the drum is called 'Bar' (Snow-Leopard, the 'pure', white-coloured, hunting animal of the high mountains). The Buryat hunt is, like the drum, circular in shape, thus containing the wild animals, and it is crossed by a line of command, by bugle or drum, which separates the right wing of the hunt from the left. Analogically to the shaman's drum, the hunt is thought of as a circular area of high ritual status in the 'outside', the Siberian taiga. The wild goat skin, which may substitute for the drum in the ongon, has qualities as a sign which are absolutely opposed to the qualities of the corresponding skin (polecat) in the Ergil-Buga ongon: the wild goat skin is (i) tanned, i.e. culturalized, (ii) from a hunted animal, (iii) from a mountain animal, (iv) from a hoofed animal (a Buryat category); the polecat skin, on the other hand, is (i) not tanned, (ii) from a hunting animal, (iii) from a lowland, burrowing animal, (iv) from a clawed animal. Furthermore, the polecat, within the category of weasels, badgers, stoats, etc., is especially 'impure' by reason of its smell and the yellow stain it leaves – which to the Buryat have a sexual significance. Similarly, the name of the procreation ongon, Ergil-Buga (Capricious Stag), can be seen as opposed to that of the hunting ongon, Friend Snow-Leopard: the stag in question is 'impure' because of its noisy sexual activity, and because it is dark-coloured, hunted, and lives in low-lying swampy land, even digging itself hollows in the ground.

Even in this brief and incomplete description of two ongon, it can be seen that they consist of bundles of objects which, in relation to one another, are, at the most superficial level of analysis, 'pure' or 'impure'. Thus the ongon convey a message, which in this case is: 'Hunting in relation to procreation is pure'; and the deeper signification of each unit, which must be immediately apparent to a Buryat though not to us, indicates the nature of this purity.

In fact, the message of the ongon is repeated on the level of behaviour. The hunting ongon must be kept inside the house at the north-west (to which its red ribbon corresponds), and the procreation ongon must be kept on the outside wall of the house to the south-east (which is the direction that accords with its yellow ribbon). The hunting ongon must be given certain foods and drinks in sacrifice; the procreation ongon must be given others which are classified as 'opposite' to them, etc.

The second type of structure of ongon – that is, the form of the expression – occurs in several series of drawings on coloured cloths (see *Figures 3*, *4*, and *5*). Here the cloth is marked out in various conventional ways – for example, by drawing the sun and the moon to indicate right and left, or by using blue and white cloth to represent earth and sky or lower and higher. The ongon spirit, and any other objects or beings the maker

Figure 3 *Ongon of the two girls of Khori lineage*

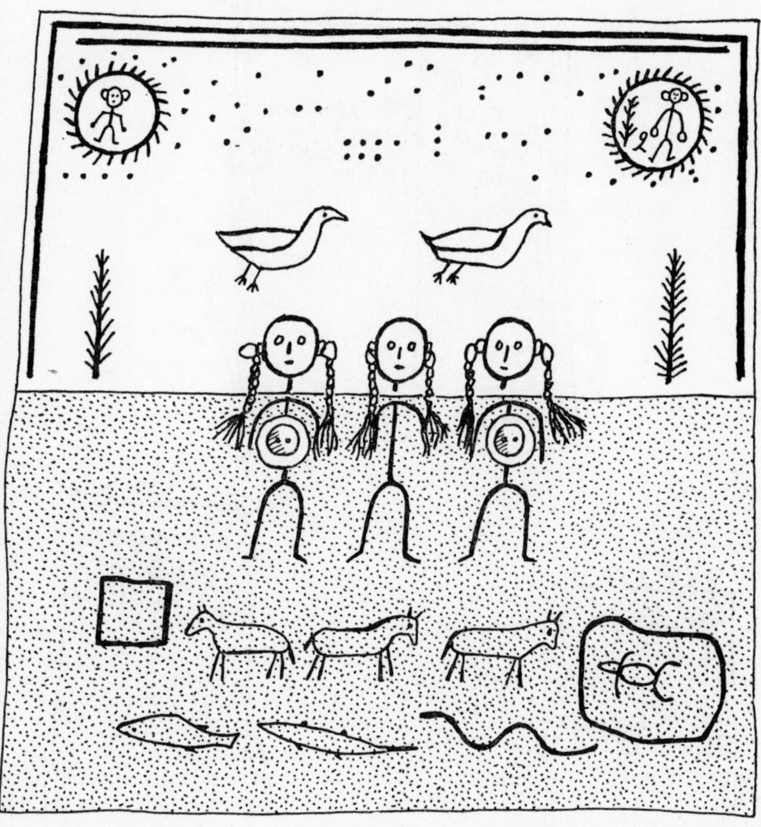

A piece of white cloth attached to a piece of dark blue cloth, together making a rectangle of 15 cm × 18 cm. Painting in red. Two brass buttons attached to the outer two figures.

(SME, collection no. 403-63)

chooses to include, are then drawn onto the cloth, and this has the effect of, as it were, putting them on a graph. Since right is 'pure' and left is 'impure', and the sky is similarly 'pure' in relation to the earth, the drawing immediately indicates the ritual position of the ongon spirit in question. In this way the ongon spirit may be compared in status with other objects or people from the myth (see *Figure 3*), and with other ongon

Figure 4 *Ongon of the tea lords*

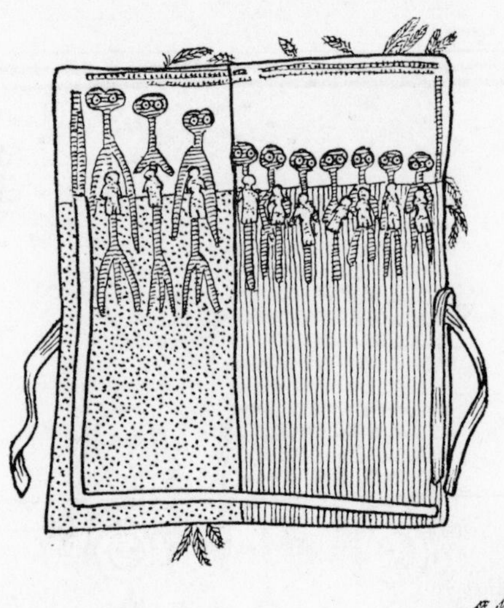

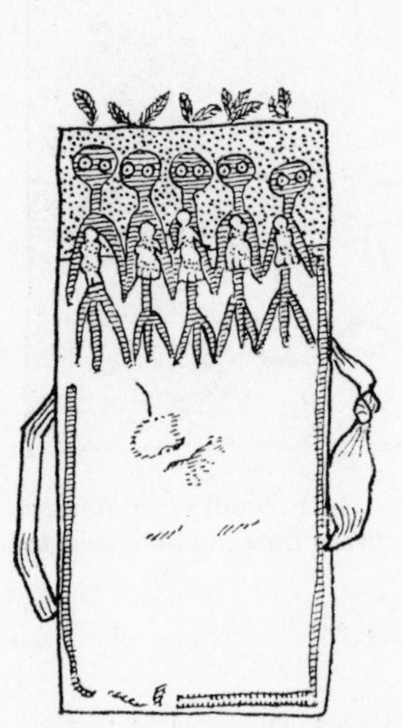

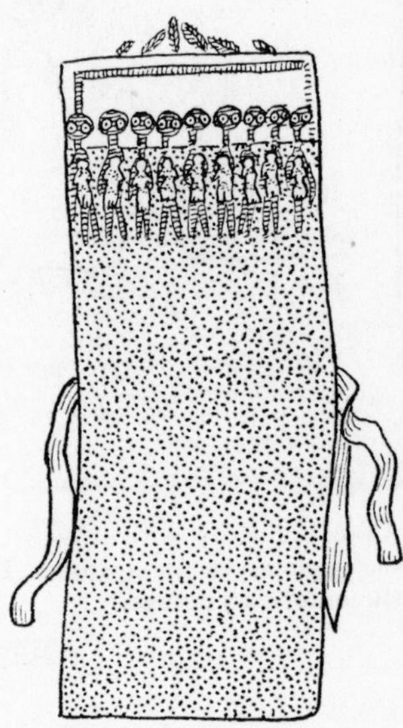

(SME, collection no. 1635-3 (a, b, v))

spirits of the same series (see *Figure 4*). This method of constructing ongon is more subtle than the first, since by it shades of ritual status can be indicated, but essentially both methods perform the same function: they arrange the signs of the ongon so that a conclusion may be drawn from them.

FIGURE 5 *Khata-Mailgan and Ukha-Solbon ongon*

(MAE, collection no. 953-3k)

It is in these ways (and most probably in others that have not yet been analysed) that the ongon are able to *answer* the contradictions posed in the myths. The ongon does two things: (i) it signifies certain concepts, and (ii) by arrangement of its signs in particular structures it is able to comment upon the situation as it is set out in the myth (or the cycle of myths). Thus the ongon could not exist without a myth. It is the existence of a myth that gives the collection of objects a meaning – and, being part of such a collection, each individual object is thereby changed from an object into a sign. In other words, the *language* of the ongon system is not enough in itself to be a means whereby new ongon are created. Although ongon are in all cases made and owned by individuals, the making of an ongon is a social event complementary to the telling of a myth.

A peculiarity of the system of ongon is that in the signifying of a concept there seems to be no difference between representing the idea in a drawing, in which case there is a perceptible relationship between the signifier and the signified (as there is also in Russian icons, for example), and indicating the idea by means of an object whose relation to the signified is distant and totally culturally determined. It is in the latter case that the ongon most closely approximates to language, while in the former it could be considered as art were it not for the fact that there seems to be a lack of concern about the appearance of the signifier provided it approximates to the conventions. If there are individual differences in the making of ongon, they seem to be differences in traditions of signification (e.g. whether to add an eagle-owl feather to Anda-Bar ongon or not) rather than in style.

The equivalence of motivated and unmotivated signs in ongon perhaps does indicate that the Buryat do not see the difference between the two as important. Certainly it is not related to any observable categories of their culture. It is not the case, for example, that some kinds of crises of life, say illnesses, are represented by one kind of ongon, while others have ongon of a different type. Although a particular spirit always has one kind of representation, perhaps a drawing on green cloth, the spirits represented by drawings as opposed to wild animals' skins or felt dolls, etc., do not form a category.

All ongon have a similar function, which is to protect or help their owners in specific circumstances. The question arises: why should a material system of signification have magical power when a system using language (e.g. myths or invocations) does not? The answer seems to be in the nature of the concept of ongon, in the full meaning of the word, that is, a material vessel for a change in spiritual state. In Buryat culture it is by ongon of one kind or another that changes are effected. Thus an ongon – a shaman in ecstasy, or a 'possessed' animal – is necessary in every ceremony effecting a change in ritual status. It is characteristic that a whole series of objects should be used, through which the spirit should pass, starting with a 'receptive' object and ending with a 'hard' object into which it is desired that the spirit should ultimately reside. In the ceremony of 'returning the soul' to an ill man, for example, the soul must pass through the following series: a horse, its bridle, a birch tree, a copper button, a thread, an arrow, and finally to a human being. It is clear that objects as used in Buryat ceremonies form a system which operates on the same level as the ongon system; both use an already existing evaluation and classification of objects in order to signify, just as poetry or myth uses an existing language to create a further statement. It seems to be characteristic of the Buryat that such meta-systems of objects become the repositories of magical power. When the objects become signs they are thought to contain the power attributed to the ideas expressed. To some extent all such systems among them, for example, writing (which is used in very restricted circumstances) or horse-branding, are also magical. Thus it is not surprising that such a system should exist in order to represent the supernatural, and that the collections of objects that make up the system should be called ongon.

NOTES

1. This paper is based on work in the archives of the State Museum of Ethnography (SME), Leningrad, and the Museum of Anthropology and Ethnography (MAE), Leningrad. The work in the USSR was done under the auspices of Moscow University (1966–67 and 1968) and Leningrad University (1969). I am greatly indebted to my supervisors, Professor Sergei Aleksandrovich Tokarev of Moscow, and Professor Rudolf Ferdinandovich Its of Leningrad, for their help and encouragement.

This work was undertaken as part of the research for a Ph.D. at Cambridge University and it was aided by a grant from the Wenner-Gren Foundation for anthropological research. I would particularly like to thank Dr Edmund Leach, who helped me to clarify the ideas in this paper and has always given sympathetic support, and Mr Edwin Ardener, for his assistance in the preparation of this article.

2. The Buryat-Mongol word *ongo*(*n*), pl. *ongud*, means primarily 'holy' or 'sacred' and may be used of any object. The meaning I have given in the text applies to more specifically shamanist context.

3. Unless otherwise stated, I shall use the word ongon to refer to the representation.

4. There are a large number of ongon expressed only in dance or mime but they form a separate group since they represent not legendary ancestors but animals and comic people, for example 'the pig ongon', 'the drunken woman ongon', etc.

5. The motivated nature of the signs in icons means that there must be fewer levels of signification.

6. As described by Barthes (1967a).

7. Saussure (1949), quoted in Barthes (1967a).

8. It must not touch the ground; it must not be approached by women; only shamans of a certain degree of consecration may own one, etc.

REFERENCES

BARTHES, R. 1964. *Éléments de sémiologie.* Paris: Le Seuil.

—— 1967a. *Elements of Semiology.* (Translation by Annette Lavers and Colin Smith of Barthes, 1964.) London: Cape.

—— 1967b. *Système de la mode.* Paris: Le Seuil.

BENVÉNISTE, E. 1966. *Problèmes de linguistique générale.* Paris: Gallimard.

IVANOV, S. V. 1951. *Proiskhozhdeniye Buryatskikh Ongonov s Izobrazheniyami Zhenshchin.* Trudy Instituta Etnografii ANSSSR, tom XIV. Moscow.

—— 1954. *Materialy po Izobrazitel'nomu Iskusstvu Narodov Sibiri* (*Materials On the Art of the Peoples of Siberia*). Moscow/Leningrad.

—— 1957. *K Semantikye Izobrazhenii na Starinnikh Buryatskikh Ongonakh.* Sbornik MAE, tom XVII. Moscow.

KHANGALOV, M. N. 1907. *Predaniya, Poveriya, i Drugiye Obychai u Buryat.* SME Archives, fond I, opus 2, files 659–696. (Unpublished.)

—— 1959. *Sobraniye Sochinenii*, tom I–III. Ulan-Ude.

LÉVI-STRAUSS, C. 1958. *Anthropologie structurale.* Paris: Plon.

—— 1962. *La Pensée sauvage.* Paris: Plon.

—— 1966. *The Savage Mind.* (Translation of Lévi-Strauss, 1962.) London: Weidenfeld & Nicolson; Chicago: University of Chicago Press.

MAE. Museum of Anthropology and Ethnography, Leningrad. Material in the Siberian section.

POTANIN, G. M. 1883. *Ocherki Severo-Zapadnoi Mongolii*, tom IV. St Petersburg.

SAUSSURE, F. DE. 1916. *Cours de linguistique générale.* Paris: Payot. Fourth edition, 1949.

—— 1959. *Course of General Linguistics.* (Translation by W. Baskin of Saussure, 1916.) New York: Philosophical Library; London: Peter Owen, 1960.

SME. State Museum of Ethnography, Leningrad. Material in the Siberian section.

ZHAMTSARANO, TS. ZH. 1901. *Ongony Aginskikh Buryat.* Zapiski IRGO po otdel. etnog., tom XXXIV. St Petersburg.

NOTES ON CONTRIBUTORS

EDWIN ARDENER

Born 1927, England; attended London University, B.A., Oxford, M.A.

Treasury Studentship, 1949–52; Research Fellow, later Senior Research Fellow WAISER/NISER, University College Ibadan, Nigeria, 1952–62; Oppenheimer Student, Oxford, 1961–62; Treasury Fellowship, 1963; Lecturer in Social Anthropology, Oxford, 1963 ; Fellow of St John's College, Oxford, 1969– .

Author of *Coastal Bantu of the Cameroons*, 1956; *Divorce and Fertility*, 1962; and papers in social anthropology.

Joint author of *Plantation and Village in the Cameroons*, 1960.

DAVID CRYSTAL

Born 1941, Northern Ireland; educated at University College London, B.A. (English), Ph.D.

Research Assistant on the Survey of English Usage, UCL, 1962–63; Assistant Lecturer, Department of Linguistics, University College of North Wales, Bangor, 1963–65; Lecturer, Department of Linguistic Science, University of Reading, 1965–69, then Reader in the Department, 1969– .

Author of *Linguistics, Language and Religion*, 1964; *What is Linguistics?*, 1968; *Prosodic Systems and Intonation in English*, 1969; *Linguistics*, 1971.

Co-author of *Systems of Prosodic and Paralinguistic Features in English*, 1964; *Investigating English Style*, 1969; *The English Language*, 1969.

NORMAN DENISON

Born 1925, England; read Modern and Medieval Languages at St John's College, Cambridge, M.A., Ph.D.

Assistant Lecturer in English, Helsinki University, 1951–54 (research in Finnish and Finno-Ugrian linguistics); Assistant Lecturer in Germanic Philology, University College of Wales, 1954–56; Lecturer in General Linguistics, University of Glasgow, 1956–64; Secondment to University of the Punjab, W. Pakistan, as Professor of English Language and Applied Linguistics and head of teaching and research centre 'The Language Unit', 1958–60; Secondment to First Institute of Foreign Languages, Moscow, 1963–64; Director, Department of Language Studies, London School of Economics, 1964– .

Author of *The Partitive in Finnish*, 1957; and of papers on sociolinguistics, plurilingualism, applied linguistics.

HILARY HENSON

Born 1946, London; studied at Oxford, St Hilda's College and St Cross College, B.A. (English), B.Litt. (Social Anthropology).

Currently working for the BBC.

CAROLINE HUMPHREY

Born 1943, London; educated at Cambridge University, B.A. (Social Anthropology); Leeds University, M.A. (Mongolian Studies).

Research at Moscow and Leningrad Universities, 1966–69 (field research among the Buryat, 1967); St Antony's College, Oxford, 1969–70; Research Student, Department of Social Anthropology, Cambridge University.

DELL HYMES

Born 1927, Portland, Oregon; educated at Reed College, B.A. (Literature and Anthropology); Indiana University, M.A., Ph.D. (Linguistics).

Field research on Chinookan language and folklore, Oregon, 1951 intermittently to present; Instructor and Assistant Professor of Social Anthropology, Harvard University, 1955–60; Associate Professor and Professor of Anthropology, University of California, Berkeley, 1960–65; Professor of Anthropology, University of Pennsylvania, 1965– .

Author of *On Communicative Competence*, 1971.

Editor of *Language in Culture and Society*, 1964; *Pidginization and Creolization of Languages*, 1971.

Co-editor (with J. J. Gumperz) of *The Ethnography of Communication*, 1964; *Directions in Sociolinguistics*, 1972.

GEORGE B. MILNER

Born 1918, Lisbon; educated at Cambridge University, M.A. 1940 (Modern Languages); London University, Dip. Anthrop. 1954, Ph.D. 1968 (Social Anthropology).

Field research in the Western Pacific 1948–50, 1955–56, 1959;

Lecturer in Oceanic Languages, School of Oriental and African Studies, 1948–64, Reader 1964– .

Author of *Fijian Grammar*, 1956; *Samoan Dictionary*, 1966; and articles in linguistics and anthropology.

JOHN B. PRIDE

Born 1929, England; educated at Edinburgh University, M.A. (English Language and Literature), after service in the Royal Navy.

Lektor in English Literature, University of Gothenburg, Sweden, 1959–60; Lecturer in English Language, University of Edinburgh, 1960–63; Lecturer to Overseas Students, Moray House College of Education, Edinburgh, 1963–65; Lecturer in English Language and General Linguistics, University of Leeds, 1965–69; Professor of English Language, Victoria University of Wellington, New Zealand, 1969.

Author of *The Social Meaning of Language*, 1971; and papers on sociolinguistics.

ROBERT H. ROBINS

Born 1921, Broadstairs, Kent; educated at Oxford University, M.A. London University, D.Lit.

Lecturer in Linguistics, School of Oriental and African Studies, 1948–54; Reader in General Linguistics, University of London, 1954–64; Professor of General Linguistics, University of London, 1965–. Research Fellow, University of California, 1951 (fieldwork on Yurok); Visiting Professor, University of Washington, Seattle, 1963; Visiting Professor, University of Hawaii, 1968; Visiting Professor, University of Minnesota, 1971; Hon. Secretary, Philological Society, 1961– .

Author of *Ancient and Mediaeval Grammatical Theory in Europe*, 1951; *The Yurok Language*, 1958; *General Linguistics: An Introductory Survey*, 1964; *A Short History of Linguistics*, 1967; *Diversions of Bloomsbury: Selected Writings on Linguistics*, 1970.

J. ELIZABETH A. TONKIN

Born 1934, England; educated at Oxford University, M.A. (English), D.Phil (Social Anthropology).

Education Officer, Kenya, 1958–63; Lecturer in English, Ahmadu Bello University, Nigeria, 1963–66; Lecturer in Social Anthropology, Centre of West African Studies, Birmingham University, 1970– .

WILFRED H. WHITELEY

Born 1924, England; read Social Anthropology at the London School of Economics, B.A., Ph.D. (Bantu Languages).

Field Research in Tanzania and Kenya, 1949–59, 1961–62, 1968–69; Senior Research Fellow, East African Institute of Social Research, Makerere University, Kampala, Uganda, 1952–58; Professor of Anthropology, University of Wisconsin, Madison, USA, 1963–64; Professor of Language and Linguistics, University College, Dar es Salaam, Tanzania, 1964–67; Professor of Bantu Languages, University of London, 1965– .

Author of *A Practical Introduction to Kamba* (with M. G. Muli), 1962; *A Study of Yao Sentences*, 1966; *Swahili: The Rise of a National Language*, 1969.

Editor of *Language Use and Social Change*, 1971.

Author Index

Subject Index

Subject Index